More Praise for *Bryson's Strategic Planning for Public and Nonprofit Organizations*, **Third Edition**

"John Bryson provides the tools leaders need to guide organizations and collaborations through a strategic planning process. His third edition should be required reading for anyone leading a nonprofit or public organization."
— Terri Barreiro, director, Donald McNeely Center for Entrepreneurship, Saint John's University, and former vice president for community impact of the Greater Twin Cities United Way

"John Bryson's book is an immensely valuable resource for leaders, professionals, researchers, and other participants in public and nonprofit settings. Anyone professing competence in public and nonprofit management needs to know what Bryson says about strategic planning."
— Hal G. Rainey, Alumni Foundation Distinguished Professor, School of Public and International Affairs, The University of Georgia, and author, *Understanding and Managing Public Organizations, Third Edition*

"The arrival of a new edition of this authoritative and highly usable book is very good news. Bryson explains strategic planning systematically and clearly in this valuable work."
— Judith E. Innes, professor of city and regional planning, University of California, Berkeley

"John Bryson's book has quickly become the classic guide for making better decisions—and getting better results. The third edition introduces new concepts like managing for results and creating public value while maintaining the powerful, disciplined thinking of previous editions. It is an indispensable guide for anyone seeking to cope with the growing challenges of managing the tough environment of the public and nonprofit world."
— Donald F. Kettl, professor of political science and public affairs, University of Wisconsin–Madison, and author, *The Transformation of Governance: Public Administration for Twenty-First Century America* and *The Global Public Management Revolution*

"If you are committed to the future effectiveness of your organization and the people it serves, this is the key resource book for you. John challenges our strategic thinking on the one hand whilst providing us with practical tools to deliver meaningful strategies and plans on the other."
— Irene Hewitt, chief executive, The Beeches Management Centre for Health and Personal Social Services, Belfast, Northern Ireland

"The new edition of *Strategic Planning for Public and Nonprofit Organizations* brings two needed gifts to this field: An excellent summary of the principles and theory behind leading and managing in a strategic way and a solid process and great set of tools that leaders and future leaders can use to make their institutions more responsive and effective."
— Bryan Barry, principal consultant, Amherst H. Wilder Foundation Center for Communities, St. Paul, Minnesota

STRATEGIC PLANNING FOR PUBLIC AND NONPROFIT ORGANIZATIONS

STRATEGIC PLANNING FOR PUBLIC AND NONPROFIT ORGANIZATIONS

A Guide to Strengthening and Sustaining Organizational Achievement

THIRD EDITION

John M. Bryson

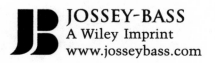

JOSSEY-BASS
A Wiley Imprint
www.josseybass.com

Published by Jossey-Bass
A Wiley Imprint
989 Market Street, San Francisco, CA 94103-1741   www.josseybass.com

Jossey-Bass books and products are available through most bookstores. To contact Jossey-Bass directly call our Customer Care Department within the U.S. at 800-956-7739, outside the U.S. at 317-572-3986, or fax 317-572-4002.

Jossey-Bass also publishes its books in a variety of electronic formats. Some content that appears in print may not be available in electronic books.

Credits are on page 431.

Library of Congress Cataloging-in-Publication Data

Bryson, John M. (John Moore), date.
  Strategic planning for public and nonprofit organizations : a guide to strengthening and sustaining organizational achievement / John M. Bryson.—3rd ed.
    p. cm.
  Includes bibliographical references and index.
  ISBN 0-7879-6755-6
  1. Strategic planning. 2. Nonprofit organizations—Management. 3. Public administration. I. Title.
  HD30.28.B79 2004
  658.4'012—dc22   2004018244

Printed in the United States of America
THIRD EDITION
HB Printing   10 9 8 7 6 5

CONTENTS

FIGURES AND EXHIBITS

Figures

Exhibits

PREFACE

How can the leaders and managers of public and nonprofit organizations cope with the challenges that confront their organizations, now and in the years ahead? How should they respond to the increasingly uncertain and interconnected environments in which their organizations operate? How should they respond to dwindling or unpredictable resources; new public expectations or formal mandates; demographic changes; deregulation or reregulation; upheavals in international, national, state, and local economies and polities; and new roles for public, nonprofit, and business organizations? What should their organizations' missions be? How can they create greater and more enduring public value? How can they build on organizational strengths and take advantage of opportunities while minimizing organizational weaknesses and overcoming challenges to their organizations? How can they formulate desirable strategies and implement them effectively? These are the questions this book addresses.

Scope

Strategic Planning for Public and Nonprofit Organizations is based on the premise that leaders and managers of public and nonprofit organizations must be effective strategists if these organizations are to fulfill their missions, meet their mandates, satisfy their constituents, and create public value in the years ahead. These leaders and managers need to exercise as much discretion as possible in the areas under their control, they need to develop effective strategies to cope with changed and changing circumstances, and they need to develop a coherent and defensible basis for their decisions.

Strategic planning is a set of concepts, procedures, and tools designed to assist leaders and managers with these tasks. Indeed, strategic planning may be defined as a disciplined effort to produce fundamental decisions and actions that shape and guide what an organization (or other entity) is, what it does, and why it does it. In the past forty years strategic planning has become a standard part of management thinking and practice in the business world. In the past twenty years strategic planning has become the standard practice of large numbers of public and nonprofit organizations.

The first and second editions of this book played an important role in promoting the use of strategic planning by public and nonprofit organizations. The practice of strategic planning has progressed substantially, and new areas of concern have emerged. Thus, although this third edition covers the same topics as the first and second editions, it also focuses on additional areas requiring special attention. All of the chapters have been updated, and new cases have been added. I have supplied new material about

- Creating public value
- Stakeholder analysis methods
- The difference between strategic issues and operational issues
- New approaches to strategic issue identification
- The importance of strategy mapping
- Performance management and balanced scorecards
- New forms of strategic management systems
- Strategic planning in collaborative settings

Four resource sections that were in the second edition have been dropped, and two new ones have been added. The dropped sections discussed an approach to external scanning and useful concepts for identifying strategic issues, formulating and implementing strategies, and establishing a vision of success. Some of the material that was in those sections has now been added to the main text; dated material has been omitted. The new resource sections are devoted to the particularly timely topics of stakeholder identification and analysis methods and strategic planning in collaborative settings.

This third edition also explicitly blends leadership, strategic planning, and management, an approach that reflects a major trend in the field. People realize that strategic planning is no substitute for leadership. Instead, strategic planning comprises a set of concepts, procedures, and tools that can help leaders and followers enhance organizational (and community) achievement. People also realize that it is not enough just to think and learn—organizations must act as well. And it is not enough just to decide what to do and how to do it—the doing matters too. Of course these points were all emphasized in the previous editions, but they are emphasized even more here. This current edition is therefore as much about strategic *management* as it is about strategic *planning*. I have kept the original title, however, because of the recognition and following the first two editions achieved.

This new edition also highlights the importance of inclusion, analysis, and speed as means of increasing organizational and community effectiveness (Bryson, 2003a), reflecting another trend in the field. The idea is to get more people of various kinds and with various skills involved, increase the sophistication and quality of analysis used to inform action, and do it all more quickly than in the past. The challenge of course is that doing any two of these three things is not so hard, but doing all three together is very hard. For example, there are methods that enable large numbers of stakeholders to be in the same room at the same time working on strategic planning, but it is hard to inform their efforts with sophisticated analysis. Alternatively, sophisticated analyses often can be done quickly but not when they involve a large group of people. One of the challenges this book presents to leaders and managers is to be inclusive, analytical, and quick all at once. Figuring out how to address that challenge effectively is not really solved here and is one of the continuing tasks for the field.

In sum, in this edition there is a renewed emphasis on the fact that strategic planning is *not* the same as strategic thinking, acting, and learning. What matters most is strategic thinking, acting, and learning. Strategic planning is useful only if it improves strategic thought, action, and learning; it is not a substitute for them. The reader should keep clearly in mind that in practice, strategies are formed (and realized) out of a variety of sources (the vision of new leaders, intuition, group learning, innovation, what already works, chance) and strategic planning is only one of them. Wise strategic thought, action, and learning take all sources into account. As Mintzberg (1994, p. 367) notes, "Strategy formation cannot be helped by people blind to the richness of its reality."

Specifically, this book

- Reviews the reasons public and nonprofit organizations (and communities) should embrace strategic planning and management as ways of improving performance.
- Presents an effective strategic planning and management process that has been used successfully by thousands of public and nonprofit organizations; this *Strategy*

Change Cycle enhances the process presented in the second edition with readiness assessment, stakeholder analysis, new approaches to strategic issue identification, strategy mapping, balanced scorecards, performance management, and strategic management systems.

- Offers detailed guidance on applying the process, including information on specific tools and techniques that might prove useful in various circumstances within organizations, across organizations, and in communities.

- Discusses the major roles that must be played by various individuals and groups for strategic planning to work, and gives guidance on how to play the roles.

- Clarifies the various ways in which strategic planning may be institutionalized so that strategic thinking, acting, and learning may be encouraged and embraced across an entire organization.

- Describes many new examples of successful (and unsuccessful) strategic planning practices.

- Relates the entire discussion to relevant research and literature.

Audience

This book is written for two main groups. The first consists of elected and appointed policymakers, managers, and planners in governments, public agencies, and nonprofit organizations who are responsible for and who want to learn more about strategic planning and management. This book will help these individuals understand what strategic planning and management are and how to apply them in their own organizations and, to a lesser extent, their communities. Thus this book speaks to city council members, mayors, city managers, administrators, and planners; sheriffs, police chiefs, fire chiefs, and their staffs; school board members and school administrators and staff; county commissioners, administrators, and planners; governors, state cabinet secretaries, and state administrators and planners; legislators; chief executive officers, chief administrative officers, chief financial officers, and chief information officers; executive directors, deputy directors, and unit directors; presidents and vice presidents; elected and appointed officials of governments and public agencies; and boards of directors of nonprofit organizations.

The second major audience consists of academics and students of strategic planning and management. Courses on strategic planning and management are now typically offered in schools of public affairs, public administration, public planning, and public policy. This book offers participants in these courses a useful blend of theory and practice.

Others who will find the book interesting are businesspeople and citizens interested in increasing their understanding of how to improve the operations of governments, public agencies, and nonprofit organizations. This book can help these individuals understand and improve their communities.

Overview of the Contents

Part One introduces the reader to the dynamics of strategic planning. Chapter One introduces the concept of strategic planning and explains why such planning is important for governments, public agencies, nonprofit organizations, and communities. Attention is focused on strategic planning for (1) public agencies, departments, and major organizational divisions; (2) general purpose governments; (3) nonprofit organizations; (4) functions, such as transportation, health care, or education, that bridge organizational and governmental boundaries; (5) interorganizational networks; and (6) entire communities, urban or metropolitan areas, regions, and states seen as economic, social, and political entities. The benefits of strategic planning are emphasized, as are the conditions under which strategic planning should *not* be undertaken. In this chapter I also argue that public and nonprofit strategic planning is an innovation that is here to stay. The reason is that at its best, strategic planning can accommodate both substantive rationality and political acceptability. Finally, readers will be introduced to three organizations whose experience with strategic planning will be used throughout the book to illustrate key points. The three comprise two public organizations (a school district and a U.S. Navy organization) and one nonprofit organization (a housing, training, and social service organization).

In Chapter Two, I present my preferred approach to strategic planning and management, which I call the Strategy Change Cycle. This approach has been used effectively by a large number of governments, public agencies, and nonprofit organizations in the United States, Canada, the United Kingdom, and Australia, and indeed has been applied successfully on every continent—except perhaps Antarctica! (Readers of the second edition will find that the Strategy Change Cycle described here differs slightly from the process outlined previously; the changes reflect changes in my own thinking—often resulting from the advice of colleagues—as well as changes in the field more generally.)

Chapters Three through Ten, which make up Part Two, describe in detail how to apply the approach.

Chapter Three covers the initial agreement, or readiness assessment and *plan for planning*, phase of the strategic planning process. Chapter Four focuses on identification of mandates and the clarification of mission and values. Chapter Five addresses the assessment of an organization's external and internal environments. Chapter Six discusses strategic issues—what they are, how they can be identified, and how to critique them. Chapter Seven is devoted to the development of effective strategies and plans and also discusses strategy review and adoption. Chapter Eight covers the development of the organization's *vision of success,* that is, what the organization should look like as it fulfills its mission and achieves its full potential. Chapter Nine attends to the development of an effective implementation process. Chapter Ten covers reassessment of strategies and the strategic planning process as a prelude to a new round of strategic planning. Chapters Three through Seven thus emphasize the planning aspect of the Strategy Change Cycle, whereas Chapters Eight through Ten highlight the management aspects.

Part Three offers two chapters designed to help leaders know what they will need to do to get started with strategic planning and to make it work. Chapter Eleven covers the many roles and responsibilities necessary for effective strategic leadership of public and nonprofit organizations. These roles include sponsoring, championing, and facilitating the process in such a way that an organization's situation is clearly understood, wise decisions are made and implemented, residual conflicts are handled well, and the organization is prepared for the next round of strategy change. Chapter Twelve assesses the strategic planning experiences of the three organizations used as examples throughout the text. This chapter also provides guidance on how to begin strategic planning.

Finally, three resource sections are provided. Resource A presents an array of stakeholder identification and analysis methods designed to help organize participation, create strategic ideas worth implementing, organize a coalition of support for these ideas, and protect these ideas during implementation. Resource B offers process guidelines for using *ovals* to develop *strategic issues maps,* discusses how these maps can be converted into *strategy maps,* and describes additional uses for the oval mapping process. Resource C provides guidance on applying the Strategy Change Cycle in collaborative settings, a growing area of need.

Strategic Planning for Public and Nonprofit Organizations will provide most of the guidance leaders, managers, and planners need to engage in a strategic planning and management process aimed at making their organizations (and communities) more effective and responsive to their environments. This book reveals a simple yet effective strategic planning and management process designed specifically for public and nonprofit organizations, detailed advice on how to apply the process, and examples of its application. The entire exposition is grounded in the relevant research and literature, so readers will know where the process fits in with prior research and practice and can gain added insights on applying the process.

The Strategic Planning Workbook

The second edition benefited from having a companion strategic planning workbook that groups and organizations could use to work through the nuts and bolts of the strategic planning and management process. I have again teamed with Farnum Alston, a highly skilled and experienced consultant, to coauthor a second edition of *Creating and Implementing Your Strategic Plan* (Bryson and Alston, 2004).

This workbook is designed primarily to help those who are relatively new to strategic planning to guide themselves through the Strategy Change Cycle. However, those who are experienced old hands are also likely to find it useful.

The workbook is in no way a substitute for this book. Effective strategic planning is an art that involves thoughtful tailoring to specific contexts. *Strategic Planning for Public and Nonprofit Organizations* provides considerable guidance on how to think about the tailoring process, including many process guidelines, caveats, and case examples. Thus this book should be read before the workbook is used, and should be consulted on a regular basis throughout the course of a Strategy Change Cycle.

Minneapolis, Minnesota
July 2004

John M. Bryson

ACKNOWLEDGMENTS

Space limitations prevent me from rethanking by name all those who contributed to the first and second editions of this book. Nonetheless, I remain deeply grateful to them. Without their insights, thoughtfulness, advice, and other forms of help, neither those editions nor this one would have been written. I carry their wisdom with me every day.

There is space, however, for me to thank the people who contributed their insights, advice, and support to this third edition. Deep thanks and appreciation must go to Colin Eden and Fran Ackermann, two colleagues at the University of Strathclyde in Glasgow, Scotland; Charles "Chuck" Finn, a colleague at the College of Saint Rose in Albany, New York; and David Andersen and George Richardson, colleagues at the Rockefeller College of Public Affairs at the State University of New York at Albany. The six of us have been carrying on a dialogue about public and nonprofit strategic management for well over a decade, and this continuing "seminar" has been one of the most significant sources of my own learning.

A number of academic colleagues (many of whom are also skilled consultants and practitioners) at various institutions in the United States, the United Kingdom, and elsewhere have contributed to the third edition through writing to me or conversing with me. They include Stuart Albert, Sandra Archibald, Franco Archibugi, Robert Backoff, Michael Barzelay, Nic Beech, Robert Behn, Kimberly

Boal, Richard Bolan, Herman "Buzz" Boschken, Barry Bozeman, Phil Bromiley, Jim Bryant, George Burt, David Chrislip, Steve Cropper, Barbara Crosby (who is also my spouse), Andre Delbecq, Tim Delmont, Bob Denhardt, Jane Dutton, Dean Eitel, Andreas Faludi, Martha Feldman, Marlena Fiol, John Forester, George Frederickson, Lee Frost-Kumpf (now deceased), Arie Halachmi, Alf Hattan, Patsy Healey, Ronald Heifetz, Chris Huxham, Judy Innes, Gerry Johnson, Phyl Johnson, Robert Kaplan, Don Kettl, Martin Krieger, Paul Light, Russell Linden, Jeff Luke (now deceased), Larry Lynn, Seymour Mandelbaum, Brint Milward, Henry Mintzberg, Mark Moore, Sam Myers, Paul Nutt, Stephen Osborne, Larry O'Toole, Michael Patton, Guy Peters, Ted Poister, Beryl Radin, Hal Rainey, Sue Richards, Peter Ring, Nancy Roberts, Tore Sager, Melissa Stone, John Clayton Thomas, Fred Thompson, Andy Van de Ven, David Van Slyke, Siv Vangen, Bart Wechsler, Karl Weick, Chris Wheeland, and many others.

A number of practitioners also provided immense help. I am reminded of the adage "A practitioner is a theorist who pays a price for being wrong." These thoughtful, public-spirited, good-hearted friends and colleagues have shared with me their hard-won insights and have provided invaluable knowledge and encouragement. Their number includes Farnum Alston, a friend for almost thirty years and coauthor of *Creating and Implementing Your Strategic Plan* (2nd ed.), the companion piece to this book. Farnum has an amazing store of experience, insights, techniques, and wisdom gained as a political appointee serving former governor Pat Lucey in Wisconsin (where we first met), as a high-ranking federal civil servant, as head of Peat-Marwick's national consulting practice for strategic planning in the public sector, and as deputy mayor and budget director for San Francisco. I am indeed fortunate that Farnum has been willing to share his prodigious talents with me. Farnum now heads The Crescent Company, a strategic planning and management consulting firm located in San Anselmo, California.

Three other truly outstanding and generous practitioners deserve special mention: Gary Cunningham and Tom Walkington, both of whom work for Hennepin County, Minnesota, one of the largest local governments in the United States, and Captain William "Bill" Frentzel (U.S. Navy Ret.), who headed the strategic planning effort of the U.S. Naval Security Group (NSG) in the 1990s. Gary serves in a number of roles for Hennepin County, Minnesota. He is director of primary care and also director of the North Point Health and Wellness Center (which until mid-2004 was called Pilot City Health Center). Prior to those assignments, he was director of the county's Office of Planning and Development. It was in that role that he got me involved in the African American Men Project (of which he is still the director), a major county-led effort to improve outcomes for African American men between the ages of eighteen and thirty. Gary pushed me to develop my ideas about stakeholder identification and analysis, and the results will be seen throughout this book. He has also involved me in other county initiatives through which I gained as much in knowledge as I might have contributed. Tom Walkington (who holds a Ph.D. degree in public administration) has played a key role in developing Hennepin County's strategic management system, which is discussed in several places in this book. Tom's patient explanations of what has and has not worked, and why, have greatly improved my own understanding of strategic management systems. Bill Frentzel helped the NSG respond effectively to drastic changes in the world geopolitical situation, overall Navy strategy, organizational funding arrangements, technological changes, and interorganizational relationships. Bill also read virtually the entire manuscript for this book; his extremely helpful comments and editorial advice have greatly improved it. In short, I have learned and been helped so much by all three that it is hard to know how to thank them.

Other practitioners (several of whom have also been academics) who have advanced my knowledge of strategic planning and deserve special thanks include Norman Anderson, Sharon Anderson, Bryan Barry, Renee Berger, Ronnie Brooks, David Byfield, Beth Carlson, Anne Carroll, Steve Cramer, George Dow, John Garry, Bill Gaslin, Leah Goldstein, Lonnie Helgeson, Mike Hopkins, Barbara Johnson, Richard Johnson, Tom Kingston, Milne Kintner, Melissa Krull, Karl Kurtz, Tony Mounts, David O'Fallon, David Osborne, Jon Pratt, David Riemer, Jim Scheibel, Randy Schenkat, Bev Stein, Becky Stewart, Sandra Vargas, Mike Winer, and Lyle Wray. I also want to make special mention of Robert W. "Bob" Terry. Bob died in 2002 and is sorely missed. He was a former colleague at the Humphrey Institute before entering private practice in the early 1990s. You will see the influence of his books (Terry, 1993, 2001) in many places in this book. I must also express deep gratitude to the many readers who gave me valuable feedback on the previous editions of this book.

Since 1987, I have served as a strategic planning consultant to various health and social service organizations in Northern Ireland, and I must thank several people there who have been especially helpful. They include David Bingham, Richard Black, Seamus Carey, David Finegan, Clive Gowdy, Irene Hewitt, Stephen Hodkinson, Stephen Leach, Hugh McCaughey, Shirley McCaughey, William McKee, Denis McMahon, Paul Simpson, and Brian White, among many others. The opportunity to work over a long period of time on strategic planning projects in a different country, in a sector undergoing often radical change, and in especially difficult political circumstances has immeasurably improved my understanding of both the limits and possibilities of strategic planning.

At the Humphrey Institute, I would like to thank, in addition to those already mentioned, Dean Brian Atwood; Harry Boyte; former dean John Brandl; Gary DeCramer; Kathy Fennelly; Marsha Freeman; Lee Munnich; Stephen Sandell; Jodi Sandfort; my research assistants Meredith Anderson, Lisa Garner-Springer, and Joshua Zepnick; my always helpful secretary, Donna Kern; and scores of students for their ideas, assistance, and support. Sharon Anderson (whom I also mentioned earlier) was at the Humphrey Institute in a variety of administrative capacities until 2002 and is now in private practice. She is an absolutely wonderful strategic planning process designer and facilitator and has been a tremendous source of advice, support, and "heavy lifting" on various projects over the years.

Much of this third edition was written while Barbara Crosby and I were on sabbatical leave in Glasgow, Scotland, for the 2002–03 academic year. While there, we were visiting professors in the Graduate School of Business (GSB) at the University of Strathclyde. I would like to thank everyone at the university for the many kindnesses and warmth we were shown. Members of the faculty who helped in various ways and have not already been mentioned include John Bothams (now retired), George Cairns (now at the University of Durham), Peter McInnes, Jill Sheppard, and George Wright (now at the University of Leeds). I especially wish to thank Sharon Gribben and Val Turner, secretaries at GSB, for their marvelous and much-appreciated efforts to make us welcome and see that we had what we needed. I would also like to thank a wonderful group of doctoral students who welcomed us into "the research studio"—Shima Barakat, Paul Hibbert, Peter McInnes (who has since joined the faculty), and Aiden McQuade.

Of course no mention of our year in Glasgow would be complete without mentioning our wonderful neighbors. I particularly want to express my heartfelt thanks to Malcolm Foley and Gayle McPherson, two charming, funny, friendly, learned Scottish academics who welcomed Barbara and me (and our children when they visited) into their home and into their lives. They have become dear friends and we hope to see them often in the coming years. And I also want to thank David Andersen (whom I also mentioned earlier) and his spouse, Deborah Andersen, also an academic, for their great friendship while they were our downstairs neighbors and were also on sabbatical leave in Glasgow. I treasure the times we had with these four fabulous human beings.

At Jossey-Bass, I wish to thank my editor, Dorothy Hearst, and Allison Brunner, Xenia Lisanevich, and Elspeth MacHattie for all the help they gave. The book was greatly improved as a result.

Some of the material in this book appeared elsewhere, and I thank the editors and publishers of these earlier publications for allowing revised versions to be printed here. Some ideas in Chapter One appeared in Bryson and Einsweiler (1987); Bryson and Roering (1987); and in a book coedited with Bob Einsweiler (Bryson and Einsweiler, 1988). Parts of Chapter Seven appeared in Bryson (1988). Parts of Chapter Four and Resource A appeared in Bryson (2004b). Earlier versions of some material in Chapters Nine, Ten, and Eleven appeared in Bryson and Crosby (1992). Resource C is a major revision of Bryson, Crosby, and Ackermann (2003).

Finally, I must thank my spouse, Barbara Crosby, herself a skilled academic, and our two wonderful children, Jessica Ah-Reum Crosby and John Kee Crosby Bryson, for their love, support, understanding, intelligence, and good humor. Barbara is my best friend, closest adviser, and the person who more than any other has helped me understand and appreciate what love can be. She has also taught me a great deal about leadership and strategic planning. Our children are marvels, and I love them very deeply and am very proud of them. My hope for this book is that it will help make the world a better place for them and their children—and everyone's children. If it does, I could not be more thankful.

—*J.M.B.*

To Andre Delbecq, Robert Einsweiler, Frederick Fisher, Jerome Kaufman, June Spencer, and Bernard Taylor—who got me going down this path and provided help of many kinds along the way

THE AUTHOR

JOHN M. BRYSON is professor of planning and public affairs at the Hubert H. Humphrey Institute of Public Affairs at the University of Minnesota, where he has also served in a variety of administrative roles. He was a visiting professor at the London Business School for the 1986–87 academic year, where the first edition of *Strategic Planning for Public and Nonprofit Organizations* was written. During the 1993–94 academic year, when most of the second edition was written, he was a visiting professor in the Department of Management Science, University of Strathclyde; the School of Planning, Oxford Brookes University; and Nuffield College, Oxford University. During the 2002–03 academic year, when much of the third edition was written, he was a visiting professor in the Graduate School of Business at the University of Strathclyde. He received a B.A. degree (1969) in economics from Cornell University and holds three degrees from the University of Wisconsin, Madison: an M.A. degree (1972) in public policy and administration, an M.S. degree (1974) in urban and regional planning, and a Ph.D. degree (1978) in urban and regional planning.

Bryson's interests include public leadership and policy change, strategic planning, and the design of participation processes. His research explores ways to improve the theory and practice of policy change and planning, particularly through situationally sensitive approaches. He has received numerous awards for his work, including the General Electric Award for Outstanding Research in Strategic Planning from the Academy of Management and awards for best article from the *Journal of the American Planning Association* and the *Journal of Planning Education and Research*. He is the coauthor (with Barbara C. Crosby) of *Leadership for the Common Good* (Jossey-Bass, 1992), which received the Terry McAdam Award for "outstanding contribution to the advancement of the nonprofit sector" and was named the Best Book of 1992 by the Public and Nonprofit Division of the Academy of Management. *Leadership for the Common Good* (2nd ed., with Barbara Crosby as first author) is forthcoming. The second edition of *Strategic Planning for Public and Nonprofit Organizations* was named the Best Book of 1995 by the Public and Nonprofit Division of the Academy of Management. His most recent book (with Fran Ackermann, Colin Eden, and Charles Finn) is *Visible Thinking: Unlocking Causal Mapping for Practical Business Results* (2004).

Bryson is a regular presenter in many practitioner-oriented training programs. He has served as a strategic planning and leadership consultant to a wide variety of public, nonprofit, and for-profit organizations in North America and Europe.

STRATEGIC PLANNING FOR PUBLIC AND NONPROFIT ORGANIZATIONS

PART ONE

UNDERSTANDING THE DYNAMICS OF STRATEGIC PLANNING

The environments in which public and nonprofit organizations operate have become not only increasingly uncertain in recent years but also more tightly interconnected; thus changes anywhere in the system reverberate unpredictably—and often chaotically and dangerously—throughout the society. This increased uncertainty and interconnectedness requires a fourfold response from public and nonprofit organizations (and from communities). First, these organizations must think, act, and learn strategically as never before. Second, they must translate their insights into effective strategies to cope with their changed circumstances. Third, they must develop the rationales necessary to lay the groundwork for the adoption and implementation of their strategies. And fourth, they must build coalitions that are large enough and strong enough to adopt desirable strategies and protect them during implementation.

Strategic planning can help leaders and managers of public and nonprofit organizations think, learn, and act strategically. Chapter One introduces strategic planning, its potential benefits, and some of its limitations. It discusses what strategic planning is not and in what circumstances it is probably not appropriate. It also describes why strategic planning is a "smart practice" that is here to stay—because of its capacity, at its best, to incorporate both substantive and political rationality. The chapter concludes by introducing three organizations that have used a strategic planning process to produce significant changes. Their experiences will be used throughout the book to illustrate the dynamics of strategic planning.

Part One concludes with an overview of my preferred strategic planning process (Chapter Two). This process, the Strategy Change Cycle, was designed specifically to help public and nonprofit organizations (and communities) think, act, and learn strategically. It is typically fluid, iterative, and dynamic in practice but nonetheless allows for a reasonably orderly, participative, and effective approach to determining how best to achieve what is best for an organization and create real public value. Chapter Two also highlights several process design issues that are addressed throughout the book.

A key point that is emphasized again and again is that strategic *thinking, acting,* and *learning* are the activities that are important, not strategic planning per se. Indeed, if any particular approach to strategic planning gets in the way of strategic thought, action, and learning, that planning approach should be scrapped!

CHAPTER ONE

WHY STRATEGIC PLANNING IS MORE IMPORTANT THAN EVER

Usually, the main problem with life conundrums is that we don't bring to them enough imagination.

THOMAS MOORE, *CARE OF THE SOUL*

Leaders and managers of governments, public agencies, nonprofit organizations, and communities face numerous and difficult challenges. Consider, for example, the dizzying number of trends and events affecting the United States in the past two decades: an aging and diversifying population; changes in the nature of families; an apparent shift to political conservatism; tax cuts, levy limits, and indexing; dramatic shifts in federal and state responsibilities and funding priorities; a huge bull market in equities followed by one of the longest bear markets in history; a closing of the gap between rich and poor and then a reopening of that gap; the emergence of children as the largest group of poor Americans; dramatic growth in the use of information technology, e-commerce, and e-government; the changing nature of work and a redefinition of careers; fears about international terrorism; and the emergence of obesity as an important public health concern. Perhaps most ominously, we have experienced a dramatic decline in social capital in recent decades (Putnam, 2000), and citizens in the United States and other developed countries appear to be less happy now than they were thirty years ago (Lane, 2000; Institute of Education, 2003).

Not surprisingly, we have seen sustained attention to governmental and nonprofit organizational design, management, performance, and accountability as part of the process of addressing these and other concerns. Indeed, in the public sector, change—though not necessarily dramatic or rapid change—is the rule rather than the exception (Peters, 1996, p. vii, Rainey, 1997, p. 317; Light, 1997, 2000; Kettl, 2002).

Globally, the spread of democracy and a beneficent capitalism seemed almost inevitable after the collapse of the Soviet Union (Schwartz, Leyden, and Hyatt, 1999; Giddens, 2002). Now, progress seems far more uneven (Huntingdon, 1998; Friedman, 2000; Sardar and Davies, 2002). Dictators—even tyrants—still abound; concerns about labor dislocations and exploitation persist; unemployment rates are high in many, perhaps most, developed and developing countries; many of the world's fish stocks are depleted, and so on. Poverty and ill health are far too widespread, even when some of the worst effects of ill health might be removed for literally pennies per person per day through ensuring clean water and sanitation facilities and easy access to immunization and generic drugs. Global environmental change shows up in hotter average temperatures, changed rainfall patterns, prolonged droughts, an increasing number of catastrophic storms, and increased skin cancer rates. The Worldwatch Institute (2004) claims in *State of the World 2004: Richer, Fatter, and Not Much Happier,* that worldwide consumerism has put us on a collision course with environmental disaster. Terrorism is real and deeply threatening, and must be countered if democracy, sane economic growth, and peaceful conflict management are to occur. And Sir Martin Rees, a renowned astrophysicist and Britain's astronomer royal, guesses the world has only a fifty-fifty chance of escaping a devastating global catastrophe of some kind sometime in this century (Rees, 2003).

So do I have your attention? Organizations that want to survive, prosper, and do good and important work must respond to the challenges the world presents. Their response may be to do what they have always done, only better, but they may also need to shift their focus and strategies. Although organizations typically experience long periods of relative stability when change is incremental, they also typically encounter periods of dramatic and rapid change (Gersick, 1991; Baumgartner and Jones, 1993; Mintzberg, 1994). These periods of organizational change may be exciting, but they may also be anxiety producing—or even terrifying. As geologist Derek V. Ager notes, "The history of any one part of the earth . . . consists of long periods of boredom and short periods of terror." (Gould, 1980, p. 185).

These environmental and organizational changes are aggravated by the interconnectedness of the world. Changes anywhere typically result in changes elsewhere. Or as novelist Salman Rushdie (1981) says, "Most of what matters in our lives takes place in our absence" (p. 19). This increasing interconnectedness is perhaps most apparent in the blurring of three traditionally important distinctions—between domestic and international spheres; between policy areas; and between public, private, and nonprofit sectors (Cleveland, 2002; Kettl, 2002). These changes have become dramatically apparent since the mid-1970s.

The U.S. economy is now intimately integrated with the economies of the rest of the world, and events abroad have domestic repercussions. My wife and I own two U.S.-made cars—whose engines and drivetrains are Japanese. Deflation in Japan in the last few years has aroused fears of deflation in the United States and elsewhere. When I was growing up, the Soviet Union was the enemy; now the Evil Empire, as President Ronald Reagan called it, does not exist, and Russia is an ally on many fronts. Threats to U.S. oil supplies from abroad prompt meetings in and actions by the White House, the intelligence agencies, and the Departments of State, Defense, and Homeland Security.

Distinctions between policy areas are also hard to maintain. For example, educational policy is now seen as a type of economic development and industrial policy to help communities and firms compete more effectively. Strengthening the economy will not eliminate the human service costs incurred by the government, but letting it falter will certainly increase them. Physical education programs, educational programs promoting healthy lifestyles, and parks and recreation budgets are viewed as ways of controlling health care costs.

Finally, the boundaries between public, private, and nonprofit sectors have eroded. National sovereignty has "leaked up" to multinational corporations, international organizations, and international alliances. Sovereignty has "leaked out" to businesses and nonprofit organizations. Taxes are not collected by government tax collectors but are withheld by private and nonprofit organizations from their employees and turned over to the government. The nation's health, education, and welfare are public responsibilities, yet increasingly, we rely on private and nonprofit organizations to produce services in these areas. Weapons systems are not produced in government arsenals but by private industry. When such fundamental public functions as tax collection; health, education, and welfare; and weapons production are handled by private and nonprofit organizations, then surely the boundaries between public, private, and nonprofit organizations are irretrievably blurred. But beyond that, sovereignty has also "leaked down"—state and local governments have been the big gainers in power in the last fifteen years, and the federal government the big loser. Now, as *Governing* magazine's editors note, "In the first decade of the new century, the federal government is no longer the instrument of first resort when it comes to dealing with the most complex social and economic problems. State and local governments are the problem-solvers—uncertain, under-funded and disunited as they frequently are" ("The Way We Were and Are," 2002, p. 37). The result of this "leakage" of sovereignty up, out, and down and this blurring of boundaries between public, private and nonprofit sectors has been the creation of what Brinton Milward and his colleagues call the *hollow state,* in which government is simply an actor—and not necessarily the most important actor—in the networks we rely on to do the public's work (Milward, Provan, and Else, 1993; Provan and Milward, 2001).

The blurring of these boundaries means that we have moved to a world in which no one organization or institution is fully in charge and yet many are involved, affected, or have a partial responsibility to act (Cleveland, 2002; Kettl, 2002; Crosby and Bryson, forthcoming). This increased jurisdictional ambiguity—coupled with the events and trends noted previously—requires public and nonprofit organizations (and communities) to think, act, and learn strategically as never before. Strategic planning is designed to help them do so. The extensive experience of public, nonprofit, and private organizations with strategic planning in recent decades offers a fund of research and advice on which we will draw throughout this book.

Definition, Purpose, and Benefits of Strategic Planning

What is strategic planning? Drawing on Olsen and Eadie (1982, p. 4), I define *strategic planning* as *a disciplined effort to produce fundamental decisions and actions that shape and guide what an organization (or other entity) is, what it does, and why it does it.* At its best, strategic planning requires broad-scale yet effective information gathering, clarification of the mission to be pursued and issues to be addressed along the way, development and exploration of strategic alternatives, and an emphasis on the future implications of present decisions. Strategic planning can facilitate communication and participation, accommodate divergent interests and values, foster wise and reasonably analytical decision making, and promote successful implementation and accountability. In short, at its best strategic planning can prompt in organizations the kind of imagination—and commitment—that psychotherapist and theologian Thomas Moore thinks is necessary to deal with individuals' life conundrums.

Figure 1.1 presents the ABCs of strategic planning, a capsule summary of what strategic planning is all about. Detail can be added as needed to this basic understanding. *A* is figuring out where you are, *B* is figuring out where you want to go, and *C* is figuring out how to get there. Leaders and managers come to understand *A*, *B*, and *C* as they formulate, clarify, and resolve strategic issues—the fundamental policy choices or challenges the organization has to face. The content of *A* and *B* are the organization's existing or new mission, structure and systems, communications, programs and services, people and skills, relationships, budgets, and other supports. The content of *C* is the strategic plan; plans for various functions; ways to redesign, restructure, or reengineer; budget allocations; and other vehicles for change. Getting from *A* to *C* involves clarifying vision, mission, and goals.

FIGURE 1.1. THE ABCS OF STRATEGIC PLANNING.

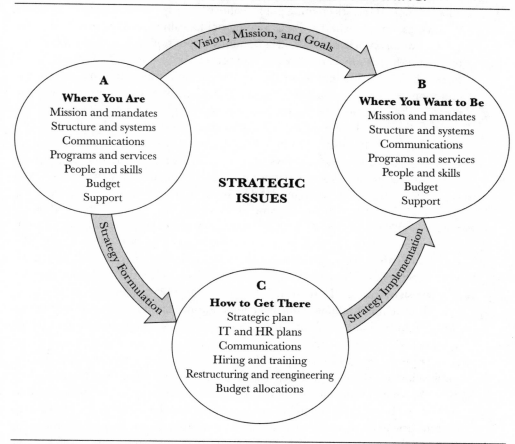

Source: Bryson and Alston, 2005.

Getting from *A* to *C* is the process of strategy formulation, whereas getting from *C* to *B* is strategy implementation. To do strategic planning well, you need to figure out *A*, *B*, and *C* and how they should be connected. You accomplish this principally by understanding the issues that *A*, *B*, *C*, and their interconnections must address effectively. This summary also makes it clear that strategic planning is not a single thing but a set of concepts, procedures, and tools.

So that is how strategic planning is defined and briefly what it is. But why engage in strategic planning? At its best the purpose of strategic planning in the United States and elsewhere is to help public and nonprofit organizations "create public value," in Mark Moore's compelling and evocative phrase (Moore, 1995, 2000). Moore discusses creating public value primarily as the responsibility of individual managers, whereas I see creating public value more broadly as an individual, group, organizational, and community responsibility. Creating public value means producing enterprises, policies, programs, projects, services, or infrastructures (physical, technological, social, etc.) that advance the public interest and the common good at a reasonable cost. In the United States, creating public value means enhancing life, liberty, and the pursuit of happiness for all while also fostering a more perfect union. It means ensuring that the beneficial effects of our institutions and efforts carry on into the indefinite future and that we change what we must so that the world is always left better off than we found it. Strategic planning is about listening to "the better angels of our nature," as Abraham Lincoln called them in his First Inaugural Address—it is about organizing our best and most noble hopes and dreams, making them reasonable and actionable, and bringing them to life. In this sense, strategic planning is about "the manufacture of transcendence" (Krieger, 2000) and finds its inspiration in the deepest sources of "the real American Dream" (Delbanco, 1999). Beyond that, strategic planning in the United States and elsewhere is meant to help its practitioners and beneficiaries "pursue significance" (Denhardt, 1993)—in short, to create public value.

Most of the thinking about strategic planning has focused on its use in for-profit organizations. Until the early 1980s, strategic planning in the public sector was applied primarily to military strategy and the practice of statecraft on a grand scale (Quinn, 1980; Bracker, 1980). That situation changed, however, with the publication in 1982 of J. B. Olsen and D. C. Eadie's *The Game Plan: Governance with Foresight,* which marks the beginning of sustained applications of strategic planning to the broad range of public organizations and the inception of scholarship on how best to do so. Strategic planning for nonprofit organizations has proceeded in parallel, with the most important early publication being Barry (1986). I am pleased to be able to say that the first and second editions of this book, published in 1988 and 1995, respectively, also played an important role in expanding the use of strategic planning by public and nonprofit organizations.

Experience has clearly demonstrated that strategic planning can be used successfully by

- Public agencies, departments, and major organizational divisions (for example, Dair, 1999a, 1999b; Abramson and Lawrence, 2001; Barzelay and Campbell, 2003)
- General purpose governments, such as city, county, state, and tribal governments (for example, Berry and Wechsler, 1995; Jurkiewicz and Bowman, 2002; Eitel, 2003; Hendrick, 2003)

- Nonprofit organizations providing what are basically public services (for example, Medley, 1999a, 1999b; Allison and Kaye, 1997; Crittenden, 2000; Kaplan, 2001; Berger and Vasile, 2002)
- Specific functions—such as transportation, health, or education—that bridge organizational and governmental boundaries (for example, Nelson and French, 2002; Poister, 2003; Burby, 2003)
- Interorganizational networks—such as partnerships, collaboratives, alliances, and coalitions—in the public and nonprofit sectors (for example, Stone, 2000; Linden, 2002)
- Entire communities, urban or metropolitan areas, regions, and states (for example, Chrislip, 2002; Wheeland, 2003)

This book concentrates on strategic planning for public and nonprofit organizations. It also considers, in lesser detail, the application of strategic planning to communities and services that bridge organizational boundaries. (The term *community* is used throughout to refer to communities, urban or metropolitan areas, regions, and states.) Although the process detailed in this book is applicable to all the entities just listed, the specifics of its implementation may differ for each case. When strategic planning is focused on an organization, it is likely that most of the key decision makers will be *insiders,* even though considerable relevant information may be gathered from outsiders. Certainly, this will be true of public agencies, local governments, and nonprofit organizations that deliver "public" services. When most of the key decision makers are insiders, it will likely be easier to get people together to decide important matters, reconcile differences, and coordinate implementation activities. (Of course, whether or not the organization's board of directors or governing body consists of insiders or outsiders may be an open question, particularly when the members of this body are publicly elected. For instance, are city council members insiders, outsiders, or both? Regardless of the answer, it remains true that typically a major proportion of the key decision makers will be insiders.)

In contrast, when strategic planning is focused on a function—often crossing organizational or governmental boundaries—or on a community, almost all the key decision makers will be *outsiders* (Huxham, 2003). In these situations the focus will be on how to organize thought, action, and learning more or less collaboratively within an interorganizational network or among networks where no one person, group, organization, or institution is fully in charge but where many are involved, or affected, or have a partial responsibility to act. We should expect that it might be more difficult to organize an effective strategic planning process in such a *shared-power* context (Bardach, 1998; Huxham, 2003). More time will probably need to be spent on organizing forums for discussion, involving diverse constituencies, negotiating agreements in existing or new arenas, and coordinating the activities of numerous, relatively independent people, groups, organizations, and institutions (Innes, 1996; Burby, 2003; Huxham, 2003).

Organizations engage in strategic planning for many reasons. Proponents of strategic planning typically try to persuade their colleagues of its value with one or more of the following kinds of statements (Nutt and Backoff, 1992, pp. 9–17; Barry, 1997, pp. 3–4; Borins, 1998, pp. 41–49):

"We face so many conflicting demands we need to figure out what our focus and priorities should be."

"The rules are changing on us. We are being told to emphasize measurable outcomes, the competition is stiffer, funding is getting tighter, collaboration is being pushed, and we need to figure out what we do or can do well that fits with the changing picture."

"We have gone through Total Quality Management, reinvention and reengineering, downsizing, and rightsizing, along with the revolution in information technology. Now people are asking us to take on process improvement, performance management, balanced scorecards, knowledge management, and who knows what else? How can we make sure all of this effort is headed in the right direction?"

"We can expect a severe budget deficit next year, and the public will suffer unless we drastically rethink the way we do business. Somehow we need to figure out how to do more with less through better integration of our activities, finances, human resources, and information technology."

"Our city is changing, and in spite of our best efforts, things do not seem to be getting better."

"This major issue is staring us in the face, and we need some way to help us think about its resolution, or else we will be badly hurt."

"We need to integrate or coordinate better the services we provide with the services of other organizations. Right now, things are just too fragmented and poorly resourced, and our clients needing more than one service are suffering."

"Our principal funder [or board of directors or new chief executive] has asked us to prepare a strategic plan."

"We know a leadership change is coming, and want to prepare for it."

"We want to use strategic planning to educate, involve, and revitalize our board and staff."

"Our organization has an embarrassment of riches, but we still need to figure out how we can have the biggest impact; we owe it to our stakeholders."

"Everyone is doing strategic planning these days; we'd better do it, too."

Whatever the reasons that drive public and nonprofit organizations to engage in strategic planning, similar *benefits* are likely to result. Many authors argue that strategic planning can produce a number of benefits for organizations (for example, Nutt and Backoff, 1992; Barry, 1997; Nutt, 2002). The first and perhaps most obvious potential benefit is the *promotion of strategic thinking, acting, and learning,* especially through dialogue and *strategic conversation* among key actors (Van der Heijden, 1996). Strategic thinking, acting, and learning are promoted by systematic information gathering about the organization's external and internal environment and various actors' interests, thoughtful examination of the organization's successes and failures, clarification of future direction, establishment of organizational priorities for action, and in general, attention to the acquisition and use of knowledge and skills. For many organizations, "strategic planning has become a natural part of doing business." Regular dialogues about key concerns are a central feature of "moving the organization forward and increasing its effectiveness" (Barry, 1997, p. 10). In short, strategic planning can be used to help organize and manage effective organizational change processes in which the organization figures out what to change but also keeps the best.

The second benefit is *improved decision making.* Improved decision making is crucial, because recent studies have indicated that at least half of all strategic decisions fail as a result of poor decision-making processes (Nutt, 2002)! Strategic planning focuses attention on the crucial issues and challenges the organization faces and helps key decision makers figure out what they should do about them. It can help them make today's decisions in light of the likely future consequences of those decisions. It can help them develop a coherent and defensible basis for decision making and then coordinate the resulting decisions across levels and functions. It can help them exercise maximum discretion in the areas that are under their organization's control, and influence actions and outcomes in those areas that are not. Strategic planning thus can help organizations formulate and clearly communicate their strategic directions and intentions to relevant audiences and also act on those intentions.

The third benefit is *enhanced organizational effectiveness,* which flows from the first two. Organizations engaging in strategic planning are encouraged to clarify and address major organizational issues, respond wisely to internal and external demands and pressures (including those for accountability), and deal effectively with rapidly changing circumstances. They are encouraged, in other words, to be well managed. And although it sounds almost tautological to say so, it clearly is not: organizations that are managed well perform better, are more responsive, more innovative, have greater influence, and are more accountable than organizations that are not managed well (Light, 1998; Borins, 1998; Rainey and Steinbauer, 1999; Gill and Meier, 2001; O'Toole and Meier, 2003; Coggburn and Schneider, 2003; Boyne and Gould-Williams, 2003). Good management creates good organizational systems; in other words, good management is a *process* that draws on *resources* to produce the *outputs and outcomes* that indicate organizational effectiveness and that trigger the resource flows the organization needs to sustain itself and continue to create public value into the future (Bryson, Gibbons, and Shaye, 2000). Porter (1985, pp. 33–61) refers to this linkage of inputs, processes, and outputs in firms as a *value chain,* and if this chain does not produce value in the marketplace at reasonable cost, the firm is in danger of going out of business. In the case of public and nonprofit organizations, we can say that the value chain must create public value at reasonable cost or serious consequences are likely to ensue. Increasingly, integrated use of human resources, information technology, and financial management are crucial elements of organizing, strengthening, protecting, and sustaining organizational capabilities for creating public value (Bryson, 2003a).

Fourth, beyond organizational effectiveness, strategic planning can produce *enhanced effectiveness of broader societal systems.* Most of the public problems we face these days stretch beyond any one organization's boundaries. As Donald Schön (1971) pointed out long ago, our big challenges in education, health, employment, poverty, the environment—you name it—typically need to be conceptualized at the supraorganizational, or *system,* level, not the *organizational* level. Those systems are what need to work better if our lives and the world are to be made better. Organizations can contribute to better functioning of these systems but typically must do so in partnership with others or by somehow taking those others into account (Kettl, 2002; Crosby and Bryson, forthcoming). Strategic planning can help organizations take the broader environment into account and help them figure out how best to partner with other organizations so that they can jointly create better environments (Joyce, 1999). The result probably should be some sort of concerted institutional redesign effort at the system level (for example, Brandl, 1998; Lake, Reis, and Spann, 2000) that enhances intellectual, human, and social capital at both the societal and organizational levels (Nahapiet and Ghoshal, 1998).

Finally, strategic planning can directly *benefit the people involved.* Policymakers and key decision makers can be helped to fulfill their roles and responsibilities, and participants in the process can improve their teamwork and expertise (Kim, 2002). Further, both employees and organizations that can create real, demonstrable public value are more likely to have a job in the future. Public and nonprofit organizations are externally justified in that they exist to provide real service; those that do and that continue to find ways to do so as circumstances change typically continue to exist (Pinsonneault and Kraemer, 2002; Holzer, Lee, and Newman, 2003).

In short, strategic planning at its best surely must count as a *smart practice*, which Bardach defines as a "method of interacting with a situation that is intended to produce some result . . . [and] also involves taking advantage of some latent opportunity for creating value on the cheap" (1998, p. 36). Strategic planning is smart because it is relatively easy to do; is not all that time and resource intensive, particularly when matched against the costs of potential failure; and would seem to go hand in hand with the craft of creating public value (Lynn, 1996; Bardach, 1998). Strategic planning can be a highly cost-effective tool for creating useful ideas for strategic interventions and for figuring out how to organize the participation and coalition needed to adopt the ideas and protect them during implementation. When not overly formalized, bereft of participation, and obsessed with numbers, strategic planning can be a very effective route to enhanced organizational responsiveness, performance, and accountability.

Although strategic planning *can* provide all these benefits, there is no guarantee it *will*. Indeed, it is highly unlikely that any organization will experience all or even most of the benefits of strategic planning the first time through—or even after many cycles of strategic planning. For one thing, strategic planning is simply a set of concepts, procedures, and tools. Leaders, managers, and planners need to engage in strategic planning carefully because their success will depend at least in part on how they tailor the process to their situations. This book presents a generic strategic planning process for governments, public agencies, and nonprofit organizations that is based on considerable research and experience. It offers advice on applying the process in different circumstances. But the process will work well only when enough key decision makers and planners support it and use it with common sense and a sensitivity to the particulars of their situation. And even then success is never guaranteed, particularly when difficult and fraught strategic issues are addressed.

Furthermore, strategic planning is not always advisable (Mintzberg, 1994; Barry, 1997; Mintzberg, Ahlstrand, and Lampel, 1998). There are two compelling reasons for holding off on a formal strategic planning effort. First, strategic planning may not be the best first step for an organization whose roof has fallen in— keeping in mind, of course, that every crisis should be managed strategically (Mitroff and Pearson, 1993; Weick and Sutcliffe, 2001). For example, the organization may need to remedy a cash flow crunch before undertaking strategic planning. Or the organization may need to postpone strategic planning until it fills a key leadership position. Or it could be that showing compassion for people who have faced some sort of disaster is the first order of business (Dutton, Frost, Worline, Kanov, and Lilius, 2002). Second, when the organization's key decision makers lack the skills, resources, or commitment to produce a good plan or when implementation is extremely unlikely, strategic planning will be a waste of time. Such a situation embodies what Bill Roering and I have called the "paradox of strategic planning": it is most needed where it is least likely to work, and least needed where it is most likely to work (Bryson and Roering, 1988, 1989). If strategic planning is undertaken in such a situation, it probably should be a focused and limited effort aimed at developing the necessary skills, resources, and commitment.

A number of other reasons can be offered for not engaging in strategic planning. Too often, however, these "reasons" are actually excuses, used to avoid what should be done. For example, one might argue that strategic planning will be of little use if the costs of the process are likely to outweigh any benefits or if the process takes time and money that might be better used elsewhere. These concerns may be justified, but recall that the purpose of strategic planning is to produce fundamental decisions and actions that define what an organization (or other entity) is, what it does, and why it does it. In Chapter Three I will argue that strategic planning probably should not take more than 10 percent of the ordinary work time available to any key decision maker during a year. When is the cost of that 10 percent likely to outweigh the benefit of focusing that time on the production of fundamental decisions and actions by the organization? In my experience, hardly ever.

Many organizations—particularly small nonprofit organizations—may prefer to rely on the intuition and vision of gifted leaders instead of on formal strategic planning processes. When these leaders are strategically minded and experienced, there may be no need for formal strategic planning. It is rare, however, for any leader to have all the information necessary to develop an effective strategy, and rarer still for any strategy developed by a single person to engender the kind of commitment necessary for effective implementation. A reasonably structured and formalized strategic planning process helps organizations gather the information necessary for effective strategy formulation. It also provides the discipline and commitment necessary to effectively implement strategies.

In addition, many organizations—particularly those that have enormous difficulty reaching decisions that cut across levels, functions, or programs—find that incremental decision making and mutual adjustments of various sorts among interested partisans constitute the only process that will work. *Muddling* of this sort, as Charles Lindblom (1959) described it, legitimizes the existing distribution of power and resources in the organization and allows the separate parts of the organization to pursue opportunities as they arise. Interesting and useful innovations may develop that enhance learning and promote useful adaptations to changing circumstances. In fact, if the muddling occurs within a general agreement on overall direction, everyone may be better off (Quinn, 1980; Behn, 1988; Mintzberg, Ahlstrand, and Lampel, 1998). Unfortunately, muddling typically results in chronic suboptimization of organizational performance, with the result that key external and internal constituencies may be badly served (Osborne and Plastrik, 1997; Barzelay, 1992, 2001).

Strategic planning should also probably not be undertaken when implementation is extremely unlikely. To engage in strategic planning when effective implementation will not follow is the organizational equivalent of making the average New Year's resolution. Nevertheless, when armed with the knowledge that implementation will be difficult, key decision makers and planners can focus extra attention on ensuring implementation success.

Finally, organizations may simply not know how and where to start and stop the process. The good news is that strategic planning can begin almost anywhere—the process is so interconnected that you end up covering most phases via conversation and dialogue, no matter where you start.

What Strategic Planning Is Not

Strategic planning is no panacea. As noted, strategic planning is simply a set of concepts, procedures, and tools designed to help leaders, managers, and planners think, act, and learn strategically. Used in wise and skillful ways by a coalition of interested parties, it can help organizations focus on producing effective decisions and actions that create public value, further the organization's mission, meet organizational mandates, and satisfy key stakeholders. Strategic planning should not be a substitute for strategic thinking, acting, and learning carried out by caring and committed people. Unfortunately, when used thoughtlessly, obsessively, or excessively formally, strategic planning can drive out precisely the kind of strategic thinking, acting, and learning it was supposed to promote.

Furthermore, strategic planning is not a substitute for leadership. In my experience there is *no* substitute for leadership when it comes to strategic planning. At least some key decision makers and process champions must be committed to strategic planning, or any attempts to use it are bound to fail.

A standard distinction is to argue that leadership is "doing the right things" whereas management is "doing things right." My own view is that *both* leadership and management involve *both* doing the right things *and* doing them well, but if we stick with this rather simplistic distinction for a moment, strategic planning is first and foremost about clarifying mission, mandates, vision, goals, and the nature of the common good and public value to be created—doing the right things—whereas management is about making sure those things are done well through strategies and operations at reasonable cost. But no matter what your view of the similarities of and differences between leadership and management, both matter and both are needed if strategic planning is to succeed—because it won't succeed by itself!

In addition, strategic planning is not synonymous with creation of an organization's strategy. Organizational strategies have numerous sources, both planned and unplanned. Strategic planning is likely to result in a statement of organizational *intentions,* but what is *realized* will be some combination of what is *intended* and what *emerges* along the way (McCaskey, 1974; Mintzberg, Ahlstrand, and Lampel, 1998). Strategic planning can help organizations develop and implement effective strategies, but organizations should also remain open to unforeseen opportunities as well. Too much attention to strategic planning and reverence for strategic plans can blind organizations to unplanned and unexpected—yet incredibly useful—sources of information, insight, and action.

It should be clear now that the *discipline* highlighted in my definition of strategic planning can be of two sorts. The first harkens back to the Latin roots of the word and emphasizes instruction, training, education, and learning. The second embodies later interpretations and emphasizes order, control, and punishment. I personally prefer the emphasis on education and learning, although there clearly are occasions when imposing order, taking control, and imposing well-chosen sanctions are appropriate. Key leaders, managers, and planners can best use strategic planning as an educational and learning tool, to help them figure out what is really important and what should be done about it. Sometimes this means following a particular sequence of steps and preparing formal strategic plans, but not necessarily. The ultimate end of strategic planning should not be rigid adherence to a particular process or the production of plans. Instead, strategic planning should promote wise strategic thought, action, and learning on behalf of an organization and its key stakeholders. It should be used to create public value. What steps to follow, in what sequence, and whether or not to prepare formal plans are subsidiary concerns.

Why Strategic Planning Is Becoming Standard Smart Practice

The vast majority of public and nonprofit organizations now claim to engage in strategic planning (Poister and Streib, 1994; Berry and Wechsler, 1995; Berman and West, 1998; Joyce, 1999). Exactly what they mean when they say that is unclear. All that is really clear is that strategic planning is an idea whose time appears to have come. The idea that strategic planning is something that skilled leaders and managers do has passed the "tipping point" (Gladwell, 2000) and is now an idea "in good currency" (Schön, 1971). Doing strategic planning has become accepted practice—and indeed, when done well, it is a smart practice.

That said, many leaders and managers no doubt groan at the prospect of having to go through another round of strategic planning. They may have "been there, done that," and depending on their experience, may not want to do it again. They have seen cost-benefit analysis, planning-programming-budgeting systems, zero-based budgeting, management by objectives, continuous improvement, downsizing, contracting out, reinvention, reengineering, and a host of other techniques trumpeted by a cadre of authors and management consultants. They have also, all too often, seen these techniques fall by the wayside after a burst of initial enthusiasm. Managers, in particular, frequently and justifiably are tired of "buzzword bingo" and feel as if they are the victims of some sort of perverse management hazing or "status degradation ritual" (Schein, 1987, pp. 84–86).

But strategic planning, at least the sort of strategic planning proposed in this book, is far from a passing fad. The strategic planning process presented here is durable because it takes account of *political* intelligence, rationality, and decision making. Many other management techniques fail because they ignore, try to circumvent, or even try to counter the political nature of life in private, public, and nonprofit sector organizations. Too many planners and managers, at least in my experience, just do not understand that such a quest is almost guaranteed to be quixotic. *Politics* is the method we humans use to find answers to the analytically unresolvable questions of what should be done for collective purposes, how it should be done, and why it should be done (Moore, 1995, p. 54; Christensen, 1999; Van Horn, Baumer, and Gormley, 2001; Stone, 2002).

Many management innovations have tried to improve government decision making and operations by trying to impose a formal rationality on systems that are not rational, at least in the conventional meaning of that word. Public and nonprofit organizations (and communities) embody a *political* intelligence and rationality, and any technique that is likely to work well in such organizations must accept and build on the nature of political rationality (Wildavsky, 1979; March and Olsen, 1995; Stone, 2002).

We can pursue this point further by contrasting two kinds of decision making: the "rational" planning model and political decision making. The rational planning model is presented in Figure 1.2. This rational-deductive approach to decision making begins with goals; policies, programs, and actions are then deduced to achieve those goals. If there is a traditional planning theology, this model is one of its icons. Indeed, if there had been a planning Moses, Figure 1.2 would

FIGURE 1.2. RATIONAL PLANNING MODEL.

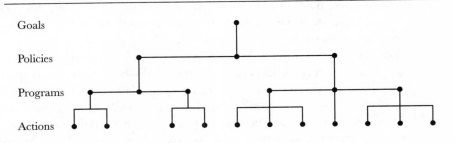

have been etched on his tablets when he came down from the mount. Now consider a fundamental assumption of the rational planning model—that in the fragmented, shared power settings that characterize many public and nonprofit organizations, networks, and communities, either there will be a *consensus* on goals, policies, programs, and actions necessary to achieve organizational aims or there will be someone with enough *power and authority* that consensus does not matter. This assumption just does not hold in most circumstances. Only in fairly centralized, authoritarian, and quasi-military bureaucracies will this assumption hold— maybe (Roberts and Wargo, 1994).

Now let us examine a model that contrasts sharply with the rational planning model, the political decision-making model presented in Figure 1.3. This model is inductive, not deductive. It begins with issues, which almost by definition involve conflict, not consensus. The conflicts may be over ends, means, timing, location, political advantage, reasons for change, or philosophy and values—and the conflicts may be severe. As efforts proceed to resolve these conflicts and learn how to move ahead, policies and programs emerge that address the issues and that are politically rational, that is, they are politically acceptable to involved or affected parties. Over time, more general policies may be formulated to capture, frame, shape, guide, or interpret the policies, programs, and learning developed to deal with the issues. These various policies and programs are in effect treaties among the various stakeholder groups, and even though they may not record a true consensus, they do represent a reasonable level of agreement among stakeholders (Lindblom, 1965, 1980; March and Olsen, 1989, 1995).

Now, the heart of the strategic planning process discussed in Chapter Two is the identification and resolution of strategic—that is, very important and consequential—issues. The process, in other words, accepts political decision making's emphasis on issues and seeks to inform the formulation and resolution of those issues. Effective strategic planning therefore should make political decision

FIGURE 1.3. POLITICAL DECISION-MAKING MODEL.

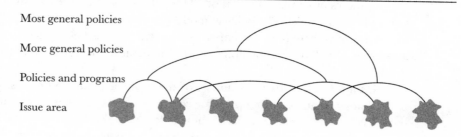

Most general policies

More general policies

Policies and programs

Issue area

makers more effective, and if practiced consistently, might even make their professional lives easier (Janis, 1989; Nutt, 2002). Because every key decision maker in a large public or nonprofit organization is in effect a political decision maker (Van Horn, Baumer, and Gormley, 2001; Bolman and Deal, 2003), strategic planning can help these decision makers and their organizations. Strategic planning—at least as described in this book—therefore will last in government and nonprofit organizations because it accepts and builds on the nature of political decision making. If done well, it actually improves political decisions, as well as programs, policies, and learning how to do better.

Having drawn a sharp distinction between the rational planning model and political decision making, I must now emphasize that the two models are not inherently antithetical. Indeed, research by Judith Innes (1996) and her colleagues demonstrates that multiparty efforts to reach consensus on important issues fraught with conflict often can look extremely messy in practice yet meet very high standards of rationality after all the political, technical, and legal issues have been sorted out. The challenge in this case is simply to sequence the approaches appropriately. Use of the political decision-making model is necessary to work out consensual agreements on what programs and policies will best resolve key issues. Then the rational planning model can be used to recast that consensus in the form of goals, policies, programs, and actions. Although the planning and decision making that goes into the formulation of a strategic plan may look fairly sloppy to an outsider, once a consensus is reached on what to do, the resulting strategic plan can be rewritten in a form that is rational in the ordinary sense of the term. Furthermore, the rational planning model may be used to sort out and address any minor (and perhaps major) inconsistencies embedded in the political consensus. Clear goals, when backed by political agreement and authority, can help foster and guide organizational innovation and effectiveness (Behn, 1999a; Nutt, 2002).

To use another example, in many organizations and communities people display a broad-based consensus on basic purposes and values—and often on many policies, programs, and actions as well. They may even possess a consensus on the organization's or community's vision. This consensus can be recast using the rational planning model. The political model can then be used to address remaining issues on which there is no agreement. These remaining issues are likely to revolve around what will have to be done in order to achieve the agreed-upon goals or vision.

To summarize, a great advantage of the strategic planning process outlined in this book is that it does not presume consensus where consensus does not exist, but it can accommodate consensus where it does exist. Because this process makes no presumption of consensus, it is more suitable for politicized circumstances than are purely rational approaches. An intense attention to stakeholders and their interests, external and internal environments, and strategic issues means that the actions ultimately agreed upon are more likely to be *politically* wise and that organizational survival and prosperity are therefore more likely to be ensured. Furthermore, because it gathers relevant information, asks probing questions, and focuses on how best to raise the issues, the process can be used to inform political decision making in such a way that virtuous public and nonprofit purposes are better served than they would be if only the rawest forms of political decision making prevailed (Flyvbjerg, 1998). The process, in other words, provides a way of blending substantive rationality *and* political intelligence—content *and* process—in wise ways to the betterment of the organizations and communities that use it (March and Olsen, 1989, 1995; Nutt, 2002; Stone, 2002).

Three Examples of Strategic Planning

Throughout this book the experiences of three organizations (two public and one nonprofit) are used to illustrate key points about strategic planning—including its capacity for accommodating substantive rationality and political intelligence. Each of these organizations used the strategic planning process outlined here, explicitly or implicitly adapting it for their own purposes. I was a strategic planning consultant for all three organizations, although the extent of my involvement varied from extensive to minimal. Each project represented an action research project in which the aims included developing theory and guidance for practice (Eden and Huxham, 1996).

The three organizations described here are a suburban school district (School District), a major U.S. Navy organization (the Naval Security Group), and a nonprofit organization providing affordable housing, jobs, training, and other support services (Project for Pride in Living). (The identities of the School District and its members have been masked to preserve their privacy.) A number of other less detailed examples are used as well to clarify the discussion.

School District

The School District is located in one of the fastest-growing suburbs of a major Midwestern metropolitan area. This primarily middle-class community has a reputation for being well planned and well managed, which the citizenry expects and which is important given the community's rapid growth. When the School District's strategic planning process began in 1996, the community's population was approximately 50,000 and was projected to increase to 60,000 in the first decade of the twenty-first century. The school census was expected to increase in parallel with the general population increase. In the decade leading up to initiation of the strategic planning process, the student population had more than doubled, to approximately 9,750, with demographic studies predicting a peak of approximately 10,500 students shortly after the millennium.

The School District has enjoyed a strong reputation for providing a quality education and has high graduation rates, a large number of National Merit Scholars, and more than its share of championship sports teams. But by 1996 the district's existing strategic plan, *Vision 2001,* was seven years old, and a number of changes were prompting initiation of a new round of planning. First, the school-age population was growing, and the fact that 60 percent of the students were in grade 6 or below indicated that a significant population bulge was working its way through the system. Second, changes in technology and physical facilities were changing ways of working and interacting and producing a range of new opportunities and challenges. When the *Vision 2001* plan was written in 1989, little thought had been given to laptop computers for students; voice-mail and e-mail communications; the Internet, intranets, and Web sites; and the creation of a sports facility under an inflatable bubble and of an activity center and a performing arts center in the high school. All of these were important realities in 1996. Third, a new superintendent had been hired in late 1995. The school board and the district had made a major commitment to quality improvement under the previous superintendent. The board was intent on making sure the new superintendent was also committed to quality education as well as to partnerships; two-way, open communications; effective decision making; and customer service. The new superintendent was committed—and also believed that strategic planning was an important front end for all of those processes.

The new superintendent had worked with me and my colleague Charles "Chuck" Finn before, on a strategic planning effort for a school district on the other side of the metropolitan area. (That case is presented in the 1995 edition of this book, where it is also called "the school district.") That effort was very successful, and he wanted to repeat the process in his new assignment, with us once again as consultants. He gained the commitment of the board to strategic planning as its top priority, encouraged the assistant superintendent (who would become the day-to-day manager of the process and later superintendent herself) to embrace the idea, and gained buy-in incrementally from other key actors.

As the process unfolded, a number of changes occurred. The vision and mission were rethought; the commitment to quality was reinterpreted, within the new strategic framework; and facilities and transportation issues were addressed. In addition, an underlying issue of mistrust between administration and staff emerged. The previous superintendent, although highly regarded outside the organization, was known to be abusive to many inside the organization who disagreed with him. The new superintendent's open and participatory style thus was initially met by a deep skepticism bordering on fear. This issue had to be dealt with—which it was—before the process could go very far. Also, the process was delayed for a time in the fall of 1997 by a successful referendum to fund facilities. Ultimately, in 1998, a new strategic plan was produced that brought with it the broad understanding and commitment that an open and participatory process at its best can produce. A new, trimmed-down strategic plan (discussed in Chapter Twelve) was produced in 2004.

The Naval Security Group

The Naval Security Group (NSG) is a major Navy organization in the U.S. Department of Defense. NSG provides cryptological personnel, products, and services for Navy ships and aircraft and for the National Security Agency (NSA). It comprises a headquarters staff of about 200 personnel in the Washington, D.C., area and over 10,000 additional personnel scattered around the world on ships, aircraft, and shore stations. NSG—along with comparable branches in the U.S. Army, Marines, and Air Force—is responsible for protecting, detecting, and analyzing communications that affect U.S. security and military preparedness.

In early 1992, NSG headquarters had not yet engaged in formal strategic planning, and the organizational culture was still reactive and crisis driven. At the height of the Cold War, NSG had had very little need for strategic planning, because most of the group's systems, people, and training were fully and effectively directed against Cold War enemies. The group was highly successful in accomplishing its mission and enjoyed good support from its two major stakeholders, the Navy and NSA. Thus the senior leadership had never been forced to consider major changes in direction. From time to time the group had introduced major new cryptological systems, but they amounted merely to a more effective methodology, not a major overhaul or redirection.

NSG did draft a formal strategic plan in July 1992, in response to the Navy's first attempt at Total Quality Management (TQM). As is typical of many first strategic planning efforts, the plan fulfilled a step in the TQM process, but it was hardly a strategic guide to action. The plan had high-level goals and "lots of slogans and New Year's resolutions" (Frentzel, Bryson, and Crosby, 2000, p. 405). Furthermore, the headquarters' six functional departments (administration, training, communications, operations, logistics, and programs and budget) had provided separate inputs to the first plan, resulting in a segmented product with no integration or common goals and objectives.

But the winds of change were already blowing. The Soviet Union had disintegrated in August 1991 and with it went NSG's primary enemy, focus, and reason for funding. Citizen groups and supportive politicians—including the next president, Bill Clinton—were clamoring for a "peace dividend." A major reduction in personnel was a real possibility. In response the Navy changed its basic doctrine. The primary Navy strategy for the future shifted from fighting an open-ocean conflict to projecting force from the sea onto land in coastal areas—in other words, an expeditionary warfare strategy. So at least two issues that NSG had to confront simultaneously were how to protect its personnel and how to reorient its own strategy in response to changes in Navy strategy. Another major issue concerned NSG's other major stakeholder, NSA. NSA badly needed to invest in new technology and was likely to cut funding for military cryptological personnel dedicated to the old technologies. So NSG's personnel needed to be reinvested, away from legacy Cold War areas and toward areas that were more programmatically secure. And finally, in the Goldwater-Nichols Act of 1986, Congress had mandated joint operations involving collaboration across the services. Implementation had been sparse, but now increasing budget cuts and base closings were forcing the issue, and intense interservice rivalry was erupting over control of the remaining infrastructure.

An effective strategic planning process seemed the only way to confront all these issues successfully. The NSG comptroller initiated what eventually turned into a full-blown strategic planning process when he asked his subordinates, in October 1992, to focus on the issues around reinvesting personnel resources. Captain William Y. Frentzel II became what I call the *process champion* for the overall effort—the person who keeps organizing and pushing the process along. Eventually, he and some of his senior and junior colleagues succeeded in prompting the entire headquarters staff and senior cryptological officers on the major fleet staffs to engage in a full-blown coordinated strategic planning process. Along the way, major refocusing, restructuring, and reinvesting occurred, and ultimately a new mission emerged. This case stands as an interesting example of how strategic planning can be led initially from the middle by a group of committed managers.

Project for Pride in Living

Project for Pride in Living (PPL) is a prominent nonprofit organization headquartered in Minneapolis, Minnesota. Joseph Selvaggio, a charismatic and committed ex-priest, founded PPL in 1972. The organization's work began on a winter's day when Selvaggio and several other PPL founders started restoring a house in a poverty-stricken area in south Minneapolis. The project would take months. Thirty years later PPL has built or renovated over 1,400 houses, duplexes, and apartment units throughout Minneapolis, St. Paul, and some first-ring suburbs. The organization was and is inspired by Selvaggio's vision of a "hand up" for the poor, including decent housing, self-sufficient families, and stronger neighborhoods in the lowest-income areas of the metropolitan area. The organization has come to be one of the most trusted human service organizations in the Twin Cities, and its pioneering approaches to fostering self-sufficiency among its participants are widely admired. In September 2002, when the new strategic plan was adopted, PPL's three divisions—affordable housing and development, employment and job training, and human services—touched the lives of over 5,000 people. The organization's annual budget was just shy of $11 million, and it employed 108 people.

Steve Cramer, a former Minneapolis city council member (and former student of mine), became PPL's executive director in 1997 and served for three years before heading on to direct the Minneapolis Community Development Agency in mid-1999. During Cramer's time the organization experienced substantial growth and became involved in very large projects. The transition from Selvaggio to Cramer went smoothly because it was carefully planned, the board was fully involved, and Selvaggio worked to ensure its success. Cramer was succeeded by Jim Scheibel in late 1999, after a somewhat lengthy search. Scheibel was a former mayor and city council member of St. Paul. He was returning to the Twin Cities after serving the Clinton administration as a senior official with the Corporation for National Service, which includes AmeriCorps, VISTA, and the National Senior Service Corps. Scheibel had been an advocate for strategic planning ever since the mid-1980s, when he served as president of the St. Paul city council (a group for which I was a strategic planning consultant when it was under Jim's leadership), and he was joining an organization with a history of strategic planning and a commitment to it.

PPL has engaged in formal strategic planning every five years. When Scheibel joined the organization, the end of the 1998–2002 strategic plan was approaching, and there was a broad consensus within the organization and among the board members that it was time to begin work on the next plan. PPL did not begin the process with any specific issues highlighted but was clear that a new plan was needed that better reflected the emerging environment and PPL capacities. For example, competition for funding was becoming more severe, pressures for accountability were rising, maintaining dynamism and sustainability was a real challenge, the organization's *core competencies* needed attention, and PPL needed to do something to affect the broader policy environment within which it had to operate.

Scheibel therefore initiated a participatory planning process that involved many people over approximately a year, from September 2001 to September 2002. During the process the issues that had been in the backs of people's minds were sharpened and often redefined. Extended discussions of the organization's mission, its core competencies, and the meaning of self-sufficiency occurred. A deeper understanding by key stakeholders resulted, and greater integration across organizational functions occurred. Not all these discussions were finished, however, before the final plan was adopted at a board meeting in September 2002. Debate on many points continues, which is healthy and to be expected. Scheibel stepped down in 2003, and Cramer became executive director once again. He has demonstrated a commitment to the plan while also getting PPL to attend to some new issues (discussed in Chapter Twelve).

Comparisons and Contrasts

These three organizations offer a number of comparisons and contrasts. They differ in size, staff, budget, and legal status. The School District is a unit of local government. The Naval Security Group is a single-function governmental agency located down the organizational hierarchy. And Project for Pride in Living is an independent nonprofit organization.

The strategic planning efforts made by these organizations differed in the extent to which they focused directly on the organization and what it should do or on what should happen in the community of which the organization is a part. The School District and PPL focused on both organizational and community planning. The NSG focused on itself and its key stakeholders.

In addition, the three organizations engaged in strategic planning for different reasons. The School District was growing rapidly but faced an emerging crisis. A demographic bulge in elementary school students was working its way through the system, and because of a quirk in the state education funding formula, the district received significantly less money per pupil than did surrounding districts. Parents expected all the same services that the other districts offered, but the School District's revenues were capped at a significantly lower level. Parents found the discrepancy hard to understand and changing the state law was problematic. The school board and the new superintendent wanted to undertake strategic planning to cope with both the immediate and longer-term issues and to take the district to a new level of excellence. PPL had a habit of regular strategic planning, and the time had come to produce the next plan. PPL did not face an emerging crisis, but its environment had become tougher, and the match with the organization's capabilities and distinctive competencies had to be explored. A new leader and his board and staff wanted to use the process to ensure the organization's survival and success in an increasingly challenging operating environment. Finally, NSG was being rocked by the loss of its raison d'être, severe budget cuts, and dramatic changes in technology. A group of middle managers saw strategic planning as a way of coping with these changes and used the process to prepare the way for changes ultimately adopted by the organization's senior leadership. The NSG case thus is one of, at least initially, leading from the middle.

The three cases have a number of similarities as well. First, each organization succeeded because it had leaders willing to act as *process sponsors,* endorsing and legitimizing the effort. The sponsors were not always particularly active participants, and they were not always at the top of the organizational hierarchy, but they did let it be known that they wanted important decision makers and managers to give the process a good try. Second, each organization had process champions, people committed to making the process work. The champions did not have preconceived ideas about the specific issues and answers that would emerge from the process, although they may have had some good hunches. They simply believed that the process would result in good answers and pushed until those answers emerged (Bryson and Roering, 1988, 1989). Third, each organization ultimately developed a fairly clear understanding and agreement among key decision makers about what strategic planning was and what they expected from the process. Fourth, each followed a reasonably structured strategic thinking, acting, and learning process. Fifth, each established a decision-making or advisory body to oversee the process. Sixth, each designated a strategic planning team to manage the process, collect information and prepare for meetings, engage in serious strategic dialogue, and draft a strategic plan. Seventh, each identified critical issues that required effective action if the organization were to capitalize on important opportunities or to avoid being victimized by serious challenges or threats, or both. Eighth, each worked hard to develop strategies that created public value and were politically acceptable, technically workable, and ethically responsible. Ninth, each relied on outside assistance, including consultants, to help with the process. Tenth, each made a point of not getting so bogged down in the process that participants lost sight of what was truly important—strategic thought, action, and learning. And finally, each gained many of the potential benefits of strategic planning outlined previously.

Summary

This chapter has discussed what strategic planning is and why it is important. Its importance stems from its ability to help organizations and communities anticipate and respond to change in wise and effective ways. Not only have the environments of public and nonprofit organizations and communities changed dramatically in the recent past but more upheaval is likely in the future. The postindustrial, postmodern, and post-9/11 era is one in which continual progress can hardly be taken for granted. The norm in fact consists of periods of stability and small changes—interrupted by instability and significant change, uncertainty and ambiguity, happy surprises but also unhappy jolts, and occasional terror. In the last century we experienced world wars, big booms, big busts, modernism, postmodernism, and major new roles for government and nonprofit organizations. The last half century in the United States was marked by the Korean War, the civil rights movement, the women's movement, major student protests, the disastrous war in Vietnam, the environmental movement, the collapse of the Soviet Union, dramatic shifts in the dominant political ideology in the United States, scandals besmirching Republican and Democratic administrations, the HIV/AIDS epidemic, growing public cynicism, staggering new technologies, unprecedented economic growth, a dramatic spread of democracy in the world, and globalization—plus all the other changes noted in the opening paragraphs of this chapter. The current century opened with the hope of a new millennium—and was quickly followed in the United States by the appalling problems with the presidential election process in 2000, the terrorist attack on the World Trade Center and the Pentagon, the collapse of Enron and a host of other once-famed, now infamous corporations, wars in Afghanistan and Iraq, and the biggest federal debt in our history. It all reminds me of a handwritten sign on a jar filled with coins at a coffee shop cash register in Portland, Oregon: "If you don't like change, leave it here." If only it were that simple!

Strategic planning is one way to help organizations and communities deal with their changed circumstances. Strategic planning is intended to enhance an organization's ability to think, act, and learn strategically. It can help organizations clarify and resolve the most important issues they face. It can help them build on strengths and take advantage of major opportunities while they also overcome or minimize weaknesses and serious challenges. It can help them be much more effective in what seems to be a more hostile world. If it does not do that, it probably was not worth the effort, even though it may have satisfied certain legal mandates or symbolic needs.

The ABCs of strategic planning (Figure 1.1) show how strategic planning helps an organization (or other entity) think about how it might get from where it is to where it wants to be. Figure 1.4 shows a way to think about strategic planning that more forcefully demonstrates its importance in functional terms—namely, that it is meant to help public and nonprofit organizations and communities create public value through meeting their mandates and fulfilling their missions. In order to do so it must produce fundamental decisions and

FIGURE 1.4. PURPOSES AND FUNCTIONS OF STRATEGIC PLANNING.

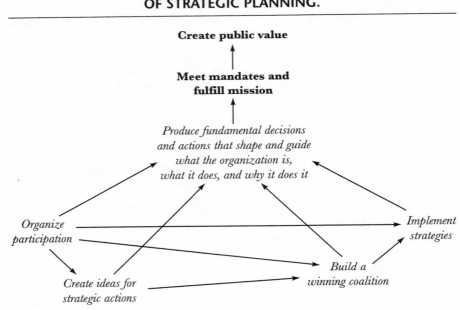

Source: Adapted from Bryson, 2004b, p. 25.

actions that shape and guide what the organization is, what it does, and why it does it. Producing those decisions and actions requires an interconnected set of activities that organize participation, create ideas for strategic actions, build a winning coalition, and implement strategies.

Strategic planning is a leadership and management innovation that is likely to persist because, unlike many other recent innovations, it accepts and builds on the nature of *political* decision making. Raising and resolving important issues is the heart of political decision making, and the heart of strategic planning. Strategic planning seeks to improve on raw political decision making, however, by ensuring that issues are raised and resolved in ways that benefit the organization, its key stakeholders, and society.

Chapter Two presents my preferred approach to strategic planning for governments, public agencies, nonprofit organizations, boundary-crossing services, and communities. Subsequent chapters will discuss how to apply the process to help public and nonprofit organizations, service networks, and communities create public value, fulfill their missions, meet their mandates, and serve their stake-holders effectively, efficiently, and responsibly. The good news in this book is of two sorts: There is lots of good work to do, and strategic planning can help you do it. The bad news is also of two sorts: strategic planning is not necessarily easy, and there is no guarantee of success. That's when it helps to remember the words of former senator and vice president Hubert H. Humphrey (1968): "Sometimes we get so overwhelmed by the problems of today that we forget the promise of tomorrow."

CHAPTER TWO

THE STRATEGY CHANGE CYCLE

An Effective Strategic Planning Approach

No, I can't say as I ever was lost, but once I was bewildered pretty bad for three days.

DANIEL BOONE

Make-believe is at the heart of play, and also at the heart of so much that passes for work. Let's make-believe we can shoot a rocket to the moon.

DIANE ACKERMAN, *DEEP PLAY*

This chapter presents my preferred approach to strategic planning for public and nonprofit organizations, boundary-crossing services, and communities. This process, called the Strategy Change Cycle, does what Poister and Streib (1999, pp. 309–310) assert strategic planning should do. Specifically, they believe strategic planning should

- Be concerned with identifying and responding to the most fundamental issues facing an organization
- Address the subjective question of purpose and the often competing values that influence mission and strategies
- Emphasize the importance of external trends and forces as they are likely to affect the organization and its mission
- Attempt to be politically realistic by taking into account the concerns and preferences of internal, and especially external, stakeholders
- Rely heavily on the active involvement of senior level managers, and [in the case of public planning] sometimes elected officials, assisted by staff support where needed

- Require the candid confrontation of critical issues by key participants in order to build commitment to plans
- Be action oriented and stress the importance of developing plans for implementing strategies, and
- Focus on implementing decisions now in order to position the organization favorably for the future

The Strategy Change Cycle becomes a *strategic management* process—and not just a *strategic planning* process—to the extent that it is used to link planning and implementation and to manage an organization in a strategic way on an ongoing basis. As Poister and Streib (1999) argue, "The overall purpose of strategic management is to develop a continuing commitment to the mission and vision of the organization (both internally and in the authorizing environment), nurture a culture that identifies and supports the mission and vision, and maintain a clear focus on the organization's strategic agenda throughout all its decision processes and activities" (pp. 311–312). The Strategy Change Cycle draws on a considerable body of research and practical experience, applying it specifically to public and nonprofit organizations. (Subsequent chapters provide detailed guidance on moving through the cycle.)

The epigraphs chosen for this chapter help make the point that strategic thinking, acting, and learning are more important than any particular approach to strategic planning. Consider the humorous statement of Daniel Boone, the famous eighteenth-century American frontiersman (Faragher, 1992, p. 65). When you are lost in the wilderness—*bewildered*—no fixed plan will do. You must think, act, and learn your way to safety. Boone had a destination of at least a general sort in mind but not a route. He had to wander around reconnoitering, gathering information, assessing directions, trying out options, and in general thinking, acting, and learning his way into where he wanted to be. In Karl Weick's words (1995), he had to "act in order to think." Or in Robert Behn's words (1988), he had to "manage by groping along." Ultimately—but not initially or even much before he got to a place he wanted to be—Boone was able to establish a clear destination and a route that worked to get him there. Boone thus had a strategy of purposeful wandering, and it is true that he was not exactly lost; rather he was working at finding himself where he wanted to be. So wandering with a purpose is an important aspect of strategic planning, in which thinking, acting, and learning clearly matter most.

Diane Ackerman's statement makes the point that almost anything is possible with enough imagination, ambition, direction, intelligence, education and training, organization, resources, will, and staying power. We have been to the moon, Mars, Venus, and a host of other places. We have won world wars and cold wars, ended depressions, virtually eliminated small pox, unraveled the human genome, watched a reasonably united and integrated Europe emerge, and seen democracy spread where it was thought unimaginable. Now, let's think about such things as having a good job for everyone, adequate food and housing for everyone, universal health care coverage, drastically reduced crime, effective educational systems, secure pensions and retirements, a dramatic reduction in greenhouse emissions, the elimination of weapons of mass destruction, the elimination of HIV/ AIDS, and the realization in practice of the Universal Declaration of Human Rights. And then let us get to work. We can create institutions, policies, projects, products, and services of lasting public value by drawing on our diverse talents— and have done so again and again throughout history (Boyte and Kari, 1996; Light, 2002a). And we can use strategic planning to help us think, act, and learn strategically—to figure out what we should want, why, and how to get it. Think of strategic planning as the organization of hope, as what makes hope reasonable (Baum, 1997).

A Ten-Step Strategic Planning Process

Now, with the caution that strategic thinking, acting, and learning matter most, let us proceed to a detailed exploration of the ten-step Strategy Change Cycle. The process (presented graphically in Figure 2.1) is more orderly, deliberative, and participative than the process followed by an essayist such as Ackerman or a wanderer like Boone. It is designed to organize participation, create ideas for strategic interventions, build a winning coalition, and implement strategies (see Figure 1.4). The Strategy Change Cycle may be thought of as a *process strategy* (Mintzberg, Ahlstrand, and Lampel, 1998, p. 199), *processual model of decision making* (Barzelay, 2001, p. 56), or *activity-based view of strategizing* (Johnson, Melin, and Whittington, 2003), in which a leadership group manages the main activities in the process but leaves much of the content of individual strategies to others. The ten steps (or occasions for dialogue and decision) are as follows:

1. Initiate and agree on a strategic planning process.
2. Identify organizational mandates.
3. Clarify organizational mission and values.
4. Assess the external and internal environments to identify strengths, weaknesses, opportunities, and threats.
5. Identify the strategic issues facing the organization.
6. Formulate strategies to manage the issues.
7. Review and adopt the strategies or strategic plan.

FIGURE 2.1. THE STRATEGY CHANGE CYCLE.

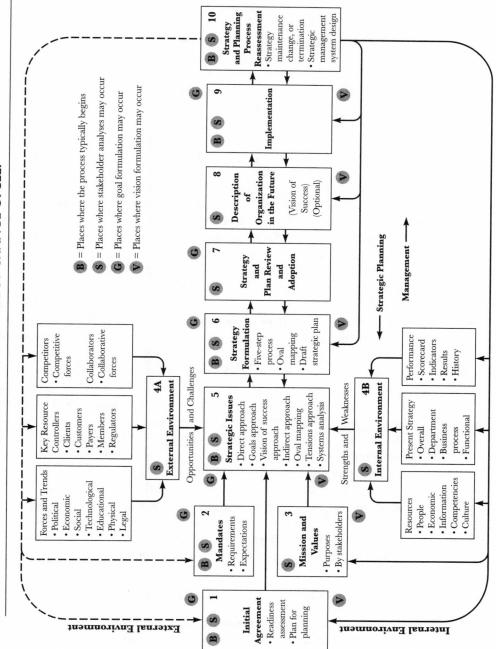

8. Establish an effective organizational vision.
9. Develop an effective implementation process.
10. Reassess the strategies and the strategic planning process.

These ten steps should lead to actions, results, evaluation, and learning. It must be emphasized that actions, results, evaluative judgments, and learning should emerge at each step in the process. In other words, implementation and evaluation should not wait until the "end" of the process but should be an integral and ongoing part of the process.

The process is applicable to public and nonprofit organizations, boundary-crossing services, interorganizational networks, and communities. The only general requirements are a *dominant coalition* (Thompson, 1967), or at least a *coalition of the willing* (Cleveland, 2002), able to sponsor and follow the process and a process champion willing to push it. In small organizations well-informed strategic planning teams that are familiar with and believe in the process should be able to complete most of the steps in a two- or three-day retreat, with an additional one-day meeting three to four weeks later to review the resulting strategic plan. Responsibility for preparing the plan can be delegated to a planner assigned to work with the team, or the organization's chief executive may choose to draft the plan personally. Additional time might be needed for reviews and sign-offs by key decision makers. Additional time might also be necessary for securing information or advice for specific parts of the plan, especially its recommended strategies. Large organizations, however, are likely to need more time and effort for the process. And when applied in a network or community, the effort is likely to be considerably more time consuming because of the need to involve substantial numbers of leaders, organizations, and in a community, citizens.

As you learn more about the steps of the Strategy Change Cycle, you will see that it bears little resemblance to the rigid, formal, detached process—a caricature of strategic planning—occasionally found in the literature (for example, Mintzberg, Ahlstrand, and Lampel, 1998). Instead, the Strategy Change Cycle is intended to enhance strategic thinking, acting, and learning; to engage key actors with what is as well as with what can be; to engage with the important details while abstracting strategic messages from them; and to link strategy formulation with implementation in wise, technically workable, and politically intelligent ways.

Step 1: Initiate and Agree on a Strategic Planning Process

The purpose of the first step is to negotiate agreement among key internal (and perhaps external) decision makers or opinion leaders about the overall strategic planning effort and the key planning steps. The support and the commitment of key decision makers are vital if strategic planning in an organization is to succeed.

Further, the involvement of key decision makers outside the organization is usually crucial to the success of public and nonprofit programs when implementation will involve multiple parties and organizations (Nutt and Backoff, 1996; Eden and Ackermann, 1998; Light, 1998; Rainey and Steinbauer, 1999; Huxham, 2003).

Obviously, some person or group must initiate the process. One of the initiator's first tasks is to identify exactly who the key decision makers are. The next task is to identify which persons, groups, units, or organizations should be involved in the effort. These two steps will require some preliminary stakeholder analysis, which is discussed in more detail later in this chapter. The initial agreement will be negotiated with at least some of these decision makers, groups, units, or organizations. In practice a *series* of agreements typically must be struck among various parties as support for the process builds and key stakeholders and decision makers sign on. Strategic planning for a public or nonprofit organization, network, or community is especially likely to work well when an effective policymaking body is in place to oversee the effort.

The initial agreements should cover

- The purpose of the effort
- The preferred steps in the process
- The form and timing of reports
- The role, functions, and membership of any group or committee empowered to oversee the effort, such as a strategic planning coordinating committee (SPCC)
- The role, functions, and membership of the strategic planning team
- The commitment of the resources necessary for proceeding with the effort
- Any important limitations on or boundaries for the effort

As noted, at least some stakeholder analysis work will be needed in order to figure out whom to include in the series of initial agreements. A *stakeholder* is defined as any person, group, or organization that can place a claim on an organization's (or other entity's) attention, resources, or output or that is affected by that output. Examples of a government's stakeholders are citizens, taxpayers, service recipients, the governing body, employees, unions, interest groups, political parties, the financial community, other businesses, and other governments. Examples of a nonprofit organization's stakeholders are clients or customers, third-party payers or funders, employees, the board of directors, volunteers, other nonprofit organizations providing complementary services or involved as coventurers in projects, banks holding mortgages or notes, and suppliers.

Attention to stakeholder concerns is crucial: *the key to success in public and nonprofit organizations (and communities) is the satisfaction of key stakeholders* (Rainey, 1997, p. 38; Light, 1998). A stakeholder analysis is a way for the organization's decision makers and planning team members to immerse themselves in the networks and politics surrounding the organization. An understanding of the relationships—actual or potential—that help define the organization's context can provide invaluable clues for identifying strategic issues and developing effective strategies (Moore, 1995; Bryson, 2004a). In this regard, note that the stakeholder definition is deliberately broad, for both practical and ethical reasons. Thinking broadly, at least initially, about who the stakeholders are is a way of opening people's eyes to the various webs of relationships within which the organization exists (Rainey, 1997, p. 96; Feldman and Khademian, 2002) and of ensuring that the organization is alert to its ethical and democratic accountability responsibilities, because these responsibilities always involve clarifying *who* and *what* counts (Lewis, 1991; Mitchell, Agle, and Wood, 1997; Behn, 2001).

Many public and nonprofit organizations will give the label *customer* to their key stakeholder, particularly when the organization is trying to *reinvent* itself (Osborne and Plastrik, 1997, 2000), *reengineer* its operations (Hammer and Champy, 1993; Cohen and Eimicke, 1998), or employ continuous improvement processes (Cohen and Brand, 1993; Cohen and Eimicke, 1998). The customer label can be useful, particularly for organizations that need to improve their *customer service* (Light, 1997, p. 204). In other situations such *customer* language may be problematic. One danger is that focusing on a single customer may lead these organizations inadvertently to ignore other important stakeholder groups. Another danger is that the customer label can undermine the values and virtues of active citizenship (deLeon and Denhardt, 2000; Denhardt and Denhardt, 2000). The public sector is not as simple as the private sector; public entities typically have many *bottom lines* (Rainey, 2003). In addition, many community-based nonprofit organizations and those relying on government funding also face complex stakeholder environments.

Resource A, at the end of this book, provides an overview of a range of stakeholder identification and analysis techniques, and Chapter Three presents more detail on how to get started. The organizers of the planning effort should count on using several techniques, including what I call the *basic analysis technique* (discussed in Chapter Four). This technique requires the strategic planning team to brainstorm in order to produce a list of the organization's stakeholders, to identify the criteria these stakeholders use for judging the organization's performance (that is, the definitions of their *stakes* in the organization or its output), and to determine how well the organization performs against those criteria *from the stakeholders' points of view.* If there is time, additional steps (perhaps involving additional analysis techniques) should be considered, including reaching an understanding of the ways in which the stakeholders influence the organization, identifying what the organization needs from each stakeholder (e.g., money, staff, political support), and determining in general how important the various stakeholders are. Looking ahead, a stakeholder analysis will help the organization decide whether it needs different missions and perhaps different strategies for different stakeholders, whether it should seek to have its mandates changed, and in general what its strategic issues are.

Step 2: Identify Organizational Mandates

The formal and informal mandates placed on the organization consist of the various "musts" it confronts—that is, the various requirements, restrictions, expectations, pressures, and constraints it faces. It is surprising how few organizations know precisely what they are (and are not) formally mandated to do. Typically, few members of any organization have ever read, for example, the relevant legislation, policies, ordinances, charters, articles, and contracts that outline the organization's formal mandates. Even when they have read these materials, it is likely that their organization's strategic plans will fail to address at least some of the formal mandates and that these mandates may be overlooked (Piotrowski and Rosenbloom, 2002). Many organizational members also do not understand the informal mandates—typically political in the broadest sense—that their organization faces. It may not be surprising, then, that most organizations make one or more of three fundamental mistakes. First, by not articulating or knowing what they must do, they are unlikely to do it. Second, they may believe they are more tightly constrained in their actions than they actually are. And third, they may assume that if they are not explicitly told to do something, they are not allowed to do it.

Step 3: Clarify Organizational Mission and Values

An organization's mission, in tandem with its mandates, provides the organization's most important justification for its existence. An organization's mission and mandates also point the way toward the ultimate organizational end of creating public value. For a government, governmental agency, or nonprofit organization, this means there must be identifiable social or political demands or needs that the organization seeks to fill. Viewed in this light, these organizations must always be seen as a means to an end, not as an end in and of themselves (Frederickson, 1997). For the entities in a collaborative, this means identifying the *collaborative advantage* to be gained by working together, that is, what they can gain together that creates public value that they cannot achieve alone (Huxham, 2003). Communities too must justify their existence by how well they address their various stakeholders' values and meet those stakeholders' social and political needs—including the need for a sense of community. Communities, however, are less likely than other groups to think in terms of having a *mission;* they are more likely to talk about their purposes, values, and identity.

Identifying the mission or purpose of the organization does more than justify the organization's existence. Clarifying purpose can eliminate a great deal of unnecessary conflict in an organization and can channel discussion and activity productively (Terry, 2001; Thompson, 2001; Nutt, 2002). Agreement on purpose also defines the arenas within which the organization will collaborate or compete and, at least in broad outline, charts the future course of the organization. Agreement on purpose thus serves as a kind of *primary framework* (Goffman, 1986; Bryant, 2003, pp. 96–99) that bounds the plausibility and acceptability of arguments. Agreement on purpose can go even further and provide a kind of *premise control* that constrains thinking, learning, and acting (Perrow, 1986; Weick, 1995), and even legitimacy (Suchman, 1995). Moreover, an important and socially justifiable mission is a source of inspiration and guidance to key stakeholders, particularly employees (Weiss and Piderit, 1999; Kouzes and Posner, 2002). Indeed, it is doubtful whether any organization ever achieved greatness or excellence without a basic consensus among its key stakeholders on an inspiring mission (Collins and Porras, 1997; Rainey and Steinbauer, 1999).

I think careful stakeholder analysis work should precede development or modification of an existing mission statement, so that attention to purpose can be informed by thinking about purpose *for whom.* If the purposes of key stakeholders are not served, then the organization may be engaging in what historian Barbara Tuchman (1984) aptly calls "folly." The mission statement itself might be very short, perhaps not more than a sentence or a paragraph. But development of the mission statement should grow out of lengthy dialogue about the organization's identity, its abiding purpose, its desired responses to key stakeholders, its philosophy and core values, and its ethical standards. These discussions may also produce a basic outline for a description of the organization in the future, or its *vision of success,* described in step 8. Considerable intermediate work is necessary, however, before a complete vision of success can be articulated.

Step 4: Assess the External and Internal Environments

The planning team should explore the environment outside the organization to identify the opportunities and challenges the organization faces (step 4a). It should explore the environment inside the organization to identify strengths and weaknesses (step 4b). Basically, *outside* factors are those not under the organization's control, and *inside* factors are those that are (Pfeffer and Salancik, 1978). Opportunities and challenges are usually (though not necessarily) more about the future than the present, whereas strengths and weaknesses are usually about the present and not the future (Nutt and Backoff, 1992). Note that communities are more likely to think in terms of assets rather than strengths (Kretzmann and McKnight, 1993).

Monitoring a variety of forces and trends, including the political, economic, social, educational, technological, and physical environmental ones, can help planners and decision makers discern opportunities and challenges. Unfortunately, organizations all too often focus only on the threats they see in serious challenges and ignore the genuine opportunities these challenges may also present, so care must be taken to ensure a balanced view (Dutton and Jackson, 1987; Borins, 1998; Nutt, 2001b). In other words, attending to challenges and weaknesses should be seen as an opportunity to build strengths and improve performance (Weick and Sutcliffe, 2001).

Besides monitoring trends and events, the strategic planning team also should monitor important external stakeholder groups—especially those that affect resource flows (directly or indirectly)—such as customers, clients, payers or funders, dues-paying members, regulators, and relevant policy bodies. The team should also attend to competitors, competitive forces, and possible sources of competitive advantage as well as to collaborators, collaborative forces, and potential sources of collaborative advantage.

The organization might construct various scenarios to explore alternative futures in the external environment, a practice typical of much strategic planning in large private sector organizations. Scenarios are particularly good at demonstrating how various forces and trends are likely to interact and which forces and trends are amenable to organizational influence and which are not. Scenarios also offer an effective way of challenging the organization's *official future* when necessary. The official future is the presumed or taken-for-granted future that makes current strategies sensible. Organizations unwilling to challenge this future are the ones most likely to be blindsided by changes (Schwartz, 1991; Van der Heijden and others, 2002; Barzelay and Campbell, 2003). Communities too may wish to develop scenarios (Neuman, 1998; Myers and Kitsuse, 2000).

Members of an organization's governing body (particularly when elected) are often better than the organization's employees at identifying and assessing external opportunities and challenges (particularly present ones). This is partly due to the board's responsibility for relating an organization to its external environment and vice versa (Scott, 1987). Unfortunately, neither governing boards nor employees usually do a systematic or effective job of external scanning. As a result, most organizations are like ships trying to navigate troubled or treacherous waters without benefit of human lookouts, global positioning systems, radar, or sonar. All too often the result is a very unwelcome surprise (Marcus and Nichols, 1999; Weick and Sutcliffe, 2001).

That is why both employees and board members should consider supplementing their informal efforts with a somewhat formal external assessment process. The technology of external assessment is fairly simple and allows organizations to cheaply, pragmatically, and effectively keep tabs on things happening in the larger world that are likely to have an effect on the organization and the pursuit of its mission. Basically, the organization takes these three steps: scanning the environment to identify key trends, analyzing those trends to interpret their importance and identify issues, and compiling reports that are useful for planning and decision making (Pflaum and Delmont, 1987). Clipping services, discussion groups, and periodic retreats, for example, might be used to explore forces and trends and their potential impact. The key is to avoid being captured by existing categories of classification and search, because they tend to formalize and routinize the past rather than to open people to the surprises of the future (Mintzberg, Ahlstrand, and Lampel, 1998; Weick and Sutcliffe, 2001).

Attention to opportunities and challenges, along with a stakeholder analysis, can identify the organization's *critical success factors* (Johnson and Scholes, 2002, pp. 145–198). These success factors may overlap with mandates in the sense that they are the things the organization must do or criteria it must meet in order to be successful in the eyes of its key stakeholders, especially those in the external environment. Ideally, the organization will excel in these areas, and it must do so in order to outperform or stave off competitors.

To identify internal strengths and weaknesses, the organization might monitor resources (inputs), present strategy (process), and performance (outputs). Most public and nonprofit organizations have volumes of information on many of their inputs, such as salaries, supplies, physical plant, and full-time-equivalent (FTE) personnel. Unfortunately, too few organizations have a clear idea of their philosophy, core values, distinctive competencies, and culture, a crucial set of inputs both for ensuring stability and for managing change.

Organizations also tend to have an unclear idea of their present strategy, either overall, by subunit, or by function. And typically they cannot say enough about their outputs, let alone the effects, or outcomes, those outputs create for clients, customers, or payers, although this too is changing. For example, schools have traditionally been able to say how many students they graduate—an output—but most cannot say how educated those students are. National requirements for standardized testing at certain grade levels are an attempt to measure outcomes in order to remedy this shortcoming. We know tests of this sort are almost always imperfect, but the need to demonstrate accountability for performance to politicians and the citizenry virtually requires that believable testing of some sort be used (Behn, 2003).

A lack of performance information presents problems both for the organization and for its stakeholders. Stakeholders judge an organization according to the criteria *they* choose, which are not necessarily the same criteria the organization would choose. For external stakeholders in particular, these criteria typically relate to performance. If an organization cannot effectively meet its stakeholders' performance criteria, then regardless of its inherent worth, the stakeholders are likely to withdraw their support (Epstein, Wray, Marshall, and Griffel, 1998; Poister, 2003). The need to address this potential threat—particularly from key stakeholders, or customers—is one of the reasons organizations initiate reinvention, reengineering, or continuous improvement efforts (Light, 1997; Kettl, 2002).

An absence of performance information may also create or harden major organizational conflicts. Without performance criteria and information, the organization cannot objectively evaluate the relative effectiveness of alternative strategies, resource allocations, organizational designs, and distributions of power. As a result, organizational conflicts are likely to occur more often than they should, serve narrow partisan interests, and be resolved in ways that don't further the organization's mission (Terry, 1993; Flyvbjerg, 1998).

The difficulties of measuring performance with reasonable objectivity are well known (Osborne and Plastrik, 2000; Ingraham and Donahue, 2000; Kaplan, 2001; Poister, 2003). But regardless of these difficulties, organizations are continually challenged to demonstrate effective performance to their stakeholders. Employees of governmental agencies and nonprofit organizations receiving governmental funds might see the public's desire to limit or decrease taxation and funding as selfishness. It may be that for some people; however, one might also interpret these limitations on public expenditure as a sign of unwillingness to support organizations that cannot demonstrate unequivocally effective performance. The desire for demonstrable performance was clearly behind the Government Performance and Results Act (GPRA) of 1993 (Public Law 103-62), which requires all federal agencies to complete a strategic plan based on outcomes rather than inputs or throughputs. The assessment of GPRA's effectiveness is mixed (Radin, 2000; Frederickson, 2001), but the impulse behind the act will remain. Several states initiated performance-oriented systems prior to GPRA (Broom, 1995), and large numbers of local governments embrace performance management as well (Berman and West, 1998).

A consideration of the organization's strengths and weaknesses can also lead to identification of its *distinctive competencies* (Selznick, 1957), or what have been termed more recently *core competencies* (Prahalad and Hamel, 1990; Johnson and Scholes, 2002) or *capabilities* (Stalk, Evans, and Shulman, 1992). These are the organization's strongest abilities, most effective strategies and actions, or best resources (broadly conceived), on which it can draw routinely to perform well. What makes these abilities distinctive is the inability of other organizations to replicate them easily, if at all, because of the way they are interlinked with one another (Eden and Ackermann, 2000).

Finally, a consideration of the ways in which inputs, process, and outputs are linked can help the organization understand what its strategies are and the *value proposition* that it offers its stakeholders (Moore, 2000, p. 197). In other words, what story does this linkage tell about the *logic model* (Millar, Simeone, and Carnevale, 2001; Poister, 2003) or *value chain* (Porter, 1985, pp. 33–61) that the organization pursues to convert inputs into outputs that meet its mandates, fulfill its mission, satisfy its stakeholders and create public value? Being clear about what *is* can be an extraordinarily helpful prelude to discerning what *ought to be* (Terry, 1993; Weick, 1995). For one thing, understanding what the strategy is in practice can open people's eyes to what is going on in the environment more generally. As Mintzberg, Ahlstrand, and Lampel (1998) note, "The very encouragement of strategy to get on with it—its very role in protecting people in the organization from distraction—impedes their capacity to respond to changes in the environment" (p. 28). Understanding the current strategy can also sensitize people to the ways in which an integration of human resource management, information technology, and financial management might be used to sustain, strengthen, and protect desirable strategies.

Step 5: Identify the Strategic Issues Facing the Organization

Together, the first four steps of the Strategy Change Cycle lead to the fifth, the identification of strategic issues. *Strategic issues* are fundamental policy questions or critical challenges affecting the organization's mandates, mission and values, product or service level and mix, clients, users or payers, cost, financing, structure, processes, and management. Finding the best way to frame these issues typically requires considerable wisdom and dialogue, informed by a deep understanding of organizational operations, stakeholder interests, and external demands and possibilities. The first four steps of the process are designed to slow things down so that planning team members have enough information and interaction for the needed wisdom to emerge. The process is designed, in other words, to *unfreeze* people's thinking (Lewin, 1951; Dalton, 1970; Fiol, 2002) so that knowledge exploration and development may occur (March, 1991; Crossan, Lane, and White, 1999). This knowledge is then exploited in this and later phases.

Strategic planning focuses on achieving the best *fit* between an organization and its environment. Attention to mandates and the external environment therefore can be thought of as planning from the outside in. Attention to mission and organizational values and the internal environment can be considered planning from the inside out. Usually, it is vital that pressing strategic issues be dealt with expeditiously and effectively if the organization is to survive and prosper. An organization that does not respond to a strategic issue can expect undesirable results from a threat, a missed opportunity, or both.

The iterative nature of the strategic planning process often becomes apparent in this step when participants find that information created or discussed in earlier steps presents itself again as part of a strategic issue. For example, many strategic planning teams begin strategic planning with the belief that they know what their organization's mission is. They often find out in this step, however, that one of the key issues their organization faces is exactly what its mission ought to be. In other words the organization's present mission is found to be inappropriate, given the team members' new understanding of the situation the organization faces, and a new mission must be created.

Strategic issues, virtually by definition, involve conflicts of one sort or another. The conflicts may involve ends (what), means (how or how much), philosophy (why), location (where), timing (when), and the entities advantaged or disadvantaged by different ways of resolving the issue (who). In order for these issues to be raised and resolved effectively, the organization must be prepared to deal with the almost inevitable conflicts that will occur. Conflict, shifts in understanding, and shifts in preferences will all evoke participants' emotions (Weick, 1995; Bryant, 2003). It is therefore in this stage that the importance of emotion will become dramatically apparent, along with the concomitant need for emotional intelligence on the part of participants if the emotions are to be dealt with effectively (Goleman, 1995; Heifetz, 1994; Goleman, Boyatzis, and McKee, 2002).

A statement of a strategic issue should contain three elements. First, the issue should be described succinctly, preferably in a single paragraph. The issue should be framed as a question that the organization can do something about. If the organization cannot do anything about the issue, it is best not to think of it as an issue for the organization; it is simply a condition (Wildavsky, 1979). An organization's attention is limited enough without wasting it on issues the organization cannot address effectively. The question should also have more than one answer, as a way of broadening the search for viable strategies. Too often organizations jump to a solution before fully understanding other options; reaching this understanding helps the planning team learn more about the issue (Eden and Ackermann, 1998; Nutt, 2002).

Second, the team should list the factors that make the issue a fundamental challenge. In particular, what is it about the organization's mandates, mission and values, or internal strengths and weaknesses and external opportunities and challenges that makes this issue a strategic one for the organization? This list will be useful in the next step, strategy development. Every effective strategy builds on strengths and takes advantage of opportunities while it minimizes or overcomes weaknesses and challenges. The framing of each strategic issue is therefore very important because it will provide much of the basis for that issue's resolution (Eden and Ackermann, 1998; Nutt, 2002; Bryant, 2003).

Finally, the planning team should prepare a statement of the consequences of failure to address the issue. This will help organizational leaders decide just how strategic, or important, various issues are. If no consequences will ensue from failure to address a particular issue, then it is not a strategic issue. At the other extreme, if the organization will be destroyed or will miss a valuable opportunity by failing to address a particular issue, then the issue is clearly *very* strategic and is worth attending to immediately. Thus the step of identifying strategic issues is aimed at focusing organizational attention on what is truly important for the survival, prosperity, and effectiveness of the organization.

Once statements of the issues are prepared, the organization will know what kinds of issues it faces and just how strategic they are. There are several kinds of strategic issues:

- Issues that alter the organization and especially its *core business* (or what might be called *developmental* issues), and those that do not (or what might be called *nondevelopmental* issues) (Nutt, 2001b). Developmental issues involve a fundamental change in products or services, customers or clients, service or distribution channels, sources of revenue, identity or image, or some other aspect of the organization. They are also issues for which there is no real organizational precedent. In other words the resolution of these issues may well hinge on defining a new vision or set of goals. Nondevelopmental issues involve less ambiguity because most aspects of the organization's overall strategy will not change. Resolving these issues is likely to require reprogramming strategies rather than altering the vision and goals.
- Issues that require no organizational action at present but that must be continuously monitored.
- Issues that are on the horizon and likely to require some action in the future and perhaps some action now. For the most part they can be handled as part of the organization's regular strategic planning cycle.
- Issues that require an immediate response and therefore cannot be handled in a routine way.

Seven basic approaches to the identification of strategic issues are discussed in detail in Chapter Six. Briefly, the *direct* approach goes straight from a discussion of mandates, mission, and SWOCs (strengths, weaknesses, opportunities, and challenges) to the identification of strategic issues. The *indirect* approach begins with brainstorming about different kinds of options before identifying issues. These options include actions the organization could take to meet its mandates, fulfill its mission, and create public value; to meet stakeholders' performance expectations; to build on strengths, take advantage of opportunities, and minimize or overcome weaknesses and challenges; and to deal with any other important knowledge from background studies. These options are then merged into a single set of potential actions and clustered into potential issue categories. The *goals* approach starts with goals (or performance indicators) and then identifies issues that must be addressed before the goals (or indicators) can be achieved. And the *vision of success* approach starts with at least a sketch of a vision of success in order to identify issues that must be dealt with before the vision can be realized. This approach is probably necessary in situations involving developmental issues—where fundamental change is needed but the organization lacks a precedent (Nutt, 2001b). For example, development of a vision of success is often recommended for organizations about to engage in a serious way in e-government or e-commerce (Abramson and Means, 2001). In addition, many community strategic planning efforts use a visioning approach to identify issues (Chrislip, 2002).

The *oval mapping* approach involves creation of word-and-arrow diagrams in which ideas about actions the organization might take, how it might take them, and why, are linked by arrows indicating cause and effect or influence relationships. In other words the arrows indicate that action A may cause or influence B, which in turn may cause or influence C, and so on; if the organization does A, it can expect to produce outcome B, which in turn may be expected to produce outcome C. These maps may display hundreds of interconnected relationships, showing differing areas of interest and their relationships to one another. Important clusters of potential actions may constitute strategic issues. A strategy that responds to the issue will then describe the specific choices of actions to undertake in the issue area, how to undertake them, and why (Eden and Ackermann, 1998; Bryson, Ackermann, Eden, and Finn, 2004). This approach is particularly useful when participants are having trouble making sense of complex issue areas, time is short, the emphasis must be on action, and commitment from those involved is particularly important.

The *tensions* approach was developed by Nutt and Backoff (1992) and elaborated by Nutt, Backoff, and Hogan (2000). These authors argue that any strategic issue always presents four basic tensions that involve, in various combinations, human resource and especially *equity* concerns, *innovation* and *change*, maintenance of *tradition*, and *productivity improvement*. They suggest critiquing the way issues are framed by highlighting these tensions, separately and in combination, in order to find the best way to frame the issue. The critiques may need to run through several cycles before the wisest way to frame the issue is found. Finally, the *systems analysis* approach can discern the best way to frame issues when a system contains complex feedback effects and must be formally modeled in order for the organization to fully understand it (Senge, 1990; Sterman, 2000).

By offering seven different approaches to the identification of strategic issues, I may raise the hackles of some planning theorists and practitioners who believe you should *always* start with issues or goals or vision or analysis. I argue in contrast that what will work best depends on the situation and that the wise planner should choose an approach accordingly.

Step 6: Formulate Strategies to Manage the Issues

A *strategy* can be defined as a pattern of purposes, policies, programs, actions, decisions, or resource allocations that define what an organization is, what it does, and why it does it. Strategies vary by level, function, and time frame. Organizations develop strategies to deal with the issues they have identified.

This definition is purposely broad in order to focus attention on achieving consistency across *rhetoric* (what people say), *choices* (what people decide on and are willing to pay for), *actions* (what people do), and the *consequences* of those actions. Effective strategy formulation and implementation processes link rhetoric, choices, actions, and consequences into reasonably coherent and consistent patterns across levels, functions, and time (Eden and Ackermann, 1998). They are also tailored to fit an organization's culture, even when the purpose of a strategy is to reconfigure that culture in some way (Johnson and Scholes, 2002). Draft strategies, and perhaps drafts of formal strategic plans, are formulated in this step to articulate desired patterns. Strategies may also be reviewed and adopted at the end of this step if the strategic planning process is relatively simple, small scale, and involves a single organization. (Such a process merges steps 6 and 7.)

There are numerous approaches to strategy development (Mintzberg, Ahlstrand, and Lampel, 1998; Holman and Devane, 1999; Bryson and Anderson, 2000; Bryson, 2001, 2003a). I generally favor either of two approaches. The first is a five-part, fairly speedy process based on the work of the Institute of Cultural Affairs (Spencer, 1989). The second, a mapping process, can be used when the planning team needs or desires to articulate the relationships among multiple options so as to show how they fit together as part of a pattern.

Developing Strategies Through a Five-Part Process. The first part of the five-part process begins with identification of practical alternatives and of dreams or visions for resolving the strategic issues. Each option should be phrased in action terms: that is, it should begin with an imperative, such as *do, get, buy, achieve,* and so forth. Phrasing options in action terms makes them more "real" to participants.

Next, the planning team should enumerate the barriers to achieving those alternatives, dreams, or visions. Focusing on barriers at this point is not typical of most strategic planning processes, but it is one way of ensuring that any strategies developed deal with implementation difficulties directly rather than haphazardly.

Once the alternatives, dreams, and visions and the barriers to their realization are listed, the team develops major proposals for achieving these alternatives, dreams, and visions, either indirectly (through overcoming the barriers) or directly. (Alternatively, the team might solicit proposals from key organizational units, various stakeholder groups, relevant task forces, or selected individuals.) For example, a major Midwestern city government did not begin to work on strategies to achieve its major ambitions until it had overhauled its archaic civil service system. That system was a barrier that had to be changed before the city government could have any hope of achieving its more important objectives.

After major proposals are submitted, two final tasks remain in this five-part process. Actions that must be taken over the next two to three years to implement the major proposals must be identified. And a detailed work program for the next six to twelve months must be spelled out to implement the actions. These last two tasks shade over into the work of step 9, but that is good, because strategies should always be developed with implementation in mind. As Mintzberg (1994) explains, "Every failure of implementation is, by definition, also a failure of formulation" (p. 25). In some circumstances, steps 6 and 9 may be merged—for example, when a single organization is planning for itself. In addition, in interorganizational or community settings, the various parties often must work out implementation details before they are willing to commit to shared strategic plans (Innes, 1996; Bardach, 1998; Bryant, 2003). In situations such as these, implementation planning may have to precede strategy or plan adoption.

Developing Strategies by Structuring Relationships Among Strategic Options.
The second method of developing strategies is based on the strategic options development and analysis (SODA) method, developed by Colin Eden and Fran Ackermann and their associates (Eden and Ackermann, 1998; Eden and Ackermann, 2001; Bryson, Ackermann, Eden, and Finn, 2004). This method involves listing multiple options for addressing each strategic issue, once again phrasing each option in imperative, action terms. The options are then linked by arrows indicating which options cause or influence the achievement of other options. Each option may be part of more than one chain. The result is a *map* of action-to-outcome (cause and effect, means-to-an-end) relationships; those options toward the end of a chain of arrows are possible goals or perhaps even mission statements. Presumably, these goals can be achieved by accomplishing at least some of the actions leading up to them, although additional analysis and work on the arrow chains may be necessary to determine and clearly articulate action-to-outcome

relationships. Option maps can be reviewed and revised and particular action-to-outcome chains selected as strategies. (See Resource B for more information on how to develop maps of this sort. Additional detail and numerous examples can be found in Bryson, Ackermann, Eden, and Finn, 2004.)

An effective strategy must meet several criteria. It should be technically workable and administratively feasible, politically acceptable to key stakeholders, and results oriented. It must also fit the organization's philosophy and core values, even if the purpose is to change them. Further, it should be ethical, moral, and legal. It must also deal with the strategic issue it was supposed to address, and it must create public value. All too often I have seen strategies that were technically, administratively, politically, morally, ethically, and legally impeccable but that did not deal with the issues they were presumed to address or did not create public value. Effective strategies thus meet a severe set of tests. Careful, thoughtful dialogue—and often bargaining and negotiation—among key decision makers who have adequate information and are politically astute is usually necessary before strategies can be developed that meet these tests. Some of this work typically must occur in this step; some is likely to occur in the next step.

Step 7: Review and Adopt the Strategies or Strategic Plan

Once strategies have been formulated, the planning team may need to obtain an official decision to adopt them and proceed with implementation. The same is true when a formal strategic plan has been prepared. This decision will affirm the desired changes and move the organization toward *refreezing* in the new pattern (Lewin, 1951; Dalton, 1970; Fiol, 2002), where the knowledge exploration of previous steps can be exploited (March, 1991). When strategies and plans are developed for a single organization, particularly a small one, this step may merge with step 6. But a separate step is likely to be necessary when strategic planning is undertaken for a large organization, a network of organizations, or a community. The SPCC will need to approve the resulting strategies or plan; relevant policymaking bodies and other implementing groups and organizations are also likely to have to approve the strategies or plan, or at least parts of the plan, in order for implementation to proceed effectively.

In order to secure passage of any strategy or plan, the planning team must continue to pay attention to the goals, concerns, and interests of all key internal and external stakeholders (Borins, 2000). Finding or creating inducements that can be traded for support can also be useful. But there are numerous ways to defeat any proposal in formal decision-making arenas. So it is important for the plan to be sponsored and championed by actors whose knowledge of negotiating the intricacies of the relevant arenas can help ensure passage (Bryson and Crosby, 1992; Crosby and Bryson, forthcoming).

Step 8: Establish an Effective Organizational Vision

In this step the organization develops a description of what it should look like once it has successfully implemented its strategies and achieved its full potential. This description is the organization's *vision of success*. Few organizations have such a description or vision, yet its importance has long been recognized by well-managed companies, organizational psychologists, and management theorists (Locke, Shaw, Saari, and Latham, 1981; Collins and Porras, 1997; Kouzes and Posner, 2002). Such descriptions may include the organization's mission, its values and philosophy, its basic strategies, its performance criteria, its important decision rules, and the ethical standards it expects of all employees.

This description, to the extent that it is widely circulated and discussed within the organization, informs organizational members about what is expected of them without constant managerial oversight. Members are freed to act on their own initiative on the organization's behalf to an extent not otherwise possible. The result should be a mobilization of members' energy toward pursuing the organization's purposes and a reduced need for direct supervision (Nutt, 2001b).

Some might question why developing a vision of success comes at this point in the process rather than much earlier. There are two basic answers. First, it does not have to come here for all organizations. Some organizations are able to develop a clearly articulated, agreed-upon vision of success much earlier in the process. Communities, in fact, often start with *visioning* exercises in order to develop a consensus on purposes and values sufficient to guide issue identification and strategy formulation efforts (Chrislip, 2002; Wheeland, 2003). (Figure 2.1 displays the many different points at which participants may find it useful to develop some sort of guiding vision.) Some planning teams may start with a visionary statement. Others may develop a vision to help them figure out what the strategic issues are or to help them develop strategies. And still others may use visions to convince key decision makers to adopt strategies or plans, or to guide implementation efforts. The further along in the process a vision is found, the more fully articulated it is likely to be.

Second, most organizations typically will not be able to develop a detailed vision of success until they have gone through several iterations of strategic planning—if they are able to develop a vision at all. A challenging yet achievable vision embodies the tension between what an organization wants and what it can have (Senge, 1990). Often several cycles of strategic planning are necessary before organizational members know what they want, what they can have, and what the difference is between the two. A vision that motivates people will be challenging enough to spur action yet not so hard to achieve that it demotivates and demoralizes people. Most organizations, in other words, will find that their visions of success serve as guides more for strategy implementation than for strategy formulation.

Further, most organizations do not need to develop a vision of success in order to achieve marked improvements in performance. In my experience, most organizations can demonstrate a substantial improvement in effectiveness if they simply identify and satisfactorily resolve a few strategic issues. Most organizations simply do not address often enough what is truly important; just gathering key decision makers to deal with a few important matters in a timely way can enhance organizational performance substantially. For these reasons step 8 is labeled "optional" in Figure 2.1.

Step 9: Develop an Effective Implementation Process

Just creating a strategic plan is not enough. The changes called for by the adopted strategies must be incorporated throughout the system for these strategies to be brought to life and for real value to be created for the organization and its stakeholders. Thinking strategically about implementation and developing an effective implementation plan are important tasks on the road to realizing the strategies developed in step 6. For example, in some circumstances direct implementation at all sites will be the wisest strategic choice, but in other situations some form of staged implementation may be best (Joyce, 1999, pp. 80–83).

Again, if strategies and an implementation plan have been developed for a single organization, particularly a small one, or if the planning is for an interorganizational network or community, this step may need to be incorporated into step 7, strategy formulation. However, many multiunit or intergovernmental situations will require a separate step to ensure that relevant groups and organizations do the action planning necessary for implementation success.

Action plans should detail the following:

- Implementation roles and responsibilities of oversight bodies, organizational teams or task forces, and individuals
- Expected results and specific objectives and milestones
- Specific action steps and relevant details
- Schedules
- Resource requirements and sources
- A communication process
- Review, monitoring, and midcourse correction procedures
- Accountability procedures

The organization must build into action plans enough sponsors, champions, and other personnel—along with enough time, money, attention, administrative and support services, and other resources—to ensure successful implementation. It must "budget the plan" wisely to ensure implementation goes well. In inter-organizational or community situations, it is almost impossible to underestimate the requirements for communications, nurturance of relationships, and attention to operational detail (Huxham, 2003). It is also important to work quickly to avoid unnecessary or undesirable competition with new priorities. Whenever important opportunities to implement strategies and achieve objectives arise, they should be taken. In other words it is important to be opportunistic as well as deliberate. And it is important to remember that what happens in practice will always be some blend of what is intended and what emerges along the way (Mintzberg, Ahlstrand, and Lampel, 1998).

Successfully implemented and institutionalized strategies result in the establishment of a new *regime,* a "set of implicit or explicit principles, norms, rules, and decision-making procedures around which actors' expectations converge in a given area" (Krasner, 1983, p. 2; see also Lauria, 1996; Crossan, Lane, and White, 1999). Regime building is necessary to preserve gains in the face of competing demands. Unfortunately, regimes can outlive their usefulness and must be changed, which involves the next step in the process.

Step 10: Reassess Strategies and the Strategic Planning Process

Once the implementation process has been under way for some time, the organization should review the strategies and the strategic planning process, as a prelude to a new round of strategic planning. Much of the work of this phase may occur as part of the ongoing implementation process. However, if the organization has not engaged in strategic planning for a while, this will be a separate phase. The organization should focus on successful strategies, asking whether they should be maintained, replaced by other strategies, or terminated. Unsuccessful strategies should be replaced or terminated. The strategic planning process also should be examined, its strengths and weaknesses noted, and modifications suggested to improve the next round of strategic planning. Effectiveness in this step depends on effective organizational learning, which means taking a hard look at what is really happening and being open to new information. As Weick and Sutcliffe (2001) say, "The whole point of a learning organization is that it needs to get a better handle on the fact that it doesn't know what it doesn't know" (p. 18). Viewing strategic planning as a kind of action research can embed learning throughout the entire process and make sure that the acquisition of information, the feedback, and the dialogue necessary for learning occur (Eden and Huxham, 1996).

Tailoring the Process to Specific Circumstances

The Strategy Change Cycle is a general approach to strategic planning and management. Like any general planning and management process, it must be tailored carefully to specific situations if it is to be useful (Christensen, 1999). A number of adaptations—variations on the general theme—are discussed in this section.

Sequencing the Steps

Although the steps (or occasions for dialogue and decision) are laid out here in a linear sequence, it must be emphasized that the Strategy Change Cycle, as its name suggests, is iterative in practice. Participants typically rethink what they have done several times before they reach final decisions. Moreover, the process does not always begin at the beginning. Organizations typically find themselves confronted with a new mandate (step 2), a pressing strategic issue (step 5), a failing strategy (step 6 or 9), or the need to reassess what they have been doing (step 10), and that leads them to engage in strategic planning. Once engaged, the organization is likely to go back and begin at the beginning, particularly with a reexamination of its mission. (Indeed, in my experience, it does not matter where you start, you always end up back at the mission.)

In addition, implementation usually begins before all the planning is complete. As soon as useful actions are identified, they are taken, as long as they do not jeopardize future actions that might prove valuable. In other words, in a linear, sequential process, the first eight steps of the process would be followed by implementing the planned actions and evaluating the results. However, implementation typically does not, and should not, wait until the first eight steps have been completed. For example, if the organization's mission needs to be redrafted, then it should be. If the SWOC analysis turns up weaknesses or challenges that need to be addressed immediately, they should be. If aspects of a desirable strategy can be implemented without awaiting further developments, they should be, and so on. As noted earlier, strategic thinking *and* acting *and* learning are important, and all of the thinking does not have to occur before any actions are taken. For one thing, often it is action that leads to real learning (Weick, 1995). Or as Mintzberg, Ahlstrand, and Lampel (1998) note: "Effective strategy making connects acting to thinking which in turn connects implementation to formulation. We think in order to act, to be sure, but we also act in order to think" (p. 71)— and to learn, they might have added. Strategic planning is iterative, flexible, and action-oriented and that is often precisely what makes it so attractive to public and nonprofit leaders and managers.

Making Use of Vision, Goals, and Issues

In the discussion of step 8 I noted that some organizations and communities may wish to start their process with a vision statement. Such a statement, even if less detailed than a statement developed later in the process, may foster a consensus and provide important inspiration and guidance. As indicated in Figure 2.1, there are other points at which organizations might develop a vision statement (or statements). A vision may thus be used to prompt the identification of strategic issues, guide the search for and development of strategies, inspire the adoption of strategic plans, or guide implementation efforts. The Amherst H. Wilder Foundation (2000) of St. Paul, Minnesota, for example, presents this vision in its 2000–05 strategic plan: "A vibrant Saint Paul where individuals, families and communities can prosper, with opportunities for all to be employed, to be engaged citizens, to live in decent housing, to attend good schools, and to receive support during times of need." The foundation also formed a vision for each of its previous plans and used each one to help it identify issues to be addressed and to develop strategies for realizing the vision. U.S. Air Force planners also used a vision to help them identify issues and develop strategies in the 1990s; a dramatic reorientation of mission and strategies resulted (Barzelay and Campbell, 2003). The decision to develop a vision statement should hinge on whether one is needed to provide direction to subsequent efforts; whether people will be able to develop a vision that is meaningful enough, detailed enough, *and* broadly supported by key stakeholders; and whether there will be enough energy left after the visioning effort to push ahead.

Similarly, as indicated in Figure 2.1, it is possible to develop goals at many different places in the process (Borins, 1998; Behn, 1999a; Roberts, 1999). Some strategic planning processes will begin with goals set by new boards of directors, elected policy bodies, chief executive officers, judges, or other top-level decision makers. These goals embody a reform agenda for the organization (or network or community). Other strategic planning processes may start with goals that are part of mandates. For example, legislation often requires implementing agencies to develop plans that include results and outcome measures that will show how the intent of the legislation is being achieved. A *starting* goal for these agencies therefore is to identify results and outcomes they want to be measured against that also are in accord with legislative intent. This goal helps these agencies identify an important *strategic issue*—namely, what should the results and outcomes be? Subsequent strategic planning efforts are then likely to start with the outcomes the organization and legislature thinks are still important.

Still other strategic planning processes will articulate goals to guide strategy formulation in response to specific issues or to guide implementation of specific strategies. Goals developed at these later stages of the process are likely to be more detailed and specific than those developed earlier. Goals may be developed any time they will be useful to guide process efforts *and* will have sufficient support among key parties to produce desired actions.

In my experience, however, strategic planning processes generally start neither with vision nor with goals. In part, this is because in my experience strategic planning rarely starts with step 1. Instead, people sense something is not right about the current situation—they are facing strategic issues or they are pursuing a strategy that is failing or about to fail—and they want to know what to do (Borins, 1998; Nutt, 2001b). One of the crucial features of issue-driven planning (and political decision making in general) is that you do not have to agree on goals to agree on next steps (Innes, 1996; Bryant, 2003; Huxham, 2003). You simply need to agree on a strategy that will address the issue and further the organization's (or community's) and the key stakeholders' interests. Goals are likely to be developed once viable strategies have been developed to address the issues. These goals will typically be strategy specific.

Articulating goals or describing a vision may give strategic planners a better feeling for where a strategy or interconnected set of strategies should lead (Behn, 1999a; Nutt, 2001b). Goals and vision are thus more likely to come toward the end of the process than the beginning. But there are clear exceptions—as the examples of the Wilder Foundation and the Air Force revealed earlier—and process designers should think carefully about why, when, and how—if at all—to bring goals and vision into the process.

Applying the Process Across Organizational Subunits, Levels, and Functions

Strategic thinking, acting, and learning depend on getting key people together, getting them to focus wisely and creatively on what is really important, and getting them to do something about it. At its most basic the technology of strategic planning thus involves deliberations, decisions, and actions. The steps in the Strategy Change Cycle make the process reasonably orderly to increase the likelihood that what is important is recognized and addressed and to increase the number of people who participate in the process. When the process is applied to the organization as a whole or at least to significant parts of it on an ongoing basis (rather than in a one-shot effort), it is usually necessary to construct a *strategic management system*. This system encourages integration of the various parts of the process in appropriate ways and engages the organization in strategic management, not just strategic planning (Poister and Streib, 1999). In the best circumstances the system will include the actors and the knowledge necessary to foster systems thinking and prompt quick, wise, and effective action, because inclusion, systems thinking, and speed are increasingly required of public and nonprofit organizations (Schachtel, 2001; Linden, 2002; Bryson, 2003a).

The Strategy Change Cycle might be applied across organizational subunits, levels, and functions as outlined in Figure 2.2. This application is based on an *integrated units of management* system used by many corporations. The system's first cycle consists of bottom-up development of strategic plans within a framework established at the top, followed by reviews and reconciliation at each succeeding level. In the second cycle operating plans are developed to implement the strategic plans. Depending on the situation, decisions at the top of the organizational hierarchy may or may not require policy board approval (which is why the line depicting the process flow diverges at the top).

The system may be supported by a set of performance indicators and strategies embodied in a *balanced scorecard* (BSC) (Kaplan and Norton, 1996, 2004; Niven, 2003). An example of a BSC, from the city of Charlotte, North Carolina, is presented in Figure 2.3. The theory behind the balanced scorecard is that learning and growth outcomes should enhance the effectiveness of internal processes, which in turn should facilitate achievement of desirable financial outcomes. Achieving desirable outcomes in all three areas should produce better customer outcomes. The theory implies that an organization that has gone through the process of developing an organization-wide balanced scorecard and supporting scorecards for departments and lines of business should be more effective in meeting its mandates, fulfilling its mission, and creating public value. (The Hennepin County, Minnesota, strategic management system relies in part on the use of balanced scorecards and is discussed in detail in Chapter Ten.)

Strategic planning systems for public and nonprofit organizations are usually not as formalized and integrated as the one outlined in Figure 2.2. More typical is a *strategic issues management* system, which attempts to manage specific strategic issues without seeking integration of the resultant strategies across all subunits, levels, and functions (Roberts and Wargo, 1994; Joyce, 1999; Hendrick, 2003). Tight integration is often not necessary, because most issues do not affect all parts of an organization, are subject to differing political requirements, and have their own time frame.

Baltimore, Maryland, and a number of other cities have institutionalized strategic issues management through use of the CitiStat system (Schachtel, 2001; Linden, 2002). In this system a central analysis staff uses geographically coded data to spot trends, events, and issues that need to be addressed by line departments. The heads of the relevant units meet regularly with the mayor and the mayor's key advisers, including the heads of finance, human resources, and information technology, to examine the data and address the issues face to face. Actions

FIGURE 2.2. STRATEGIC PLANNING SYSTEM FOR INTEGRATED UNITS OF MANAGEMENT.

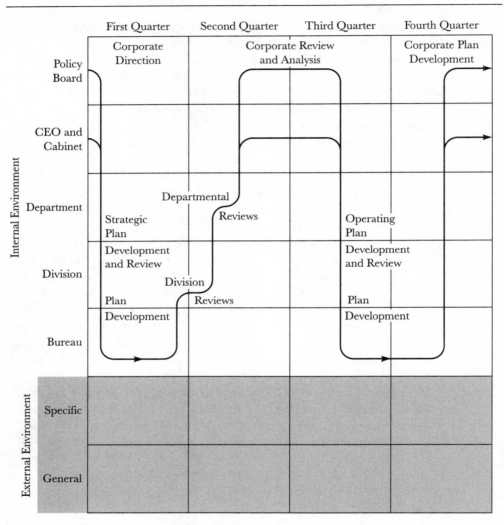

Source: Adapted from Bryson and Roering, 1987, p. 16.

FIGURE 2.3. BALANCED SCORECARD FOR A GOVERNMENT.

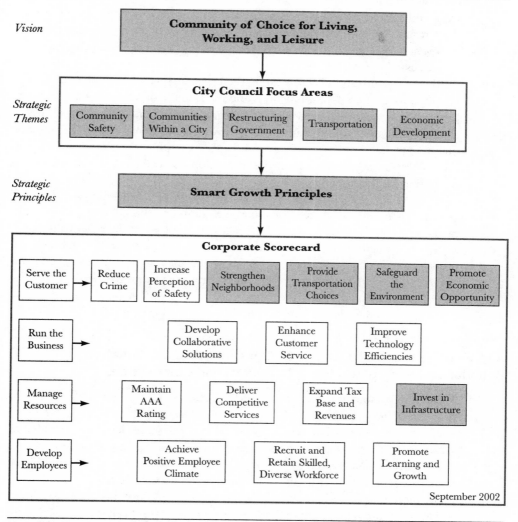

Note: Corporate Scorecard shaded boxes are specifically related to Smart Growth Principles.

Source: City of Charlotte, North Carolina, 2004. Reprinted with permission.

and follow-up procedures are agreed upon on the spot. Notable successes have occurred in which better outcomes were produced, money was saved, or teamwork and competence were enhanced. Many cities have experienced all three of these results. Other common public and nonprofit strategic planning systems are the *contract model, collaboration,* the *portfolio model,* and the *goal model.* (These systems are discussed in Chapter Ten.)

If the organization is fairly large, then specific linkages will be necessary to join the process to different functions and levels in the organization so that it can proceed in a reasonably orderly and integrated manner. One effective way to achieve such a linkage is to appoint the heads of all major units to the strategic planning team. All unit heads can then be sure that their units' information and interests are represented in strategy formulation and can oversee strategy implementation in their unit.

Indeed, key decision makers might wish to form themselves into a permanent strategic planning committee or cabinet. I recommend this approach when it appears workable for the organization, because it emphasizes the role of line managers as strategic planners and the role of strategic planners as facilitators of decision making by the line managers. Pragmatic and effective strategies and plans are likely to result. Temporary task forces or strategic planning committees or cabinets can work, but whatever the arrangement, there is no substitute for the direct involvement of key decision makers in the process (Borins, 1998).

Applying the Process to Functions That Cross Organizational Boundaries, Interorganizational Networks, and Communities

When applied to a function or network that crosses organizational boundaries or to a community, the Strategy Change Cycle usually needs to be sponsored by a committee or task force of key decision makers, opinion leaders, "influentials," or "notables" representing important stakeholder groups. Additional working groups or task forces usually need to be organized at various times to deal with specific strategic issues or to oversee the implementation of specific strategies. Because so many more people and groups need to be involved and because implementation has to rely more on consent than authority, the process is likely to be much more time consuming and iterative than strategic planning applied to an organization. However, the additional time spent on exploring issues and reaching agreement may be made up later through speedy implementation (Innes, 1996; Bardach, 1998; Bryant, 2003; Huxham, 2003). Resource C provides additional information on how to pursue strategic planning in collaborative settings.

In addition, when a community is involved, special efforts are necessary to make sure that important connections are made and any incompatibilities are resolved between the strategic plans and the community's comprehensive plan and the various devices used to implement it, such as the government's capital improvement program, subdivision controls, zoning ordinances, and official maps. Making these connections, however, should not unduly hamper the process. Strategic planning and comprehensive planning can be complementary, and efforts should be made to ensure that they are so that the interests of the community and its various stakeholders can be advanced (Innes, 1996; Burby, 2003; Wheeland, 2003).

Roles for Planners, Decision Makers, Implementers, and Citizens

Planners can play many different roles in a strategic planning process. In many cases the planners are not people with the job title of planner but are policymakers or line managers (Mintzberg, Ahlstrand, and Lampel, 1998). The people with the title of planner often act primarily as facilitators of decision making by policymakers or line managers, as technical experts in substantive areas, or as both. Planners also operate in a variety of other roles. Sometimes the planner is an "expert on experts" (Bolan, 1971), easing different people with different expertise in and out of the process for different purposes at different times. At other times planners act as technicians, politicians, or hybrids of these roles (Howe, 1980). At still other times they are finders of strategy, interpreting existing actions and recognizing important patterns in the organization and its environment; analysts of existing or potential strategies; catalysts for promoting strategic thought and action; or strategists themselves (Mintzberg, 1994, pp. 361–396).

Because the most important thing about strategic planning is the development of strategic thought, action, and learning, it may not matter much which person does what. However, it does seem that strategic planning done by policymakers or line managers is most likely to be implemented. (Line managers in government are not usually charged with making important political trade-offs—politicians are. Therefore an effective governmental strategic planning process probably needs participation from both policymakers and line managers.)

Public organizations engaged in strategic planning often have little citizen participation in the process other than that of elected or appointed policy board members. One reason for this may be that the organization already possesses the necessary knowledge and expertise in-house, making citizen involvement redundant and excessively time consuming. In addition, insiders typically are the chief implementers of strategies, so their ownership of the process and resultant decisions may be what is most crucial. Further, the direct involvement of an elected or appointed policy board may be sufficient to legitimize the process, in keeping with the idea that this country has a representative, not a direct, democracy. The absence of participation by ordinary outsiders would parallel much private sector corporate planning practice. Nonetheless, it is easy to be wrong about how much one "knows," or needs to know, and how much perceived legitimacy the process needs (Suchman, 1995; Nutt, 2002). Interviews, focus groups and surveys of outsiders, and external sounding boards of various sorts are often worth their weight in gold because they open insiders' eyes to information they have missed, add legitimacy to the effort, and keep the organization, network, or community from reaching wrong conclusions or making poor decisions (Thomas, 1995; Feldman and Khademian, 2000). So a word of caution is in order: remember, as the ancient Greeks believed, that nemesis always walks in the footsteps of hubris!

Program-focused strategic planning appears to be much more likely to involve citizens, particularly in their capacity as customers. Citizen involvement in program planning thus is roughly analogous to consumer involvement in private sector marketing research and development projects. For example, the School District relied on a variety of citizen involvement techniques (for example, committees, task forces, surveys, public meetings) to figure out what it should be doing. More generally, transportation planning typically involves a great deal of citizen participation. Citizens may provide information concerning their travel needs and desires, reactions to various transportation system design alternatives, and advice on ways to resolve conflicts that arise during the process. Park planning also typically involves substantial citizen participation. Unfortunately, because the use of transportation systems or parks by citizens is generally broad based, actual users are often assumed to be identical with citizens at large. This equation is hardly ever justified, however, as it probably masks great variety in stakeholder concerns about and contributions to the process. A stakeholder analysis can help keep the interests and contributions of different groups of citizens analytically separate (Eden and Ackermann, 1998; Bryson, 2004b).

Finally, planning on behalf of a community almost always involves substantial citizen participation. Unfortunately, community-focused strategic plans often assume that all citizens can be treated alike and that all citizens are interested in the community as a whole—two assumptions at odds with most studies of political participation (see, for example, Putnam, 2000). Application of the stakeholder concept to community strategic planning would help avoid some of these errors, as it did in the case of the School District's efforts, where the interests of parents, businesses, taxpayers, elected officials, and other stakeholder groups were all explored. Beyond that, broad citizen involvement usually results in better plans and implementation processes (Chrislip, 2000; Burby, 2003; Wheeland, 2003).

Summary

This chapter has outlined the Strategy Change Cycle, a process for promoting strategic thinking, acting, and learning in governments, public agencies, nonprofit organizations, networks, communities, and other entities. Although the process is presented in a linear, sequential fashion for pedagogical reasons, in practice it proceeds iteratively as groups continuously rethink the connections among the various elements of the process, take action, and learn on their way to formulating effective strategies. In addition, the process often does not start with step 1 but instead starts with some other step and then cycles back to step 1. The steps are not steps precisely but rather occasions for deliberations, decisions, and actions within a continuous flow of strategic thinking, acting, and learning; knowledge exploration and exploitation; and strategy formulation and implementation. Mintzberg, Ahlstrand, and Lampel (1998) assert that "all real strategic behavior has to combine deliberate control with emergent learning" (p. 195). The Strategy Change Cycle is designed to promote just this kind of strategic behavior.

Figure 2.4 shows how the Strategy Change Cycle is designed to further the functions of strategic planning outlined in Figure 1.4. It also displays the iteration that is likely to occur as planning teams work to organize participation, create ideas of strategic significance, build a winning coalition, and implement the ideas so that the decisions and actions produced lead to meeting the organization's mandates, fulfilling its mission, and creating real public value.

As previously mentioned, my colleague Farnum Alston and I have prepared a strategic planning workbook designed to help individuals, teams, groups, and organizations work through the process (Bryson and Alston, 2004). The workbook should not be used without this book, however, because the Strategy Change Cycle typically requires careful tailoring to specific circumstances. Owing to space limitations, the workbook contains little advice on how to adapt the process to different situations, whereas this book offers a great deal of the advice and guidance necessary to design and manage a successful process.

In Chapter Three I discuss how to negotiate an initial agreement among key internal (and perhaps external) decision makers or opinion leaders on the purpose and process of a strategic planning effort. This agreement will shape the nature and direction of deliberations, decisions, and actions designed to deal with what is truly important to the organization or community.

FIGURE 2.4. STRATEGIC PLANNING PURPOSES AND FUNCTIONS AND STRATEGY CHANGE CYCLE STEPS.

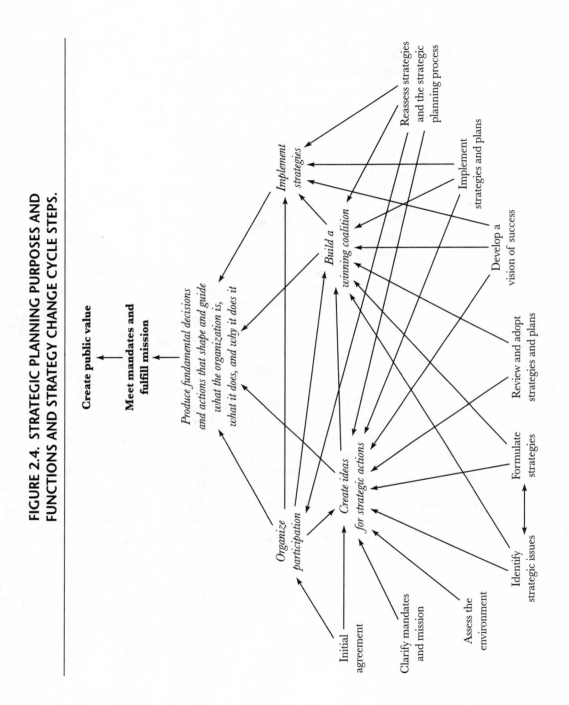

PART TWO

KEY STEPS IN USING THE STRATEGY CHANGE CYCLE

The ten-step strategic planning process is presented in detail in Part Two. It is a reasonably orderly, deliberative, and participative approach to facilitating strategic thought, action, and learning by key decision makers.

Chapter Three covers the initial agreement phase, the "plan for planning." Chapter Four focuses on clarifying organization mandates and mission. Chapter Five describes how to assess an organization's strengths and weaknesses, as well as the opportunities and challenges it faces. Chapter Six discusses strategic issues—what they are, how they can be identified, and how to critique them. Chapter Seven is devoted to formulating and adopting effective strategies and plans.

The final three chapters in Part Two move from planning to management. Chapter Eight covers development of the organization's vision of success, a description of what the organization should look like as it fulfills its mission, meets its mandates, and achieves its full potential for creating public value. Chapter Nine focuses on implementing strategies and plans, and Chapter Ten on reassessing and revising them.

An organization that completes this Strategy Change Cycle should be well on its way toward improving and maintaining its effectiveness, pursuing its mission, meeting its mandates, and creating genuine public value. It should be clearly focused on satisfying key stakeholders in ways that are politically acceptable, technically and administratively workable, and legally and ethically defensible.

CHAPTER THREE

INITIATING AND AGREEING ON A STRATEGIC PLANNING PROCESS

The beginning is the most important part of the work.

PLATO, *THE REPUBLIC*

The purpose of the first step in the Strategy Change Cycle is to develop among key internal decision makers or opinion leaders (and key external leaders as well if their support is necessary for the success of the effort) an initial agreement about the overall strategic planning effort and main planning steps. This represents a kind of "plan to plan" (Steiner, 1979), intended to point the way toward the ultimate end of creating public value.

The support and the commitment of key decision makers are vital if strategic planning and change in an organization are to succeed. But the importance of these decision makers' early involvement goes beyond the need for their support and commitment. They supply information vital to the planning effort: who should be involved, when key decision points will occur, and what arguments are likely to be persuasive at various points in the process. They can also provide critical resources: legitimacy, staff assignments, a budget, and meeting space.

Every strategic planning effort is in effect a drama that must have a correct setting; themes; plots and subplots; actors; scenes; a beginning, a middle, and a conclusion; and interpretation (Mangham and Overington, 1987; Brower, 1999; Bryant, 2003). Only key decision makers have access to the information and resources needed for the effective development and direction of such a drama. But unlike the outcome of a scripted play, the end of this drama is not known to anyone in advance. The end will be as much *emergent* as it is deliberate. Indeed, strategic planning and management at their best involve the ongoing crafting of "the subtle relationships between thought and action, control and learning, stability and change" (Mintzberg, Ahlstrand, and Lampel, 1998, p. 209).

Planning Focus and Desired Outcomes

Ideally, this first step will produce agreement on several issues:

1. The purpose and worth of the strategic planning effort
2. The organizations, units, groups, or persons who should be included, and the ways in which they should participate
3. The specific subsequent steps to be followed
4. The form and timing of reports

A strategic planning coordinating committee (SPCC) and a strategic planning team probably should be formed and given a charge statement or charter. Finally, the necessary resources to begin the endeavor must be committed.

As a general rule the strategic planning effort should focus on that part of the organization (or function or community) controlled, overseen, or strongly influenced by the key decision makers interested in engaging in strategic planning. In other words, only under unusual circumstances does it make sense to develop strategic plans for organizations or parts of organizations over which the key decision makers involved in the effort have no control or for which they have no responsibility. The exception to this rule is externally initiated reform programs designed to demonstrate how an organization might conduct itself if it took the reformers' aims seriously. For example, candidates running for elective office often issue campaign platforms that propose new strategies for the governments they wish to lead. Newspaper editorial and opinion pages, book and magazine discussions of public affairs, and think tank reports also often offer what are in effect reformers' strategic plans for public or nonprofit organizations.

The agreement achieved in this first step should also make clear what the *givens* are at the beginning of the process. In other words, what things relating to the organization's history, arrangements, and practices are off limits, at least for the time being, and what things are open for revision? On the one hand, if everything is a candidate for far-reaching change, potential participants may be scared off, and resistance to change in the organization may harden. On the other hand, if everything is sacred, then there is no reason for strategic planning. There should be enough tension to prompt change and make it worth the effort, but not so much that it paralyzes potential participants with fear and anxiety (Dalton, 1970; Schein, 1987; Nutt, 2001b; Fiol, 2002).

The process of reaching an initial agreement is straightforward in concept but often circuitous in practice. It usually proceeds through the following stages:

1. Initiating the process
2. Introducing the concept of strategic planning
3. Developing an understanding of what strategic planning means in practice
4. Thinking through the important implications of the process
5. Developing a commitment to strategic planning
6. Reaching the actual agreement

The more numerous the decision makers who must be involved and the less they know about strategic planning, the more time consuming the process will be and the more indirect the route to agreement. Indeed, typically a series of agreements must be reached before the strategic planning process can begin in earnest.

Benefits

A number of significant benefits flow from a good initial agreement (Benveniste, 1989; Janis, 1989; Nutt, 2002). The first is simply that the purpose and worth of the strategic planning effort is likely to be widely recognized by the affected parties, leading to broad sponsorship and legitimacy. *Broad sponsorship* dispels any suspicion that the effort is a power play by a small group. And it ensures that the results of the efforts are likely to be seen as objective (that is, as not manipulated to serve narrow partisan interests). Broad sponsorship also is a source of psychological safety, which can help people address what might otherwise be highly threatening or anxiety- or guilt-producing prospects of change (Schein, 1997; Fiol, 2002; Bryant, 2003). *Legitimacy* justifies the occasions, content, and timing of the discussions and ensuing actions in the next stages of the planning process (Herson, 1984; Suchman, 1995). Such discussions—particularly when they involve key decision makers from a variety of functions and levels and thus cross organizational boundaries of various sorts—are unlikely to occur without prompting. And they are unlikely to be prompted without authorization. As Borins (1998) notes, "Collaboration across boundaries does not happen naturally, it must be made to happen" (p. 47). *Authorization* of such discussions is an enormous resource for the planners who organize them because the planners gain considerable control over the forums in which these discussions occur, the agendas, the information provided, and the framing of the issues. The planners gain leverage because the discussions typically will be cross-functional, rather than under the control of any unit or department, and the planners will then be the discussion facilitators. Control of this sort is not manipulative in a partisan sense; instead, it ensures that the organization as a whole is looked at and discussed and not just the separate parts (Bryson and Crosby, 1996).

In the School District, for example, a group made up of the seven-member school board, the superintendent, the assistant superintendent, and the directors of finance, personnel, community education, and communications began the strategic planning process. These participants saw the initiation of strategic planning by this group as a way for them to engage each other in extended, reasonable, balanced, and holistic discussions about what was best for the district. Not coincidentally, it was also a way to limit the possibility that each board member would pursue his or her own agenda. The School District also needed better coordination across district departments and levels, in part because the board had not provided updated policy guidance and in part because of the previous superintendent's management style. The new superintendent (the planner who had initiated the process) was interested in strategic planning precisely because he hoped it would further the board's expressed desire for holistic thinking in pursuit of organizational excellence.

A second benefit is that a well-articulated initial agreement provides a clear definition of the network to be involved and the process by which it is to be maintained. A good network management process will provide involved or affected stakeholders with a sense of *procedural justice*—that is, with a sense that both the procedures used to reach decisions and the decisions themselves are fair (Eden and Ackermann, 1998, pp. 53–55). For example, adopting a doctrine of "no surprises" can be a good idea when developing a network and moving toward major decisions. This doctrine means that major stakeholders are at least kept informed of progress, events, and impending decisions, and perhaps consulted or even involved in decision making. Nothing is dropped on them out of the blue. This doctrine may be particularly useful when the need for cooperation and the risks of failure are high (Janis, 1989). Adopting a doctrine of no surprises may be best in other situations as well—even when there seem to be good reasons for keeping certain stakeholders in the dark. In an era when a basic characteristic of information seems to be that it leaks (Cleveland, 1985), full and prompt disclosure may be advisable. As Ben Franklin said, "Three may keep a secret, if two of them are dead."

Third, a good initial agreement includes an outline of the general sequence of steps in the strategic planning effort. This sequence should contribute to stakeholders' sense that the process is *procedurally rational*. According to Eden and Ackermann (1998), *procedural rationality* means that "the procedures used for strategy making make sense in themselves—they are coherent, follow a series of steps where each step is itself understood (not opaque) and relates to prior and future steps" (p. 55). Eden and Ackermann add that a procedurally rational process needs to be "sensible and reasonably thorough going, but neither too time-consuming nor too hurried," and the process must allow for "cognitive and emotional commitment." As a result, any decisions made are seen to be the outcome of appropriate deliberation. To be effective the sequence of steps must ensure that the process is tied to key decision-making points in the relevant arenas (for example, budget decisions, elections, or the rhythm of the legislative cycle). Time in organizations is not linear; it is *junctural* (Bryson and Roering, 1988, p. 1001; Bryson and Roering, 1989; Bromiley and Marcus, 1987; Albert and Bell, 2002). And the most important junctions are decision points.

To revert to our drama metaphor, a good initial agreement will name the actors, describe the general character of the story and themes to be followed, spell out as much of the plot as it is possible to know in advance, specify the way the drama will be broken into acts and scenes, designate the stage on which it will be played, and clarify who the audience is. Thus the initial agreement step is extremely important because what follows depends significantly on the specifics of the beginning. The epigraph that begins this chapter captures the fatefulness embodied in this early work, particularly in systems prone to unpredictable or chaotic behavior (Kingdon, 1995). As Gleick (1988) notes, chaotic systems demonstrate a "sensitive dependence on initial conditions" (p. 23).

Fourth—and this will dramatically affect the story that develops—the agreement should specify exactly what is to be taken as given—at least at the start. For example, an organization's existing legal commitments, mandates, personnel complements, organizational designs, mission statements, resource allocations, job descriptions, or crucial aspects of its culture may need to be taken as givens in order to gain agreement. It is very important to be clear from the start what is off limits for the exercise; otherwise several key decision makers are unlikely to participate. When too much is up for grabs, the process will be too threatening or dangerous, will result in unconstructive or downright damaging conflict, or will produce a strategic plan that is useless because it lacks adequate support. At the same time, the more that is taken as given, the less useful strategic planning is likely to be. It is important, therefore, to find the right tension between what is given and what is possible (Mangham and Overington, 1987).

Fifth, a good agreement also provides mechanisms, such as a strategic planning task force or coordinating committee, for buffering, consulting, negotiating, or problem solving among units, groups, or persons involved in or affected by the effort. Without these mechanisms, conflicts are likely to stymie or even destroy the effort (Ury, Brett, and Goldberg, 1988; Borins, 1998). These mechanisms also allow errors to be detected and corrected as the process proceeds; a strategic planning task force or coordinating committee can make needed midcourse corrections.

A task force or committee can also be a valuable sounding board for ideas. And another important function of such a group is to keep planners' attention focused on strategic concerns and to refer operational matters to appropriate groups and individuals.

A sixth benefit is that a good initial agreement guarantees the necessary resources. Money typically is not the most needed resource for strategic planning; the time and the attention of key decision makers are more important. The time of staff is also needed to gather information and provide logistical and clerical support. (This will probably involve one staff person part-time in a small organization, several people either full-time or part-time in a larger organization.)

Seventh, a good agreement provides useful preparation for any major changes that may be forthcoming. For example, if planning initiators envision pursuing an ultimate big win rather than a series of small wins, the groundwork will probably need to be laid in this first phase. Achieving a big win may require changing the conceptual frame underpinning current strategy, dramatically changing goals or guiding visions, changing basic technologies, altering dominant coalitions, or making some other fundamental change. Needed groundwork may involve having people other than the "usual suspects" on the planning committee or planning team; highlighting the planning effort or separating it from ongoing processes in such a way that its power and influence are increased; gaining authorization for a range of background studies, such as benchmarking analyses, reengineering studies, or system analyses; and so forth. Such groundwork can lead to undesirable fear and rigidity among stakeholders, so the way it is undertaken must be thought through carefully. Consider these words, spoken by a character in Amy Tan's *The Bonesetter's Daughter* (2001): "And Precious Auntie flapped her hands fast: '*A person should consider how things begin. A particular beginning results in a particular end*'" (p. 153).

Finally, an eighth benefit is that a good initial agreement signifies the political support of key decision makers or opinion leaders at several levels in the organization, and it helps maintain that support throughout the process. For strategic planning to work, a coalition must develop that is large enough and strong enough to formulate and implement strategies that deal effectively with key strategic issues. Such coalitions typically do not develop quickly (particularly in interorganizational or community planning efforts; see Denis, Lamothe, and Langley, 2001; Huxham, 2003). Instead, they coalesce around the important strategic ideas that emerge from the sequence of discussions, consultations, times of mutual education, and reconceptualizations that are at the heart of any strategic planning effort (Mintzberg and Westley, 1992; Sabatier and Jenkins-Smith, 1993; Crosby and Bryson, forthcoming).

Developing an Initial Agreement

So far we have covered the purpose, desired outcomes, and benefits of this first step in the Strategy Change Cycle. Now we can go into greater depth on specific aspects of the process of developing an initial agreement.

Whose Process Is It, and Who Should Be Involved?

Obviously, some individual or some group must initiate and champion the strategic planning process. This champion will need to make the initial decisions about what the process should focus on and who should be involved. If the process is going to affect the entire organization, then the organization's key decision makers (and perhaps representatives of key external stakeholders) should be involved. For example, the School District chose a four-tiered system of involvement for its strategic planning effort. The first tier had eight people: the seven school board members and the superintendent, who also led the second tier. The second tier was made up of the superintendent and the six members of his cabinet. The third tier was the strategic planning steering committee, which included twenty-four representatives of internal stakeholder groups. The fourth tier consisted of task forces charged with developing responses to the strategic issues. Those in the first tier obviously were the key decision makers, but they chose to involve the other groups in a consultative role in order to get the information, support, commitment, and resources necessary to make the strategic planning effort work for the district as a whole. This first group decided not to involve representatives of key external stakeholder groups in major decision-making roles; as the official, legally responsible decision-making body for the district, it could not easily share this responsibility. (Outsiders did cochair and serve on the advisory task forces created to make recommendations for addressing the strategic issues identified by the board and the superintendent. Outsiders were also involved in focus groups and community information-gathering meetings.)

If the strategic planning focus is on an organizational subunit, a boundary-crossing service, or a community, then the key decision makers (and possibly other stakeholders) for that entity should be involved, even if they are not immediate members of that entity. For example, key decision makers or stakeholders for a community, such as the owners of major businesses, may not live in the community. Elected or appointed policy board members may be either insiders or outsiders. Drafting the initial agreement for the Project for Pride in Living strategic planning effort involved the president, senior staff, and the board of directors, whose forty-six members came from various segments of the community. The initial agreement made for the Naval Security Group (NSG), after everyone was on board, involved the admiral commanding NSG and his deputy (the top policy decision makers) as well as the major NSG functional department heads (the main policy implementers). Other participants were key officer representatives from the main Navy staff of the chief of Naval Operations (a major external stakeholder and resource provider critical to NSG's success), several commanding officers of key NSG field sites (representing NSG's frontline operations and including NSG's key technology research and development organization), and officers from the fleet and joint service staffs (representing NSG's key customers). The admiral also kept the director of the National Security Agency (NSA) (NSG's other critical stakeholder, customer, and resource provider) involved through direct personal liaison. Additionally, lower NSG field elements were involved through a series of *rollout* briefings and e-mail exchanges. As e-mail became more pervasive and virtual involvement became feasible, it became much easier to involve a wider NSG insider audience from multiple levels in the organization in the planning efforts.

For organizations it may be advisable to involve insiders from three organizational levels: top policy- and decision makers, middle managers, and technical core or frontline personnel (Thompson, 1967; Nutt and Backoff, 1992). Top policy- and decision makers should be involved for several reasons. First, they are formally charged with relating the organization to its domain. Second, because of their responsibilities they are often highly effective *boundary spanners,* with links to many people and entities both inside and outside the organization. Third, they are often among the first to perceive mismatches between the organization and its environment and therefore may be the most responsive to external threats and opportunities affecting the organization (Hampden-Turner, 1990; Schein, 1997). Finally, they control the resources necessary to carry out the strategic planning effort and implement the recommendations that grow out of it. It is simply very difficult to plan around these people, so they should be included from the start if at all possible (Rainey, 2003).

In governments and public agencies the initial planning group is likely to include members of an elected or appointed board as well as high-level executives. In council-manager cities, for example, the initial agreement typically is negotiated among council members, the city manager, and key department heads. As noted earlier, the initial agreement that framed the School District's effort involved the elected school board, the appointed superintendent, and key managers. In nonprofit organizations the key decision-making group is likely to include the senior managers and board of directors. The initial agreement for Project for Pride in Living's effort was negotiated among the organization's board, president, senior managers, and persons who served as process facilitators.

Middle management personnel should be included because of their vital role in translating policies and decisions into operations. Further, middle managers are likely to bear the brunt of any managerial changes that result, and therefore should be involved to reduce unnecessary resistance and make transitions smoother (Kanter, 1983, 1989; Block, 1987; Oshry, 1995).

Technical core or frontline personnel may also be needed when fashioning an initial agreement. Again, there are several reasons to consider involving them or their representatives (Benveniste, 1989; Normann, 1991, Cohen and Eimicke, 1998). First, they are in charge of the day-to-day use of the core technologies contributing to or affected by strategic change. As a result, they are likely to be the most knowledgeable about how the organization's basic technologies work in practice and also most likely to be immediately helped or hurt by change. Their early involvement may be necessary to ensure that needed changes can be understood, wise changes implemented, and resistance to change minimized. Second, technical core or frontline personnel are likely to be asked for their opinions by key decision makers anyway, so anything that makes them receptive to strategic change is a plus. Finally, because of their technical knowledge or their daily contact with customers, clients, or users, these personnel can severely hamper strategic changes they do not support. In extreme cases they might undermine or even sabotage change efforts. Co-opting these groups early on can be an important key to strategic planning success.

An important caveat is in order, however. If it is clear from the start that strategic planning will result in the elimination of certain positions, workgroups, or departments—as may be the case in major reengineering efforts, for example—then it may be both unnecessary and downright harmful to involve people who are in the affected areas. The effective and humane approach may be to involve them in planning for their transition to new jobs, offering retraining, placement assistance, and severance arrangements (Behn, 1983; Nutt, 2001a; Holzer, Lee, and Newman, 2003).

How Do You Find the Right People?

Typically, some initial stakeholder analysis work will need to be done before the "right" group of people can be found to forge an effective initial agreement. The purpose of stakeholder analyses at this point is to help process sponsors decide who should be involved in negotiating an initial agreement, either because they have information that cannot be gained otherwise or because their support is necessary to ensure successful implementation of initiatives built on the analyses (Thomas, 1993, 1995).

First, of course, process sponsors must choose who should do the stakeholder analyses and how. Again, in general, people should be involved when they have information that cannot be gained otherwise or when their participation is necessary to ensure a successful strategic planning process. Fortunately, this choice can be approached as a sequence of choices in which an individual or a small planning group begins the effort and then others are added later as the advisability of doing so becomes apparent (Finn, 1996; Chrislip, 2002; Bryson, 2004b).

One way to approach the task is with a five-step process in which a decision can be made to stop any time after the first step. Stopping might be advisable when, for example, enough information and support to proceed have been gained, timelines are short, or the analyses are too sensitive. The five steps are as follows:

1. An individual or a small planning group initiates the process with a preliminary stakeholder analysis, using, for example, the basic analysis technique (discussed in more detail in Chapter Four) or the power versus interest grid, stakeholder influence diagram, or participation planning matrix (discussed in Resource A). This step is useful in helping sponsors and champions of the change effort think strategically about how to create the ideas and coalitions needed to reach a successful conclusion. This step is typically backroom work (Eden and Ackermann, 1998). Necessary information may be garnered through interviews, questionnaires, focus groups, or other targeted information-gathering techniques in this and subsequent steps or in conjunction with the other techniques outlined in Resource A.

2. After the results of the first analysis have been reviewed, a larger group of stakeholders can be assembled. This meeting can be viewed as the more public beginning of the change effort. The assembled group should be asked to brainstorm to produce a list of stakeholders who might need to be involved in the change effort. Again, the basic analysis technique, power versus interest grid, stakeholder influence diagram, or participation planning matrix might be used as a starting point.

3. After the second analysis has been completed, the group should be encouraged to think carefully about who is not at the meeting who should be at subsequent meetings. The group should consider actual or potential stakeholder power, legitimacy, and urgency (defined as a composite of the stakeholder's need for a timely organizational response and the importance of the claim of or relationship to the stakeholder) (Mitchell, Agle, and Wood, 1997). The group should think carefully through the positive and negative consequences of involving—or not involving—other stakeholders or their representatives and the best ways of involving them.

4. After these conversations have been completed, the full group should be assembled—that is, everyone who should be involved in the stakeholder analyses. The previous analyses may need to be repeated, at least in part, with the

full group present, in order to ensure that everyone has the same information and understands and accepts the analyses and premises (is on board, is on the same page, and has bought in) and to make any needed corrections or modifications to prior analyses.

5. After the full group has met, it should be possible to finalize the various groups who will have some role to play in the change effort: sponsors and champions, the coordinating group, the planning team, and various advisory or support groups (Bryson and Roering, 1988; Friend and Hickling, 1997, pp. 257–65; Chrislip, 2002; Linden, 2002). It may make sense to fill out a participation planning matrix (see Resource A).

Note that this staged process embodies a kind of technical, political, and ethical rationality. The process is designed to gain needed information, build political acceptance, and address at least some concerns about the legitimacy, representation, and credibility of the process. Stakeholders are included when there are good and prudent reasons to do so but not when their involvement is impractical, unnecessary, or imprudent. A certain amount of collective wisdom is used to inform these choices. Clearly, the choices of whom to include, how, and when are freighted with questions of value, and are perhaps fraught as well, but the effort to make wise and ethical judgments is essential if an organization's mission and the common good are to be advanced (Vickers, 1995; Frederickson, 1997).

Should You Hold an Opening Retreat?

For an organization, often the best way to reach initial agreement is to hold a retreat (Weisman, 2003). Begin the retreat with an introduction to the nature, purpose, and process of the strategic planning effort. Often key decision makers need such an introduction before they are willing fully to endorse a strategic planning effort. Orientation and training methods might include a lecture and discussion; presentations by representatives of organizations that have used strategic planning, followed by group discussion; analysis by key decision makers of written case studies, followed by group discussion; circulation of reading materials; strategy films; and so on. Because strategic planning means different things to different people, such an introduction can be useful even when many key decision makers have considerable experience with strategic planning. The discussions can help participants agree on what the process might mean in practice for the organization.

Here is a possible format for the first day of a strategic planning retreat:

Morning: presentation and discussion about the nature, purpose, and process of the strategic planning effort

Lunch: presentation by a representative from a similar organization that engages in strategic planning, highlighting the benefits and liabilities of the process

Afternoon: analysis and discussion of a written case study, and instruction in any special techniques necessary for successful strategic planning, such as brainstorming, the nominal group technique (Delbecq, Van de Ven, and Gustafson, 1975), the snow card technique (Spencer, 1989), or the oval mapping process (see Resource B)

By the end of the first day it should be clear whether or not the key decision makers wish to proceed. If so, the second day might be organized as follows:

Morning: basic stakeholder analysis (see Chapter Four), power versus interest grid (See Resource A), review of mandates, and development of a draft mission statement

Lunch: a speaker presenting another case example

Afternoon: SWOC analysis and preliminary identification of strategic issues and next steps

Organizations that have little experience with strategic planning but are committed to it nonetheless might skip the activities outlined for the afternoon of the first day in order to begin the second day's activities earlier. Organizations that have used strategic planning before might spend much of the first morning identifying the strengths of their previous processes and modifications that would improve the processes. They would then begin the second day's activities in the afternoon of the first day.

The retreat might conclude at the end of the second day, after the next steps have been consensually mapped out, or it might continue for a third day. The morning of the third day might be devoted to further identifying and discussing strategic issues, establishing priorities among issues, and developing possible strategies for addressing issues. The afternoon might carry this discussion further and outline possible next steps in the process. The retreat should not end until participants reach agreement on the next steps in the process and identify who will be responsible for what in each step.

If a group can reach quick agreement at each point, less than three days might be sufficient. If quick agreement is not possible, more time may be necessary to complete the various tasks, and sessions may have to be spread out over several weeks. Quick agreement is particularly unlikely when the strategic issues imply the need for a major change. It takes a group time to cope with the anxiety, fear, anger, and denial that may accompany profound change, particularly if the group senses that its culture and basic beliefs about the world are being threatened (Hampden-Turner, 1990; Schein, 1997; Fiol, 2002; Bryant, 2003).

A retreat might also help decision makers reach agreement about the nature of the strategic planning effort for a network or a community. Such a retreat, however, might be more difficult to organize than an organizational retreat. More groundwork will probably be necessary to build trust and to gain agreement from decision makers on the purposes, timing, and length of the retreat. The retreat itself will probably have to run less than three days, and post-retreat logistics, coordination, and follow-through will probably take more time and effort. Nonetheless, a retreat can function as an important signal and symbol that the network or community is about to address its most important issues and concerns, can provoke desirable media attention and pressure to continue, and can prompt stakeholders who have been lukewarm about the process to participate (Bardach, 1998; Chrislip, 2002; Ray, 2002; Wheeland, 2003).

How Many Initial Agreements Do You Need?

Sometimes it may be necessary to make sequential agreements among successively larger groups of key decision makers until everyone is on board. For example, the School District had several "initial" agreements. The board and superintendent had seen that the district might benefit from strategic planning. That led to the first agreement, between the superintendent and the board, which was contained in a jointly negotiated 1996 work program that included an assignment for the superintendent to initiate a strategic planning process for the district. The board therefore expected strategic planning of some sort but was waiting for the superintendent to propose a process. A second agreement was reached after the superintendent had spoken with the assistant superintendent, me, and my colleague Chuck Finn. This agreement included an outline of a proposed process, including specific steps, a timeline, and likely consulting costs. It was used to involve the rest of the key administrators, who signed on after they had had a chance to meet Chuck and me and to review, discuss, and modify the process in a retreat setting. A final agreement was reached with the board after the board members had had a chance to meet Chuck and me and to review, discuss, and modify the process informally. The "official" initial agreement was completed at a regular meeting of the board. This series of agreements was necessary to build understanding of what strategic planning would mean for the district, tailor the process to the district and its needs, establish trust in the consultants, and develop the necessary commitment among key decision makers to move ahead (Bryson, Ackermann, Eden, and Finn, 1996). The strategic planning efforts of the Naval Security Group and Project for Pride in Living also began with several initial agreements. Strategic planning in collaborative settings will almost certainly require a series of initial agreements (Chrislip, 2002; Linden, 2002; Huxham, 2003).

Indeed, it is worth keeping in mind that forging agreements of various sorts will go on throughout the Strategy Change Cycle. Coalitions are built incrementally, by agreement, and strategies and plans are adopted and implemented incrementally as well, also through various agreements. The achievement of each agreement may be signaled by various means, including handshakes, letters or memoranda of agreement, formal votes, and celebrations.

It is important for sponsors and champions also to keep in mind that a number of tangible and intangible, process- and content-oriented outcomes are likely to be needed throughout a Strategy Change Cycle if the process is to succeed. Figure 3.1 classifies outcomes according to these dimensions. The process versus content dimension is probably familiar—at least in a negative way—to most people. It is, for example, this dimension that we are referring to when we complain that "process is getting in the way of substance." Less obvious, because it is less frequently discussed, is the distinction between tangible and intangible outcomes (Friend and Hickling, 1997, p. 100; Innes and Booher, 1999; Baum, 2001). Here, I have sorted this dimension into three subcategories, following my interpretation of Schein's three levels of culture (1997). The most obvious aspects of culture are things we can see: namely, artifacts, plans, documents, and similar items. These visible items are symbolic or representative of things in the second and less visible subcategory: values, beliefs, and interpretive schemes. Even less obvious, almost invisible but in many ways the most important of all, are basic assumptions and worldviews. They are most important because they serve as the underpinnings of what is above them; they are the platform on which values, beliefs, and interpretive schemes and subsequently artifacts, plans, and documents are built. As Innes (1998) notes, *"When information is most influential, it is also most invisible"* (p. 54). Strategic planning and management grow out of organizational or community cultures, and thus any outcomes produced must tap into that culture, even if the purpose—as it usually is—is to change the culture in some ways, possibly even some of its basic assumptions (Schein, 1997; Khademian, 2002; Crosby and Bryson, forthcoming).

Figure 3.1 illustrates that the most obvious outcome—but in some ways the least important one—is the *tangible, content-oriented outcome* of adopting the strategic plan itself. Recall that the purpose of strategic planning is to produce fundamental decisions that shape and guide what an organization is, what it does, and why it does it—and not to produce a strategic plan. Strategic plans, however, will sit on the shelf if they are not based on positive outcomes in the other three quadrants of the figure.

The initial agreement is primarily about developing *tangible, process-oriented outcomes:* specifically, a commitment—probably in the form of a written agreement—

FIGURE 3.1. OUTCOMES LIKELY TO BE NEEDED FOR THE STRATEGIC PLANNING PROCESS TO SUCCEED.

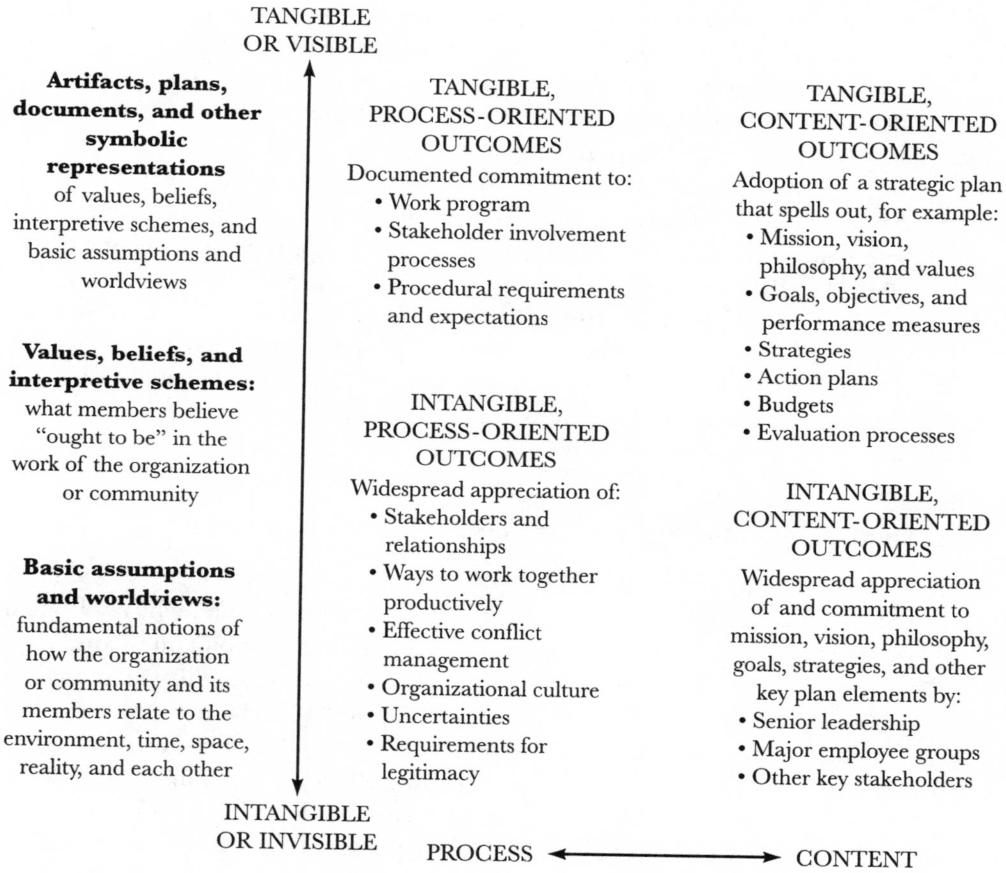

TANGIBLE
OR VISIBLE

Artifacts, plans, documents, and other symbolic representations
of values, beliefs, interpretive schemes, and basic assumptions and worldviews

Values, beliefs, and interpretive schemes:
what members believe "ought to be" in the work of the organization or community

Basic assumptions and worldviews:
fundamental notions of how the organization or community and its members relate to the environment, time, space, reality, and each other

TANGIBLE,
PROCESS-ORIENTED
OUTCOMES

Documented commitment to:
• Work program
• Stakeholder involvement processes
• Procedural requirements and expectations

INTANGIBLE,
PROCESS-ORIENTED
OUTCOMES

Widespread appreciation of:
• Stakeholders and relationships
• Ways to work together productively
• Effective conflict management
• Organizational culture
• Uncertainties
• Requirements for legitimacy

TANGIBLE,
CONTENT-ORIENTED
OUTCOMES

Adoption of a strategic plan that spells out, for example:
• Mission, vision, philosophy, and values
• Goals, objectives, and performance measures
• Strategies
• Action plans
• Budgets
• Evaluation processes

INTANGIBLE,
CONTENT-ORIENTED
OUTCOMES

Widespread appreciation of and commitment to mission, vision, philosophy, goals, strategies, and other key plan elements by:
• Senior leadership
• Major employee groups
• Other key stakeholders

INTANGIBLE
OR INVISIBLE   PROCESS ←——————→ CONTENT

to process steps, procedures, and requirements; a general work program for carrying out those steps; and stakeholder involvement processes. The initial agreement will be meaningless, however, unless it is based on some *intangible, process-oriented outcomes.* These include appreciations of stakeholders and stakeholder relationships, ways to work together productively, effective approaches to conflict management, organizational culture, uncertainties surrounding the process and the organization, and requirements for legitimacy. If these appreciations are not deepened and widened over the course of the process, the process will fail. If they are enriched and spread throughout relevant networks, then crucial *intangible, content-oriented outcomes* will be produced. These include a widespread appreciation of and commitment to the organization's mission, vision, philosophy, core values, goals, strategies, and other key elements of a successful change effort on the part of senior leadership, major employee groups, and other key stakeholders.

When these last outcomes are in place in a small organization, then the strategic plan will basically implement itself. When they exist in a large organization, boundary-crossing service, or community, then implementation will be far easier than it would be otherwise. The plan will simply record the changes that have *already* occurred in the hearts and minds of key stakeholders. Said differently, if the intangible elements are in place, then the tangible outcomes will follow. As Mintzberg (1994) observes: "Organizations function on the basis of commitment and mindset. In other words, it is determined and inspired people who get things done" (p. 252). Commitment, mindset, determination, and inspiration are not directly visible. What matters most in strategic planning thus is what is *not visible,* so sponsors, champions, and facilitators must pay careful attention to the production of those *intangible* but highly consequential outcomes; if they do not, the plan will be mostly worthless. It may satisfy certain mandates or reporting requirements, but it will certainly not be a living document.

What Should the Initial Agreement Contain?

The initial agreement should cover the desired outcomes listed at the beginning of this chapter: agreement on the purpose of the effort (including by implication what the effort will not achieve) and its worth; the organizations, units, groups, or persons who should be involved, and how; a shared understanding about the nature and sequence of the steps in the process; and agreement on the form and timing of reports. Typically, three more actions are taken. First, a committee is established to oversee the strategic planning effort. The committee should be headed by someone with enough standing and credibility in the organization to give the effort visibility and legitimacy. Ideally, this person will be trusted by all or most factions in the organization so that the effort will not be seen as a narrow partisan affair. The committee can be an existing group, such as a board of directors or city council, that adds strategic planning oversight to its responsibilities, or it can be a group established for this specific purpose. In the School District the board and superintendent were the official overseers of the process, and the cabinet and a strategic planning team also shared responsibility for strategic planning. Each cabinet member cochaired with a community leader one of the task forces set up to address some of the strategic issues. In the Naval Security Group the process was overseen by the deputy commander, as the process sponsor, and by a committee composed of the major functional department heads, chaired by one of the department heads acting as the process champion. And in Project for Pride in Living, the process was overseen by the board's planning and development committee. The oversight committee is often the body with whom the initial agreement is formulated, although it may be necessary to work out agreements first with various groups and factions who then send representatives to sit on the oversight body.

Second, a team to carry out the staff work is usually set up. This team should include planners and change advocates and also helpful critics, to make sure that any difficulties arising over the course of the process are recognized and constructively addressed (Janis, 1989). For example, the School District's team at first was made up of the superintendent, assistant superintendent, and the two consultants, and the consultants also served as constructive critics. Later, specific tasks were assigned to the board and the superintendent, to individuals supervised by the superintendent, and to task forces cochaired by cabinet members and community leaders.

Finally, the necessary resources to begin the endeavor must be committed. Obtaining needed financial resources may not be difficult because these amounts will be relatively minor in comparison with an organization's overall budget. The more important—and typically scarce—resources needed for a successful effort are the attention and the involvement of key decision makers (Light, 1998; Van de Ven, Polley, Garud, and Venkataraman, 1999). Depending on the scale of the effort, strategic planning may demand from five to twenty-five days of attention from an organization's key decision makers over the course of a year—in other words, up to 10 percent of ordinary work time. Is this too much? Not for what is truly important for the organization. If there is not enough time for everything, then something else—not strategic planning—should go. Recall the great German philosopher Goethe's admonition: "Things which matter most must never be at the mercy of things which matter least."

The end of this first step in the Strategy Change Cycle is typically the first major decision point in the process when the organization (or community) is large, when the situation is complex, or when many people need to be involved. (When the organization is small, few people are involved, or the situation is simple, the first major decision point will come later, although precisely when will depend on the situation.) If agreement has been reached on the various content items, then it makes sense to go ahead with the process.

If agreement has not been reached, then either the effort can go on anyway—with little likelihood of success—or step 1 can be repeated until an effective agreement is worked out. It usually makes sense either to repeat the step or to scale the effort down to focus on a smaller area where agreement is possible. Part of the scaled-down effort might be to develop effective strategies to involve the other areas later. This was the strategy of the initial strategic planning team in the Naval

Security Group case. At first the initial agreement involved only the major functional department heads and not the key decision makers or major external stakeholders. However, this early effort successfully identified key strategic issues facing the organization and taught the department heads the power of the process and how to think strategically. Eventually, the key decision makers were impressed by the results of these early efforts and officially sponsored and became involved in the process and, in so doing, sanctioned the creation of the Department of Strategic Planning, Policy, and Readiness to oversee the process. Successive iterations of strategic planning gradually widened the initial agreement to include the most important external stakeholders as well as other key elements of the NSG organization.

Process Guidelines

The following process guidelines, summarizing the procedures discussed in this chapter, may be helpful in developing an initial agreement:

1. *Some person or group must initiate and champion the process.* Strategic planning does not just happen—involved, courageous, and committed people make it happen. In each of the three cases examined in this book the process worked in large part because there were people involved—usually key decision makers and leaders— who acted as process champions (Kanter, 1983, p. 296; Bryson and Roering, 1988, 1989). These people believed in the process and were committed to it (not to any preconceived solutions). They may have had good hunches about what might emerge, but their main belief was that following the process would produce good answers. Indeed, these champions were willing to be surprised by the answers that emerged. Process champions may or may not be process initiators as well. For example, one of the main champions of the School District's process was the assistant superintendent, but she was not the initiator. The superintendent was the initiator, as well as a champion of the process. Similarly, the president of Project for Pride in Living was the formal initiator of the process as well as a champion, but key champions also included a senior project manager, the chair of the board's planning and development committee, and a consultant hired to work on the process.

2. *It may be desirable for the initiators to do a quick assessment of the organization's readiness to engage in strategic planning.* This assessment should cover the organization's current mission; its budget, financial management, human resource, information technology, and communications systems; its leadership and management capabilities; the expected costs and benefits of a strategic planning process; and ways of overcoming any expected barriers. Depending on the results of this assessment,

the initiators may decide to push ahead, focus on improving the organization's readiness, or drop the effort. (Readiness assessment worksheets can be found in this book's companion workbook [Bryson and Alston, 2004].)

3. *Some person or group must sponsor the process to give it legitimacy.* Sponsoring a strategic planning process is different from championing it, even though sponsors and champions may be the same people. Sponsorship is necessary to provide legitimacy to the process, whereas championing the process provides the energy and commitment to follow through. In the case of the School District, for example, the superintendent was the initial sponsor, but the board soon became a sponsor as well. The strategic planning coordinating committee or task force, discussed later in this chapter, often serves as this legitimizing body.

4. *Some initial stakeholder analysis work is likely to be needed before the right group of people can be found to forge an effective initial agreement.* The purpose of a stakeholder analysis at this point is to help process sponsors decide who should be involved in negotiating an initial agreement either because they have information that cannot be gained otherwise or because their support is necessary to ensure successful implementation of initiatives built on the analyses. The five-step process outlined earlier is a good way to figure out who should be involved.

5. *Decide whether or not a detailed, jointly negotiated initial agreement is needed.* An informal understanding may suffice when the organization is small, few people need to be involved in the process, and the situation faced is relatively straightforward. Conversely, a detailed, jointly negotiated initial agreement is likely to be needed when the organization is large, many people need to be involved, and the situation is complex or when a strategic plan for a network or community is to be developed. A formal contract is probably unnecessary (except, of course, for contracts with outside consultants), but someone should prepare a written memorandum that outlines the content of the agreement, including statements on the following items: the purpose and worth of the effort; the organizations, units, groups, or persons who should be involved; the steps to be followed; the form and timing of reports; the role, functions, and membership of the strategic planning coordinating committee; the role, functions, and membership of the strategic planning team; and the commitment of necessary resources to begin the effort. The agreement might be summarized in chart form and distributed to all planning team members, as illustrated in Exhibits 3.1 and 3.2. Exhibit 3.1 outlines the planning process followed by North End Area Revitalization (N.E.A.R.), a small, community-based development organization in St. Paul. Exhibit 3.2 displays the elements of the initial agreement used to organize the strategic planning effort of a large human service organization. This organization's process is considerably lengthier and more complex than N.E.A.R.'s process because many more people needed to be involved in various ways.

EXHIBIT 3.1. OUTLINE OF STRATEGIC PLANNING PROCESS DEVELOPED BY N.E.A.R.

Steps	Responsible Person or Group	By When
1. Select a steering group. (The board's executive committee and executive director will serve in this role.)	Board chair and executive director	Feb. 1
2. Select a consultant to assist in design and facilitation of the process.	Steering group	Feb. 15
3. Get agreement on the planning steps, responsibilities, and resources required.	Steering group, consultant	Feb. 25
4. Gather information via a questionnaire—from board members, staff, other neighborhood representatives, and others familiar with N.E.A.R.—regarding our image, strengths, weaknesses, opportunities, and critical issues or choices. Also conduct focus group discussions with staff, the Neighborhood Housing Agenda Committee, and Community Building Initiative Committee about their hopes for the future and issues that need attention in the planning. Summarize this information.	Consultant, staff, steering group	Mar. 20
5. At a six-hour planning retreat with board and staff: • Review N.E.A.R.'s history and accomplishments since inception; note when participants got involved and what lessons they've learned. Use timeline. • Review progress toward our mission and goals over the past year. • Review summary of questionnaire responses and information on neighborhood changes. In small groups, identify key issues or choices for N.E.A.R. • Determine N.E.A.R.'s future direction. • Review steps to complete the strategic plan.	Participants, consultant	Apr. 1

EXHIBIT 3.1. OUTLINE OF STRATEGIC PLANNING
PROCESS DEVELOPED BY N.E.A.R., CONT'D.

Steps	Responsible Person or Group	By When
6. Summarize the retreat.	Consultant, executive director	Apr. 12
7. At two follow-up meetings (approximately two hours each), develop a draft of the strategic plan. The executive director will develop the initial draft for discussion and refinement with the steering group.	Steering group, consultant as needed	May 15
8. Review the draft with staff, board, other community representatives, and a key funder. Make needed revisions based on these reviews.	Steering group, consultant as needed	June 10
9. Approve the plan.	Board	June 25
10. Implement the plan.	Those indicated	July 1
11. Monitor progress at six months, and update the plan yearly.	Steering group	Feb. 1

Meeting time required:

Approximately eighteen to twenty hours for steps 1 through 8, plus staff work to prepare for the retreat and draft the plan.

Source: Adapted from Barry, 1997, p. 30. Copyright 1997 Amherst H. Wilder Foundation. Used with permission.

6. *Form a strategic planning coordinating committee or task force, if one is needed.* Again, if the organization is small, few people need to be involved, and the situation is easy to comprehend, then a coordinating task force or committee probably will not be needed. But if the organization is large, many people need to be involved, and the situation is complex, then this task force or committee should probably be appointed. Such a group should not be formed too early, however. It is easier to add a needed person after the committee is formed than it is to drop a troublesome person who is already a member. Consult with trusted advisers before inviting people to participate. Also keep in mind that there is a big difference between giving people a seat on a committee and consulting with them as part of the process. People can supply a great deal of information and advice—and legitimacy for the process—

EXHIBIT 3.2. OUTLINE OF STRATEGIC PLANNING PROCESS DEVELOPED BY A LARGE HUMAN SERVICE ORGANIZATION.

Steps	Responsible Person or Group	By When
1. Get agreement on planning steps, responsibilities, and timelines. Review the planning process with the board and staff.	Executive director and board chair	Feb. 1
2. Meet informally with neighborhood groups, user groups, other nonprofits, public officials, funders, and others to solicit ideas on how our organization might better serve this community. Summarize this information.	Executive director and designated staff	May 1
3. In preparation for the board and management planning retreat, summarize information on (1) the organization's mission, success, and limitations over the past twenty years; (2) human service and community trends; and (3) several options and scenarios for how the organization might have the greatest impact in coming years.	Executive director with staff support	July 1
4. At a two-day board and management retreat, review and discuss the information above and determine the organization's future focus and emphasis. Use scenario approach. Invite two resource people with knowledge of these issues to participate in the retreat. (See workbook for a description of the scenario approach.)	Participants, guests, facilitator	Aug. 1
5. Summarize the retreat, develop a proposed focus statement for the organization, and discuss implications with staff.	Executive director, management staff	Sept. 15
6. Review implications and approve the focus statement.	Board	Oct. 15
7. Draft strategic plans for each of the organization's three divisions describing how they will implement the new focus over the next five years. Involve potential partner groups in developing these plans.	Executive director, management staff	Jan. 1

EXHIBIT 3.2. OUTLINE OF STRATEGIC PLANNING PROCESS DEVELOPED BY A LARGE HUMAN SERVICE ORGANIZATION, CONT'D.

Steps	Responsible Person or Group	By When
8. Review division plans. Note any recommended change areas that require coordination across the organization, and implications for administrative support services.	Executive director, management staff	Jan. 15
9. Draft overall strategic plan for the organization.	Executive director	Mar. 1
10. Review draft plan with staff, the board, and six to eight community representatives. Make revisions based on these reviews.	Executive director	Apr. 1
11. Approve strategic plan.	Board	May 1
12. Implement the plan. Review progress and update the plan yearly.	Executive director and those indicated	

Meeting time required:

Sixty to sixty-five hours for steps 1 through 10 (includes strategic planning for each division), plus staff time for informal meetings with community representatives, development of background materials for the retreat, and drafting the plan.

Source: Adapted from Barry, 1997, p. 31. Copyright 1997 Amherst H. Wilder Foundation. Used with permission.

without actually having a vote on a committee. Unless membership is limited, the committee may balloon in size and become unmanageable and unproductive. If an organization is the focus of attention, the coordinating committee might include top-level decision makers, midlevel managers, technical and professional opinion leaders, persons representing outside resources, representatives of key stakeholder groups, process experts, and critics. Remember, however, that there may be a trade-off between having a broadly representative committee (which may be very large) and an effective one (which probably should number no more than nine). Two groups may ultimately be necessary: a large representative and legitimizing body and a small executive committee that engages in the most extensive discussions and makes recommendations to the larger group. For a community, a large, representative legitimizing body could coordinate the process, and smaller representative bodies could attend to specific issue areas.

7. *If a coordinating committee is formed, use it as a mechanism for consultation, negotiation, problem solving, or buffering among the organizations, units, groups, and persons involved.* This committee is likely to be the body that officially legitimizes the initial agreement and makes subsequent decisions, although it also may serve as an advisory body to official decision makers. For example, the School District's strategic planning committee acted as an advisory body to the superintendent and to the school board. The Naval Security Group's strategic planning team acted as an advisory body to the commander, deputy commander, and the key NSG officers on the fleet staffs, the area directors. Project for Pride in Living's strategic planning team advised the president and board of directors. Committee decisions should be recorded in writing and probably should be circulated to key stakeholder groups. In some situations the committee should include more than one representative from each key stakeholder group so that a clearer picture of stakeholder preferences, interests, and concerns emerges. Also, if the group is to be a standing committee that oversees annual strategic planning efforts, it is probably wise to rotate membership to keep new ideas flowing and widen involvement in the process. You will not necessarily be asking for a major commitment of time from committee members, but they should expect to spend from five to twenty-five days on strategic planning over the course of a year. And that time must be quality time, typically away from the office, and concentrated in one- to three-day blocks. The group should focus its attention on strategic concerns and refer operational matters to appropriate individuals and groups.

8. *The process is likely to flow more smoothly and effectively if the coordinating committee and any other policy board that is involved are effective policymaking bodies.* Recall that strategic planning has been defined as a disciplined effort to produce fundamental decisions and actions that shape and guide what an organization (or other entity) is, what it does, and why it does it. It is hard to produce those decisions unless the process is overseen by effective policymaking bodies. In other words the work of strategic planning forums, no matter how good, will not be worth much unless it is linked to arenas in which effective policies can be adopted and decisions made. Effective policymaking bodies

- Discipline themselves to focus most of their attention on their policymaking role.
- Have a mission statement that clearly states their purposes as policymaking bodies.
- Establish a set of policy objectives for the organization, function, or community they oversee.
- Concentrate their resources to be more effective as policymakers.
- Control managers primarily through the questions they ask. The general form

of these questions is, "How does this recommendation [a proposal, a strategy, a budget, or the like] serve our purposes, values, or policies?"

- Have staff help group members become better policymakers.
- Rely on various media (press releases, newsletters, television, Web sites, and so forth) to transmit information to key stakeholders and the general public.
- Hold periodic retreats to develop strategic plans and work programs for subsequent years.
- Monitor appropriate performance data in appropriate ways (Houle, 1989; Carver, 1997; Bryce, 2000; Robinson, 2001).

Not many public or nonprofit organizations, boundary-crossing services, collaboratives, or communities are governed by effective policymaking bodies (see, for example, Gurwitt, 2003). A strategic issue that often arises therefore is how to make the governing bodies more effective policymaking bodies. The School District's elected board, for example, wanted to be an effective policymaking body and wanted to make sure the strategic planning process would help the board in this regard before it was willing to commit to the process. The Naval Security Group's strategic planning team used the process to enhance the policymaking of the commander, deputy commander, and area directors (NSG's equivalent of a board of directors). Project for Pride in Living had a forty-six-member board of directors during its strategic planning process (the number of members was subsequently reduced to thirty-three), and so the process was intended to help the board better fulfill its policymaking duties.

9. *Form a strategic planning team if one is needed.* In theory a team is assigned the task of facilitating decision making by the strategic planning coordinating committee. The team gathers information and advice and produces recommendations for committee action. The committee legitimizes the process, provides guidance to the team, and makes decisions on team-produced recommendations. In practice, a team may or may not be formed and may or may not facilitate decision making by the coordinating committee. A team may not be needed when the organization or community is small, few people need to be involved in the effort, and the situation is relatively easy to handle. In these cases a single planner, perhaps with the assistance of an outside consultant, will probably suffice. However, when the organization is large, many people need to be involved, and the situation is complex, a team will probably be necessary. Most of the team members probably will not need to work full-time on the effort, except for brief periods. But formation of a team will allow many different skills to be brought forward at important times. The team should be headed by an organizational diplomat and should include members skilled in boundary spanning, process facilitation, technical analysis, advocacy, and self-criticism. Such a team will almost certainly be needed for a large community effort.

Whether the team does much of the strategic planning itself or facilitates strategic planning by key decision makers will depend on a number of factors. On the one hand, if team members possess most of the information needed to prepare the plan and if they hold positions of substantial power, then they may prepare the plan themselves. In this situation the planners are themselves the key decision makers. On the other hand, if there are a number of key decision makers who already possess much of the necessary information and if the planners who make up the team are not themselves powerful by virtue of their position or person, then these planners will need to serve primarily as facilitators of the process. In my experience, planners typically find that they can be of greatest service by serving as facilitators of cross-functional and cross-level planning, policymaking, and decision making by key decision makers (Bryson and Crosby, 1996). Nevertheless, planners typically must have at least some substantive knowledge of the topic areas under discussion in order to be good facilitators. Thus a blend of process skill and content knowledge is typically required of strategic planners and strategic planning teams. The specific proportions vary by situation, however.

Once it is decided that a strategic planning team is needed, the sponsors and champions can turn their attention to procedures that will make the team more effective. First, to recruit skilled, committed team members, they may need to use special personnel hiring, transfer, or compensation procedures. People must see how their careers might be helped by joining the team; otherwise they are not likely to join voluntarily. If the assignment is to be temporary, people must be assured that they can return to their old jobs—or better ones—when the effort is completed. Second, clear and positive working relationships need to be negotiated among team members and supervisors. Third, the team should meet frequently and communicate effectively to foster sharing of information and joint learning. In the case of strategic planning for a community, the team or teams may have many volunteer members. Personnel hiring, transfer, and compensation procedures may not be an issue for volunteers, but clear and positive working relationships and effective communication are likely to be very important.

10. *Key decision makers may need orientation and training about the nature, purpose, and process of strategic planning before they can negotiate an initial agreement.*

11. *A sequence of initial agreements among a successively expanding group of key decision makers may be necessary before a full-scale strategic planning effort can proceed.* In expanding the circle, sponsors, champions, planners, and facilitators need to be attentive to building trust among involved stakeholders (Huxham, 2003). They need to be aware that this is a slow process. They also need to be attentive to the range of tangible and intangible content and process outcomes that are necessary for a successful effort (see Figure 3.1). Remember that the outcomes that are not visible are considerably more important than the ones that are.

12. *Recognize that things will change over the course of the Strategy Change Cycle.* For example, in studying the strategic planning efforts of many nonprofit organizations, Berger and Vasile (2002) found that "decisions regarding plan breadth and detail, the mechanics of how it would be written, and the look of its final form were made as the process unfolded" (p. 25).

13. *Keep in mind that a good initial agreement should provide useful preparation for any major changes that may be forthcoming.* For a strategic planning process to be successful, the process itself must be thought about strategically. The initiators of the planning process should play out various scenarios about how it might unfold and then use what they have learned to shape the initial process design. (This same kind of strategic thinking about the process itself should occur throughout the process.) For example, a successful process for a major transformation of some kind is likely to be different from a successful process for a series of incremental changes (see Chapter Seven). Similarly, if major data collection and analysis efforts are likely to be needed, the groundwork should be laid in this step.

14. *In complex situations, development of an initial agreement will culminate in the first big decision point.* If an effective agreement cannot be reached among key decision makers, then the effort should not proceed. The initiators may want to try again or focus on areas in which key decision makers can reach agreement. In relatively simple situations the first major decision points are likely to be reached later in the process, although precisely when will depend on the particular situation.

Have Realistic Hopes for the Process

The initiation of strategic planning for many organizations primarily involves a series of three simple activities: (1) gathering key actors (preferably key decision makers); (2) working through a strategic thinking, acting, and learning process; and (3) getting people to do something practical about what is truly important for the organization. Although these activities may be conceptually simple, they are difficult to implement because strategic planning is a process deliberately designed to produce change.

Organizations prefer to program, routinize, and systematize as much as they can (Thompson, 1967; Bolman and Deal, 2003). Strategic planning, however, is designed to question the current routines and even the treaties that have been negotiated among stakeholders to form a coalition large enough and strong enough to govern the organization. The strategic planning process is therefore inherently prone to fail because it is deliberately disruptive. Only strong sponsors, unflagging champions, skillful planners and facilitators, a supportive coalition, and a clear view of the potential benefits can make it succeed. Even then the best efforts can still be derailed by unexpected events, changes, crises, or intractable conflicts. Initiating strategic planning can be worth the effort, but the process will not necessarily be a smooth or successful one. Potential sponsors and champions should go into it with their eyes open (Bryson and Roering, 1988, 1989; Nutt, 2001b, 2002; Huxham, 2003).

In part because of the disruption strategic planning can cause during strategy formulation (as opposed to implementation), Mintzberg argues (1994, p. 333) that the *only* role for strategic planning is strategic *programming*, by which he means the codification, articulation, and elaboration of strategies that are already in place. As he asserts, "planning works best when the broad outlines of a strategy are already in place, not when significant change is required from the process itself" (p. 176). I do not second this extreme view, although I can empathize with it. I obviously think strategic planning can play an important role in strategy formulation, but I also think no one should expect the process to succeed automatically.

One way to develop reasonable hopes for the process is to have the members of the sponsoring group and planning team explicitly discuss, together or separately, their hopes and concerns (or fears) for the process. The hopes can be a source of goals for the organization or community, or at least for the process, and the process can be designed in such a way that it deals effectively with the concerns.

Summary

The initial agreement is essentially an understanding among key internal (and at times also external) decision makers or opinion leaders concerning the overall strategic planning effort. The agreement should cover the purpose and worth of the effort; the persons, units, groups, or organizations to be involved; the steps to be followed; the form and timing of reports; the role, functions, and membership of the strategic planning coordinating committee, if such a committee is formed; the role, functions, and membership of the strategic planning team, if one is formed; and the commitment of necessary resources to begin the effort.

The importance of an initial agreement is highlighted if one thinks of each strategic planning effort as a drama in which the most important questions the organization faces are raised and resolved. For the drama to have a successful ending, the agreement needs to sketch out the setting, the themes, perhaps the plots and subplots, the actors, the scenes, the beginning, the climax, and the desired conclusion. As the tale unfolds, content and detail will be added to this sketch, along with surprise twists and turns, making it a rich, instructive, and emotional drama that is lived by the actors. In the absence of such an agreement, the story may never reach a climax or conclusion.

An effective initial agreement helps leaders, managers, and planners raise and resolve key issues. Discussion and deliberation concerning these issues helps effective political coalitions coalesce (Riker, 1986; Benveniste, 1989; Roberts, 1997). Without such an agreement, issues and answers are likely to flow randomly through the organization, disconnected from the resources and decisions necessary for effective action (Cohen, March, and Olsen, 1972; Kingdon, 1995). Organizational survival, let alone effectiveness, will itself become random, and key decision makers will have abdicated their responsibility to focus on organizational purposes and their pursuit (Selznick, 1957; Terry, 2001).

In the next chapter we will move to steps 2 and 3 in the Strategy Change Cycle: the identification of mandates and the clarification of mission and values. Together, these two steps stipulate the organizational purposes to be strategically pursued.

CHAPTER FOUR

CLARIFYING ORGANIZATIONAL MANDATES AND MISSION

Three outstanding attitudes—obliviousness to the growing disaffection of constituents, primacy of self-aggrandizement, and the illusion of invulnerable status—are persistent aspects of folly.

BARBARA TUCHMAN, THE MARCH OF FOLLY

This chapter covers steps 2 and 3 of the Strategy Change Cycle, identifying mandates and clarifying mission and values. Together, mandates, mission, and values indicate the *public value* the organization will create and provide the social justification and legitimacy on which the organization's existence depends.

Public and nonprofit organizations are *externally justified*. This means that they are chartered by the state to pursue certain public purposes (Bryce, 2000; Rainey, 2003), and their legitimacy is conferred by the broader society (Scott, 1987; Suchman, 1995; Frederickson, 1997). These organizations must find ways to show that their operations do indeed create public value, or they risk losing the social justification for their existence, legitimacy, and any tax-exempt status they have.

Democratic governments can create public value through a number of overlapping activities, some of which are more appropriate to one level or type of government than another (Moore, 1995; Weimer and Vining, 1998; Bozeman, 2002). These activities include

- Providing a constitutional framework of laws and supporting the rule of law—not least by the government itself
- Creating open, transparent government
- Fostering and relying on the democratic process, including making sure that mechanisms for articulating and aggregating values function in a democratic way

- Protecting human rights, human dignity, and the core of subsistence
- Ensuring that a long-term, holistic view is taken and that stewardship of the public interest and the common good is seen as a crucial function of government, albeit shared with other actors and usually subject to contest
- Inspiring and mobilizing the government itself and other key entities and actors to undertake individual and collective action in pursuit of the common good (Crosby and Bryson, forthcoming), which includes promoting both within-group social connections (or what Robert Putnam calls "bonding social capital") and across-group social connections (what he calls "bridging social capital") (Putnam, 2000; Nelson, Kaboolian, and Carver, 2003), and catalyzing *active* citizenship, in which diverse groups of citizens create programs, projects, products, or services of lasting public value (Boyte and Kari, 1996; Luke, 1998)
- Maintaining an economy with reasonable levels of growth, employment, unemployment, inflation, debt, savings, investment, and balance of payments figures
- Relying on markets when they can be expected to work, including correcting market imperfections and freeing, facilitating, and stimulating markets, and not relying on markets when they cannot be expected to work. Serving this purpose might include

    Providing needed public goods that private markets will not provide on their own or else will provide poorly (for example, defense, large infrastructure projects, common spaces, free parks), and ensuring that the benefits of publicly provided goods and serviced are not inappropriately captured by some subset of the population for whom they are intended (for example, unnecessarily restricting public access to public lands)

    Subsidizing activities that have positive spillover effects for the general public (for example, K–12 and higher education, basic research, certain economic development activities, block clubs)

    Taxing or regulating activities with actual or potential negative spillover effects for the general public (for example, food and drug production and distribution, building construction, automobile operation)

    Addressing problems created by asymmetries in information availability, distribution, or use (for example, licensing or certification programs, product labeling requirements)

    Addressing problems of loss and uncertainty (for example, government-organized or -subsidized insurance schemes, the national Strategic Petroleum Reserve)

    Making sure that conservation of resources (for example, oil and fossil fuels) is emphasized rather than assuming substitutable resources will be found or invented

Protecting a common heritage when it might otherwise be lost (for example, historic and architectural preservation programs, protection of areas of outstanding natural beauty, establishment of memorials to outstanding public service)

- Providing public goods and services in a cost-effective way (for example, transportation infrastructure and systems, health and social services, police and criminal justice services)
- Using information and cost-benefit and cost-effectiveness analyses that are as objective as possible to inform public decisions
- Making use of civic-minded public servants and their professional expertise (Frederickson, 1997)

Nonprofit organizations in the United States can create public value by a number of means. The array of types of nonprofit organizations and their specific purposes is extraordinary (Bryce, 2000, pp. 684–695). Section 501(c)(3) of the Internal Revenue Code identifies the most commonly seen tax-exempt organizations. They are granted tax concessions because they are presumed to create public value when they

- Express the First Amendment right of assembly
- Promote public welfare directly rather than privately, as a firm might, or promote the welfare of a definable subgroup, as an association might
- Promote public welfare in a manner that goes beyond what government does, as a religion might, or in a way that substitutes for government action, as an organization that provides housing or health care might
- Serve public purposes at a cost less than government would incur and therefore produce a savings in terms of taxes foregone
- Serve public purposes in a charitable way, so that public or community welfare rather than individual welfare is served (Bryce, 2000, pp. 32, 40)

There are three tests that an organization must pass to be granted 501(c)(3) status (Bryce, 2000, pp. 40–41, 49–50). The *organizational* test requires that the nonprofit be organized to improve public welfare, rather than to benefit individuals or owners, by pursuing one or more of eight specific purposes: the purpose of education, religion, charity, science, literary interests, testing that promotes public safety, fostering certain national or international sports competitions, or preventing cruelty to children or to animals. The *political* test requires the nonprofit organization to have a charter that forbids it from participating in any political campaign on behalf of a candidate. And the *asset* test requires that the charter must prohibit any distribution of assets or income to benefit individuals as owners or managers, except for fair compensation for services rendered, and must forbid the use of the organization for the personal benefit of founders, supporters, managers, their relatives, or associates.

Nonprofit organizations can fail in a variety of ways, so public value can also be created by working to avoid such failures. Salamon (1995) identifies four categories of voluntary failure:

- *Philanthropic insufficiency.* The sector's "inability to generate resources on a scale that is both adequate enough and reliable enough to cope with the human service problems of an advanced industrial society" (p. 45).
- *Philanthropic particularism.* "The tendency of voluntary organizations and their benefactors to focus on particular subgroups of the population. . . . As a result, serious gaps can occur in the coverage of subgroups by the existing voluntary organizations" (pp. 45–46).
- *Philanthropic paternalism.* The "nature of the sector comes to be shaped by the preferences not of the community as a whole, but of its wealthy members" (p. 47).
- *Philanthropic amateurism.* Care that requires professional training and expertise is "entrusted to well-meaning amateurs" (p. 48).

Communities can create public value by promoting a sense of individual and collective identity, belonging, recognition, and security; by providing people a place to live, work, learn, enjoy, and express themselves; by building and maintaining physical, human, intellectual, social, and cultural capital of various sorts; and by fostering a civically engaged, egalitarian, trusting, and tolerant democratic society (Boyte and Kari, 1996; Chrislip, 2002). Social capital in particular has been shown to have a broad range of positive effects on health, education, welfare, safety, and civic activism (Putnam, 2000). Communities are necessary for our existence as human beings, and serving communities provides a justification for our existence as humans (see, for example, Friedmann, 1982; Becker, 1997; Grayling, 2003).

Mandates

Although step 3, clarifying mission, is usually more time consuming than step 2, identifying organizational mandates, step 2, is no less important. Before an organization can define its mission and values, it must know exactly what it is formally and informally *required* to do (and not do) by external authorities. Formal requirements are likely to be codified in laws, regulations, ordinances, articles of incorporation, charters, and so forth, and therefore may be easier to uncover and clarify than the organization's mission. In addition, organizations typically must meet a variety of informal mandates that may be embodied in norms or in the expectations of key stakeholders, such as the electorate or duly elected representatives. These informal mandates may be no less binding than formal ones. For example, newly elected officials often talk about the "mandate" they have received from the voters—and if that mandate is widely recognized and strong, woe unto to those who ignore it. Real clarity, however, about these informal mandates may have to await a stakeholder analysis, discussed in a subsequent section.

An interesting example is provided by the British National Health Service (NHS) (Johnson and Scholes, 2002, p. 202). In the 1990s, in the United Kingdom and elsewhere, governments wanted to increase the voice of the "customer" through various means. In the UK one of these means has been the *citizen's charter*. These charters outline the rights of citizens and the standards they should expect from public services. Each public service is required (mandated) by the central government to adopt its own charter. These charters may be thought of as outlining goals for the service, but in effect they are self-imposed mandates—what the service must do. The Labor government elected in 1997 decided to revise and extend the citizen's charter idea and in 2001, after extensive consultation, *Your Guide to the NHS* (National Health Service, 2001) was published to fulfill the government mandate. The government wanted this citizen's charter to restate some values on which the NHS (founded in 1948) had been built and to emphasize the idea of partnership between the NHS and patients. According to the charter, patients are expected not only to receive rights but to accept responsibilities as well. Patients, in other words, have some mandates to meet, too.

The NHS core principles, or commitments, state that the NHS will

- Provide health care on the basis of clinical need, not the ability to pay
- Provide comprehensive services
- Shape services to fit the needs of patients, families, and carers
- Respond to different needs of different populations
- Work toward continuous improvement of quality and minimization of errors
- Value NHS staff
- Use public funds only for NHS patients
- Work with others to create seamless services
- Work to keep people healthy and reduce inequities in health
- Respect confidentiality and provide open access to information

The responsibilities of patients include the following:

- Leading a healthy lifestyle
- Caring for yourself where possible
- Giving blood and carrying a donor card
- Listening to advice on treatment
- Treating NHS staff with respect
- Keeping your appointments
- Returning equipment after use
- Paying charges promptly
- Using the *Guide* to find services

The guide also lays out national standards, including quantitative targets (such as patients' being seen at outpatient clinics within thirty minutes of their appointment time) and qualitative targets (such as standards of cleanliness). Each NHS organization is required to develop its own *patient's prospectus* that reflects local priorities and states the mandates for the organization and for its patients. The idea that patients, clients, customers, or citizens also have responsibilities is worth emphasizing in any situation, such as health care, education, or public safety, where *coproduction* is a central feature of effective service provision (Normann, 1991; Osborne and Plastrik, 1997, 2000).

Purpose and Outcomes

The purpose of step 2 is to identify and clarify the nature and meaning of the externally imposed mandates, both formal and informal, affecting the organization. Four outcomes should be sought from this step:

1. Identification of the organization's formal and informal mandates, including who is mandating what and with what force
2. Interpretation of what is required as a result of the mandates (leading perhaps to explicit goals or performance indicators)
3. Clarification of what is forbidden by the mandates (which might also lead to explicit goals or performance indicators)
4. Clarification of what is not ruled out by the mandates (that is, the rough boundaries of the unconstrained field of action)

It is very important to clarify what is explicitly required, explicitly forbidden, and not explicitly ruled out. Attending to the first two can alert organizational members to what they *must* or *must not* do. For example, research on state-imposed local government planning mandates in Florida indicates that much of the variation in local compliance is directly attributable to variation in the emphasis given to different mandates by the state Department of Community Affairs (Deyle and Smith, 1998). Clearly not all mandates are of equal interest to both the state and local governments. Whether more public value would have been created if they were is unclear. In a time of constrained resources and competing demands, choices must no doubt be made about which mandates to emphasize and which to downplay or try to change, but doing either is not without risk.

By considering what the organization *might* or *should* do, organizational members and other key stakeholders can engage in valuable discussions about which mandates are useful, which mandates may need to be changed, and what the organization's mission ought to be. Too many organizations think they are more constrained than they actually are and, indeed, make the fundamental error of assuming that their mandates and mission are the same. They may be, but leaders and planners should not start out with that assumption.

A situation involving the Minnesota Department of Transportation (MNDOT) offers an interesting example of the interplay of mandates and mission. In the late 1990s, a vocal state legislator strongly criticized the use of existing ramp meters to govern access to freeways in the Twin Cities area. Many professionals in MNDOT thought the organization's mission might be served by a study in which the existing ramp meters were turned off and the impact of that change on travel times and accidents was observed. But they did not think MNDOT *could* turn off the meters because of the state's liability laws. Victims of accidents might sue MNDOT on the supposition that turning off the meters had led to the accidents. Then a 2000 state law mandated such a study. As a result of the carefully designed study, in which ramp meters were turned off for thirty days, MNDOT was able to make several adjustments to the system (Krause and Milgrom, 2002). The change in mandates helped MNDOT better pursue its mission and create more public value.

The Naval Security Group provides another interesting example. Prior to its strategic planning efforts, NSG limited its mission to its mandate of providing cryptological personnel, products, and services for the purposes of protecting, detecting, and analyzing communications that affect U.S. security and military preparedness. At the height of the Cold War, NSG had felt little need for thinking beyond its mandates, because most of its systems, people, and training were fully and effectively directed against Cold War enemies. The group was highly successful in accomplishing its mission and enjoyed good support from its two major stakeholders, the Navy and the National Security Agency (NSA). However, in the early 1990s, NSG simultaneously faced three major forces for change: the loss of its primary Cold War enemy owing to the dissolution of the Soviet Union and a corresponding need to focus on a more global set of targets; the explosion in telecommunications capabilities, products, and services, including cheap methods of encryption; and congressional mandates for reduction in personnel through consolidation and joint actions among the various military branches of service. Thus, when the world changed around it, NSG was forced to think beyond its mandate if it expected to survive as an organization. NSG planners could see a growing emphasis on the value of information in warfare. This analysis enabled NSG to identify a new possible organizational niche: *information warfare* (IW), that is, attempting to deny critical battlefield decision information to one's enemy while simultaneously safeguarding one's own information. This work was a significant expansion from its traditional cryptological mission and former prescribed mandates. Indeed, had the NSG continued to limit its mission to meeting its mandates, it might well have *jeopardized* its ability to meet those mandates and have produced less public value.

Benefits and Guidelines

Step 2 offers two potential benefits. First, clarity about what is mandated—what must be done and not done—will increase the likelihood that mandates will actually be met and public value created (Nelson and French, 2002; Piotrowski and Rosenbloom, 2002). Research on goal setting indicates that one of the most important determinants of goal achievement is the clarity of the goals themselves. The more specific the goal, the more likely it will be achieved (Behn, 1999a; Sawhill and Williamson, 2001; Nutt, 2002). Second, the possibility of developing a mission that is not limited to mandates is enhanced. Once people know what is not explicitly forbidden, they can more readily examine *potential* purposes of organizational action for creating public value.

The process guidelines for step 2 are straightforward:

1. *Have someone compile a complete list of the formal and informal mandates that apply to the organization.* A straightforward summary in plain English should be produced. In a governmental organization it is important to include the democratic and constitutional values that legislatures and the courts have been trying to enforce for decades, such as representation, participation, transparency, and individual rights (Piotrowski and Rosenbloom, 2002).

2. *Review the mandates in order to clarify what is required, what is forbidden, and what is allowed.* Part of this exercise may include gaining clarity about who is mandating what and with what force. This activity can provide a major clarification of organizational goals and performance indicators. These goals can then be used, along with goals from stakeholder analyses and the mission statement, to identify issues.

3. *Regularly remind organizational members of what the organization is required to do and forbidden to do, as a way of ensuring conformity with the mandates.* In other words, institutionalize attention to the mandates. Certainly, strategic plans, annual reports, staff retreats, and orientation sessions for new employees should include a section (perhaps a brief one) on mandates. Other methods of focusing people on mandates might prove useful as well. Failure to do so can diminish public value and undermine legitimacy. For example, recent research on federal annual performance plans required by the Government Performance and Results Act has revealed disturbing failures of those plans to attend to some important mandates, specifically requirements under the Freedom of Information Act. This leads one to wonder if an important mandated element of creating public value is being ignored (Piotrowski and Rosenbloom, 2002).

4. *Undertake a regular review of the mandates and discuss which seem to be current, which may need to be revised, and which should be dropped.* NSG, for example, concluded that aspects of its mandate should be changed and then built the case for doing so with its superiors. In a review of state-imposed mandates in Minnesota, local government respondents saw a need for dialogue with the state to ensure mandates are reasonable, flexible, adequately funded, and less burdensome in terms of their cumulative impact (Grossback, 2002).

Mission

Yogi Berra, the famous New York Yankees baseball player and manager, once said, "You've got to be very careful if you don't know where you're going, because you might not get there." His maxim emphasizes that without a sense of purpose we are literally lost. Mission provides that sense of purpose. In addition, an organization may, if it wishes, be able to expand its mission into an early vision of success, which may then guide subsequent efforts at issue identification and strategy development (see Figure 2.1). Without a vision of success, organizational members may not know enough to fulfill the mission. Communities, in particular, may find it useful to develop a guiding vision that embodies important purposes and values. They are unlikely to have a mission statement as such, but a guiding vision can provide the sense of purpose, values, and common ground that enables disparate and essentially independent groups and organizations to strive together for the common good (Wheeland, 2003).

Mission, in other words, clarifies an organization's purpose, or *why* it should be doing what it does; vision clarifies *what* it should look like and *how* it should behave as it fulfills its mission. Chapter Eight discusses constructing a vision of success; for now it is enough to note that the foundation of any good vision of success is an organization's mission statement or a community's statement of purpose and values.

Consider the distinction between Yogi Berra's maxim and J.R.R. Tolkien's observation in *The Fellowship of the Ring* that "All who wander are not lost" (1965). Tolkien was referring to the need to confront evil wherever it showed up—and of the challenge of doing so when it was not clear where or when evil would show up. In this situation, wandering with a sense of purpose was a rational strategy. Purposeful wandering is quite different from the mindless wandering to which Yogi Berra alludes. Purposeful wandering is also what Daniel Boone is alluding to in the statement that appears as an epigraph to Chapter Two.

In the statement quoted at the head of this chapter, Barbara Tuchman (1984) makes a point about the corruption of mission: any organization that becomes an end in itself is doomed—eventually, if not immediately—to failure. The collapse of the former Eastern Bloc nations and the Soviet Union illustrates how self-aggrandizement, illusions of invulnerability, and disregard for constituents' desires can lead to disaster. Indeed, most planning disasters probably meet Tuchman's criteria for folly (Hall, 1980; Bryson, Bromiley, and Jung, 1990; Bryson and Bromiley, 1993; Nutt, 2002).

Purpose and Outcomes

Ultimately, strategic planning is about purpose, meaning, values, and virtue. Nowhere is this more apparent than in the clarification of mission and the subsequent development of a vision of success. The aim of mission clarification is to specify the purposes of the organization and the philosophy and values that guide it. Unless the purposes focus on socially useful and justifiable ends and unless the philosophy and values are themselves virtuous, the organization cannot hope to command indefinitely the resources needed to survive, including high-quality, loyal, committed employees (Selznick, 1957; Burns, 1978; Terry, 1993, 2001; Collins and Porras, 1997). Unfortunately, as Paul Light (1998) points out, some organizations can plod along in ignorance and inertia for some time: "One of the great mysteries of organizational life is how agencies survive year after year without a clue as to their mission" (p. 187).

Step 3 has two main desired outcomes: a stakeholder analysis (if one has not been completed already) and a mission statement. A stakeholder analysis provides useful information and valuable preparation for a mission statement. Agreement on the stakeholder analysis and mission statement by key decision makers should clarify the organization's arenas of action, many of the basic rules of the game within these arenas, the implicit if not explicit goals of the organization, and possible performance indicators. In addition, the agreement on mission—particularly if it is consensual—will itself be a source of power for the organization that can have positive effects on performance (Pfeffer, 1992). Much of this power comes from framing and communicating the mission (including measurable goals) in such a way that employees and other actors can commit to and identify with the organization and its mission (Weiss and Piderit, 1999; Wright and Davis, 2003). Finally, agreement on an organizational mission that embraces socially desirable and justified purposes should produce legitimacy internally and externally for the organization (Suchman, 1995), as well as enthusiasm and even excitement among organizational members (Kouzes and Posner, 2002).

Benefits

A number of benefits flow from clarifying and agreeing on the organization's mission. Perhaps the most important benefit is simply that it fosters a habit of focusing discussion on what is truly important. Too often key decision makers in a public or nonprofit organization never come together to discuss cross-functional issues or, more important, the organization as a whole. The board of the School District particularly wanted to find time to focus on what was important for the district, and used strategic planning specifically for this purpose. The president, board, and staff of Project for Pride in Living and the middle managers of the Naval Security Group had similar concerns and saw strategic planning as a way to get key decision makers to focus on what was best for the organization as a whole.

When key decision makers do gather—for example, at a staff meeting—most of their time is often taken up with announcements or with discussion of relatively trivial matters, such as allocating parking spaces or scheduling floating holidays. Although such discussions may serve to introduce key decision makers to one another and may provide some of the social glue necessary to hold any organization together, they are relatively useless and may in fact be a colossal waste of everyone's time.

When important issues are not being addressed, it is important to know *why*. Participants may simply not know how to do so, particularly when serious conflicts might be involved, in which case targeted training might help. Or they may not be comfortable with one another—they may be unsure of one another's motives, for example—and therefore fearful of the consequences of raising difficult issues. Team building might be used to build trust and address these fears. In addition, avoiding discussion of real issues can be a way for senior decision makers to control the agenda and enhance their own power (Benveniste, 1989). In this last case, senior personnel might be persuaded of the benefits of more participatory decision making or else might somehow be persuaded to leave the organization.

The second important benefit, of course, is the clarification of organizational (or community) purpose, or the organization's *strategic intent* (Hamel and Prahalad, 1994). Depending on how this is done, the performance payoffs can be significant. For example, quantitative comparative evidence from public schools in Michigan demonstrates that the existence of a mission statement that is focused and activist and that emphasizes a commitment to measurable achievement is linked to a measurable positive effect on students' math and reading achievement (Weiss and Piderit, 1999). There is case evidence to indicate similar positive, measurable impacts of similarly well-formulated mission statements in a number of other public and nonprofit organizations (for example, Bryson, 1999; Sawhill and Williamson, 2001).

Because defining the mission may be thought of as the central function of leadership, more effective leadership is another benefit (Selznick, 1957). Clarity of organizational purpose helps leaders in other ways as well. In particular, it helps clarify the purposes of organizational structures and systems, including the resource allocation system. Agreed-upon purpose provides a kind of *premise control* (Perrow, 1986; Bryant, 2003, p. 36) or criterion against which organizational structures and systems can be judged. In addition, it may help leaders to guide internal conflict so that it furthers organizational ends. Leaders are required to guide the "play of the game" within the structure of the rules, but they also need to change the rules on occasion. Clarity of purpose establishes a valuable basis for guiding conflict productively and for understanding which rules help with that task and which need to be changed (Ury, Brett, and Goldberg, 1988; Hampden-Turner, 1990; Schein, 1997; Terry, 2001).

A key point about managing conflict is that organizational conflicts typically are about something other than what is nominally in dispute. For that reason, resolving them requires reframing them at a higher level of abstraction (Watzlawick, Weakland, and Fisch, 1974; Schön and Rein, 1994; Nadler and Hobino, 1998). Terry (1993, 2001), for example, describes a hierarchy of human action. *Fulfillment* is at the top and is the embodiment of all that is underneath. Then comes *meaning*, or why people act; then *mission*, which guides one in a meaningful direction; then *power; structures and systems; resources;* and finally the *givens* of existence. Terry argues that disputes at any level in this hierarchy are usually really about what is at the next level up. Thus power struggles in general are usually about the purposes the power is to serve. Arguments about organizational structures and systems are really about who is empowered or disempowered by different designs. Disputes over resources are typically about how the use of those resources should be regulated in structures and systems. Conflicts over givens are about what counts as a resource and what is to be discounted, de-valued, or ignored. A focus on the purpose and ultimate meaning of organizational efforts—to the extent that there is agreement on them—can therefore frame most conflicts in such a way that they facilitate the pursuit and fulfillment of organizational ends.

Agreement on purpose can also help the parties in a conflict disconnect ends from means and be clear about goals to be pursued or problems to be addressed prior to exploration of solutions. The advantage of doing so is that most conflicts are about solutions; that is, there usually is no agreement or clear understanding about what problems the solutions are to meant to solve (Nadler and Hobino, 1998; Nutt, 2002; Bryant, 2003). Further, the organization cannot really know what problems it ought to address without some sense of the purpose it serves. Once an organization understands its purpose, it can define the problems it is meant to solve and can better understand how to choose among competing solutions. David Osborne and Ted Gaebler based their best-selling book *Reinventing Government* (1992) in part on this very point: if governments stick to *steering* (purpose and problem definition), then they are less likely to be captives of any one approach to *rowing* (solutions) (see also Osborne and Plastrik, 1997, 2000; Osborne and Hutchinson, 2004).

Agreement on purpose therefore gets the organization to pursue what is often a normatively preferable sequence of conflict resolution activities: agree on purposes, identify problems or issues, and then explore and agree on solutions. The likelihood that successful solutions will be found is increased because this sequence narrows the focus to fulfillment of the mission and broadens the search for acceptable solutions to include all that would further the mission (Nadler and Hobino, 1998; Nutt, 2002).

Agreement on purpose acts as a powerful means of social control. To the extent that purposes are socially justified and virtuous, agreement about them will invest organizational discussions and actions with a moral quality that can constrain self-serving and organizationally destructive behavior on the part of organizational members. Said differently, agreement on purpose can lead to a mobilization of organizational energies based on pursuit of a morally justifiable mission beyond self-interest (Lewis, 1991; Suchman, 1995).

Another benefit of this step is the explicit attention decision makers must give to philosophy, values, and culture. Organizational members rarely discuss these matters directly. As a result they are likely to misread strengths and weaknesses and therefore to make mistakes in the internal assessment step to come. Also, when they lack an understanding of their organization's philosophy, values, and culture, decision makers and planners are likely to make serious errors in the strategy formulation step. They may choose strategies that are not consonant with organizational philosophy, values, and culture and that are therefore doomed to fail, unless a well-conceived strategy for culture change is pursued as well (Hampden-Turner, 1990; Schein, 1997; Johnson and Scholes, 2002).

Finally, as a result of answering the six questions that lead to a mission statement (presented later in this chapter), the organization will be well on its way to developing a clear vision of success. Indeed, answers to the six questions may provide organizational members with the conception that must precede any actual perceptions of success. In other words, it is conceiving and believing that make seeing possible (Weick, 1995).

Stakeholder Analysis

A stakeholder analysis is a valuable prelude to a mission statement, a SWOC analysis, and effective strategies. Indeed, I usually argue that if an organization has time to do only one thing when it comes to strategic planning, that one thing ought to be a stakeholder analysis. Stakeholder analyses are critical because the key to success in the public and nonprofit sectors—and the private sector too for that matter—is the satisfaction of key stakeholders. If an organization does not know who its stakeholders are, what criteria they use to judge the organization, and how the organization is performing against those criteria, there is little likelihood that the organization (or community) will know what it should do to satisfy those stakeholders (Boschken, 1994, 2002; Rainey and Steinbauer, 1999; Rainey, 2003).

An example may prove instructive at this point. It shows how a misreading of who one's key stakeholders are can cause serious trouble for an organization, how a better reading can improve things dramatically, and how building on a series of stakeholder analyses can lead to far greater fulfillment of one's mission. The story plays out over almost twenty years and comes from the Division of Fisheries and Wildlife of the state Department of Natural Resources in a Midwestern state. The department (as the state's agent) is one of the major landowners in the United States. It manages a vast area, including water, forest, mineral, and land resources and huge populations of fish and wildlife. The fish and wildlife resources are important to in-state and out-of-state anglers and hunters and to the large recreational and tourist industry that depends on them. Something like a quarter of the state's residents identify themselves as anglers and hunters, and an almost equal number enter the state each year to fish and hunt.

You would think that the Division of Fisheries and Wildlife would be one of the most protected and supported units of this state's government, that legions of interest groups from the National Rifle Association to resort-industry groups to recreational equipment dealer associations would be continually lobbying state legislators and the governor to maintain, if not increase, public financial support for the division. When our story begins, however, such was most emphatically not the case. The division was instead under frequent attack from some of its key stakeholders—hunters and anglers. They argued that the division saw itself primarily as a regulator of and naysayer to them. They felt it was completely uninterested in their satisfaction.

The division decided to engage in strategic planning to turn around an increasingly bad situation. One of its first steps was a stakeholder analysis. The most important piece of information to emerge from that analysis was that the professionals in the division operated under the assumption that in effect their prime stakeholders were fish and deer. They felt their job was to regulate anglers and hunters so that the state's fish and wildlife resources could be protected and managed over the long term. There would have been little problem with this view if fish and deer could vote, spend money, and pay taxes. But they cannot. But anglers, hunters, and their families can, along with the owners of resorts and sporting goods establishments. Although the division's maintenance of fish and wildlife resources was obviously one criterion anglers and hunters used to judge its performance, they had other criteria as well (such as its ability to provide enjoyable recreational opportunities), and the division was failing in many instances to perform well against these stakeholder standards. The result was hostility on the part of these stakeholders and attempts in the legislature to cut the division's budget and curtail its powers. As a result of insights gained from its stakeholder analysis, the division began pursuing several strategies to manage fish and wildlife resources effectively in the long term while also increasing the satisfaction of hunters and anglers (and not simultaneously alienating environmentalists), and it has in fact dramatically increased support from the sports groups.

But the division and its encompassing department did not stop there. The department embraced strategic planning and began to work on issues that mattered to the department's key stakeholders and developed a synthesis of divisional missions and mandates. By taking a big-picture view the department developed a new mission focused on what is now called *ecosystem-based management*, which includes working with citizens to protect and manage the state's natural resources (not just those that are state owned), to provide outdoor recreation opportunities, and to provide for commercial uses of natural resources in a way that creates a sustainable quality of life. The new mission has the support of all the major stakeholders (even though they do not all support the department on every issue) because the department took their interests into account. The mission and the strategies used to pursue it have won the department accolades nationally and internationally for innovative approaches to involving the public and to pursuing the common good. And it all began with a simple stakeholder analysis almost twenty years ago.

Resource A presents a variety of stakeholder analyses. In general the three analyses that are most useful for developing a mission statement are the basic analysis technique, power versus interest grid, and stakeholder influence diagram. Organizations may have produced these analyses already as part of developing an initial agreement (step 1), in which case they should be revisited in this step. If these analyses have not been conducted, then now is the time. Here I present the basic analysis technique in detail and the power versus interest grid and stakeholder influence diagram (which are discussed in Resource A) in brief.

The basic analysis technique consists of a minimum of three steps. The first step is to identify exactly who the organization's stakeholders are. Figure 4.1 presents a typical stakeholder map for a government. The stakeholders are numerous (although many organizations have even more). Five additional points are suggested by this figure. First, the diagram makes clear that any organization (and especially a government) or network is an arena in which individuals and groups contest for control of its attention, resources, and output (Bryant, 2003; Huxham, 2003; Crosby and Bryson, forthcoming). A major purpose of a stakeholder analysis is to get a more precise picture of the players in the arena. Second, it is important to

FIGURE 4.1. STAKEHOLDER MAP FOR A GOVERNMENT.

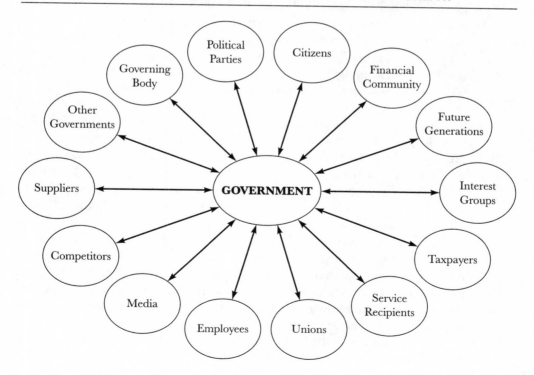

identify stakeholders at the right level of aggregation. For example, in the NSG case it is certainly true that the Navy is a key stakeholder, but saying so does not help much because, looked at more closely, the Navy encompasses a host of stakeholders with different stakes or interests in NSG, such as the Chief of Naval Operations, individual departments and directorates, particular admirals, fleet staffs, and so on. There is an art to knowing what level of aggregation to pick, and the choice can influence the results of subsequent analyses of how well the organization is doing in meeting stakeholders' expectations and obtaining what it needs from specific stakeholders. In general, stakeholders should be differentiated if doing so would make a difference in the expectations placed on the organization and the responses it might make (Eden and Ackermann, 1998). Third, special note should be made of future generations. I believe strongly that organizations (and especially governments) have an obligation to leave the world in as good a shape as they found it, if not better. It is important in this era of special interest groups and a strong lurch to the political right to keep this public trust in mind. As proverbial wisdom puts it, "We do not inherit the earth from our ancestors, we borrow it from our children." Fourth, it is very important for key employee groups to be explicitly identified. Not all employees are the same. There are different groups with different roles to play, and they will use different criteria to judge organizational performance. Clarity about these groups is necessary to ensure organizational responses sufficiently differentiated to satisfy each group. I worked with a public library that presents an interesting example in this regard. It took considerable encouragement on my part to get the librarians to identify themselves as key stakeholders. Their self-effacing and altruistic view of themselves as public servants was admirable but misplaced. By definition they were key stakeholders of the organization, and their own satisfaction was important to the success of their services. Indeed, one of the issues driving the strategic planning process for the library was that the librarians were experiencing increased stress and even burnout as a result of heightened demands on their services. Something had to be done to alleviate the stress. Furthermore, several of the key criteria they used to judge organizational performance related to professional standards (such as guaranteeing First Amendment protections). In other words, it was usually the professional librarians themselves, not other stakeholders, who held the library to exacting professional standards of service. Fifth, some key stakeholders for many organizations and communities are likely to be geographically distant yet nonetheless must be considered carefully. For example, federal and state governments and distant corporate headquarters of local establishments typically have a significant impact on local communities.

The second step in the basic analysis is to specify the criteria the stakeholders use to assess the organization's performance. There are two approaches to this task. One is to guess what the criteria are; the other is to ask the stakeholders themselves. The strategic planning team should always make its own guesses, but at some point it may prove instructive and politically useful to ask stakeholders (through such means as surveys, interviews, or group discussions) what their professed criteria are. The compatibility of strategic planning with many newer governance and management approaches is directly related to this emphasis on addressing the needs of key stakeholders, particularly those who might be called customers. For example, one hallmark of reinvention (Osborne and Gaebler, 1992; Osborne and Plastrik, 1997, 2000), reengineering, and continuous quality improvement (Cohen and Eimicke, 1998) is an emphasis on meeting customer expectations. And nonprofit organizations are exhorted by the Drucker Foundation (Stern, 1998) to clearly identify their *primary* and *supporting* customer needs as part of their organizational assessment efforts.

Why should the team always make its own guesses? First, it is faster. Second, the stakeholders may not be completely honest. In the case of city council members, for example, city employees will usually say that a key criterion for this important stakeholder group is whether the performance of city departments enhances their reelection prospects. Council members are unlikely to declare this criterion in public, even though it is important to them. Nonetheless, asking stakeholders what their criteria are can be instructive because the team's own guesses may be incomplete or wrong (Normann, 1991; Nadler and Hobino, 1998).

The third step in the basic analysis technique is to judge how well the organization performs against the stakeholders' criteria. These judgments need not be sophisticated. Simply noting whether or not the organization does poorly, OK, or very well is enough to prompt a useful discussion. Topics of discussion should include areas of organizational strength and weakness; overlaps, gaps, conflicts, and contradictions among the criteria; and opportunities and challenges posed by the organization's current performance.

These three steps should help set the stage for a discussion of the organization's mission (or a community's purposes and values). In particular, a stakeholder analysis forces strategic planning team members to place themselves in the shoes of others—especially outsiders—and make a dispassionate assessment of the organization's performance from the outsiders' points of view. This activity is one of the best possible ways to avoid the attributes of folly that Tuchman describes. It is also likely to be a necessary precursor of ethical action (Lewis, 1991). In addition, the stakeholder analysis provides a valuable prelude to the SWOC analysis (step 4 of the Strategy Change Cycle), strategic issue identification (step 5), and strategy development (step 6).

If time permits or circumstances demand it, completing three additional steps in the basic analysis technique may be advisable. First, the strategic planning team may wish to discuss exactly how the various stakeholders influence the organization (Eden and Ackermann, 1998). Many members of the team may not know precisely how the organization is influenced, and this discussion may also highlight the really important stakeholders. Use of the power versus interest grid and stakeholder influence diagram can move this discussion forward. Second, the strategic planning team may wish to discuss what the organization needs from each stakeholder group. I have emphasized the need for the organization to satisfy key stakeholder groups, and the usual assumption is that if the organization does this, it can survive and prosper. But that may not be the case, especially when there is a difference between funders and service recipients (as is often the case for public and nonprofit organizations). So it may be important for the organization to focus directly on what it needs to survive and prosper. This focus may reveal an important strategic issue for the organization to address: how can the organization secure the resources necessary to continue pursuit of its mission when it does not already receive all of the resources it needs from its key stakeholders? Finally, the team may wish to establish a rough order among the stakeholders according to their importance to the organization. The order, of course, might vary with different issues, but this rough ordering will give the team an idea of which stakeholders demand the most attention.

A power versus interest grid arrays stakeholders according to their power to place a claim on the organization's attention, resources, or output and according to their interest in the organization's attention, resources, or output. Four categories of stakeholders result. Those with high power and high interest are called *players*. Those with high power and low interest are called *context setters*, because their power helps set the context but they are not interested enough to be players. Those with high interest and low power are called *subjects*, because they are subject to the power of others. And those with low interest and low power form the *crowd* (Eden and Ackermann, 1998). The mission certainly must take the players and context setters into account in some way, even if the organization's ultimate purpose is to serve the subjects or crowd (Bryson, Cunningham, and Lokkesmoe, 2002).

A stakeholder influence diagram begins with the use of a power versus interest grid. Once stakeholders are located on the grid, arrows are drawn to show which stakeholders influence other stakeholders. (A power versus interest grid and stakeholder influence diagram can be used in tandem to facilitate and formalize completion of the three final steps in the basic analysis technique.)

The strategic planning team will have to decide whether or not to circulate the stakeholder analysis (or analyses) outside the team. The analysis is primarily an input to other steps in the process (mission statement, SWOC analysis, strategic issue identification, strategy development, implementation), so there may be no good reason for more public discussion of it (especially if a major purpose of the strategic planning effort is to change the power, interest, influence, or other aspects of the organization's current stakeholders).

The Mission Statement

A mission statement is a declaration of organizational purpose. Mission statements vary in length based on their purpose, but they are typically short—no more than a page, and often not more than a punchy slogan. They should also be targeted, activist in tone, and inspiring. And they should lead to measures that will indicate whether or not the mission is being achieved.

A mission statement should grow out of discussions aimed at answering the six questions that follow. (Answering questions is often highly instructive for those supplying the answers, as the late movie mogul Sam Goldwyn clearly realized when he said, "For your information, let me ask a few questions.") The mission statement should at least touch on most answers to these questions, even though for some purposes it may be distilled into a slogan. Answers to the six questions will also provide the basis for developing a vision of success later in the process.

Developing answers to the questions is a valuable but very demanding process. Several hours (and in some cases days) of discussion by the members of the strategic planning team may be required to reach consensus on the answers, and additional time for reflection may be necessary. In the case of the Naval Security Group, new driving forces in the environment required NSG to revise its mission statement over several strategic planning cycles. A certain amount of time was required for NSG planners to fully understand the ramifications of these forces, to determine the direction in which the organization should proceed, and then to build political support for a changed mission, both inside and outside the organization. The School District and Project for Pride in Living also changed their missions, though not as much, as a result of changes in their environments and corresponding changes in the thinking of key decision makers about what these organizations' purposes ought to be.

At times the discussions may seem too philosophical or academic to be of much use. When discussions seem bogged down in grand abstractions or minutiae, by all means move ahead. Assign someone the task of writing up what has been discussed so far, including points of agreement and disagreement, and come back for further discussions when the time seems right or when decisions must be reached. Strategic planning should not be allowed to get in the way of useful action. However, it is also important to remember that strategic planning *is* ultimately about purpose, meaning, value, and virtue, and therefore it is philosophical at its base. To paraphrase management guru Peter Drucker, strategic planning involves responding to a series of Socratic questions. The six questions that follow structure one of the most important parts of that Socratic dialogue.

1. *Who are we?* If your organization were walking down the street and someone asked it who it was, what would the answer be? The question is one of *identity*, defined as what organizational members believe is distinct, central, and enduring about their organization (Dutton and Dukerich, 1991; Ackerman, 2000). Clarity about identity is crucial because often the most effective way to influence people is not to tell them what they *do* but to communicate who they *are*. So too with organizations. To say that we are the Internal Revenue Service or the U.S. Marine Corps or the School District or the Naval Security Group or Project for Pride in Living carries a great deal of meaning and implies a great deal about what the organization can and ultimately will do, at least to the members of these organizations (Ashforth and Mael, 1989; Alvesson and Wilmott, 2002). It is important to ask about identity in order to help the organization draw a distinction between what it is and what it does. Too many organizations make a fundamental mistake when they assume they are what they do (Osborne and Plastrik, 1997). It is true that it can be hard to know what something is without seeing what it does, but it is still important not to assume that something is only what it appears to do. When that mistake is made, important avenues of strategic response to environmental conditions can be unwittingly sealed off. At best the organization may fail to create as much public value as it can; at worst it becomes irrelevant. Collins and Porras (1997), in their influential work on companies "built to last" (such as 3M, Johnson and Johnson, and Sony), argue that "the only truly reliable source of stability is a strong inner core and the willingness to change and adapt everything but that core" (p. xx). They define *inner core* as the organization's guiding purpose and fundamental values combined. And one of the important values has to be to appreciate and embrace change in pursuit of the purpose (Brown and Starkey, 2000). Paul Light (1998) found much the same thing in his research on public and nonprofit organizations. The organizations in his sample—including Project for Pride in Living—that have been able to sustain innovation over long periods of time have held fast to their missions (although they may have tinkered with them around the edges) but have been willing to change many other things. Finally, if collaboration is important to the organization, it is also important to be aware that the organization's identity may well change at least some as collaborative relationships develop and the identity of the collaboration itself evolves. This is to be expected and should be acknowledged as part of the process of collaborating (Stone, 2000; Fiol, 2001; Beech and Huxham, 2003). The fact that cycles of identity change typically occur in collaborative relationships underscores

the need for the partners to value change in the pursuit of their missions (Brown and Starkey, 2000). It also emphasizes the need to honor the previous identity while partially estranging people from it (Bryson, Ackermann, Eden, and Finn, 1996), in keeping with the idea that if you want change you should emphasize stability (Collins and Porras, 1997; Johnson 1996).

2. *What are the basic social and political needs we exist to meet, or what are the basic social or political problems we exist to address?* The answer to this question, along with the organization's mandates, describes the basic social justification for the organization's existence and much of the source of its legitimacy. The purpose of the organization is to meet the needs or address the problems. The organizations can then be seen as a means to an end and not as an end in itself, and that end is to create public value in areas that need it. This question may need to be asked stakeholder by stakeholder.

3. *In general, what do we do to recognize, anticipate, and respond to these needs or problems?* This question prompts the organization to stay actively in touch with the needs it is supposed to fill or problems it is supposed to address, typically through continuing informal and formal research. Left to their own devices organizations will generally talk primarily to themselves, not to those outside (March and Olsen, 1989; Wilson, 1989). When we see individuals talking mainly to themselves, we often suspect mental illness. When we see organizations talking primarily to themselves, we should suspect some sort of pathology as well. In order to remain healthy, organizations must be encouraged to stay in touch with the outside world that justifies their existence and provides the resources to sustain it. Furthermore, constant attention to external needs or problems is likely to prompt any adjustments to the organization's mission (though these would probably be rare), mandates, product or service level and mix, costs, financing, management, structure or processes needed for it to remain effective. Successful innovations typically are a response to real needs or problems; mere technological feasibility is not enough (Van de Ven, Polley, Garud, and Venkataraman, 1999). Furthermore, most of the information critical to the creation of innovations usually comes from outside the organization. The more people in the organization as a whole attend to external needs and problems, the more likely it is that a climate conducive to innovation and effectiveness will prevail and the easier it will be to justify desirable innovations to internal audiences (Light, 1998; Osborne and Plastrik, 1997; Rainey and Steinbauer, 1999). Finally, people often need to be reassured that they will not be punished for returning from the outside world with bad news. We have all seen messengers shot down because key decision makers didn't like their messages. An explicit endorsement of contact with the outside world is likely to make the organization safer for messengers who carry bad news that should be heard (Nutt, 2002).

4. *How should we respond to our key stakeholders?* This question asks the organization to decide what relations it wishes to establish with its key stakeholders and what values it seeks to promote through those relations. For example, it almost always pays to be open to what people have to say (King, Feltey, and Susel, 1998), to listen (Stivers, 1994), and to engage in constructive dialogue (Roberts, 1997). This question also focuses on what the stakeholders value and what the organization does, or might do, to provide stakeholders with what they value. If the key to success in the public and nonprofit sectors is the satisfaction of key stakeholders, what will the organization do to understand and satisfy those stakeholders? Obviously, a detailed discussion of what the organization might do may have to wait until step 6, but discussions of this sort can be pursued usefully throughout the strategic planning process. In this step it is particularly important to get people to talk and think in terms of creating public value.

5. *What are our philosophy, values, and culture?* The importance of reflecting upon and clarifying an organization's philosophy, core values, and culture becomes most apparent in the strategy development step. Only strategies that are consonant with the philosophy, core values, and culture are likely to succeed; strategies that are not consonant are likely to fail unless culture change is a key part of the strategy (Hampden-Turner, 1990; Schein, 1997; Johnson and Scholes, 2002). Unfortunately, because organizations rarely discuss their philosophies, values, and culture, they often adopt strategies doomed to failure. Clarity about philosophy and values in advance of strategy development is one way to avoid this error. Perhaps even more important, however, clarity about philosophy, core values, and culture will help an organization maintain its integrity. When an organization understands its philosophy and core values, it can more easily refuse any proposals or actions likely to damage its integrity and recognize and accept those that maintain or enhance its integrity. In a time when public confidence in most institutions is low, it is vital to maintain organizational integrity. Once this integrity is damaged, it is very difficult to reestablish public confidence in the organization. The difficult but successful turnarounds in the 1990s at the Federal Emergency Management Administration and the National Aeronautics and Space Administration demonstrate how hard creating or rebuilding integrity is; how important it is to be clear about philosophy, core values, and culture; and how much effort must be expended on changing them (Abramson and Lawrence, 2001; Khademian, 2002).

A caution must accompany this question, however. It might be argued that open discussion of philosophy, values, and culture might actually damage an organization's effectiveness in some cases. Because only publicly acceptable aspects of philosophies, values, and culture are generally discussed in public, an organization whose success depends in part on pursuit of publicly unacceptable values could suffer. For example, a local economic development agency might in effect further the ends of wealthy land developers as part of its strategy of encouraging private development and investment to boost the local economy. No matter how beneficial such a strategy appears to be to the community, it is probably unacceptable in most parts of the country for a governmental agency to say publicly that as a by-product of successful pursuit of its mission, it helps the rich get richer. Public discussion of this aspect of the agency's philosophy and values might require the agency to change its strategy and, as a result, perhaps become less effective. At the very least the agency might need to engage in some public education about the virtues of private markets and the fact that there is no guarantee private developers and investors will survive in those markets. Key decision makers will have to decide whether to go public with a discussion of the organization's philosophy, values, and culture. Those persons interested in "reform" are likely to favor public discussion; those against reform are not. The point to be taken to heart, of course, is that *any* discussion of philosophy, values, and culture, whether public or not, will have political consequences (Stone, 2002).

6. *What makes us distinctive or unique?* There was a time in the not too distant past when it seemed public organizations were, in Herbert Kaufman's (1976) term, *immortal*. Not any more. *Cutback management* and *downsizing* are now terms familiar to most public managers, and many public organizations or parts of public organizations have disappeared, and the number of public functions being carried out by private or nonprofit organizations has increased. Privatization is here to stay, and its domain may be expected to increase (Light, 1997; Osborne and Plastrik, 1997; Peters and Pierre, 2003). Public organizations must be quite clear about what makes them or the functions they perform distinctive or unique, or they will be likely candidates for privatization. Indeed, if there is nothing distinctive or unique about a public organization or function, then perhaps it should be privatized. Nonprofit organizations also need to be clear about what makes them distinctive or unique, or they too may find themselves at a competitive disadvantage (Light, 1998; Bryson, Gibbons, and Shaye, 2001). The world has become increasingly competitive, and those organizations that can't point to some distinct contribution they make may lose out.

Some Examples

Some examples can illustrate how these mission questions might be answered or at least touched upon in mission statements. The mission statements for the School District, the Naval Security Group, and Project for Pride in Living are presented in Exhibits 4.1, 4.2, and 4.3. Although all are relatively short, each grew out of extensive discussions, emphasizes important purposes to be served, and articulates what many employees would see as a *calling* worthy of their commitment (although NSG's statement does seem rather dry).

EXHIBIT 4.1. MISSION STATEMENT OF THE SCHOOL DISTRICT.

Educating for success in our diverse and changing world

EXHIBIT 4.2. MISSION STATEMENT OF THE NAVAL SECURITY GROUP.

[The Naval Security Group's mission is] to perform cryptologic and related functions, and to exercise command authority over, and be responsible for the primary support of the shore activities of the Naval Security Group as a naval service-wide system and such other activities and resources as may be assigned.

Source: Commander Naval Security Group (CNSG), 2004. Printed with permission.

EXHIBIT 4.3. MISSION STATEMENT OF PROJECT FOR PRIDE IN LIVING.

PPL's mission is to assist low-income people to become self-sufficient by providing housing, job training, and support services.

Source: Project for Pride in Living, 2002. Printed with permission.

Another example comes from the Amherst H. Wilder Foundation, a large, nonprofit operating foundation located in St. Paul, Minnesota. It provides a wide range of effective and often innovative social services and programs. Its mission statement, presented in Exhibit 4.4, is somewhat lengthy but also clearly authorizes and prompts the foundation to seek the biggest impact it can in its chosen domain.

A final example comes from Hennepin County, Minnesota, the county that contains Minneapolis (see Exhibit 4.5). (Hennepin County's approaches to strategy making and to strategic management systems are discussed in Chapter Seven and Chapter Ten, respectively.)

Process Guidelines

Several process guidelines should be kept in mind as the strategic planning group works to clarify mission and mandates:

EXHIBIT 4.4. MISSION STATEMENT OF THE AMHERST H. WILDER FOUNDATION.

[The Foundation's purpose is] to promote the social welfare of persons resident or located in the greater Saint Paul metropolitan area consisting of the counties of Ramsey, Washington, Dakota, and Anoka, by all appropriate means, including relief of the poor, care of the sick and aged, care and nurture of children, aid of the disadvantaged and otherwise needy, promotion of physical and mental health, support of rehabilitation and corrections, provision of needed housing and social services, operation of residences and facilities for the aged, the infirm and those requiring special care, and in general the conservation of human resources by the provision of human services responsive to the welfare needs of the community, all without regard to, or discrimination on account of, nationality, sex, color, religious scruples or prejudices.

Source: Amherst H. Wilder Foundation, Articles of Incorporation. Used with permission.

EXHIBIT 4.5. MISSION STATEMENT OF HENNEPIN COUNTY, MINNESOTA.

The mission of Hennepin County is to enhance the health, safety and quality of life of our residents and communities in a respectful, efficient and fiscally responsible way.

Source: Hennepin County, 2002c.

1. *Someone should be put in charge of compiling the organization's formal and informal mandates.* The group should then review and discuss this list and make any modifications that seem appropriate. The group should pay particular attention to what is required, what is not ruled out, and what mandates the organization should try to change.

2. *The group should complete a stakeholder analysis.* Guidance on how to conduct a basic stakeholder analysis is presented in this chapter. The worksheets in Bryson and Alston (2004) also can be used to guide a group in the use of the basic analysis technique. See Resource A for guidance on how to construct power versus interest grids and stakeholder influence diagrams.

Public and nonprofit organizations typically contain shifting coalitions involving networks of internal and external stakeholders. Organizational purpose should be crafted at least in part out of a consideration of these stakeholders' interests. Otherwise, successful agreement on organizational purposes is unlikely (Fisher and Ury, 1981; Thompson, 2001).

3. *After completing the stakeholder analysis the group should answer the six organizational questions presented earlier in this chapter.* (The same questions will be found on the mission statement worksheets in Bryson and Alston, 2004.) Group members should answer these questions as individuals first and then gather together to discuss their answers. Extra time must be reserved for a *culture audit* if it is necessary to identify organizational philosophy, values, and culture. (Guidelines for performing a culture audit can be found in Schein, 1997; Hampden-Turner, 1990, pp. 185–207; Johnson, 1998, pp. 137–151; Khademian, 2002, pp. 108–123.)

4. *After answering the questions and discussing the answers, the group should turn the task of developing a draft mission statement (and perhaps a separate values statement) over to an individual.* It is important to allow the group sufficient time to discuss and debate the draft mission statement, particularly if any changes in mission are contemplated. Quick agreement may occur but should not be expected. It is particularly important that the degree to which the mission is being fulfilled be measurable, either directly or indirectly through closely associated directly measurable goals. Otherwise the mission may well be a "mission impossible" and the satisfaction of employees and other key stakeholders may suffer (Wright and Davis, 2003; Poister, 2003). Sawhill and Williamson (2001) found that the nonprofit organizations they studied had the most success with the indirect measurement approach, although the direct approach could work as well. The best of the measurable missions or goals are as follows: "(1) set the bar high, (2) helped focus the organization on high-leverage strategies, (3) mobilized the staff and donors, and (4) served multiple purposes, such as setting the larger public agenda about a certain issue" (p. 383). Further, organizations found that it was best to keep measures simple and easy to communicate, that the measures and performance against them made the organization "marketable" to boards of directors and donors interested in effectiveness and accountability, and that the measures made management easier (pp. 384–385).

After an agreed-upon mission statement is developed, the group may also wish to brainstorm a slogan that captures the essence of the mission. Another option is to run a contest among organizational members or stakeholders for an appropriate slogan. For example, a public library with which I worked came up with the wonderful slogan "Mind of the City," which emphasizes intelligence, learning, information and information technology, community, and wholeness, rather than the older view of libraries as book warehouses.

5. *The group should avoid getting stalled in its development of a mission statement.* If the group hits a snag, record areas of agreement and disagreement, and then move on to the next steps in the strategic planning process. Return to the mission discussion later, incorporating any additional information and solutions that turn up in future steps.

6. *Strategic planning teams should expect to reexamine the draft mission statement as they move through the process, either to reaffirm the statement or to redraft it in light of additional in-*

formation or reflection. Even if the organization has a satisfactory mission statement, it still should expect to reexamine that statement periodically during the process. Steps 4 through 6 provide additional opportunities to discuss the mission. As the process proceeds, more detail may be added to the mission statement, such as specific programs, products, services, or relationships that will be offered to stakeholders, particularly those who are customers.

7. *Once the strategic planning group reaches agreement on a mission statement, that statement should be kept before the group as it moves through the planning process.* The group should refer to the mission as it seeks to formulate goals, identify strategic issues, develop effective strategies, prepare a vision of success, and in general resolve conflicts among group members. Keeping the mission in mind should help the group resolve conflicts in ways that serve organizational purposes and interests, not individuals' positions (Fisher and Ury, 1981; Thompson, 2001; Schwarz, 2002).

8. *Once the group agrees on the form of the mission, the mission statement should be highly visible to all organizational members.* The mission should be referred to in preambles to official organizational actions and posted on walls and in offices—it should become a *physical* presence in the organization. Otherwise it is likely to be forgotten at the very times it is most needed. Explicit reference to the mission should be the standard first step in resolving conflicts. The organization that forgets its mission will drift, and opportunism and loss of integrity are likely to spread and perhaps become rampant. Organizational survival itself—or at least the survival of the organization's leadership—will then be in serious question (Selznick, 1957; Terry, 2001; Kouzes and Posner, 2002).

9. *Adoption of the organization's mission should mark an important decision point.* Agreement may not occur at the end of step 3, however, as the draft mission may be revised over the course of the strategic planning process. Formal agreement on the organization's mission should definitely be reached by the end of the strategy development step.

10. *Organizations not engaged in a full-blown strategic planning process may still want to hold mission retreats periodically to reaffirm or revisit and modify their mission.* Retreats that prompt organizational members to focus on mission (and vision) may be helpful during the organization's formative period and at multiyear intervals after that (Angelica, 2001, pp. 11–12). The dialogue at such retreats may bring to light the need for some organizational tinkering that can be dealt with promptly or a strategic issue to be addressed later.

Summary

This chapter has discussed identifying the mandates an organization faces and clarifying the mission it wishes to pursue. Mandates are imposed from the outside and can be considered the *musts* that the organization is required to pursue (and of course it may desire to do them as well). Mission is developed more from the inside; it identifies the organization's purposes. Mission may be considered what the organization *wants* to do. Rarely is an organization so boxed in by mandates that its mission is limited to meeting those mandates. Mandates and mission jointly frame the domain within which the organization seeks to create public value.

CHAPTER FIVE

ASSESSING THE ENVIRONMENT TO IDENTIFY STRENGTHS AND WEAKNESSES, OPPORTUNITIES AND CHALLENGES

You wouldn't think that something as complexly busy as life would be so easy to overlook.

DIANE ACKERMAN, *A NATURAL HISTORY OF THE SENSES*

So it is said that if you know others and know yourself, you will not be imperiled in a hundred battles; if you do not know others, but do know yourself, you win one and lose one; if you do not know others and do not know yourself, you will be imperiled in every single battle.

SUN TZU, *THE ART OF WAR*

To respond effectively to changes in their environments, public and nonprofit organizations (and communities) must understand the external and internal contexts within which they find themselves so that they can develop effective strategies to link these two contexts in such a way that public value is created. The word *context* comes from the Latin for "weave together," and that is exactly what well-done external and internal environmental assessments help organizations do: weave together their understandings and actions in a sensible way so that organizational performance is enhanced. As Weick (1995) observes, "Sensemaking is about context. Wholes and cues, documents and meanings, figures and ground, periphery and center, all define one another. Sensibleness derives from relationships, not parts" (p. 104).

The sheer pace of change in the world at large heightens the need for effective assessments. There are disputes about whether or not the pace of change is accelerating (Land and Jarman, 1992; Mintzberg, 1994; Gleick, 1999; Barkema, Baum, and Mannix, 2002). Regardless of whether it is or not, there is enough change all around that wise organizational leaders feel compelled to pay attention. They do this in part because change so often occurs in the places, at the times, and in the forms least expected—which of course is exactly what you *should expect* in a complex, richly interconnected world (Senge, 1990; Kelly, 1994).

Purpose

The purpose of step 4 in the strategic planning process, therefore, is to provide information on the strengths and weaknesses of the organization in relation to the opportunities and challenges it faces. This information can be used, as Figure 2.4 indicates, to create ideas for strategic interventions that can shape and guide organizational decisions and actions designed to create public value. Strengths and weaknesses are usually internal and refer to the present capacity of the organization, whereas opportunities and challenges are typically external and refer to future potentials for good or ill. These distinctions between internal and external and between present and future are fluid, however, and people should not worry too much about whether they have made them properly.

In addition, networks and communities may wish to focus not on strengths, weaknesses, opportunities, and challenges but on people's hopes and concerns for the community. For one thing, the distinction between internal and external ceases to be very meaningful when applied to networks or communities, which typically have an extremely wide range of decision makers, stakeholders, and implementers. Beyond that, attention to hopes and fears is likely to elicit value concerns (Weick, 1995, pp. 30, 127), which can be central to network or community-oriented strategic planning (Provan and Milward, 2001; Stone, 2002). Interestingly, delineation of hopes often may lead directly to an articulation of goals (and perhaps strategic issues), and enumerating fears helps identify strategic issues that must be addressed in order to achieve the goals, allowing the network or community to avoid what might be called *negative goals*, or damaging outcomes (see Bryson, Ackermann, Eden, and Finn, 2004, pp. 161–163).

The approach to external and internal environmental assessments outlined in this chapter sets the stage for the identification of strategic issues in step 5. It also provides valuable information that can be used in step 6, strategy development. Strategic issues typically concern how the organization (what is inside) relates to the larger environment it inhabits (what is outside). Every effective strategy will take advantage of strengths and opportunities at the same time as it minimizes or overcomes weaknesses and challenges. In other words it will link inside and outside in effective ways.

Chapter One highlighted several major trends and events that are currently forcing often drastic changes on governments, public agencies, and nonprofit organizations. Unfortunately, for various reasons, public and nonprofit organizations typically are not very savvy about perceiving such changes quickly enough to respond effectively (Light, 1998, p. 66; Weick and Sutcliffe, 2001). Instead, a crisis often has to develop before organizations respond (Wilson, 1989). A crisis may open up significant *opportunity spaces,* but for the unprepared organization many useful avenues of response will usually be closed off by the time a crisis emerges (Bryson, 1981, pp. 185–189; Mitroff and Pearson, 1993; Mitroff and Anagnos, 2000). Also, in crisis situations people typically stereotype, withdraw, project, rationalize, oversimplify, and otherwise make errors likely to produce unwise decisions (Janis, 1989). The result can be colossal errors and debacles (Tuchman, 1984; Nutt, 2002). A major purpose of any strategic planning exercise therefore is to alert the organization to the various external threats and challenges that may prompt or require an organizational response in the foreseeable future. In other words a major purpose of strategic planning is to instill the kind of *mindfulness* (Weick and Sutcliffe, 2001, pp. 41–46) or "support for sensemaking" (Weick, 1995, p. 179) that prompts timely learning and action and prepares an organization to respond effectively to the outside world either before a crisis emerges or when one cannot be avoided. Even in a crisis, however, organizations can use many of the concepts, procedures, and tools of strategic planning to help them think and act strategically (Mitroff and Pearson, 1993).

However, any effective response to potential challenges or opportunities must be based on an intimate knowledge of the organization's capabilities and the strengths and weaknesses they entail. Strategic planning, in other words, is concerned with finding the best or most advantageous fit between an organization and its environment based on an intimate understanding of both.

Desired Outcomes

In step 4, the strategic planning team produces documented lists of external or future-oriented organizational opportunities and challenges and internal or present strengths and weaknesses. Ordered differently, these four lists constitute a SWOC analysis, a popular strategic planning tool. (Traditionally *challenges* have been called *threats,* but experience and research indicate that talking about threats may be too threatening to many strategic planning participants. When people see something as a threat, this perception can lead to rigidity in their thinking or, alternatively, excessively risky behavior in response to the threat; see, for example, Staw, Sandelands, and Dutton, 1981; Dutton and Jackson, 1987; Chattopadhyay, Glick, and Huber, 2001). My own experience and that of other consultants with whom I work indicates that the more neutral label *challenges* seems to do a better job of encouraging people to consider a range of possible futures and actions. (When the threat category is used, the SWOC analysis becomes a SWOT analysis, a more commonly used term; see Bryson, 2001, 2003a.)

The SWOC analysis, in conjunction with a stakeholder analysis, can help the team to identify the organization's *key success factors* or *critical success factors* (Leidecker and Bruno, 1984; Jenster, 1987; Johnson and Scholes, 2002). These are the things the organization must do, the criteria it must meet, or the performance indicators it must do well against (because they matter to key stakeholders) in order to survive and prosper. In addition, the team should be encouraged to clarify the organization's *distinctive competencies* (Selznick, 1957; Prahalad and Hamel, 1990; Stalk, Evans, and Shulman, 1992; Van der Heijden, 1996; Eden and Ackermann, 2000). Here, some definitions are helpful. A *competency* is a capability, set of actions, or strategy that helps the organization perform well on its key success factors. Alternatively, a competency may be thought of as the resources (broadly construed) on which the organization can easily draw to perform well on its key success factors. In other words, an organization may have a competency, but if it does not help the organization do well on a key success factor, it is not much of a competency—unless stakeholders can be convinced to change their key success factors. Competencies usually arise and are perfected through "learning by doing" (Joyce, 1999, p. 35). A *distinctive competency* is a competency that is very difficult for others to replicate and so is a source of enduring organizational advantage. A *core competency* is one central to the success of the organization. A *distinctive core competency* is not only central to the success of the organization but also helps the organization produce more public value than alternative providers do. Distinctive core competencies might, for example, be the means by which the organization maintains a strong reputation and an abiding trust in the organization among key stakeholders, specific tangible or intangible assets, and the uniqueness and quality of products and services. Usually, distinctive core competencies arise from the interrelationships among a group of competencies and core competencies. It is the interrelationships that are particularly hard for others to replicate. They may, for example, be based on tacit knowledge and be long term (Eden and Ackermann, 1998, pp. 102–110; Eden and Ackermann, 2000). (Guidance on identifying competencies can be found in Resource B.)

Before completing a SWOC analysis, it may be necessary to prepare various background reports on external forces and trends; key resource controllers, such as clients, customers, payers, or dues-paying members; and competitors and collaborators, with additional reports on internal resources, present strategy, and performance. It may also be necessary to prepare and then assess various *scenarios,* or stories, that capture important elements of possible futures for the organization and the organization's strengths, weaknesses, opportunities, and challenges, along with its key success factors and competencies (Schwartz, 1991, 2003; Van der Heijden, 1996; Myers and Kitsuse, 2000; Van der Heijden and others, 2002). Further, once the lists of SWOCs, key success factors, and competencies is prepared (with or without the help of scenarios), it may be necessary to commission careful analyses of some listed items in relation to the overall strategic posture of the organization.

Another important outcome of a SWOC analysis may be specific actions to deal with challenges and weaknesses, build on strengths (including distinctive core competencies), and take advantage of opportunities (including improving performance on key success factors). As soon as appropriate moves become apparent, key decision makers should consider taking action. It is not only unnecessary but probably also undesirable to draw a sharp temporal distinction between planning and implementation. As long as the contemplated actions are based on reasonable information, have adequate support, and do not foreclose important strategic options, serious consideration should be given to taking them. The feedback arrows in Figure 2.1 try to capture this continuous blending and interplay of thinking and acting, planning and implementation, and strategic and operational concerns. This kind of prompt action in response to a rich appreciation of the interconnectedness of the organization's operations and its environment is the essence of mindfulness (Weick and Sutcliffe, 2001, p. 42).

Completion of step 4 of the Strategy Change Cycle may be an impetus for establishing a formal environmental scanning operation if the organization does not have one already (Pflaum and Delmont, 1987). It will need adequate staff—typically an in-house coordinator plus volunteer in-house scanners, including, ideally, persons with major decision-making responsibility. Added staff may be needed for special studies. Scanning should result in periodic meetings to discuss what people are learning, plus a newsletter or some other form of regular report distributed widely within the organization. Special studies that produce detailed analyses may also need to be distributed widely. Environmental scanning, however, should never be allowed to become a bureaucratic, paper-pushing exercise. It should be kept simple and relatively informal; otherwise it will deaden strategic thought and action, not promote it. One important way for the scanning staff to stay on track is to always let purpose—meeting mandates, fulfilling mission, and creating public value—be their guide. Paying attention to purpose can help them engage in limited, rather than overwhelming and useless, information collection (Nadler and Hobino, 1998).

The most effective scanning operations will be conducted by people who form a network of scanners from several organizations. These organizational boundary spanners can exchange information and mutually develop scanning and boundary spanning skills and insights. If this network does not exist, it may be possible to create it through regular meetings and electronic mail communications. The point is for people to keep their eyes open and to talk about what they see—rather than overlook what might be important, which can easily happen, as Diane Ackerman points out in the quotation that begins this chapter. Paying attention also means not being blinded by existing categories or expectations, which will reveal some things and hide others. Categories are a necessary part of sensemaking; they trim the amount of information that we must absorb. But what is trimmed and then hidden may turn out to be what is most important (Mintzberg, 1994; Weick and Sutcliffe, 2001). So paying attention also means being open to surprises. As J.R.R. Tolkien says in *The Hobbit*, "You certainly find something if you look, but it is not always quite the something you were after" (1999).

Completion of step 4 should also prompt development of an effective management information system (MIS) that includes input, process, and output categories, if one does not already exist. An effective MIS is usually expensive and time consuming to develop, but without it the organization may be unable to assess, relatively objectively and unambiguously, its strengths, weaknesses, efficiency, and effectiveness. If an organization is using a balanced scorecard (discussed in Chapters Two and Seven), the MIS should support the use of the scorecard. Again, the MIS should not be allowed to become excessively bureaucratic or cumbersome. And in no circumstances should the MIS drive out attention to the kinds of qualitative information so vital to real understanding and so useful to effective managers (Mintzberg, 1973; Innes, 1998). As Mintzberg (1994) notes, "While hard data may inform the intellect, it is largely soft data that generates wisdom" (p. 266). Beyond that the MIS should be designed to serve organizational purposes, and if these purposes change, or the strategies for achieving them change, the MIS should change too.

Thoughtful discussions among key decision makers and opinion leaders concerning strengths, weaknesses, opportunities, and challenges; key success factors; and distinctive competencies are one of the most important outcomes of this step. Such discussions—particularly when they bridge functional lines in the organization—produce important quantitative and qualitative insights into the organization and its environment and also prepare the way for the identification of strategic issues in the next step. Discussions such as these are absolutely crucial in order to move from what individuals do (intuit and interpret) to what groups do (integrate information) to what organizations do (institutionalize information) (Crossan, Lane, and White, 1999). To paraphrase marketing guru Paco Underhill (1999, p. 42), such discussions provide a way to make apparent what perhaps *ought* to be obvious but is not, and then to act on it.

Benefits

An effective external and internal environmental assessment should provide several benefits to the organization. Among the most important is information vital to the organization's survival and prosperity. It is difficult to imagine that an organization can be truly effective over the long haul unless it has an intimate knowledge of its strengths and weaknesses in relation to the opportunities and challenges it faces, as Sun Tzu observed over 2,500 years ago.

Said somewhat differently, step 4 allows the strategic planning team to see the organization as a whole in relation to its environment. This is usually one of the singular accomplishments of strategic planning. An ability to see the organizational whole in relation to its environment keeps the organization from being victimized by the present. Instead, the organization has a basis for *reasoned* optimism, in that difficulties may be seen as specific rather than pervasive, temporary rather than permanent, and the result of factors other than irremediable organizational incompetence (Seligman, 1998; Kouzes and Posner, 2002). The organization thus prepares itself to follow Hubert Humphrey's advice: "Instead of worrying about the future, let us labor to create it" (Humphrey, 1959).

Step 4 clarifies for the organization the nature of the *tension fields* within which it exists. It has been argued (Wechsler and Backoff, 1987; Nutt and Backoff, 1992, 1996) that every organization must manage the tensions among its capacities and intentions in relation to the opportunities and challenges it faces. A SWOC analysis clarifies the nature of these tensions by juxtaposing two fundamental dimensions of existence—good (strengths and opportunities) and bad (weaknesses and challenges)—as well as two temporal dimensions—present (strengths and weaknesses) and future (opportunities and challenges). A SWOC analysis in conjunction with an understanding of stakeholders, key success factors, and distinctive competencies clarifies the organizational tensions that arise when trends and events juxtapose concerns for equity, productivity, preservation, and change.

External and internal assessments also develop the boundary-spanning skills of key staff, especially key decision makers and opinion leaders. Assessments draw attention to issues and information that cross internal and external organizational boundaries. In effect, key decision makers and opinion leaders are prompted to move beyond their job descriptions in their thinking and discussions, increasing their opportunities to produce creative and integrative insights and actions that bridge organizational functions and levels and link the organization to its environment (Ford and Ford, 1995).

Once reasonably routine, formal environmental scanning and MIS operations are established, along with regular dialogues on what the information obtained from them means, then the organization has routinized attention to major and minor external trends, issues, events, and stakeholders and to internal inputs, processes, and outputs (Emmert, Crow, and Shangraw, 1993). The chances of encountering major surprises are reduced and the possibilities for anticipatory actions enhanced—particularly if the systems themselves are the subject of mindful scrutiny.

But even if external scanning and MIS systems are not institutionalized, the organization will have become more externally oriented if it engages in periodic assessments, and will gain a better understanding of its internal strengths and weaknesses in relation to what is outside. In my experience, organizations tend to be insular and parochial and must be forced to face outward. Unless they face outward, they are virtually certain not to satisfy key external stakeholders and to be overwhelmed by the unexpected.

In addition, people should never assume that the existence of formalized systems of environmental assessment and management information relieves them of the need to pay constant attention to what is going on in the outside world and to talk about it. For one thing, as noted earlier, systems are designed around categories, and the categories may be outdated or simply wrong. The categories may make it hard or impossible to see important new developments that do not fit the categories (Mintzberg, 1994; Weick and Sutcliffe, 2001). So the best advice may come from Yogi Berra, who once aptly commented, "You can observe a lot by watching." Beyond that, perhaps writer Salman Rushdie (1981) is right: "Most of what matters in your life takes place in your absence" (p. 236). But that does not mean one has to be taken completely by surprise.

Another major benefit of step 4 is that the organization may take timely actions based on the analyses and conversations. As appropriate actions become apparent, at any point throughout the strategic planning process, these actions should be taken, as long they are based on reasonable information, have adequate support, and do not prematurely close off important strategic avenues. Indeed, the organization should work to make this habit of prompt, informed action a distinctive core competency (Weick and Sutcliffe, 2001). The final benefit of this step is that it prepares the organization to focus on identification of key strategic issues stemming from the convergence of an organization's mandates, mission, strengths, weaknesses, opportunities, and challenges and its key success factors and competencies.

External Environmental Assessments

The purpose of the first part of step 4 is to explore the environment outside the organization in order to identify the opportunities and challenges the organization faces (and ideally, in conjunction with stakeholder analyses, to identify key success factors). As illustrated in Figure 2.1, three major categories might be monitored in such an exploration: (1) forces and trends, (2) key resource controllers, and (3) actual or potential competitors or collaborators and important forces affecting competition and collaboration. These three categories represent the basic foci for any effective external environmental scanning system.

Forces and trends usually are broken down into political, economic, social, technological, environmental, and legal categories (Johnson and Scholes, 2002). Organizations may choose to monitor additional categories that are particularly relevant. For example, colleges and universities often add educational trends, and public health care organizations monitor health outcomes. Strategic planners must be sure they attend to both opportunities and challenges in whatever categories are used.

What are the recent issues and trends affecting public and nonprofit sector organizations? Innumerable reviews and forecasts are available, but it is hard to know what to make of them (see, for example, Emmert, Crow, and Shangraw, 1993; Huntingdon, 1998; Glassner, 1999; Schwartz, Leyden and Hyatt, 1999; Friedman, 2000; Stiglitz, 2002; Schwartz, 2003). For example, Schwartz, Leyden, and Hyatt's book *The Long Boom,* published at the height of the economic and stock market boom of the 1990s, seems decidedly optimistic as of 2004, but these authors are looking twenty-five years ahead and, who knows, they may yet be right. Schwartz (2003) certainly continues to believe they are—and I would certainly be pleased if they were! Nevertheless, as a character in Gilbert and Sullivan's *H.M.S. Pinafore* observes, "Things are seldom what they seem, / Skim milk masquerades as cream," and the trick is to figure out which is which. What follows is a quick review of much of this literature, in the form of ten interconnected categories of forces or trends of particular importance (especially in the United States) to the public and nonprofit sectors:

1. *Social and organizational complexity.* This complexity is driven by a number of forces, including technological change, the globalization of information and economies, and the consequent interconnectedness of almost everything. Meanwhile, many of our most important institutions were designed for a world that was more stable and simple. As a result serious institutional mismatches exist between the problems or issues that need to be addressed and the institutional arrangements for doing so (Schön, 1971; Friedman, 2000; Cleveland, 2002).

2. *Reform and reinvention of governments and increased interaction among public, private, and nonprofit sectors.* Citizens in developed nations around the world have been asking for smaller, cheaper, and more effective governments, which in practical terms means there will be limited public sector resources and growth. The size of government in relation to gross domestic product (GDP) is not likely to increase, although the overall cost of public problems almost certainly will. At the same time,

citizens have also asked for more programs and better services. In order to resolve the paradox these competing desires represent, governments are experimenting with numerous ideas for becoming more productive, improving performance, and reducing costs (Peters, 1996; Light, 1997; Pollitt and Bouckaert, 2000; Kettl, 2002). Ultimately, this means changing the focus on *government* as the means to resolve public problems to an emphasis on *governance* as a phenomenon in which the institutions of the public, private, and nonprofit sectors and civil society share the effort and responsibility for the common good (Kettl, 2000, 2002). Effective governance will place a premium on inclusion of multiple organizations and perspectives, systems thinking, and speed of analysis and response, three things that are hard to do simultaneously (Bryson, 2003a). As outlined by David Osborne and his associates (Osborne and Gaebler, 1992; Osborne and Plastrik, 1997, 2000; Osborne and Hutchinson, 2004), government's principal role is to steer, not row. Governments of the future—and not just in the United States—will rely far more on the nonprofit and for-profit sectors to do much of the actual rowing (Kettl, 2000). Opportunities for increased effectiveness will be opened to organizations in each sector, but numerous challenges will arise as well through heightened competitive pressures, uncertainty, and revenue instability.

3. *Continuation of technological change.* Many futurists and economists see technological innovation as one of the major forces driving change (Schwartz, Leyden, and Hyatt, 1999; Cleveland, 2002; Schwartz, 2003). Public and nonprofit organizations' personnel will need new skills to use new technologies, and the organizations will need to adapt their processes, structures, and resource allocation patterns. The nature of work itself may change, perhaps as a result of fundamental business process reengineering (Hammer and Champy, 1993). Information technologies in particular are driving major changes likely to have dramatic impacts on organizational performance, accountability, stakeholder empowerment, and issues related to data use and privacy (Abramson and Means, 2001; Fountain, 2001; Schachtel, 2001; Cleveland, 2002; Schwartz, 2003). For many organizations moving into e-commerce or e-government, making good use of information technology is of paramount importance.

4. *Diversity of workforce, clientele, and citizenry.* This diversity will take many forms—racial, ethnic, gender, cultural, and almost any other category you can imagine. The result will be a *demassified* version of the *mass society* of the 1950s and early 1960s (Toffler, 1971). In addition, as people live longer the numbers of senior citizens will increase dramatically in most advanced economies, simultaneously increasing both the need for many public services and the fraction of people who are not part of the taxpaying workforce. In the jargon of strategic planning, the number of stakeholders is increasing, each group with its own ideas, interests, and needs. This differentiation will complicate the quest for public value, gover-

nance, service design and delivery, and workforce recruitment, retention, training, and management.

5. *Individualism, personal responsibility, and civic republicanism.* Most futurists envision a move away from reliance on large institutions, particularly governmental institutions, and toward self-reliance and greater personal responsibility. U.S. welfare reform initiatives of the 1990s emphasized these values, as do reforms of the U.S. tax code to favor saving rather than spending. There are also signs that citizenship is being reinvented to emphasize active citizen involvement in public problem solving and governance—the kind of *civic republicanism* favored by Jefferson and the Anti-Federalists, Jacksonian Democrats, Populists, John Dewey, many of the Progressives, and the present-day communitarians (Dewey, 1954; Barber, 1984; Boyte and Kari, 1996). But citizen action is going against the tide at present, when social capital of many kinds has been in decline for decades (Putnam, 2000). Social capital formation is the antidote to excessive individualism.

6. *Quality of life and environmentalism.* Concern for the quality of life is likely to increase. The sources of these concerns are numerous, including the emergence of an era when time is more scarce than money for many people (Burns, 1993; Gleick, 1999). People are also searching for meaning beyond work, expressing fears about the long-term viability of the planet, and worrying about health and physical safety issues. The increased influence of women in the workplace is bringing with it demands for changes in that arena. Flexibility and workplace improvements are likely to be needed and demanded, health care reform will be necessary, crime prevention and control will be called for yet difficult to provide, and "green" policies and practices will be preferred by a majority of the population.

7. *Struggles for legitimacy and changes in the American dream.* Governments at all levels, churches of many kinds, a host of nonprofit organizations (for example, the Red Cross, the United Way), and many corporations (for example, Enron, Adelphia, and Time Warner) have seen their legitimacy undermined as a consequence of concerted ideological attack, poor performance, or scandals. There are not many icons left to topple, and legitimacy is increasingly difficult to attain, as much of what was previously taken for granted is questioned (Suchman, 1995). In the midst of all this the American dream has been changing. Historian Andrew Delbanco (1999) argues that in the colonial era, that dream involved doing or realizing God's will in the New World. From the early republic to Lyndon Johnson's Great Society, the dream was secularized as an ideal of the "sacred nation state"—smaller than God, but larger and more enduring than the individual American citizen. Abraham Lincoln's Second Inaugural Address captures perfectly this sense of transcendence through national union. Now, however, "hope has narrowed to the vanishing point of self alone" (p. 103). Delbanco goes on to argue, however, that ironically "the most striking feature of contemporary culture is the unslaked

craving for transcendence" (p. 114). This is very dangerous for the United States, for as Brandeis University social scientist Robert Reich has argued: "Unlike the citizens of most other nations, Americans have always been united less by a shared past than by the shared dreams of a better future. If we lose that common future, we lose the glue that holds the nation together" (quoted in Glassner, 1999, p. xviii). Writers as distinguished as de Tocqueville, Emerson, Melville, and William James have all shared this view (Delbanco, 1999). The big worries, at least in the foreign policy arena, are twofold. The first is that the glue that holds us together will be a legitimate fear of terrorism and an irrational xenophobia that is used by ambitious politicians and others to muster an almost religious zeal intent on imposing its will by force no matter what the precedents, costs, destruction, and other negative consequences left in its wake (Huntingdon, 1998; Sardar and Davies, 2002; Monbiot, 2003). The second is an irrational isolationism and retreat from engagement with the broader world. Democracy, human rights, sustainable development, and a stable, prosperous, just, and humane world order are all things the United States should try to foster worldwide (Friedman, 2000).

8. *Culture of fear.* It should not be surprising that we have developed what sociologist Barry Glassner (1999) calls a "culture of fear" in a very diverse culture in which so many icons have been toppled, social capital is in decline, a transcendent faith in the purpose of life has diminished, and the American dream is increasingly focused on the self. Mainly what we fear is individuals of many kinds—black males, pedophiles, single mothers, teenagers, drug dealers, and so on. We also fear plane crashes. What is so striking about all these fears—media hype notwithstanding—is how truly small the risks really are. Take plane crashes for example: even when you take terrorism into account, you are far more likely to be struck by lightning than to die in a plane crash. Or consider crime: even though press coverage of crimes went *up* in the 1990s, crime was actually going *down*. As Glassner notes, "In just about every American scare, rather than confront disturbing shortcomings in society the public discussion centers on disturbed individuals" (p. 6). As individuals we have become a market for fears, and there are plenty of media sources, pundits, and politicians to supply them. As communities and a nation we have the wherewithal to address those fears, but we have to relearn how to be the vibrant civil society and democracy we once were if we are to succeed. Meanwhile, things we really ought to fear and do something about include the ill effects of poverty, inadequate health insurance, and poor education; the 20,000 homicides and 30,000 suicides that occur each year (National Center for Vital Statistics, 2003); and the untold misery resulting from the almost unbelievable proliferation of handguns. We should also fear the serious decline in social capital, because this loss makes us more vulnerable to fearmongers and less able to respond wisely and collectively to what we genuinely should fear. Finally,

we should fear the media that sensationalize the unusual, play to our fears, seriously distort our perceptions of risk, and overemphasize personal rather than systemic causes of behavior.

9. *An emphasis on learning.* Individuals, jobs, organizations, and communities cannot stand still, given the pace of change. People, organizations, and communities must constantly be learning how to do their work better and how to make the transitions they are likely to face if they are to play constructive roles in shaping the future (Senge, 1990; Weick, 1995; Light, 1998; Crossan, Lane, and White, 1999; Weick and Sutcliff, 2001).

10. *Transitions with continuity, not revolution.* The American tradition emphasizes "disjointed incrementalism" involving "partisan mutual adjustment" among actors (Braybrooke and Lindblom, 1963; Lindblom, 1965). We have had the American Revolution and many major convulsions such as the Civil War and the Great Depression, but generally, "muddling through" (Lindblom, 1959) has been our preferred strategy as a nation. The good news is that continuous improvement in institutions is possible; the bad news is that typically it is very difficult to stimulate major institutional change in the absence of a crisis (Baumgartner and Jones, 1993; Kingdon, 1995). Clearly, it is a leadership challenge to inspire and mobilize others to undertake collective action in pursuit of the common good—producing wise changes, small or big, in response to the situation at hand (Crosby and Bryson, forthcoming).

In addition to keeping an eye on various trends, public and nonprofit sector organizations might monitor important stakeholder groups, especially actual or potential clients, customers, payers, or members (for voluntary organizations) and also competitors and collaborators and the forces driving competition or collaboration.

As I mentioned earlier, in my experience, members of a public or nonprofit organization's governing board, particularly if they are elected, are often better at identifying and assessing external threats and opportunities than are the organization's employees. Partly this is a reflection of differing roles; unlike most employees a governing board typically has formal responsibility for relating an organization to its external environment (Thompson, 1967; Carver, 1997). In the public sector there is a further reason. Employees get their mandates from laws, rules, and policies. Elected officials and politicians get their mandates primarily from elections. There can be major differences between legal or quasi-legal mandates and political mandates. Politicians pay attention mostly to political mandates, because they must. Indeed they typically employ "external environmental assessors" (pollsters, that is) to keep them informed about mandates likely to be externally imposed. So it may be easier to sell external scanning to elected officials than to planners and public administrators, because politicians live or die by how well they scan.

Even though board members may be better than staff members at identifying external opportunities and threats, typically neither group does a systematic or effective job of external scanning. Thus both groups should rely on a more or less formal and regular process of external assessment. The technology is fairly simple and allows organizations to keep tabs cheaply, pragmatically, and effectively on outside trends and events that are likely to have an impact on the organization and its pursuit of its mission. A simple process is outlined later in this chapter.

In addition to performing external scanning, organizational members can construct scenarios to help them pinpoint possible opportunities and challenges (as well as internal strengths and weaknesses). A simple method of scenario construction is outlined in Resource B. More complicated yet still relatively simple methods can be found in Schwartz (1991, pp. 226–234) and Van der Heijden and others (2002, pp. 187–228).

Internal Environmental Assessments

The purpose of the second part of step 4 is to assess the organization's internal environment in order to identify its strengths and weaknesses: that is, those aspects of the organization that help or hinder accomplishment of the organization's mission and fulfillment of its mandates. (Communities are more likely to think in terms of assets rather than strengths; see Kretzmann and McKnight, 1993.) This step may also lead to clarification of the organization's distinctive core competencies. The three major categories that should be assessed (again, as displayed on Figure 2.1) are the basic elements of a simple systems model: resources (inputs), present strategy (process), and performance (outputs). Not only are these categories basic to any internal organizational assessment, they also are the fundamental categories around which any effective management information system should be built (Kearns, 1996; Kaplan and Norton, 1996; Poister, 2003). Indeed, organizations with effective MIS systems should be in a better position than organizations without such systems to assess their strengths and weaknesses. The caveat of course is that no MIS system can provide all the information the organization needs—especially qualitative information, which is absolutely crucial. Culture, for example, is largely qualitative and rarely shows up in an MIS system, and yet culture is a crucial bridge across inputs, process, and outputs and between the inside and outside worlds (Khademian, 2002).

In my experience, most organizations have plenty of quantifiable information about inputs—salaries, supplies, physical plant, full-time-equivalent (FTE) personnel, and so on—readily available. They typically have far less command of qualitative information about inputs, such as the nature of the organization's culture—even though culture typically is crucial to performance (Johnson and Scholes, 2002; Khademian, 2002). Also, organizations generally cannot say succinctly what their present strategy is—overall, by business process, or by function. One of the most important things a strategic planning team can do is simply to articulate clearly what strategies the organization currently practices. This role of finders of strategy—codifying the organization's apparent *logic model* (McLaughlin and Jordan, 1999; Millar, Simeone, and Carnevale, 2001; Poister, 2003) or *value chain* (Porter, 1985, pp. 33–61)—is a very useful role for planners (Mintzberg, 1994). The recognition of patterns and the discovery of pockets of innovative strategies in various parts of the organization can be immensely instructive and can give the strategic planning team a better-informed basis for assessing strengths and weaknesses. Additionally, clarifying the current strategy helps people understand exactly what *value proposition* the organization offers its stakeholders—that is, precisely how the organization is going about converting inputs into outputs intended or presumed to meet its mandates, fulfill its mission, satisfy its stakeholders, and create public value (Moore, 2000, p. 197). As noted in Chapter Two, being clear about what *is* can be an extraordinarily helpful prelude to discerning what *ought* to be (Terry, 1993; Weick, 1995). As psychiatrist Fritz Perls once observed, "Nothing changes until it becomes what it is."

Organizations typically can also say little, if anything, about their outputs, either historically or in the present, let alone about the effects those outputs have on clients, customers, or payers. For example, social welfare agencies can say a lot about their budgets, staff, physical facilities, and so on, but they usually can say very little about the effects they have on their clients, and schools typically can say little about how educated their students are (Abramson and Kamensky, 2001).

The relative absence of performance information presents problems both for the organization and for its stakeholders. Stakeholders will judge the worth of an organization by how well the organization meets the criteria for success the stakeholders have chosen. For external stakeholders in particular, these criteria typically relate to performance. If the organization cannot demonstrate its effectiveness against the criteria, then stakeholders are likely to withdraw their support. Public schools, for example, are now finding their management, budgets, staffing patterns, and curricula judged by how well their pupils score on standardized educational achievement tests. Schools that fail to produce "educated" students may be forced to do better or close their doors (Behn, 2003). If educational voucher schemes become widespread, public schools may even have to compete directly with one another for revenues, students, and staff, in the same way that private and nonprofit schools must compete with each other and with the public schools. In fact some voucher schemes would allow public monies to be spent on education delivered in private and nonprofit schools, including religiously affiliated ones, so that *all* schools, regardless of legal status, might need to compete with one another. In part it was this kind of competition that prompted the School District's strategic planning effort. The district wanted to be a winner in the competition for students in a state that had open enrollment and educational voucher policies in place. Similarly, nonprofit organizations that rely on government financing, foundation support, or charitable contributions to provide social services may find their funding sources drying up unless they can demonstrate effective performance against relatively objective measures (Sawhill and Williamson, 2001).

The absence of performance information may also create or harden major organizational conflicts. Without performance criteria and information, there is no way to judge the relative effectiveness of different resource allocations, organizational designs, and distributions of power. Without such judgments, organizational conflicts are likely to occur unnecessarily, be more partisan, and be resolved in ways that undermine the organization's mission.

The difficulties of measuring performance in the public and nonprofit sectors are well known (Sawhill and Williamson, 2001; Niven, 2003; Poister, 2003). Nevertheless, stakeholders will continue to demand that organizations demonstrate effective performance and thereby justify their existence. Indeed, the federal Government Performance and Results Act of 1993 and similar acts passed by states across the nation—and legislatures around the world—mandate strategic plans and annual or multiyear performance plans geared to key criteria held by external stakeholders (Frederickson, 2001). This managerial push goes by different names—for example, strategic management, performance management, managing for results, results-oriented budgeting, and so on—but regardless of its name, the push is in large part a response to stakeholders' demanding demonstrably better performance and value for money (Kettl, 2000, 2002; Poister, 2003; Osborne and Hutchinson, 2004).

The Assessment Process

Here are two techniques for carrying out a SWOC analysis. The first is often a useful prelude to the second.

The Organizational Highs, Lows, and Themes Exercise

Often it is helpful for organizations to look forward by first looking backward. Indeed, organizations will find it easier to look forward for any period of time (five, ten, twenty years) if they first look backward for an equivalent period of time. An extremely useful technique for helping organizations assess strengths, weaknesses, opportunities, and challenges in a historical context is the *organizational highs, lows, and themes* exercise. This exercise is patterned after an exercise for individuals outlined in Bryson and Crosby (1992, pp. 349–351), which is in turn based on a more elaborate charting exercise described by Kouzes and Posner (1987). The organizational highs, lows, and themes exercise consists of the following steps:

1. Reserve a room with a large wall. A room with a whiteboard that covers a whole wall is ideal. Alternatively, you might wish to cover a wall with sheets of flipchart paper taped together (in two rows, with eight sheets in each row), so that the results of the exercise may be saved intact.

2. Divide the wall into top and bottom halves. This can be done by drawing a line on the whiteboard or flipchart sheets or by using a long strip of masking tape.

3. At the right-hand end of the line, write in the current year. At the left-hand end, write in the date that is as far *back* as you wish the strategic planning team to ultimately look *forward* (typically five or ten years).

4. Ask group members to individually and silently brainstorm, on a sheet of scratch paper, all of the organizational "highs" and "lows" they can recall that occurred within the agreed time frame. These might include the organization's founding, arrivals or departures of respected leaders, successful or unsuccessful management of crises, particularly useful or disastrous innovations, and so on. Ask participants to date each item and label it as a high or low.

5. Have participants transcribe their highs and lows (or some specified number of each) onto half-sheets of paper, one high or low per sheet, and attach a piece of tape rolled sticky side out or a small bit of self-adhesive putty to the back of each sheet.

6. Have participants stick their sheets to the wall at the appropriate places on the timeline. The height of each sheet above or below the line should indicate how high the "high" was or how low the "low" was.

7. Ask the group to identify the themes that are common to the highs, to the lows, and to both.

8. Then ask the group to analyze the data and themes by answering these questions:

> What opportunities have we had? Which have we taken advantage of, which were we unable to take advantage of, and which have we ignored?

> What challenges have we had to deal with? Which have we handled successfully, which have we handled unsuccessfully, and which have we ignored?

What strengths have we relied on to deal with challenges and take advantage of opportunities? Which strengths have we ignored?

What weaknesses have we had in dealing with challenges and opportunities? What have we done about these weaknesses?

9. Ask the group to identify patterns in the way strengths, weaknesses, opportunities, challenges, and themes have interrelated over the relevant organizational history. In particular, ask participants to identify what the organization's strategies have been *in practice*—what has actually happened, as opposed to what might be voiced in official pronouncements.

10. Have the participants move the timeline forward an equivalent distance and discuss what their previous analyses might imply for the future. In particular, have the group speculate about future opportunities and challenges and the strengths the organization might have to use to address them and the weaknesses it might encounter while doing so. What themes, patterns, and strategies from the past would the group like to see projected into the future? Which would the group not like to see projected? What new themes would the group like to see?

One example of the usefulness of this exercise is provided by a generally successful nonprofit organization in the United Kingdom devoted to addressing the needs of children (and whose patron is a member of the royal family). Its management team realized as a result of this exercise that the organization almost always performed better when it did careful planning, attended to key stakeholder interests, and took advantage of opportunities. Conversely, it did less well when it got caught in crisis management, failed to attend to key stakeholder interests, and failed to deal with important challenges. The exercise thus renewed management's commitment to strategic planning and helped it focus on some key strengths, weaknesses, opportunities, and challenges related particularly to stakeholder concerns. Mintzberg, Ahlstrand, and Lampel (1998) capture this interplay of past, present, and future well when they say, "Strategies appear first as patterns out of the past, only later, perhaps, as plans for the future, and ultimately, as perspectives to guide overall behavior" (p. 208). Delbanco (1999) more assertively captures the fatefulness of how we look at the past when he says, "The future is always at stake in how we understand the past" (p. 10).

The Snow Card Technique

The *snow card* technique (Greenblat and Duke, 1981; Spencer, 1989) is a simple yet effective group technique for developing a list of strengths, weaknesses, opportunities, and challenges. Also referred to as the *snowball* technique (Nutt and

Backoff, 1992), the method combines brainstorming—which produces a long list of possible answers to a specific question—with a synthesizing step in which the answers are grouped into categories according to common themes. Each of the answers is then written on a white card (a snow card): for example, a half-sheet of inexpensive photocopy paper, a 5-by-7-inch card, or a large self-stick note. The individual cards are then stuck to a wall with masking tape or self-adhesive putty and grouped according to common themes, producing several snowballs of cards.

This technique is extremely simple in concept, easy to use, speedy, and productive. It is particularly useful as part of a SWOC analysis and as part of the strategy development step. In a SWOC analysis the snow card process is completed four times in order to address these four questions:

- What major external or future opportunities do we have?
- What major external or future challenges do we face?
- What are our major internal or present strengths?
- What are our major internal or present weaknesses?

This quickly produces four lists for the strategic planning team to discuss, compare, and contrast, both to determine actions that should be taken immediately and to prepare for the identification of strategic issues in the next step. This SWOC analysis also will help the team prepare effective strategies in response to the issues.

Here are the guidelines for using the snow card technique:

1. Select a facilitator.
2. Form the group that will use the technique. The ideal group size is five to nine persons, but the technique can be effective with as many as fifteen. Even larger numbers of participants can be involved if they first work in subgroups of five to nine.
3. Have the members of the group seat themselves around a table in a room that has a nearby wall onto which the snows cards can be attached.
4. Focus on a single question, problem, or issue. Typically the entire process will be repeated four times in a SWOC analysis, once for each of the categories: strengths, weaknesses, opportunities, and challenges. Alternatively, you might choose to analyze strengths and weakness in one round, and opportunities and challenges in one round.
5. Have the participants silently brainstorm as many ideas as possible in response to the question, and record them on their personal worksheets.
6. Have each person pick out the five to seven best items from his or her personal worksheet and transcribe each one of them onto a separate snow card. Make

sure people write legibly enough and large enough so that items can be read when posted on the wall. Have group members attach some rolled tape or self-adhesive putty to the back of each of their snow cards.

7. Collect the cards (shuffle them if anonymity is important), and attach them one at a time to the wall, clustering cards with similar themes together. The tentative label for each category should be selected by the group. Alternatively, the participants may wish to tape all the cards to the wall at once and then, working together, rearrange the cards into thematic categories.

8. Label each cluster, using a separate card. These label cards should be differentiated in some way from the snow cards; they might be a different color of paper, use a different color of ink, or have a box drawn around the name.

9. Once all the cards are on the wall and initially clustered, rearrange them and tinker with the categories until the group agrees that a particular arrangement makes the most sense. Categories might be arranged in logical, priority, or temporal order. New items may be added and old ones deleted as necessary. Subcategories should be added as needed. In addition, structuring within categories may be advisable to highlight linkages among items (see Resource B).

10. When the group members are satisfied with the categories and their contents, ask them to discuss, compare, and contrast the results.

11. Participants' collective opinion of the relative importance of the categories (or individual items) may be visually accentuated with colored stick-on dots. For each round of a SWOC analysis, I usually give each participant seven dots and ask the participants to place one dot on each of the seven most important categories or items on the wall. The pattern formed by the dots graphically displays the pattern of group opinion.

12. When the session is over, collect the cards in order, have them typed up in outline or spreadsheet form, and distribute the results to the group. Having a notebook computer and secretary at the session will speed this process. It may also be advisable to take digital photographs of the display, both as a backup and to provide a pictorial reminder of the process.

A fascinating variation on this exercise is the *camera exercise* used on occasion in East St. Louis, Missouri, by a community planning group (Khademian, 2002, p. 74). Community members are given an inexpensive disposable camera containing at least twenty-seven shots. Group members are asked to bring to a meeting at least nine shots of things that represent community strengths, nine shots of things that represent community weaknesses, and nine shots of potential assets or opportunities for the future. The photographs are then clustered, using the technique described for the snow cards, and discussed.

Example of a SWOC Analysis

Simply creating lists of strengths, weaknesses, opportunities, and threats is not enough. The lists must be carefully discussed, analyzed, compared, and contrasted; that is, a SWOC analysis must be performed. Planners should note specific implications for the formulation of strategic issues and effective strategies as well as indications of actions that might be necessary (and could be taken) before the end of the strategic planning process.

One of the fascinating features of most SWOC analyses is that strengths and weaknesses are often highly similar to one another. That is, an organization's greatest strengths may also be its greatest weaknesses. Likewise the opportunities and challenges an organization faces are often similar to one another. Strategic planning team members should not be surprised to see such relationships. Indeed they should expect that every organization will carry the weaknesses of its strengths and face the challenges of its opportunities (and vice versa). The trick is to take advantage of the strengths and opportunities without being disadvantaged by the related weaknesses and challenges (Johnson, 1996).

The team also should not be surprised to find internal opportunities and challenges and external strengths and weaknesses. Although, as discussed earlier, opportunities and challenges are primarily external and strengths and weaknesses are primarily internal and although, as Nutt and Backoff (1992) argue, strengths and weaknesses are primarily in the present and opportunities and challenges are primarily in the future; in fact SWOCs may arise inside or outside the organization and in the present or in the future.

The strategic planning process at Project for Pride in Living (PPL) produced an interesting example of SWOC lists developed initially through the use of snow cards (see Exhibit 5.1, which contains the category labels). (The SWOC analysis that guided initial Naval Security Group efforts can be found in Frentzel, Bryson, and Crosby, 2000, pp. 422–424). Only the main category headings are discussed here, but they are enough to illustrate key points that I have been making. The basic lists were developed in a half-day retreat of three to four hours. Thirty to forty participants were involved, including board members, senior managers, and midlevel managers. After the session, rough rankings of items were established, based on the number of people who mentioned each item. A, B, and C lists were created, with the A list having the broadest support and the C list the least. The final SWOC lists also benefited from interviews and discussions held at management meetings and with program participants, other staff, advisory group members, and partners. The vast majority of PPL employees got to comment on the SWOCs at some point.

EXHIBIT 5.1. PROJECT FOR PRIDE IN LIVING SWOC LISTS.

Strengths

A list
- Holistic understanding of self-sufficiency needs
- Strong, competent, dedicated staff and board
- Expertise in low- and moderate-income housing
- Strong community reputation

B list
- Diversity of programs
- Capacity
- Partnering and collaborating ability
- Practical help
- Relations with clients
- Efficient at keeping expenses in line
- Strong track record
- Progressive external orientation

Weaknesses

A list
- Lack of focus
- Lack of integration
- Lack of analysis in project planning and program planning
- Lack of community participation in PPL leadership
- No clear definition of measures of self-sufficiency and related critical success factors
- Lack of understanding of overall scope of PPL programs
- Lack of adequate reserves; negative cash flow in key programs

B list
- Moving into areas outside our core competencies
- Edison-PPL partnership
- Classroom space
- Inadequate training materiel, for example, computers
- Too tied to current services that are successful
- Participants still too narrowly defined
- Internal checks and balances
- Private fundraising
- Housing skills lead to big projects with limited mission connection
- Confusing organization to those outside
- Job generation

Opportunities

A list
- Collaboration and partnerships
- Need for affordable housing, especially low income and larger units

EXHIBIT 5.1. PROJECT FOR PRIDE IN LIVING SWOC LISTS, CONT'D.

- Integrated programs to increase effectiveness
- Need for community among new immigrants

B list
- Expansion of high-impact programs
- Expansion in new geographic areas of service, especially suburbs
- Increasing demand for self-sufficiency services
- Expertise and influence to affect public policy on high-profile issues
- Become leaders in our community

C list
- Teach
- Partnerships with colleges to expand College House programs
- Increase effectiveness
- Acquire foreclosed properties because of the state of the economy
- New headquarters and training facility
- Support to maintain or rebuild families
- Employer demands for skilled entry-level employees
- PPL Board is willing to look at sharpening its focus and priorities
- Allows for self-sufficiency of participants
- To build stronger communities
- Public acknowledgment of need for self-sufficiency versus handouts
- Need education advocates for children from low-income families

Threats [Challenges]

A list
- Possible decreased charitable giving
- Lack of resources to solve housing crisis
- Downturn in economy
- Competition among nonprofits endangers scarce resources
- Loss of quality PPL employees
- Community opposition

B list
- Political apathy or antipathy
- More training graduates than jobs available
- Community needs become more complex and PPL doesn't respond
- Overextension of resources

C list
- Reputation damage if initiatives fail
- 5-year welfare limit and its impact on participants
- Lack of understanding of what PPL does
- Reduced support from people who don't agree
- Earned income too volatile as a result of economic, housing, and funding cycles
- Great community needs encourage us to lose focus on our mission

Note: In the PPL process the challenges were called threats.

Source: Gary, 2003. Printed with permission.

The fact that the lists of strengths, weaknesses, opportunities, and challenges were in need of further elaboration and conversation was to be expected. The snow card technique was a first crack at the task. Nonetheless that exercise and ensuing discussions helped shape the way strategic issues were identified, provided the basis for a number of decisions and actions to improve PPL's performance, and in general moved the strategic planning process forward. For example, discussions helped to open people's minds, so that they saw things less parochially and more holistically. Discussions also helped the team to identify core competencies, and they helped the group see the need for concerted attention to integration in terms of both improved communications and program offerings (items relating to this need showed up as weaknesses and as opportunities).

A few observations about PPL's complete SWOC list are in order. First, the weaknesses are more numerous than the strengths, whereas the opportunities are more numerous than challenges. Given the way the lists were constructed, this may mean simply that there was greater agreement (less dispersion) on what the strengths and the challenges were. Whatever the reason, it is hard to take advantage of an opportunity from a position of weaknesses (which is why the old cartoon character Pogo could get a laugh by referring to his "insurmountable opportunities"). Nonetheless that is in part the situation PPL faces; for example, as noted above, items relating to integration of communications and services are both weaknesses and opportunities. PPL's mission is to foster self-sufficiency among low-income individuals and families through affordable housing, job training, and social service supports. Pursuing the mission forces PPL to integrate across boundaries of all sorts—its own divisions and funding streams; governmental jurisdictions, programs, and funding; foundation programs and funding; cultural, neighborhood, and family divides; the differing timelines, deadlines, and requirements of the many stakeholders; and so on—all in an environment of increasingly tight funding. PPL clearly has strengths on which it can draw, but it also needs to work constantly at overcoming the weaknesses its opportunities create or expose and the challenges that can magnify the weaknesses or overwhelm the strengths and opportunities.

This kind of needed outward focus is the reverse of what often happens when senior managers get together. Most managers are responsible for the day-to-day operation of their departments. Their jobs often virtually preclude paying careful attention to external trends and events. Furthermore most organizations do not have well-established occasions and forums for line managers to come together to discuss external trends and events and their likely impact. Most organizations are thus in danger of being blindsided by external developments, unless they make use of external scanning practices and have organized forums so that managers can discuss information developed through external scanning or have an invited speakers program.

Second, the fact that PPL's opportunities are more numerous than its challenges is a bit unusual—and perhaps a very good sign, if it doesn't simply mean a broader dispersion of views—because challenges are quite often the longest of the four lists. When I see challenges as the longest list I wonder whether that reflects the highly stressful work climate many public servants and nonprofit employees currently face or whether it is an accurate assessment of the challenges (or opportunities) that are actually present. In psychologically punishing circumstances, it may be quite natural to focus on the things that seem to have produced the all-too-familiar climate of fear, anxiety, shame, or guilt—rather than on things that might evoke more pleasant but somehow more diffuse emotions such as satisfaction, happiness, joy, or even love (Dutton and Jackson, 1987; Ortony, Clore, and Collins, 1990; Kaufman, 1992).

The good news is that a shared perception of challenges may induce both group cohesion and action, particularly if the culture supports facing rather than avoiding failure, weakness, and threats (Weick and Sutcliffe, 2001). Indeed, as was noted in Chapter Two, most organizations get into strategic planning because they face strategic issues that they do not know how to handle or because they are pursuing strategies that are failing or likely to fail. In either case it is the perception of serious challenges that prompts strategic planning. The bad news is that without some sense of safety provided by credible leaders; inspiring missions, visions, and goals; supportive cultures; or strong facilitators, groups gripped by challenges or actual threats may become paralyzed and unable to think of or take advantage of opportunities (Schein, 1997; Weick and Sutcliffe, 2001; Kouzes and Posner, 2002; Schwarz, 2002).

Third, although PPL's list of weaknesses outnumbers its list of strengths, there are still many strengths on which to build. This is good, as it helps inoculate the group against the natural human tendency to become a captive of action inhibitors (weaknesses) rather than focusing on what facilitates action (strengths). It also protects PPL from the equally familiar human tendency to assign blame or find a scapegoat as a way of avoiding action. Whatever the reason, it is important to turn weaknesses into challenges to be overcome (Csikszentmihalyi, 1990; Bandura, 1997; Seligman, 1998).

A final point to be made about SWOC analyses is that when a general-purpose government (in contrast to most nonprofit and single-function public organizations) performs a SWOC analysis, the results will involve both the government as an organization and its jurisdiction as a place or community. This blending should be expected of governments responsible for themselves and for places. The same blending of results for both the organization and its jurisdiction occurred for the School District. This was expected, given the interdependence between the School District and its supporting community. It also was expected because the district invited representatives of key external stakeholder groups to participate in its planning process. These representatives typically were at least as concerned with the community as a whole as they were with the district's role in it. The individual lists are also informative.

Strengths. The PPL planning group identified a solid set of strengths. PPL can build on those strengths to enhance the organization's ability to fulfill its mission, meet its mandates, and create public value. Further, there are entries for all three broad internal environment categories—resources, present strategy, and performance. PPL has much of the understanding it needs to work with clients and partner programs on a case-by-case basis to enhance clients' self-sufficiency on the one hand, and to make organizational ends meet on the other hand. This web of understanding and skill represents a distinctive core competency. PPL also has a strong track record and community reputation. A strength that does not show up, however, is major cash reserves or an endowment on which PPL can draw. So although PPL knows what to do and how to do it, finding the needed financial resources is a challenge.

Weaknesses. The planning group also identified a significant set of weaknesses, although none is unusual or insurmountable. As would be expected, most of them mirror strengths. For example, although PPL has a holistic understanding of self-sufficiency needs, it has no clear definition of measures of self-sufficiency or of the critical factors in producing it—and probably no one does. Similarly, because client self-sufficiency is a product of pulling many things together on a case-by-case basis, it is no wonder that PPL planners see in the organization a lack of focus, integration, analysis, and understanding of PPL's scope. Focusing on clients engenders a kind of centrifugal force that takes a real and continuing effort to counter. Finally, the lack of adequate cash reserves and negative cash flow in key programs is a real concern. These weaknesses helped frame a number of the strategic issues PPL identified around the need to measure effectiveness; foster organizational sustainability, connectivity, and integration; and articulate its role in the larger community. These issues will be discussed in the next chapter.

Opportunities. The list of opportunities is helpful, hopeful, and a cause for optimism. It is also a bit vague and therefore in need of elaboration. As part of its mission, PPL has the opportunity to help fill the continuing need for affordable housing, especially larger units, for low- and moderate-income people; to provide integrated programs to increase effectiveness; and to address the needs of the new immigrant community. The opportunities for partnerships and collaborations can be used to take advantage of these affordable housing opportunities. PPL also has opportunities for expanding high-impact programs, expanding geographical coverage of services, and taking a more active role in community leadership and public policy around issues of concern. In addition, a number of other opportunities exist in the lowest-priority category. Many of these seem to be elaborations of higher-priority opportunities.

Challenges. The list of challenges is substantial, and often more specific than the list of opportunities. And as expected, many challenges mirror opportunities. At the head of the list are potential losses of financial and staff resources and community support. Decreases in charitable giving, loss of public tax dollars, and departures of high-quality employees all would hamper PPL's ability to do its work—that is, take advantage of its opportunities in pursuit of its mission. PPL could find itself overextended and with no political support to change the policy environment within which it operates. Its reputation might diminish, along with its ability to manage its resources effectively. Meanwhile, the self-sufficiency needs of participants are not diminishing, the five-year eligibility clock for recipients of federal welfare support keeps ticking, jobs for training graduates are not always available, and PPL might find itself unable to maintain its focus, resource flow, and base of support.

In sum PPL's planning group identified a number of strengths, weaknesses, opportunities, and challenges through the use of the snow card technique. Some specific actions were suggested based on the lists, and the identification of strategic issues was facilitated. (Interestingly, one of the most important actions—fostering greater focus and integration—was a natural consequence of the strategic planning process because of the board-staff-community and cross-divisional conversations that the process created.) The lists were not exhaustive, however, and a more extensive SWOC analysis, with more staff support, is merited in the future. PPL did use its SWOC analysis to home in on its competencies. These were identified by division (affordable housing and development, human services, and employment and job training) and included in PPL's 2003–2007 strategic plan.

Process Guidelines

One of the special features of strategic planning is the attention it accords external and internal environments. Coupled with attention to organizational mandates and mission, external and internal assessments give an organization a clear sense of its present situation and lay the basis for identifying strategic issues and developing strategies in the next two steps. As the ancient Chinese military strategist Sun Tzu (1991) might have said, without this kind of in-depth understanding an organization is likely to be continuously imperiled. And certainly successful major change will be highly unlikely (Abramson and Lawrence, 2001; Khademian, 2002). The following process guidelines may be helpful as an organization looks at its external and internal environments.

1. *Keep in mind that simpler is likely to be better.* Highly elaborate, lengthy, sophisticated, and quantified procedures for external and internal assessment are likely to drive out strategic thinking, not promote it. Let purpose be your guide. Always keep in mind the organizational mandates, mission, and need to create public value, and search for information related to them. Do not gather information indiscriminately.

2. *The organization may wish to review its mission and mandates; stakeholder analyses; existing goal statements; results of the organizational highs, lows, and themes exercise (if it was used); the competency identification exercise in Resource B (if it was used); culture audits; relevant survey results; MIS and external scanning reports; scenarios; and other information related to the organization's internal and external environments prior to performing a SWOC analysis.* Alternatively, a "quick and dirty" SWOC analysis may prompt strategic planning team members to pay attention to what they previously ignored, or it may indicate where more information is needed. Because an organization's culture can place severe limits on people's ability to perceive SWOCs and can constrain strategic responses, an analysis of the culture may be particularly useful. If key decision makers and opinion leaders are willing, a serviceable cultural analysis can be performed in one and a half days, following guidelines provided by Schein (1997, pp. 147–168; see also Hampden-Turner, 1990, pp. 185–207; Khademian, 2002, pp. 108–123).

3. *Consider using the snow card technique with the strategic planning team to develop a list of strengths, weaknesses, opportunities, and challenges.*

4. *Always try to get the strategic planning team to consider what is going on outside the organization before it considers what is going on inside.* Attending to the outside is crucial, because the social and political justification for virtually every organization's existence is what it does or proposes to do about external social or political challenges or problems. Organizations therefore should focus on those challenges or problems first and on themselves second.

5. *As part of its discussion of the SWOC list, the strategic planning team should look for patterns, important actions that might be taken immediately, and implications for the identification of strategic issues.*

6. *A follow-up analysis of the SWOC analysis developed by the strategic planning team is almost always a good idea.* Constructing logic models that capture the apparent reasoning and perceived causal chains behind existing organizational processes and strategies can be very instructive (Millar, Simeone, and Carnevale, 2001; Abramson and Kamensky, 2001; Poister, 2003).

7. *The organization should take action as quickly as possible on those items for which it has enough information.* Doing so is desirable if it does not foreclose important strategic options for the future. It is important to show continuous progress and desirable results from strategic planning if people are to stay with it when the going gets tough.

8. *The organization should consider institutionalizing periodic SWOC analyses.* The simplest way to do this is to schedule periodic meetings of the strategic planning team, say, once or twice a year, to engage in a snow card exercise to develop a SWOC list that can be a basis for discussion. A norm should be established that at least some organizational changes will result from these sessions. These periodic meetings could also be a means of establishing a quasi-permanent external and internal scanning function.

9. *The organization may wish to construct various scenarios in order to help it identify SWOCs.* The advantage to this approach is that the stories conjured up by scenarios can help many people better imagine the future. As the poet Muriel Rukeyser said, "The world is made of stories, not atoms." The often abstract categories of a SWOC analysis may be just vague "atoms" to people when what they need is a tangible story with "real" scenes, events, and actors. The story can help them see the whole rather than just the parts. I have seen effective assessments done with and without scenarios. Not using scenarios can save time, but some of the possible richness of a good assessment exercise can be lost without them. In the 1990s, both the Naval Security Group and, on a much larger scale, the U.S. Air Force (Barzelay and Campbell, 2003) made effective use of scenarios in order to understand their situations better and to set the stage for strategic issue identification in the next step of their planning processes.

Summary

Step 4 of the strategic planning process explores the organization's external and internal environments in order to identify the strengths, weaknesses, opportunities, and challenges the organization faces. Together with the steps that increase attention to mandates and mission, this step provides the foundation for identifying strategic issues and developing effective strategies to create public value in the following two steps. Recall that every effective strategy will build on strengths and take advantage of opportunities while it minimizes or overcomes weaknesses and challenges.

By far the most important strategic planning techniques are individual thinking and group discussion. Neither may look like useful work—as poet Wallace Stevens says, "Sometimes it is difficult to tell the difference between thinking and looking out the window." But do not be deceived. The organizational highs, lows, and themes exercise; the competency identification exercise; and the snow card technique can be used to build the basic SWOC list that will be the focus of the individual thinking and group discussion that will clarify what the most important issues are and much of what the organization has and can use to carry out its work.

Organizations should consider institutionalizing their capability to perform periodic SWOC analyses. To do so, they will need to establish serviceable external and internal scanning operations, develop a good MIS, and undertake regular strategic planning exercises.

As with every step in the strategic planning process, simpler is usually better. Strategic planning teams should not get bogged down in external and internal assessments. Important and necessary actions should be taken as soon as they are identified, as long as they do not prematurely seal off important strategic options.

CHAPTER SIX

IDENTIFYING STRATEGIC ISSUES FACING THE ORGANIZATION

Depend upon it, Sir, when a man knows he is to be hanged in a fortnight, it concentrates his mind wonderfully.

SAMUEL JOHNSON, IN JAMES BOSWELL, *LIFE OF JOHNSON*

Identifying strategic issues is the heart of the strategic planning process. Recall that a *strategic issue* is a fundamental policy question or critical challenge affecting an organization's mandates, mission and values, product or service level and mix, clients, users or payers, cost, financing, structure, processes, or management. The purpose of this step (step 5) therefore is to identify the fundamental policy questions—the strategic issue agenda (Nutt and Backoff, 1992)—facing the organization. The way these questions are framed can have a profound effect on the creation of ideas for strategic action and the establishment of a winning coalition— along with the associated decisions that define what the organization is, what is does, and why it does it—and therefore on the organization's ability to create public value (see Figure 2.4). If strategic planning is in part about the construction of a new social reality, then this step outlines the basic paths along which that drama might unfold (Mangham and Overington, 1987; Bryant, 2003; Bolman and Deal, 2003, pp. 270–286).

An organization's mission often is explicitly or implicitly identified as an issue during this phase. The School District's board and staff had extensive debates about exactly what *education* and *success* should mean and what role education should play in relation to the district's mission before they adopted a new mission of "educating for success in our diverse and changing world." Project for Pride in

Living board and staff members struggled with the meaning of *self-sufficiency* and what PPL's mission should be as PPL tried to develop self-sufficiency in program participants. The Naval Security Group grappled with what the emergence of information warfare might mean for its mission and role.

The organization's culture will affect which issues get on the agenda and how they are framed and will also affect which strategic options get serious consideration in step 6, strategy formulation and plan development. The need to change the organization's culture may thus become a strategic issue itself if the culture blinds the organization to important issues and possibilities for action. It is also worth keeping in mind that every major strategy change will involve a cultural change (Schein, 1997; Khademian, 2002).

As noted in Chapter Two, strategic issues are important because issues play a central role in political decision making. Political decision making begins with issues, but strategic planning can improve the process by affecting the way issues are framed and addressed. When issues are carefully framed, subsequent choices, decisions, and actions are more likely to be politically acceptable and technically and administratively workable; in accord with the organization's basic philosophy and values; and morally, ethically, and legally defensible.

Identifying strategic issues typically is one of the most riveting steps for participants in strategic planning (Ackermann, 1992). Virtually every strategic issue involves conflicts over what will be done, why it will be done, how and how much of it will be done, when it will be done, where it will be done, who will do it, or who will be advantaged or disadvantaged by it. These conflicts are typically desirable and even necessary because they clarify the issues. As Rainey (1997) observes, "In public and nonprofit organizations, one expects and even hopes for intense conflicts, although preferably not destructive ones" (p. 304). As a result a key leadership task is promoting constructive conflict aimed at clarifying exactly what the issues are that need to be addressed in order to satisfy key stakeholders and create public value. But whether the conflict draws people together or pulls them apart, participants will feel heightened emotion and concern (Ortony, Clore, and Collins, 1990; Schein, 1997; Patterson, Grenny, McMillan, and Switzler, 2002). As with any journey, fear, anxiety, and sometimes depression are as likely to be travel companions as are excitement and adventurousness. It is very important therefore that people feel enough psychological safety to explore potentially threatening situations, relationships, and ideas; in other words they need what Ronald Heifetz (1994, p. 103; see also Chrislip, 2002, pp. 45–46) calls a *holding environment* and what Karl Weick (1995, p. 179) calls a *sensemaking support system* to help them through. An effective strategic planning coordinating committee and strategic planning team will provide these necessary supports.

Desired Outcomes

This step should result in the creation of the organization's strategic issue agenda. This agenda is a product of three intermediate outcomes. The first is a list of the issues faced by the organization. The items on the list may have many sources, but the list itself is likely to be a product of strategic planning team deliberations. The second is the division of the list into two categories: *strategic* and *operational*. It often takes focused discussion to discern which issues are really strategic and which are more operational. Generally, strategic issues imply a need for exploring or creating new knowledge, whereas operational issues imply exploiting existing knowledge (March, 1991; Benner and Tushman, 2003). Operational issues should be referred to an operations management group, team, task force, or individual for further attention. And the third intermediate outcome is the arrangement of the strategic issues in some sort of order: priority, logical, or temporal. The listing and arrangement of issues should contain information that helps people consider the nature, importance, and implications of each issue.

Benefits

A number of benefits ensue from the identification of strategic issues. First, attention is focused on what is truly important. The importance of this benefit is not to be underestimated. Key decision makers in organizations usually are victimized by the 80-20 rule. That is, key decision makers usually spend at least 80 percent of their time on the least important 20 percent of their jobs (Parkinson, 1957). When this is added to the fact that key decision makers in different functional areas rarely discuss important cross-functional matters with one another, the stage is set for shabby organizational performance.

It also helps to recognize that in terms of the immediacy of the attention they require, there are three different kinds of strategic issues: (1) issues that require no action at present but that must be continuously monitored, (2) issues that can be handled as part of the organization's regular strategic planning cycle, and (3) issues that require an immediate response and therefore cannot be handled in a more routine way.

A second benefit is that attention is focused on issues, not answers. All too often, serious conflicts arise over solutions to problems that have not been clearly defined (Fisher and Ury, 1981; Janis, 1989). Such conflicts typically result in power struggles, not problem-solving sessions. More important, they are unlikely to help the organization achieve its goals, be satisfied with the outcome of its planning, or enhance its future problem-solving ability (Bryson and Bromiley, 1993; Nutt, 2002).

Third, the identification of issues usually creates the kind of useful tension necessary to prompt organizational change. Organizations rarely change unless they feel some need to change, some pressure or tension—often fear, anxiety, or guilt—that requires change to relieve or release the stress (Peters, 1996, p. 73; Light, 1998, p. 66; Fiol, 2002). The tension must be great enough to prompt change but not so great as to induce paralysis. Strategic issues that emerge from the juxtaposition of internal and external factors—and that involve organizational survival, prosperity, and effectiveness—can provide just the kind of tension that will focus the attention of key decision makers on the need for change (Nutt, 2001b). These decision makers will be particularly attentive to strategic issues that entail severe consequences if they are not addressed. As Samuel Johnson observed, albeit humorously, frightening situations quickly focus one's attention on what is important.

Fourth, strategic issue identification should provide useful clues about how to resolve each issue. By stating exactly what it is about the organization's mission, mandates, and internal and external factors (or SWOCs) that makes an issue strategic, the team gains some insight into possible ways that the issue might be resolved. Insights into the nature and shape of effective answers are particularly likely when the team follows the dictum that an effective strategy will take advantage of strengths and opportunities and minimize or overcome weaknesses and challenges (Mintzberg, 1994, p. 277). Attention to strengths and opportunities is likely to promote action-enhancing optimism, as opposed to the inaction, depression, or rigidity of thought associated with attention only to weaknesses and threats (Dutton and Jackson, 1987; Seligman, 1991; Nadler and Hobino, 1998).

Fifth, if the strategic planning process has not been *real* to participants previously, it will become real for them now. For something to be real for someone there must be a correspondence between what the person thinks about something, how he or she behaves toward that thing, and the consequences of that behavior (Boal and Bryson, 1987; Hunt, Boal, and Dodge, 1999). As the organization's situation and the issues it faces become clear, as the consequences of failure to face those issues are discussed, and as the behavioral changes necessary to deal with the issues begin to emerge, the strategic planning process will begin to seem less academic and much more real. The more people realize that strategic planning can be quite real in its consequences, the more seriously they will take it. A qualitative change in the tone of team members' discussions can often be observed at this point as the links among cognitions, behaviors, and consequences are established. Less joking and more serious discussion occur. A typical result of this *realization* is that the group may wish to recycle through the earlier steps of the process. In particular the group's initial framing of the strategic issues is likely to change as members come to realize and to discuss more fully the consequences of both addressing and failing to address the issues (Eden and Sims, 1978). Or, to go back to the theatrical metaphor, as the group members rehearse the various decision and action sequences that might flow from a particular issue framing, they may wish to reframe the issue so that certain kinds of strategies are more likely to find favor (Bryant, 2003).

A further consequence of the understanding that strategic planning will have real consequences is that key decision makers may wish to terminate the effort at this point. They may be afraid of addressing the conflicts embodied in the strategic issues. They may not wish to undergo the changes that may be necessary to resolve the issues. These decision makers may fall into "the pit," where they may experience stress, anger, depression, feelings of powerlessness, and grief (Spencer and Adams, 1990, pp. 49-60). Such feelings are quite common among individuals undergoing major changes until they let go of the past and move into the future with a new sense of direction and renewed confidence (Baum, 1999). A crisis of trust or a test of courage may thus occur and may lead to a turning point in the organization's character. If after completion of this step the organization's key decision makers decide to push on, a final very important benefit therefore will have been gained: the organization's character will be strengthened. Just as an individual's character is formed in part by the way the individual faces serious difficulties, so too is organizational character formed by the way the organization faces difficulties (Selznick, 1957; Schein, 1997). Strong characters emerge only from confronting serious difficulties squarely and courageously (Terry, 1993, 2001).

Examples of Strategic Issues

The Naval Security Group (NSG) identified six strategic issues at a strategic planning retreat in 1992, near the beginning of its six-year strategy change effort. What follows is a summary of the list of issues, framed as questions NSG could do something about, along with a brief description of what made the issue an issue (Frentzel, Bryson, and Crosby, 2000, pp. 405–407, 424–425):

- *What can NSG do to better support military operations?* This issue arose from the Navy's change in focus, after the collapse of the Soviet Union, from control of the seas to projecting U.S. power inland, in an environment in which joint operations with the other armed services are emphasized. It was clear that NSG would have to change its cryptological processes, products, and services to concentrate on coastal areas to retain the support of its major stakeholder, the Navy.

- *How does NSG maintain a global reach?* This issue arose from a number of factors. Budget constraints would drive the reduction of infrastructure and therefore the closure of a number of overseas bases and sites.
- *How does NSG best use technology to produce its products and services?* Advancing technology is introducing process challenges; cryptology will be done differently in the future. For example, NSG had to consider whether it should rely more on manned or on unmanned (*remoted*) operations. Unmanned operations, although more cost effective, presented challenges in that a certain feel for the operations would be lost. How could NSG posture itself in the *remoting* business so as to better direct its products and services toward the Navy's power projection strategy?
- *Does NSG want to be involved in other warfare areas, such as electronic warfare (EW)?* (Electronic warfare is military action aimed at retaining control over the use of the electromagnetic spectrum.) This issue had been around since the late 1970s, and NSG had some strong core competencies and experience in the area.
- *How does NSG address the growing field of information warfare (IW)?* All participants agreed that this was an important issue. IW is a broad, amorphous, and still evolving concept, but clearly cryptology plays a fundamental and critical role in IW. However, very much like the older EW issue, IW represents a broad functional area fraught with control issues and politics.
- *How does NSG define joint cryptological operations?* This was a key issue with which NSG was wrestling in both the strategic and the tactical arenas. How could NSG meet the congressional mandates for joint operations and still retain control and some sort of command structure? (In other words, how could NSG ensure a cooperative venture and not a hostile takeover?)

These issues guided the efforts of the group of middle managers that formulated them as they sought to perform their own jobs better, involve their superiors in the process, and help NSG deal with its present challenges and prepare for the future. Changes occurred in the framing of the issues over the course of the six-year change effort as more key stakeholders became involved in the process and as the implications of various strategic responses were pursued, and such changes are to be expected (Frentzel, Bryson, and Crosby, 2000, pp. 415–417, 424–425).

NSG may represent something of an extreme case when it comes to addressing major issues involving information technology, human resources, and financial management. But issues in these three areas are becoming salient for virtually every public and nonprofit organization (Bryson, 2001, 2003a). Information technology, in particular, is assuming almost paramount importance for organizations moving into e-commerce and e-government (Cassidy, 2002; Abramson and Morin, 2002; Abramson and Harris, 2003). It is imperative that issues involving information technology, human resources, and financial management be addressed in such a way that they support the organization's overall mission and efforts to meet its mandates and create public value.

Describing Strategic Issues

An adequate strategic issue description (1) phrases the issue as a question the organization can do something about and that has more than one answer, (2) discusses the confluence of factors (mission, mandates, and internal and external environmental aspects, or SWOCs) that makes the issue strategic, and (3) articulates the consequences of not addressing the issue. At the same time, this description should probably be no longer than a page or two if it is to attract the attention of and be useful to busy decision makers and opinion leaders.

The issue should be phrased as a question the organization can do something about, for several reasons. First, if there is nothing the organization can do about a situation, then there is no strategic issue, at least not for the organization. This apparent issue, in other words, is really a condition or constraint. Having said that, I must also point out that a strategic issue may exist when the organization is forced by circumstances into doing something, however symbolic or ineffective, about the condition (Edelman, 1977, 1988, 2001). Second, effective strategic planning has an action orientation. If strategic planning does not produce useful decisions and actions, then it probably was a waste of time—although it is not a waste of time to consider taking action in response to an issue and then to choose, based on careful analysis, not to act. Third, focusing on what the organization can do helps it attend to what it controls, instead of worrying pointlessly about what it does not control. Finally, organizations should focus their most precious resource—the attention of key decision makers—on issues they can do something about. Articulating strategic issues as challenges the organization can do something about, particularly when done on a regular basis, should help the organization strongly influence the way issues get framed and what might be done about them. In the vernacular, this will help the organization get out in front of the issues. An organization that waits until a crisis develops may find it very difficult to deal with that crisis with wise strategies (Heath, 1997). Strategic issues thus are typically not *current* problems or crises—although obviously there are almost always strategic implications in the ways current problems or crises are resolved and equally obviously decision makers *should* think strategically about how to address current problems and crises (Pearson and Clair, 1998). In any event, strategic issues are typically complex and potentially destructive if not satisfactorily resolved.

There are also several reasons why a strategic issue should be phrased as a challenge that has more than one solution. When a question has only one answer, it probably presents not an issue but a choice about whether to pursue a specific solution or not. In addition, when people are forced to frame issues in such a way that there might be more than one answer, they are less likely to confuse strategic issues with strategies and to consider innovative or even radical answers to those issues (Nadler and Hobino, 1998; Nutt, 2002). Innovative or radical answers may not always be chosen, but they almost always should be considered, because dramatic increases in key stakeholder satisfaction or public value creation may result.

Considering the factors that make an issue strategic is important both to clarify the issue and to establish the outlines of potential strategies to resolve the issue (Nutt and Backoff, 1992). Strategic issues arise in three kinds of situations. First, they can arise when events beyond the control of the organization make or will make it difficult or impossible to accomplish basic objectives acceptably and affordably. These situations would probably be called threats. Second, they can arise when technological, cost, financial, staffing, management, or political choices for achieving basic objectives are changing or will soon change. These situations might present either challenges or opportunities. Lastly, they arise when changes in mission, mandates, or internal or external factors suggest present or future opportunities to (1) make significant improvements in the quantity or quality of products or services delivered; (2) achieve significant reductions in the cost of providing products or services; (3) introduce new products or services; (4) combine, reduce, or eliminate certain products or services; or (5) otherwise create more public value. Unless the context surrounding the issue is understood clearly, it is unlikely key decision makers will be able to act wisely in that context, which they must do to improve the chances for successful issue resolution (Neustadt and May, 1986; Janis, 1989; Nadler and Hobino, 1998, pp. 107–126; Crosby and Bryson, forthcoming).

Finally, there should be a statement of the consequences of failure to address the issue. These consequences may be either exposure to serious threats or failure to capitalize on significant opportunities. If there are no positive or negative consequences, then the issue is not an issue. The issue may be interesting in an academic sense, but it does not involve an important or fundamental challenge for the organization. Again, the resource in shortest supply is the attention of key decision makers, so they should focus on issues that are most consequential for the organization.

Once a list of strategic issues has been prepared, the team can figure out just how strategic each issue is. Two methods for doing so, a litmus test and an issue-precedence diagram, are covered later in the process guidelines.

Seven Approaches to Strategic Issue Identification

At least seven approaches to the identification of strategic issues are possible: the direct approach, the goals approach, the vision of success approach, the indirect approach, the oval mapping approach (Eden and Ackermann, 1998; Bryson, Ackermann, Eden, and Finn, 2004), the issue tensions approach (Nutt and Backoff, 1992), and the systems analysis approach (Senge, 1990). Which approach is best depends on the nature of the broader environment and the organization's or community's characteristics. Guidelines for using the seven approaches are presented in this section; guidelines for the whole strategic issue identification step are presented in the following section.

The *direct approach* is probably the most useful to most governments and nonprofit organizations. Using this approach planners go straight from a review of mandates, mission, and SWOCs to the identification of strategic issues. The direct approach is best when (1) there is no agreement on goals, or the goals on which there is agreement are too abstract to be useful; (2) there is no preexisting vision of success, and developing a consensual vision will be difficult; (3) there is no hierarchical authority that can impose goals on the other stakeholders; or (4) the environment is so turbulent that development of goals or a vision seems unwise, and partial actions in response to immediate, important issues seem most appropriate. The direct approach, in other words, can work in the pluralistic, partisan, politicized, and relatively fragmented worlds of most public (and many nonprofit) organizations, as long as there is a *dominant coalition* (Thompson, 1967) strong enough and interested enough to make it work. That is, there must be a coalition committed to the identification and resolution of at least some of the key strategic issues faced by the organization, even if coalition members are not committed to the development of a comprehensive set of goals or a vision of success (Bolman and Deal, 2003, pp. 181–238).

In the *goals approach*—which is more in keeping with traditional planning theory—an organization first establishes goals and objectives for itself and then goes on to identify issues that need to be addressed to achieve those goals and objectives or else goes straight to developing strategies. Increasingly these goals and objectives are likely to be embedded in a balanced scorecard from a prior round of strategic planning; the issues concern how best to achieve what is in the scorecard. For this approach to work, fairly broad and deep agreement on the organization's goals and objectives must be possible, and the goals and objectives themselves must be specific and detailed enough to provide useful guidance for developing issues and strategies (but not so specific and detailed that they filter out wise strategic thought, action, and learning). This approach is likely to work best in organizations with hierarchical authority structures, in which key decision makers can impose goals on others affected by the planning exercise and in which there is not much divergence between the organization's *official goals* and its *operative goals* (Rainey, 1997, p. 127). Finally, externally imposed mandates may embody goals that can drive the identification of strategic issues or development of strategies. This approach, in other words, is more likely to work in public or nonprofit organizations that are hierarchically organized, pursue narrowly defined missions, and have few powerful stakeholders (Bolman and Deal, 2003, pp. 41–67). In contrast, organizations with broad agendas and numerous powerful stakeholders are less likely to achieve the kind of consensus (forced or otherwise) necessary to use the goals approach effectively—although they may achieve it in specific areas as a result of political appointments, elections, referenda, or other externally imposed goals or mandates. Similarly, this approach is likely to work for communities that are relatively homogeneous and have a basic consensus on values but is unlikely to work well for heterogeneous communities or those without agreement on basic values, unless extraordinary efforts are put into developing a genuine consensus on goals (Chrislip, 2002; Wheeland, 2003).

In the *vision of success* approach organizational members are asked to develop a "best" picture of the organization in the future, as it fulfills its mission and achieves success. The issues then ask how the organization should move from the way it is now to the way it might look and behave having realized its vision of success. The vision of success developed in this step will be sketchier than the more elaborate version called for in step 8 of the strategic planning process. All that is needed in the present step is a relatively short, idealized depiction of the organization in the future (Angelica, 2001). The vision of success approach is most useful when it is particularly important to take a holistic approach to the organization and its strategies—that is, when integration across a variety of organizational boundaries, levels, or functions is necessary (Kotter, 1996; Barzelay and Campbell, 2003; Bolman and Deal, 2003, pp. 214–286). As conception precedes perception (Weick, 1995), development of a vision of success can provide the concepts necessary in times of major change to enable organizational members to see what changes are necessary (Mintzberg and Westley, 1992; Morgan, 1998). Finally, many people understand the utility of beginning with a sense of vision. When enough key actors agree on this utility, it may be the best approach and may lead to truly integrated strategies, assuming the actors are able to agree on a vision. This approach is more likely to apply to nonprofit organizations than to public organizations, as public organizations are usually more tightly constrained by mandates and the conflicting expectations of numerous stakeholders. Public organizations will find this approach useful, however, when new leaders who have been elected or appointed due at least in part to their vision for the future take charge. This approach may also work for communities that are reasonably homogeneous, share an underlying value consensus, or are willing to take the time to develop a consensus (Chrislip, 2002; Wheeland, 2003).

The *indirect approach,* as its name implies, is a more indirect way to identify strategic issues than the direct approach. It works in the same situations as the direct approach and is generally as useful. In addition this approach is particularly useful when major strategic redirection is necessary but many members of the planning team and organization have not yet grasped the need for it or cannot sense where the changes might lead. This method starts with participants' existing system of ideas and helps them elaborate on the action implications of those ideas and then recombine the ideas in new ways, so that they *socially construct* (Berger and Luckmann, 1967) a new reality, one that allows them to convince themselves of the need for change (Kelly, 1963; Bryson, Ackermann, Eden, and Finn, 2004). Participation in this process of social reconstruction is a means of producing the commitment necessary to pursue new directions (Bolman and Deal, 2003, pp. 111–159). In other words, participants' own ideas, when recombined in new ways, help them see things differently and act accordingly. Innovation thus is more a consequence of recombination than of mutation (Kingdon, 1995). When using this approach, the planning team develops several sets of options, merges the sets, then sorts the combined sets into clusters of options having similar themes, using the snow card process (discussed in Chapter Five) or the oval mapping process (described in Resource B). Each cluster's theme represents a potential strategic issue. The sets consist of options to (1) make or keep stakeholders happy according to their criteria for satisfaction; (2) build on strengths, take advantage of opportunities, and minimize or overcome weaknesses and challenges; (3) fulfill the mission and mandates and in general create public value; (4) capture existing goals, strategic thrusts, and details; and (5) articulate actions stated or suggested in other relevant background studies.

The *oval mapping* approach involves creation of word-and-arrow diagrams in which statements about potential actions the organization might take, how these actions might be taken, and why are linked by arrows indicating the cause and effect or influence relationships between them. In other words the arrows indicate that action A may cause or influence B, which may in turn cause or influence C, and so on; if the organization does A, it can expect to produce outcome B, which may in turn be expected to produce outcome C. These maps can consist of hundreds of interconnected relationships, showing differing areas of interest and their relationships to one another. Important clusters of potential actions may constitute strategic issues. A strategy in response to an issue would consist of the specific choices of actions to undertake in the issue area, how to undertake them, and why (Eden and Ackermann, 1998; Bryson, Ackermann, Eden, and Finn, 2004; Ackermann, Eden, and Brown, 2004). This approach is particularly useful when participants are having trouble making sense of complex issue areas, time is short, the emphasis must be on action, and commitment on the part of those involved is particularly important. Participants simply brainstorm possible actions, cluster them according to similar themes, and then figure out what causes what. The result is an issue map (see Figure 6.1 later in this chapter). This process of producing word-and-arrow diagrams may also be called *causal mapping*, and it can be used in tandem with the other approaches to indicate whatever logic is being followed.

The *issue tensions* approach was developed by Nutt and Backoff (1992, 1993) and elaborated by Nutt, Backoff, and Hogan (2000). These authors argue that there are always four basic tensions around any strategic issue. These tensions involve human resources (especially *equity* concerns), *innovation and change*, maintenance of *tradition*, and *productivity improvement*, and their various combinations. These authors suggest critiquing the way issues are framed, using these tensions separately and in combination in order to find the best way to frame the issue. The critiques may need to run through several cycles before the wisest way to frame the issue is found. The tensions approach may be used by itself or in conjunction with any of the other approaches. Taking the extra time to critique an issue statement using the tensions approach is advisable when the costs of getting the issue framing wrong are quite high or when there is a lot of uncertainty about what the issue actually is.

Finally, *systems analysis* can be used to discern the best way to frame issues when the issue area can be conceptualized as a system (and issue areas almost always can be) and when the system contains complex feedback effects that must be modeled in order to understand the system (Senge, 1990; Sterman, 2000). Systems analysis can vary in how formal it is and whether or not it requires computer support. Many systems do not require formal modeling in order to be understood (Oshry, 1996), but others do, and it can be dangerous to act on these more complex systems without adequately appreciating what the system is and how it behaves. The more complicated the system, the more difficult it is to model and the more expert help will be needed. But there are limits to systems analysis, because there are systems no one can understand given current methodologies. Considerable wisdom is required to know when it is worth attempting sophisticated analyses, which analysts to use, and how to interpret and make use of the results.

Direct Approach

The following guidelines may prove helpful to organizations that use the direct approach.

After a review of mandates, mission, and SWOCs, strategic planning team members should be asked to identify strategic issues on their own. For each issue, each member should answer these three questions on a single sheet of paper (sample worksheets can be found in the workbook for this book, Bryson and Alston, 2004):

- What is the issue?
- What factors (mandates, mission, external and internal influences) make it a strategic issue?
- What are the consequences of failure to address the issue?

It may be best to give individuals at least a week to propose strategic issues. The identification of strategic issues is a real art and cannot be forced. People may need time to reflect on what the strategic issues really are. Also, individuals' best insights often come unpredictably, at odd moments, and outside of group settings (Isenberg, 1984; Mintzberg, Ahlstrand, and Lampel, 1998). (For example, many ideas for this book came to me while I was taking long runs.)

Each of the suggested strategic issues—phrased as a question about something the organization can do something about—should then be placed on a separate sheet of flipchart paper and posted on a wall so that members of the strategic planning team can consider and discuss them as a set. The sheets may be treated as giant snow cards, with similar issues grouped together or perhaps recast into a different form on blank sheets held in reserve for that purpose. Alternatively, ask planning team members to individually brainstorm as many strategic issues as they can—answering only the first question (What is the issue?) on individual worksheets. Then have each participant place a checkmark next to the five (or six or seven) most important issues on his or her individual list. These items are then transferred to snow cards and clustered into issue categories. The group (or subgroups) can then answer all three questions in relation to each cluster.

Whichever method is used, it is usually helpful to clarify the group's opinion about the most important issues for the short term and for the long term. I usually use colored stick-on dots for this purpose. I ask each person to place an orange dot on each of the five issues he or she thinks are the most important in the short term and a blue dot on each of the five issues most important in the long term. (The same issue can be important in both the short and the long term.) The pattern of dots will indicate where the majority opinion lies, if any exists. As with any judgmental exercise, it is usually best to have people make their individual judgments and record them on a piece of scratch paper before they publicly express their views (by placing colored dots, for example). After individuals have expressed their views, a group discussion should ensue, followed by additional individual "voting" (using the dots) if it appears people have changed their minds. A more reasoned group judgment is likely to emerge via this procedure (Delbecq, Van de Ven, and Gustafson, 1975).

When at least tentative agreement is reached on the list of strategic issues, prepare new single sheets of paper that present each issue and answer the three questions. These new sheets will provide the basis for further discussion if necessary or for the development of strategies to resolve the issues in the next step.

The Project for Pride in Living (PPL) planning team used the direct approach to identify four strategic issues over the course of several meetings. The planning team first came up with eleven possible issues, which it then winnowed down to five. After extensive explanations and discussions of the five issues at meetings of the divisions, division managers, and planning and development committee of the board, the final list consisted of the following four issues:

- How should PPL define, measure, and demonstrate its effectiveness in helping people progress toward self-sufficiency?
- How should PPL continue to be a dynamic organization?
- What should PPL's role be in the larger community—city, metropolitan area, state, and nation?
- How should we make PPL sustainable, with capacity to grow, over the next five years?

One issue that had to be dealt with before the list could be finalized was what to do with ongoing divisional planning and management efforts. PPL planners had to assure division managers that existing divisional strategies that were working well would be included in the plan—that is, there would be a "maintain and improve" agenda and not just "new" and "stop" agendas, in the plan—and that their existing planning efforts would be taken into account.

Goals Approach

The following guidelines are for organizations that choose the goals approach.

The goals approach begins with a compilation, review, and update of existing organizational goals or desired outcomes. These goals may be found in a variety of places: for example, prior strategic plans, functional area plans, key performance indicators, balanced scorecards, or mandated outcomes. Remember, however, that there may be a divergence between an organization's official goals and its operative goals.

If the organization does not have a current set of goals, then, after a review of mandates, mission, and SWOCs, members of the strategic planning team should be asked to propose goals for the organization as a basis for group discussion. Again, the snow card procedure is an effective and quick way to develop and organize a set of possible goals as a basis for further group discussion. More than one session may be necessary before the group can agree on goals that are specific and detailed enough to guide the development of strategies to achieve the goals in the next step.

It may not be necessary to identify strategic issues when this approach is used; the team may be able to move directly to the strategy development step. If strategic issues are identified, team members are likely to pose such questions as these: How do we gain the agreement of key decision makers on this set of goals? How do we establish priorities among these goals? And what are the best strategies for achieving the goals?

An alternative way to identify a set of goals for the organization is to assign one or more members of the strategic planning team the task of reviewing past decisions and actions to uncover the organization's implicit goals. (This activity can also be usefully undertaken as part of the previous step, internal assessment.) This approach can uncover the existing consensus about the organization's goals. It also can uncover any divergences between this consensus and the organization's mandates, mission, and SWOCs. Dealing with the divergences may represent strategic issues for the organization.

Whichever approach to the development of goals is used, specific objectives will be developed in the next step, strategy development. Strategies are developed to achieve goals; objectives (as opposed to goals) should be thought of as specific milestones or targets to be reached during strategy implementation.

Vision of Success Approach

New boards or elected or appointed officials may arrive with a vision already worked out. Their main task often will involve selling this vision and incorporating any useful modifications that are suggested (Kotter, 1996). Other organizations, those wanting to develop a vision of success from scratch, may wish to keep in mind the following guidelines.

After a review of mandates, mission, and SWOCs, each member of the strategic planning team should be asked to develop his or her own picture or scenario of what the organization should look like as it successfully meets its mandates, fulfills its mission, creates public value, and in general achieves its full potential. These individual visions should be no more than one page long and might be developed in response to the following instructions: "Imagine that it is three to five years from now and your organization has been put together in a very exciting way. It is a recognized leader in its field. Imagine that you are a newspaper reporter assigned to do a story on the organization. You have thoroughly reviewed the organization's mandates, mission, services, personnel, financing, organization, management, and so on. Describe in no more than a page what you see" (adapted from Barry, 1997, p. 56; Angelica, 2001).

The members of the strategic planning team should then share their visions with one another. A facilitator can record the elements of each person's vision on large sheets. Either during or after the sharing process, similarities and differences should be noted and discussed. Basic alternative visions then should be formulated (perhaps by a staff member after the session) to serve as a starting point for further discussion.

At a subsequent session, planning team members should rate each alternative vision or scenario along several dimensions deemed to be of strategic importance (such as ability to create public value, fit with mandates and mission, degree of stakeholder support, SWOCs, and financial feasibility) and should develop a list of the relative advantages and disadvantages of each vision. The team may also wish to consult internal and external advisers, critics, and possible partners to gain their insights and opinions. Discussion should follow to decide which vision is best for the organization.

An alternative approach involves asking team members to develop two lists: what the organization is moving *from* (both good and bad) and what it is moving *toward* (both good and bad) (Nutt and Backoff, 1992, pp. 168–177). This approach involves capturing the essence of the organization's past and present and then projecting what it might be into the future. The good and bad aspects inherent in future possibilities can be used to formulate best- and worst-case scenarios. A subsequent sketch of an organizational vision of success highlights what is good that the organization wants to move toward and takes account of what is bad that the organization wants to avoid.

Once key decision makers agree on the best vision, the strategic planning team may be able to move on to the next step, developing strategies to achieve the vision. A major, 3,000-member downtown church in Minneapolis pursued the vision of success approach. Its strategic planning team constructed visions to guide subsequent strategy development in areas covered by its mission statement and other areas where new strategies were clearly needed. These areas included

- Worship
- Nurture (Christian education for member families and their children)
- Global outreach (education and action abroad)
- Local outreach (local social service and community action)
- Children and youth (bringing member youth more into the life of the church and doing more for youth who are not members)

- Ministry of caring (mutual support and comfort for those in need)
- Evangelism (faith sharing and development)
- Stewardship (resource development)
- Communication with the public (radio and television broadcasts of services, public forums on timely issues)
- Facilities (redoing the sanctuary, building entrances, and education and outreach facilities)

Goals, strategies, and action steps were then formulated in each of these vision areas.

The visions developed with this approach may constitute a *grand strategy* for the organization, its overall scheme for how best to fit with its environment. The strategy development step then will concentrate on filling in the detail for putting the grand strategy into operation.

The strategic planning team may decide to identify strategic issues first, however, before developing more detailed strategies for implementation. These strategic issues typically concern how to gain broad acceptance of the vision and how to bridge the gap between the vision and where the organization is at present. It is important not to spend so much time and energy on visioning that not enough time and energy are left for developing detailed strategies, implementation guidance, and vehicles for implementation. (For a discussion of the possibility that Atlanta made this mistake in its Vision Atlanta process of the late 1990s, see Helling, 1998.)

Indirect Approach

The following guidelines may help organizations identify strategic issues using the indirect approach.

Planning team members should systematically review the organization's current mission, the summary statement of its mandates, the results of the stakeholder and SWOC analyses, any statements of present goals and strategies, and any other pertinent background studies or discussions and then brainstorm sets of possible options for organizational action. Each option should be phrased in action terms—that is, it should start with an imperative (*get, acquire, create, develop, achieve, show, communicate,* and so on). Each then should be placed on a separate snow card or oval (see Resource B). The following option sets should be created:

- Options to keep stakeholders happy where they are happy or to make them happy where they are not. (Obviously, the organization may not wish to make some stakeholders happy. For example, police forces are not likely to pursue options that will make drug dealers happy by relaxing law enforcement efforts. However, police forces might collaborate with economic development agencies, for example, to find alternative employment for drug dealers.)

- Options that enhance strengths, take advantage of opportunities, and minimize or overcome weaknesses and challenges.
- Options that are tied directly to fulfilling the organization's mission, meeting its mandates, and creating public value.
- Options that articulate the goals, thrust, and key details of current organizational strategies.
- Options that are identified or suggested by any other pertinent background studies or discussions.

The source of each option (stakeholder or SWOC analysis, mission or mandates, existing goals and strategies, or background reports or discussions) should be indicated in small print somewhere on the snow card or oval. Knowing the source can help participants assess the potential importance of options.

Once the option sets have been assembled they should be mixed and regrouped by team members into clusters that share similar themes. The theme of each grouping represents a candidate strategic issue. The oval mapping process can also be used to structure the clusters further by showing interrelationships among clusters and the various options that constitute them (see Resource B).

When suitable categories have been identified and key interrelationships noted, the team should develop one-page descriptions of the strategic issues, answering the three questions discussed earlier. The process of noting the source of each option will help the team answer the second question, about relevant situational factors, and the third question, about the consequences of not addressing the issue.

Oval Mapping Approach

People interested in the oval mapping approach will find detailed process guidelines in Resource B.

The School District used oval mapping to identify a number of goals and the strategic issues tied to achieving them. (The School District's use of oval mapping thus is related to the goals approach discussed earlier.) The potential goals and issues came from a composite map created from twenty-two separate maps. Each of the school board members, selected administrators, and a variety of stakeholder groups were mapped in detail, and these separate maps were merged to create the composite map. This map displayed 1,330 ideas and 2,050 links between ideas. This broadly based process enabled process participants to develop a deep understanding of and commitment to the final list of goals and strategic issues.

After reviewing and discussing the map, the board identified a draft mission statement ("Educating for success in our diverse and changing world") and five "strategic goals" phrased as desired outcome statements:

- Our educational environment supports all learners including students, staff, and parents.
- Our learners are becoming confident, ethical, self-directed learners.
- Our learners are prepared to become successful citizens in a democratic society.
- Our financial resources effectively support the educational program.
- Our district and community strongly support each other.

The board also noted other goals that supported each of these five, including effective technology support, communication, professional development, and measurability and assessment.

The board and superintendent then created five task forces to look at how best to achieve the goals. The task force names captured the categories of the very specific issues the task forces were charged to address. In other words, the names reflected the questions that the task forces were asked to answer:

1. What We Teach and What We Do. (*Strategic issue area:* What should we teach and how should we do it?)
2. Environment and Climate. (*Strategic issue area:* How do we make a difference in the environment and climate so that students learn to their optimum ability, teachers teach to their optimum ability, and all staff are able to grow personally and professionally?)
3. How We Learn, Teach and Work. (*Strategic issue area:* How should we teach, learn, and work?)
4. Finance. (*Strategic issue area:* How can we make sure we have strong finances and the resources we need?)
5. Communication and Community Support. (*Strategic issue area:* How can we have effective communications and build strong community support?)

Issue Tensions Approach

The following guidelines will help those who wish to explore the tensions surrounding an issue.

The tensions approach begins much like the direct approach. After a review of mission, mandates, and SWOCs, planning team members are encouraged to put forward statements of potential strategic issues. Each statement is then categorized according to whether it is essentially a question of human resources (especially equity concerns), innovation and change, maintenance of tradition, or productivity improvement. After the initial categorization, the statements are explored further to draw out any other tensions that might be involved. So, for example, an issue that concerns executive pay (human resources) may also be explored in relation to each of the other tensions: the need to foster innovation and change, the need to maintain a culture and tradition, and the need to achieve productivity improvement. Drawing out these other aspects of the issue may allow for the kind of reframing often necessary to find constructive strategies (Nutt and Backoff, 1992; Bolman and Deal, 2003, pp. 303–333). The critiques may need to run through several cycles before the wisest way to frame the issue is found. The tensions approach can be used in tandem with any of the other approaches to gain additional insight. For example, the tensions related to goals, visions, clusters of actions, or system models may be explored.

Systems Analysis Approach

Modeling a system of any complexity takes considerable skill (Sterman, 2000); therefore skilled help and facilitation should be sought if it appears that a system model will be necessary. Modeling is often done in a conference setting in order to elicit all the needed information and to build participants' understanding of and commitment to the resulting model. Andersen and Richardson (1997) offer detailed guidance, in the form of what they call *scripts*, for building a model directly with a planning team. Their approach includes the following steps:

1. Plan for the modeling conference. This involves setting goals for the conference and managing the scope of the work, dealing with the logistics, and designing and making use of the appropriate groups for specific tasks.
2. Schedule the day. This includes planning to follow a variety of guidelines, such as starting and ending with a bang, clarifying expectations and products, mixing kinds of tasks and providing frequent breaks, striving for visual consistency and simplicity in model representations, and reflecting frequently on the model as it develops.
3. Follow specific scripts for specific tasks. Andersen and Richardson have developed scripts for defining problems, conceptualizing model structure, eliciting feedback structure, supporting equation writing and parameter setting for quantified models, and developing policy.

It should be noted that these seven approaches to the identification of strategic issues are interrelated (a point that will be brought out again in discussing strategy development). It is a matter of where you choose to start. For example, an organization may frame strategic issues directly, indirectly, or through oval mapping and then in the next step can develop goals and objectives for the strategies developed to deal with the issues. Mission, strategies, goals, and objectives can then be used to develop a vision of success in step 8 in the process. Alternatively, an organization may go through several cycles of strategic planning using the direct or goals approaches before it decides to develop a vision of success. Or the organization may start with the ideal scenario approach in the present step of the process and then expand the scenario into a vision of success after it completes the strategy development step. Particular issue areas may require system modeling in order to be understood well enough for effective strategy development. At various points along the way the organization may explore issues, goals, visions, or system models further through using the tensions framework.

Finally, the planning team may use more than one approach as part of the same strategic planning effort. The differing conditions surrounding different issue areas may prompt the use of multiple approaches to the identification of strategic issues. Where useful goals or visions are already developed, they may be used to help formulate issues. Where they are not available, efforts to develop them or to use the direct or indirect approaches should be considered. Whenever sophisticated analyses are needed, they should be undertaken.

Process Guidelines

The following process guidelines should prove helpful as the strategic planning team identifies the strategic issues its organization faces:

1. *Review the organization's (or community's) mandates, mission, strengths, weaknesses, opportunities, and challenges, including any key indicators the organization watches—or should watch.*

2. *Select an approach to strategic issue identification that fits the organization's situation: direct, goals, vision of success, indirect, oval mapping, tensions, or systems analysis.* Whichever approach is used, prepare one-page descriptions of the resulting strategic issues that (a) phrase the issue as a question the organization can do something about; (b) clarify what it is about the mission, mandates, and internal and external factors that makes it an issue; and (c) outline the consequences of failure to address the issue. In the process of identifying and articulating issues, do not be surprised if (a) the mission itself is an issue, (b) you need to do issue-specific SWOC analyses in order to appropriately understand and frame the issues, and (c) the issues go through considerable reframing as the consequences of one framing versus another become clear. Also, no matter which approach is chosen, do not be surprised

if issues arise involving misalignment between or across the organization's mission, goals, strategies, staffing, technology, resources, and so on. Organizations are chronically out of alignment, and issues can be expected to arise at points of mismatch (Schön, 1971). For example, the School District created five task forces to address the strategic issues that arose in its process. The charge to each task force began with this observation: "We know a lot about how staff and students learn best, how teachers can teach best, and how best to involve parents and others who care about education in our community. And we are not organized that way!" The phenomenon of misalignment is so common that Barry (1997, pp. 59–60) advises searching for misalignments as a key approach to identifying strategic issues. I do not advise that in this step of the process (that is, I do not suggest an eighth approach to identifying strategic issues). In my experience, misalignments are more likely to be operational issues than strategic issues. Nevertheless, serious misalignments may certainly emerge as strategic issues, and planning team members should be alert to that possibility. And I do advise searching for misalignments in step 6 (strategy formulation), step 9 (implementation), and step 10 (strategy and planning process reassessment). There is almost always a need to work on appropriate alignments in those steps.

3. *Once a list of issues has been prepared, try to separate them into strategic and operational issues.* Operational issues should be assigned to an operations group, team, or task force. If an appropriate group does not exist, it should be created.

4. *If it would be helpful, use a litmus test to develop some measure of just how "strategic" an issue is.* One litmus test that might be used to screen strategic issues is presented in Exhibit 6.1. A truly strategic issue is one that scores high on all dimensions. A strictly operational issue would score low on all dimensions.

5. *Once strategic issues have been identified, arrange them in a priority, logical, or temporal order, as a prelude to strategy development.* The attention of key decision makers is probably the resource in shortest supply in most organizations, so it is very important to focus that attention effectively and efficiently. Establishing a reasonable order, or agenda, among strategic issues allows key decision makers to focus on them one at a time. (It must be recognized, however, that the issues may be so interconnected that they have to be dealt with as a set.) An effective tool for figuring out a useful issue order is an issue-precedence diagram (Nutt and Backoff, 1992), which uses arrows to indicate the influence relationships among the issues (which makes these diagrams a kind of oval map; see Resource B).

Figure 6.1 presents an issue-precedence diagram of the strategic issues facing the U.S. province of a Roman Catholic religious order. The order's members are priests and brothers who live in religious communities and work with low-income people and communities. The order employs many laypeople to teach in its

EXHIBIT 6.1. LITMUS TEST FOR STRATEGIC ISSUES.

Issue: _____ Issue is: ☐ **Primarily operational** ☐ **Primarily strategic**

	Operational ⟵		⟶ Strategic
1. Is this issue on the agenda of the organization's policy board (whether elected or appointed)?	No		Yes
2. Is this issue on the agenda of the organization's chief executive (whether elected or appointed)?	No		Yes
3. When will this issue's challenge or opportunity confront the organization?	Right now	Next year	2 or more years from now
4. How broad an impact will this issue have?	Single unit or division		Entire organization
5. How large is the organization's financial risk or opportunity?	Minor (≤10% of budget)	Moderate (10–15% of budget)	Major (≥25% of budget)
6. Will strategies for issue resolution likely require:			
a. Change in mission?	No		Yes
b. Development of new service goals and programs?	No		Yes
c. Significant changes in revenue sources or amounts?	No		Yes
d. Significant amendments in federal or state statutes or regulations?	No		Yes
e. Major staff, technology, or facility changes?	No		Yes
7. How apparent is the best approach for issue resolution?	Obvious, ready to implement	Broad parameters, few details	Wide open
8. What is the lowest level of management that can decide how to deal with this issue?	Line staff supervisor		Head of major department

EXHIBIT 6.1. LITMUS TEST FOR STRATEGIC ISSUES, CONT'D.

Issue: _____   Issue is: ☐ **Primarily operational**   ☐ **Primarily strategic**

	Operational	← — — — — →	Strategic
9. What are the probable consequences of not addressing this issue?	Inconvenience, inefficiency	Significant service disruption, financial losses	Major long-term service disruption and large cost or revenue setbacks
10. How many other groups are affected by this issue and must be involved in its resolution?	None	1 to 3	4 or more
11. How sensitive or "charged" is this issue relative to community, social, political, religious, and cultural values?	Benign	Touchy	Dynamite

Source: Adapted from a test in Hennepin County, 1983.

schools, work with target communities, produce publications, and assist with fundraising and management. The diagram indicates that in order to achieve more effective ministries, an issue closely linked with the order's mission, four additional issues must be dealt with first ("maintain or increase ministries"; clarify vision of success"; "maintain and improve income in the long run"; and "have satisfied, productive employees"). In order to maintain or increase ministries, the order will need to increase its membership ("increase vocations") and "maintain and improve income in the long run." In general, arrows leading *to* an issue indicate issues that must also be addressed if the focal issue is to be resolved. Arrows leading *from* an issue indicate potential consequences of having addressed the issue. Preparation of this diagram produced two crucial insights for the planning team members. First, they were able to see that the key to increasing vocations was the sequence of issues flowing into that issue: "improve community life" (key strategy options are indicated by the bullet points), "improve interpersonal relations," "improve attention to individual needs," "promote healthy lifestyles," and "improve governance and management processes and structures." It was this set of issues

FIGURE 6.1. ISSUE-PRECEDENCE DIAGRAM OF STRATEGIC ISSUES FACING A RELIGIOUS ORDER.

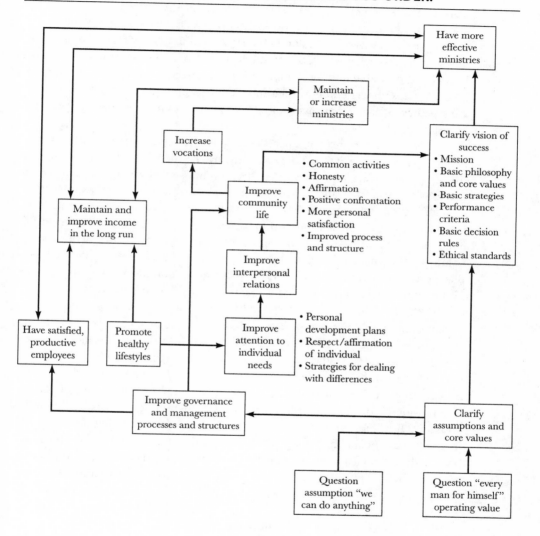

in particular, the set tied to the order's community life, that prompted members of the planning team to push for strategic planning in the first place. Second, the team was able to make the case to the members of the order who cared mainly about having more effective ministries and increased vocations that the best way to achieve these was to first address the issues tied to improving community life. The diagram thus helped all the members of the religious order understand the logical and probably temporal relationships among the issues, helped key stakeholder groups understand how their individual agendas might be served by working together on each other's issues, and helped the group decide what its priorities for attention should be.

Of course the strategic implications of an issue agenda should be considered carefully. For example, it may not be wise to have key decision makers focus first on the top priority issue, especially if key decision makers have had little prior interaction with each other and little experience with constructive conflict resolution. In such circumstances it may be best to start the process of resolving strategic issues by focusing on the least important issue, so decision makers can gain experience in dealing with one another and with conflict when the consequences of failure are the smallest. Planning team members should talk through the likely implications of different orders for the issue agenda before deciding on the appropriate sequence for action in the next step, strategy development.

6. *Remain aware that there is an art to framing strategic issues.* Considerable discussion and thoughtful revision of first drafts of strategic issues are likely to be necessary in order to frame issues in the most useful way. If the organization's mission is itself a strategic issue, the organization should expect to develop a second set of issues after the mission has been reexamined. Once the new or revised mission is in place, the "real" strategic issues can be identified. The importance of former vice president Hubert Humphrey's advice—"When in doubt, talk"—should be apparent. It is important to critique strategic issues to be sure that they really do usefully frame the fundamental policy questions the organization faces. The members of the strategic planning team should discuss several questions about the issues they have identified before they settle on a set of issues to address. Some useful questions include the following:

- What is the real issue, conflict, or dilemma?
- Why is it an issue? What is it about the organization's mission, mandates, or SWOCs that makes it an issue?
- Who says it is an issue?
- What would be the consequences of not doing something about it?
- Can the organization do something about it?
- Is there a way to combine or eliminate issues?

- Should an issue be broken down into two or more issues?
- What issues are missing from the list, including issues that the organization's culture might have kept us from recognizing?

It is especially important to remember that strategic issues framed in single-function terms will be dealt with by single-function departments or agencies. Strategic issues that are framed in multifunctional terms will have to be addressed by more than one department. And strategic issues that are framed in multiorganizational, multi-institutional terms will have to be addressed by more than one organization or institution. If one seeks to wrest control of an issue from a single department, then the issue must be framed multifunctionally. If one seeks to wrest control of an issue from a single organization, then it must be framed multiorganizationally. Strategic planners can gain enormous influence over the strategic planning process and its outcomes if the issues are framed in such a way that decision makers must share power in order to resolve the issues. Often, wresting control over the framing of the issue from the status quo ante is a crucial step in a move toward dramatic changes, or what will be called *big wins* in the next chapter (Schön, 1971; Baumgartner and Jones, 1993; Abramson and Lawrence, 2001; Barzelay and Campbell, 2003; Crosby and Bryson, forthcoming). The importance of this admonition is apparent when one examines organizations' efforts to engage in process improvement efforts, performance budgeting, or new uses of information technology. In my experience, organizations often get into such ventures without thinking through carefully why they wish to do so. This may be partly the result of particular professionals' championing causes that are the current fashion in their respective professions. Process improvement then gets assigned to a *quality czar* of some sort, performance budgeting to the budget director, and information technology improvement strategies to IT professionals. The reform agenda then becomes the captive of these particular units, and the organization-wide perspectives and goals are subverted. The means substitute for the ends and a kind of *goal displacement* occurs in which instrumental values become terminal values (Merton, 1940). Although the power of the subunits may be enhanced, organizational performance is less than it should be. The process improvement initiative ends up making continuous improvements in unwise strategies, budgets enhance performance in the wrong directions, and IT improvements are led by technology rather than by overarching organizational strategies. Convening forums in which the organization-wide perspective is developed is the best way to make sure the means serve the ends and not the reverse.

7. *Remember that different strategic issues will require different kinds of attention and treatment.* There are likely to be at least three kinds of issues here: (1) those that require no action at present but must be monitored, (2) those that can be handled as part

of the organization's regular strategic planning cycle, and (3) those that require urgent attention and must be dealt with out of sequence with the organization's regular strategic planning cycle.

8. *Focus on issues, not answers.* The answers will be developed in step 6, strategy formulation. They will be helpful only if they are developed in response to the issues that actually confront the organization. Put differently, an answer without an issue is not an answer. Keep in mind, however, that people can be counted on to put forward favored solutions, whether or not they have much to do with the real issues (Nutt, 1984; Neustadt and May, 1986). Planners can use this tendency to advantage by constantly asking team members what problems or issues their proposed solutions actually address. When this question is asked about several proposed solutions, a useful picture of what the real issues might be is likely to emerge (Eden and Sims, 1978; Nutt, 2002). Issues developed in this fashion have the advantage of emerging from what people actually can imagine doing and thus may seem more real to these individuals.

9. *Reach an agreement among key decision makers that a major fraction of their time together will be devoted to the identification and resolution of strategic issues.* Without an agreement of this sort, it will be too easy for key decision makers to forget when they get together that one of their most important tasks is to deal with what is most important to the organization. The decision-making bodies in all three organizations highlighted in this book made such a commitment: the School District's board and administrative cabinet, Project for Pride in Living's board and senior management team, and the Naval Security Group's cryptologic board of directors (CBOD), with support from the headquarters' department heads and the strategic planning department.

10. *Keep it light.* As noted at the beginning of this chapter, this step in the strategic planning process can quickly become very serious and heavy. It is important for members of the strategic planning team to keep their sense of humor, acknowledge emotions, and release tensions with good-humored mutual solicitude. Otherwise, destructive conflict or paralysis may set in, and they may find it difficult to agree on a set of strategic issues and move on to developing effective strategies to deal with these issues. Emotions may run high—or low in the case of depression and grief—and the group will have to acknowledge these emotions and deal with them constructively.

11. *Notwithstanding efforts to keep things light, remember that participants may fall into "the pit" or "hit the wall"* (Spencer and Adams, 1990). This wall often takes the form of a dilemma, vicious circle, or paradox that cannot be resolved (Senge, 1990; Hamden-Turner, 1990). For example, a public library with which I worked faced a vicious circle when its service culture collided with serious budget cuts. Existing

strategies had begun to fail because the system was at its limit and staff stress and burnout were reaching crisis proportions. Given their ethos, the librarians could not yet see what to do about it. They were all deeply committed to giving library patrons what they wanted—almost no matter what it took—but could not continue to do so without increased resources. The obvious need to narrow their role, set priorities among patrons, and adopt a more entrepreneurial and political mentality challenged their professional identities built up over many years. They felt themselves surrounded by a wall they did not know how to climb, skirt, tunnel under, or blow up. However, through lots of discussion, emotional venting, mutual support, and consideration of various options for addressing the issues, they did eventually figure out how to knock down the wall.

12. *Be aware that agreement on strategic issues to be addressed in the next step is likely to mark an important organizational decision point.* The identification of strategic issues is the heart of the planning process. Identifying the fundamental challenges the organization faces will have a profound effect on the actual choices made and ultimately on the viability and success of the organization.

13. *Manage the transition to strategy development.* This is crucial. Too often organizations move quickly to the identification of strategic issues and then back off from resolving those issues. The conflicts or choices embodied in the issues may seem too difficult or disruptive to address. Strong leadership and commitment to the strategic planning process must be exercised if the organization is to deal effectively with the basic issues it confronts.

Summary

The purpose of step 5 is to identify the fundamental challenges facing the organization concerning its mandates, mission and values, product or service level and mix, clients, users or payers, cost, financing, structure, processes, or management. At the end of this step key decision makers should agree on a strategic issue agenda—the set of strategic issues to be addressed, arranged in priority, logical, or temporal order. Effectively addressing the issues on this agenda should help the organization satisfy its key stakeholders and create real public value.

The seven approaches to identifying issues are the direct approach, the goals approach, the vision of success approach, the indirect approach, oval mapping approach, the tensions approach, and the systems analysis approach. In general, governments and nonprofit agencies will find the direct and oval mapping approaches most useful, but which approach to use depends on the situation at hand.

To return to the story metaphor, this step constitutes the framing of conflicts (issues). The climax of the story will be reached in the next two steps, when these conflicts are resolved through the construction and adoption of effective strategies. Fear, anxiety, guilt, dread, or grief relating to the ways these issues might be resolved can cause people to flee from strategic planning. Faith, hope, courage, and reasoned optimism typically are needed to press forward.

The transition to the next step in the process will require careful management. It is one thing to talk about what is fundamental, quite another to take action based on those discussions. Strong leadership, high morale, and a reasonable sense of psychological safety and optimism will all help the team and organization keep moving ahead. Unless the team and organization push on, organizational effectiveness and stakeholder satisfaction are likely to suffer, and the organization will not meet its mandates or fulfill its mission.

CHAPTER SEVEN

FORMULATING AND ADOPTING STRATEGIES AND PLANS TO MANAGE THE ISSUES

If you play with the fibers, they suggest possibilities.

ANNIE ALBERS

This chapter covers steps 6 and 7, formulating and adopting strategies and plans. Even though these two steps are likely to be closely linked in practice, they should be kept separate in planning team members' minds. Both concern creating ideas for strategic action and building a winning coalition (see Figure 2.4); however, the dynamics that surround each step may be dramatically different, especially when strategies must be adopted by elected or appointed policy boards. Strategy formulation often involves freewheeling creativity and the give and take of dialogue, whereas formal adoption of strategies and strategic plans can involve political intrigue, tough bargaining, public posturing, and high drama. The team should formulate strategies that can be adopted in politically acceptable, technically and administratively workable, results-oriented, and legally and morally defensible form.

Strategy may be thought of as a pattern of purposes, policies, programs, actions, decisions, and resource allocations that defines what an organization is, what it does, and why it does it. Strategy therefore is an extension of an organization's (or community's) mission, forming a bridge between the organization and its environment. Strategies typically are developed to deal with strategic issues: that is, they outline the organization's response to the fundamental challenges it faces. To continue the bridge metaphor, strategic issues show where bridges are needed, and strategies are the bridges. (When the goal approach to strategic issues has been taken, strategies are developed to achieve the goals; when the vision of success approach has been taken, strategies are developed to achieve the vision.) This definition of strategy is purposely very broad. It is important to recognize patterns that transcend organizational policies, decisions, resource allocations, and actions large and small. General strategies will fail if specific steps to implement them are absent. Further, strategies are prone to failure when there is no alignment or consistency among what an organization says, what it pays for, and what it does. The definition of strategy offered here—an arrangement to achieve the mission, meet the mandates, and create public value—calls attention to the importance of this alignment.

Effective strategies have effective linkages with the organization's environment, even when their purpose is to change that context. As noted in Chapter Five, the word *context* comes from the Latin for "weave together." The arrows in the strategic planning process outlined in Figure 2.1 may be thought of as the "threads" in a weaving, representing ideas about the organization's context and what might be done to respond effectively to it (Healey, 1997; Forester, 1999). Potentially useful patterns are suggested when you play with these threads, or fibers, as weaver Annie Albers proposes. The *art* of creating an effective response is also highlighted—as it should be because, in my experience, decision makers and strategic planning team members are often not creative enough in addressing strategic issues and crafting strategies (see also Mintzberg, 1987; Szulanski and Amin, 2001). The art, however, is typically not without anguish. As psychotherapist and theologian Thomas Moore (1992) observes: "Creative work can be exciting, inspiring, and godlike, but it is also quotidian, humdrum, and full of anxieties, frustrations, dead ends, mistakes, and failures" (p. 199). Rosabeth Moss Kanter (1983, 1989) goes further and asserts that basically every innovation is a failure in the middle of the change process introducing it. Innovations are failures in the middle because they *must* be. By definition, they have never been tried before (at least by the organization), and success can be determined only after they are implemented. Thus strategy is intentionally defined in a way broad enough to help ensure that strategic changes (a kind of innovation), though they may be failures initially, are successes in the end.

According to my definition every organization (or community) already *has* a strategy (or strategies). That is, every organization evidences some sort of pattern—or *logic in action* (Krogh and Roos, 1996; Millar, Simeone, and Carnevale, 2001; Poister, 2003)—across its purposes, policies, programs, actions, decisions, and resource allocations. The pattern is there—although it may not be a good one. It may need to be refined or sharpened or (less frequently) changed altogether before it can be an effective bridge between the organization and its environment. The task of strategy formulation typically involves highlighting what is good about the existing pattern, reframing or downplaying what is bad about it, and adding whatever new bits are needed to complete the picture (Mintzberg, 1987; Nutt,

Backoff, and Hogan, 2000). Culture becomes very important in strategy formulation, as whatever patterns exist are typically manifestations of the organization's culture, or cultures. This culture provides much of the glue that holds inputs, processes, and outputs together. It affects how strategic issues are framed and placed on the agenda in the first place and subsequently affects which strategy options are given serious consideration (Hampden-Turner, 1990; Schein, 1997; Khademian, 2002).

Put differently, every strategy is almost always both emergent *and* deliberate, although the balance between the two can vary a good deal (McCaskey, 1974; Mintzberg, Ahlstrand, and Lampel, 1998). The world of sports provides two useful examples of this both emergent and deliberate quality. Jean-Claude Killy of France, triple gold medal winner in alpine skiing at the 1968 Winter Olympics, was once asked why he drank wine for lunch. His reply: "What would you have me do—drink milk and ski like an American?" His unorthodox (some said wild) style of skiing revolutionized alpine ski racing. His style capitalized on his physique and psyche and, he said, was the only way he knew how to ski. In this sense his strategy was at first emergent and then became deliberate. It also became deliberate for the many racers who tried to imitate him. Francis "Fran" Tarkenton, former quarterback of the Minnesota Vikings and New York Giants, member of the National Football League Hall of Fame, and holder of several still unbroken NFL records, displayed a converse pattern. Tarkenton was known as a "scrambling" quarterback; he drove the defense crazy when he ran around in the open field, buying time until he could run or pass for a big gain. In describing his strategy as it moved from deliberate to emergent, he said, "Whenever things break down completely, I don't hesitate to roam out of the pocket and do the boogaloo."

Borins (1998), in a major study of 217 public sector innovations, explored whether each was more deliberate or more emergent. He found that politicians tended to be the initiators of innovations in times of crisis, agency heads were the initiators when they took over the reins or were overseeing an organizational change effort, and midlevel and frontline public servants were the initiators in response to internal problems or technological opportunities (pp. 48–49). But the extent to which these initiators' strategies involved deliberate comprehensive planning or emergent *groping along* (Behn, 1988) varied considerably. Formal planning was more likely when the changes involved responding to political mandates, making large capital investments, coordinating a large number of organizations, or making a well-developed theory operational. Groping (or trying lots of things and learning by doing) was more likely in the absence of large capital investments, when it was not necessary to coordinate several organizations, when there was no well-articulated theory, and when there was no political impetus. Overall, in Borins's sample, planning was more frequent than groping (pp. 64–65).

Recall also that most organizations' strategies remain fairly stable for long periods of time and then may change abruptly. Thus, most of the time, strategic planning will focus on adapting and programming strategies whose outlines are already reasonably clear (Mintzberg, Ahlstrand, and Lampel, 1998). At other times, though, strategic planning will be called on to assist with the formulation of new strategies to deal with new and different circumstances. Even in times of drastic change, however, an organization is unlikely to discontinue all of its existing strategies, so the task of blending the old with the new and the deliberate with the emergent still remains (Benner and Tushman, 2003). In effect, organizations are always called on to develop three agendas: what they will keep and improve, what they will initiate that is new, and what they will stop.

Strategies also can vary by level and time frame. Four basic levels of strategy are as follows:

1. Grand strategy for the organization as a whole
2. Subunit strategies (subunits may be divisions, departments, or units of larger organizations) (Montanari and Bracker, 1986)
3. Program, service, or business process strategies (Hammer and Champy, 1993; Cohen and Eimicke, 1998)
4. Functional strategies (such as financial, staffing, facilities, information technology, and procurement strategies)

Strategies may also be long term or short term.

Strategies are different from tactics. Tactics are the short-term, adaptive actions and reactions used to accomplish limited objectives. Strategies provide the "continuing basis for ordering these adaptations toward more broadly conceived purposes" (Quinn, 1980, p. 9). One needs to be cautious, however, about drawing a sharp distinction between the two, given the importance of changing environments and emergent strategies. As Mintzberg (1994, p. 243) observes, "The trouble with the strategy-tactics distinction is that one can never be sure which is which until all the dust has settled."

Purpose

The purpose of the strategy formulation and plan development step (step 6) is to create a set of strategies that will effectively link the organization (or community) to its environment and create public value. Typically these strategies will be developed in response to strategic issues, but they may also be developed to achieve goals or a vision of success. The purpose of the strategy and plan adoption step

(step 7) is to gain authoritative decisions to move ahead with implementing the strategies and plans.

A good example of formulated and adopted strategies is provided by the Amherst H. Wilder Foundation of St. Paul, Minnesota, a large, well-managed, highly effective, 100-year-old nonprofit operating foundation providing health, housing, education, employment, and social services in St. Paul (Bryson, 2003b). In addition, the foundation engages in a variety of partnership and advocacy efforts designed to change the institutional and policy environments affecting those most in need. As of the end of its 2003 fiscal year, the foundation had an endowment and assets worth over $226 million; spent over $58 million of income from grants, fees, trust earnings, and other sources; employed 799 people (including part-time employees); and through its 105 programs served almost 13,000 people, trained more than 28,000 persons, and provided services to 554 organizations. The foundation's four-page 2000 strategic plan outlines the organization's grand strategy through 2005 via a set of linked statements about mission, focus, vision, goals, roles, strategies, underlying principles, and internal priorities (Amherst H. Wilder Foundation, 2004). These elements are reproduced in Exhibit 7.1.

The plan begins with a very brief discussion of the strategic planning process. Approximately 500 stakeholders participated in the process, including community leaders, funders, program participants, and employees. The mission statement (Exhibit 4.4), adopted in 1974, is then presented. This statement indicates *why* the foundation exists and *what* its purpose is. Then comes the current *focus statement*. In the 1980s, the foundation's president and board of directors began the practice of clarifying the mission periodically by drafting a focus statement. The current focus statement (summarized under the "Focus" heading in Exhibit 7.1) indicates *with whom* the foundation will primarily work, *how* and *when* it will serve them, and *where* it will work. The plan also includes a vision statement that describes what a successful community would look like, as one way of articulating the foundation's roles and strategies for achieving its vision. Note that the vision is for the *community*, not for the organization. This is unusual in that visioning of this sort is more typical of governmental and community-based strategic planning. But it makes sense for a foundation that sees itself as a capacity builder and facilitator of change as well as a provider of direct service. The foundation realizes that the community's needs are so great that it cannot hope to meet them without the efforts of lots of other people and organizations, including the community as a whole and city, county, state, and federal governments. The foundation therefore finds that a vision of community success helps it figure out how best to achieve desirable outcomes in concert with other actors. The vision is not "owned" by Saint Paul's urban neighborhoods, which might be a problem except that it is hard to imagine these neighborhoods objecting to the components of this vision.

EXHIBIT 7.1. STRATEGIC PLAN FOR THE AMHERST H. WILDER FOUNDATION, 2000–2005.

Mission

Since 1906, the foundation has been committed "to relieve, aid and assist the poor, sick, and needy people of St. Paul . . . by all appropriate means . . . without regard to their nationality, place of residence, sex, color, or religious prejudices."

Focus

- Low-income people
- People who need support during critical times in their lives
- Saint Paul's urban neighborhoods

Vision

A vibrant Saint Paul where individuals, families, and communities can prosper, with opportunities for all to be employed, to be engaged citizens, to live in decent housing, to attend good schools, and to receive support during times of need

Goals

- **Healthy, resilient children, youth, and families** with strong school, neighborhood, and community support
- **Economic stability** for individuals and families through employment with strong support systems for the working poor in the areas of housing, transportation, child care, and health care
- **Successful aging in the community** through an array of affordable and flexible services and resources that sustain and enhance the quality of life for seniors
- **Vital neighborhoods and communities** in Saint Paul, with sufficient safe and affordable housing, excellent schools, opportunities for work and active citizen participation

Three Roles Wilder Will Use to Achieve Its Goals

- **Role 1: serve individuals.** Use Wilder's service delivery capabilities to address unmet needs and demonstrate approaches that work.
- **Major growth areas:** early intervention, school success, community-based youth development, low-income housing, and community services for the elderly
- **Role 2: serve organizations and groups.** Strengthen Wilder's supporting role by building the capacity of communities and organizations to meet needs, by disseminating information, and by linking public and private resources to community-based efforts.
- **Role 3: provide community leadership.** Leverage and integrate Wilder's direct services, research, and relationships to advance community improvement efforts and provide leadership in Saint Paul.

EXHIBIT 7.1. STRATEGIC PLAN FOR THE AMHERST H. WILDER FOUNDATION, 2000–2005, CONT'D.

Target issues: school success, severely troubled children and families, and housing

Wilder's Strategies

Goal 1 Healthy, Resilient Children, Youth, and Families	Goal 2 Economic Stability	Goal 3 Successful Aging in the Community	Goal 4 Vital Neighborhoods and Communities
1. Expand early intervention	5. Move people from welfare to work	9. Provide a broad, flexible, and accessible array of community-based support services	12. Build the capacity of key leaders, organizations, and coalitions
2. Increase school success	6. Address barriers to employment: housing, child care, health care, and transportation	10. Create partnerships that improve service access in neighborhoods	13. Increase private and public investment in neighborhood development
3. Provide community-based youth development efforts	7. Strengthen the financial position of the working poor	11. Mobilize community awareness and attention to aging issues	14. Reduce violence and bias in neighborhoods
4. Improve outcomes and accessibility to services for very troubled youth and their families	8. Improve the quality, quantity, and stability of low-income housing		

Principles

- **Healthy families and communities.** Wilder recognizes that children need strong families, that families benefit from a supportive community, and that healthy communities are the key to a livable city.

EXHIBIT 7.1. STRATEGIC PLAN FOR THE
AMHERST H. WILDER FOUNDATION, 2000–2005, CONT'D.   .

- **Strength-oriented practice.** Wilder helps individuals, families, organizations, and communities identify and use their strengths to meet current challenges.
- **Community engagement.** Wilder creates mechanisms that strengthen its connections and responsiveness to the communities it serves.
- **Cultural competency/equity.** Wilder develops services that are representative of, accessible to, and effective with cultural communities.
- **Partners.** Wilder seeks out, cultivates, and works with organizations that share the foundation's vision.
- **Life-span orientation.** Wilder supports the health and development of individuals throughout their life spans and fosters intergenerational ties and relationships.

Internal Priorities

Service Effectiveness and Service Accessibility	Human Resources	Financial Stability
Strengthen organization-wide approaches to managing, evaluating, and improving service effectiveness	Develop competitive and sustainable compensation and benefits programs	Strengthen the financial base of the foundation
Ensure that all Wilder Foundation programs measure outcomes, satisfaction, and accessibility	Recruit and retain a culturally diverse and culturally competent workforce	Use information systems and practices to improve organizational effectiveness and efficiency
Maximize use of foundation real estate and physical plant	Strengthen career and professional development opportunities	Understand, reflect, and recover the real cost of doing business
Strengthen administrative support systems for collaborative efforts	Develop and strengthen supervisory skills	Use endowment income strategically
Use marketing and communications strategies to increase our impact	Develop mechanisms to integrate effort across functions and departments on key strategic projects	

Source: Adapted from Amherst H. Wilder Foundation, 2000. Reprinted with permission.

The next major section in the plan outlines the foundation's four major goals and three basic roles in assisting individuals and communities. The roles include serving individuals, organizations and groups, and the community as a whole and providing community leadership. The Wilder Foundation sees that it must engage with other organizations and groups, indeed, must work to change important parts of the public policy environment if it is to maximize its impact. In other words, the foundation thinks about the complex systems that create problems for children, youth, families, and the elderly, and it seeks to intervene where it can to create systems that are more beneficial to the people, groups, and places it cares about. This focus on the system level in addition to the organizational level is unusual, special, and admirable—and represents an important way for public and nonprofit organizations to create additional public value in a complex, shared-power world in which most important public problems spill beyond any organization's boundaries (Peters, 1996). The Wilder Foundation's mission, vision, goals, and role statements essentially constitute the foundation's grand strategy. The next part of the plan presents the foundation's strategies, grouped according to the goals they serve. Then comes a series of principles the foundation thinks should be kept in mind as goals, strategies, and roles are pursued. Indeed, the foundation thinks the three roles and the principles should be reflected in all of its strategies. The plan closes with a set of internal priorities that emphasize enhancing service effectiveness and accessibility, investing in human resources, and ensuring financial stability and effectiveness.

A very different example of a grand strategy is presented by the *strategy map* drafted for Hennepin County, Minnesota (Hennepin County, 2004) (Figure 7.1). The map's design is similar to a balanced scorecard design. The map displays the priorities of the county's strategic leadership team, consisting of its most senior decision makers. The map starts with a statement of the county's vision, as adopted by the elected board of county commissioners. It then presents the county's key desired results, or outcomes, in the areas of mobility, health, self-reliance, protection and safety, and due process. These are the *above-the-line* indicators of well-being for the county as a community and place (as opposed to indicators that show how well the county government is doing its job as an organization). Achieving good results in these areas is the purpose of the strategies in the map, but the county government is only one player among many having a role to play in producing these key results. *Below the line* are the county's strategies to "improve outcomes for customers, consumers, clients and taxpayers." They include "ensure fair access to services," "improve the quality and value of service," and "inform and engage residents and communities." These three major strategies make up the *customer* category in most balanced scorecards. But note that in contrast to business-oriented balanced scorecards, the county is careful not to call

FIGURE 7.1. STRATEGY MAP FOR HENNEPIN COUNTY.

Hennepin County Vision

We envision a future where residents are healthy and successful and where our communities are safe and vibrant. We will strive to meet and exceed expectations by engaging people and communities in developing innovative solutions to challenges. We will be a diverse learning organization. We will partner with others to enhance the quality of life in Hennepin County and the region. This vision provides the foundation for Hennepin County's strategies to create change.

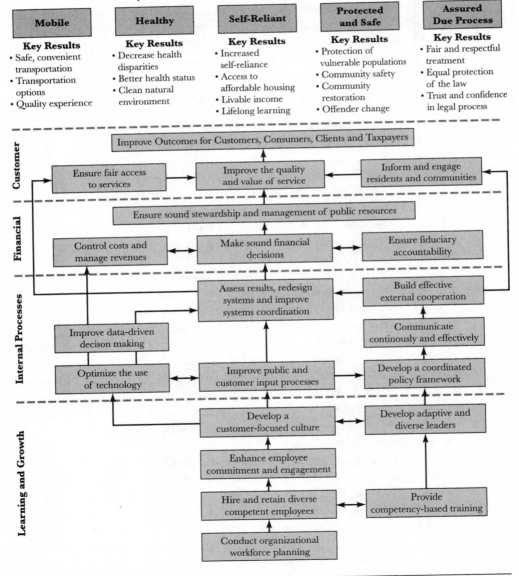

everyone a customer; instead the county recognizes different categories of key stakeholders. After the strategies for achieving key customer outcomes come the financial strategies, internal process strategies, and learning and growth strategies that can also help the county to achieve the desired results. Arrows link the strategies, indicating how one strategy relates to another, in much the way that an oval map or an issue-precedence diagram displays relationships. Thus "ensure sound stewardship and management of financial resources" (a financial strategy) depends on the county's ability to "make sound financial decisions" (another financial strategy). Similarly, the county needs to "develop a coordinated policy framework" (an internal process strategy). In order to do that, it will need to "improve public and customer input processes" (another internal process strategy), and in order to do that it will need to "develop a customer-focused culture" (a learning and growth strategy). It will also need to "develop adaptive and diverse leaders" (another learning and growth strategy). The map encapsulates a great deal of strategic thinking and conversation among key decision makers and presents it in a graphic and relatively easily understandable way—which is a very good thing for a county government that in 2004 had 11,000 employees, a budget of $1.65 billion, and served a population of over 1.1 million people. The county has also developed indicators for each of the key results above the line and high-level performance measures for each strategy area below the line. The map is thus more than a strategy map; it also serves as a performance management tool.

The overall Hennepin County strategy map provides the framework (grand strategy) for a cascade of similar strategy maps down to the departmental level, where the real work of linking with customers, consumers, clients, and taxpayers takes place. The county's North Point Health and Wellness Center strategy map offers an example (see Figure 7.2). The center is located in a low-income area of Minneapolis that is home to a diverse group of citizens. (Until mid-2004 North Point was called Pilot City Health Center; the center was founded in the 1960s as a War on Poverty initiative of the Johnson administration.)

The map begins with the center's mission: to promote and deliver quality community health care and improve the lives of individuals and families of diverse cultures. The mission is followed by an overarching goal to reduce health disparities and improve the overall physical, dental, and mental health of the community throughout the life cycle. Six key results areas are outlined: perinatal, pediatric, adolescent, adult, women's health, and geriatric—results areas that cover the life cycle. Then come the customer, financial, internal processes, and learning and growth strategy areas. Measures have been developed to track performance in each strategy area. The map thus depicts the center's overall strategy and also serves as a performance management tool.

FIGURE 7.2. STRATEGY MAP FOR NORTH POINT HEALTH AND WELLNESS CENTER.

North Point Health and Wellness Center Mission

North Point Health and Wellness Center promotes and delivers quality community health care and improves the lives of individuals and families of diverse cultures.

Overarching Goal

To reduce health disparities and improve the overall physical, dental, and mental health of this community through the life cycle.

Perinatal	Pediatric	Adolescent
Key Results	**Key Results**	**Key Results**
• Reduce the infant mortality rate among NPHWC patients. • Reduce the rate of low birth weight infants for NPHWC prenatal patients.	• NPHWC patients will have current immunizations. • Prevent and treat asthma among NPHWC pediatric users. • Provide sealants for children and educate parents about baby bottle tooth decay.	• Reduce the teen pregnancy rate among adolescent NPHWC users. • Reduce the rate of STIs among adolescent NPHWC users.

Adult	Women's Health	Geriatric
Key Results	**Key Results**	**Key Results**
• Improve the prevention and treatment of diabetes in patients. • Improve the prevention and treatment of hypertension. • Effectively treat patients with STIs/HIV. • Screen for and treat periodontal disease.	• Increase the use of birth control among sexually active teens. • Effectively screen and provide appropriate intervention for domestic violence. • Implement initiatives to improve health access for women and girls.	• Geriatric patients will have an up-to-date medication management plan. • Increase appropriate vaccinations among NPHWC geriatric patients.

FIGURE 7.2. STRATEGY MAP FOR NORTH POINT HEALTH AND WELLNESS CENTER, CONT'D.

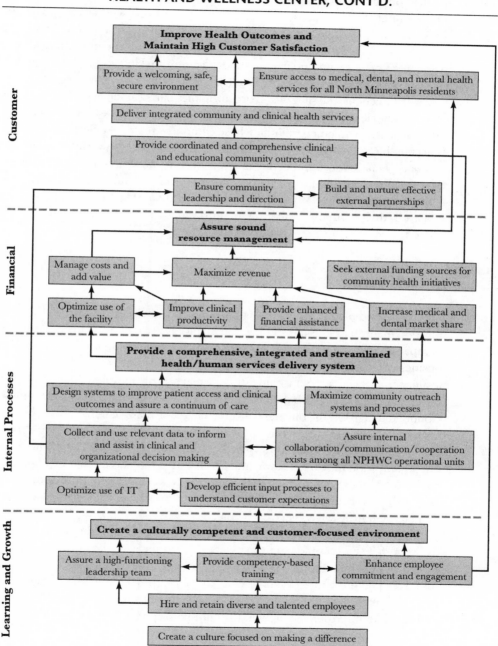

Note: NPHWC equals North Point Health and Wellness Center.
Source: North Point Health and Wellness Center, 2004.

Unfortunately, not enough governments, public agencies, and nonprofit organizations have thought as long and hard as the Wilder Foundation and Hennepin County about what they want to do and for whom, why, where, when, and how. Nor have most condensed their thinking into a succinct grand strategy, either in text or graphic form. As a result they often have little more than an odd assortment of goals and policies to guide decision making and action in pursuit of organizational purposes. In the absence of deliberate or emergent overall strategic directions, the sum of the organization's parts can be expected to add up to something less than a whole. Of course, in a period of transition from a deliberate strategy to an emergent one whose contours are not yet clear, perhaps this is acceptable—even good. Or the organization may face powerful stakeholders whose expectations are conflicting or contradictory, making it unwise or impossible for the organization to develop a coherent grand strategy. In either of these cases the organization's key decision makers and planning team should be clear, at least in their own minds, that the organization has legitimate reasons—as opposed to excuses—for not having a grand strategy.

Desired Outcomes

Several desired planning outcomes may come from steps 6 and 7. First, the organization might seek a grand strategy statement for itself, perhaps including an accompanying strategy map. It also might want subunit; program, service, or business process; and functional strategy statements for its constituent parts—again, perhaps with accompanying strategy maps. It might want to link all of these statements and maps to balanced scorecards as well, which is what Hennepin County is doing. On the one hand a complete set of these statements may be warranted if the organization has chosen the vision of success approach; this set would be necessary to clarify strategies for achieving the vision. On the other hand the organization may have more limited aims. If it has chosen the direct or indirect approaches to defining issues, it may simply want a statement of how it will deal with each issue. If it has chosen the goal approach, it may want statements that clarify how it will achieve each goal.

Second, the organization—or at least the strategic planning team and key decision makers—should gain clarity about what parts of the current strategies should be kept and improved, what will be initiated that is new, and what should stop. Keeping these three agendas clear and conceptually separate is important; otherwise what is currently being done is likely both to drive out what is new and to make it harder to stop what should be stopped (Benner and Tushman, 2003).

Third, the organization may or may not wish to have a formal strategic plan at the end of step 6, one that will be formally adopted in step 7. The contents of a strategic plan are discussed later in this chapter.

Fourth, planners may seek formal agreement to push ahead at the conclusion of step 6. If a strategic plan has been prepared and the organization is governed by an elected or appointed policymaking body, this agreement likely will mean proposing that the policy board adopt the plan (step 7). Policy board adoption then would be a fifth desired outcome. (It is likely that community-based strategic plans will need to be adopted by several organizations before they can be implemented; see Chrislip, 2002; Wheeland, 2003.) If the unit doing the planning is the board itself or if the organization does not need the approval of its board (or does not have a board), then steps 6 and 7 may be collapsed into a single step. Formal agreement by key decision makers may not be necessary, but it usually enhances the legitimacy of strategic actions and provides an occasion for widely communicating the intent and content of such actions.

Finally, as is true throughout the process, actions should be taken when they are identified and become useful or necessary. Otherwise, important opportunities may be lost or threats may not be countered in time. It is also important to ease the transition from the old reality, whatever that may have been, to the new reality embodied in the organization's emerging strategies. If the transition can be broken down into a small number of manageable steps it will be easier to accomplish than if it requires a major leap.

Benefits

Ten benefits of the strategy and plan development and adoption steps can be identified.

First, a fairly clear picture will emerge—from grand conception to many implementation details—of how the organization can create public value, meet its mandates, fulfill its mission, and deal effectively with the situation it faces. This picture provides the measure of clarity about where an organization is going, how it will get there, and why that is an important part of most successful change efforts (Kotter, 1996; Abramson and Lawrence, 2001). A new reality cannot be fully realized until it is named and understood (May, 1969; Weick, 1995).

Second, this new picture should have emerged from a consideration of a broad range of alternative strategies, a process that in itself should enhance organizational creativity and overcome the usual tendency of organizations to engage in simplistic, truncated, and narrow searches for solutions to their problems (Cyert and March, 1963; Nutt, 2002). Typically, major parts of existing strategies should continue to be applied and should be improved, some new strategies should be tried, and some things should stop.

Third, if actions are taken as they become identified and useful, a new reality will emerge in fact, not just in conception. If the strategic planning exercise has not become real for team members and key decision makers prior to this point, it will certainly become real now (Boal and Bryson, 1987).

Fourth, early implementation of at least parts of major strategies will facilitate organizational learning. The organization will find out quickly whether its strategies are likely to be effective. Thus strategies can be revised or corrected before being fully implemented. Learning of this sort is facilitated when a *formative evaluation*—designed to shape implementation as it forms—is called for in the strategic plan (Scriven, 1967; Patton, 1997).

Fifth, emotional bonding to the new reality can occur as the new reality emerges gradually through early and ongoing implementation efforts. To return to the story metaphor, no drama can reach an effective and satisfying conclusion without a catharsis phase in which the audience is allowed time to break its emotional bonds with an old reality—and perhaps experience confusion, distress, depression, and despair—so that it can forge new emotional bonds with the new reality (Kübler-Ross, 1969; Spencer and Adams, 1990; Fiol, 2002). This bonding process is likely to fail if the gap between old and new realities is large and is not bridged by a series of *acts* and *scenes* (Mangham and Overington, 1987).

Sixth, organizational members will get help with working their way through the failure-in-the-middle syndrome identified by Kanter (1983). In many of the strategic planning efforts in which I have been involved, decision makers and planning team members have experienced this sense of failure somewhere between identifying strategic issues and formulating strategies to deal with the issues. The planning groups for the School District, Project for Pride in Living, and the Naval Security Group all had difficulty coming to grips with what they should do in response to the issues they faced. The members of each of these groups had to acknowledge their difficulties, engage in constructive (though not always easy) dialogue, offer support to each other, and search for thoughtful responses to the issues before they could see their way through the difficulties and imagine a better and viable future (Roberts, 2002). In this regard, recall philosopher Jean-Paul Sartre's observation that "human life begins on the other side of despair."

Seventh, heightened morale among strategic planning team members, key decision makers, and other organizational members should result from task accomplishment and early successes in the resolution of important issues. If the organization is pursuing an important mission and dealing with the fundamental questions it faces, it can expect key organizational actors to become involved and to experience excitement (Selznick, 1957; Kouzes and Posner, 2002).

Eighth, further strategic planning team development (and indeed broader organizational development) should result from the continued discipline of addressing fundamental questions constructively. Improved communication and understanding among team (and organizational) members should occur. Strategic thinking, acting, and learning are likely to become a habit.

Ninth, if key internal and external stakeholder interests have been addressed successfully as part of the strategic planning process, a coalition is likely to emerge that is large enough and strong enough to agree on organizational strategies and pursue their implementation. If a formal strategic plan has been prepared, there is likely to be a coalition large enough and strong enough to adopt it, implement it, and use it as an ongoing basis for decision making.

Tenth, organizational members will have the permission they need to move ahead with implementation of strategies. Those who wish to preserve the status quo will find themselves fighting a rearguard action as the organization mobilizes to implement adopted strategies.

If all these benefits are realized, the organization will have achieved progress in an effective and artful way. Following Alfred North Whitehead's observation about "the art of progress," the organization will have preserved "order amid change" and "change amid order." It will have built new and more effective bridges from itself to its environment and from its past to its future. And people will be able to cross those bridges relatively easily and painlessly.

Two Approaches to Strategy Development

In this section I present two approaches to strategy development that I have found particularly effective.

The Five-Part Process

One useful approach to strategy development involves a five-part process in which planners answer five questions about each strategic issue. (This approach is adapted from one developed by the Institute of Cultural Affairs; see Spencer, 1989.) These questions should be adjusted so that they accord with the approach to strategic issue identification used by the planning team.

1. What are the practical alternatives, dreams, or visions we might pursue to address this strategic issue, achieve this goal, or realize this idealized scenario?
2. What are the barriers to the realization of these alternatives, dreams, or idealized scenarios?

3. What major proposals might we pursue to achieve these alternatives, dreams, or idealized scenarios directly or to overcome the barriers to their realization?
4. What major actions (with existing staff working within existing job descriptions) must be taken within the next year (or two) to implement the major proposals?
5. What specific steps must be taken within the next six months to implement the major proposals, and who is responsible for each step?

The five-part process begins conventionally, by asking strategic planning team members to imagine grand alternatives for dealing with a specific issue. Then comes an unconventional task—instead of being asked to develop major proposals to achieve the alternatives, the team members are asked to enumerate the barriers to realizing the alternatives. Listing barriers at this point helps ensure that implementation difficulties are dealt with directly rather than haphazardly. The third question asks for major proposals to achieve the alternatives directly or else indirectly through overcoming the barriers. Many organizations find that they must spend considerable time overcoming barriers before they can get on with achieving an alternative. For example, the Naval Security Group (NSG) planners found that they had to deal with NSG resistance to collaborating with the other armed services before they could make real headway on other issues. Project for Pride in Living planners found they had to assure divisional managers that existing divisional strategies that were working well would be included in the plan— that is, the plan would include a "maintain and improve" agenda and not just "new" and "stop" agendas.

The answer to the fourth question will consist essentially of a one- to two-year work program to implement the major proposals. Note that the work will be done by existing staff within their existing job descriptions. This question begins to elicit the specifics necessary for successful strategy implementation. It also conveys the notion that any journey must begin where one is. For example, if full-blown implementation of the strategy will require more staff and resources, this question requires strategists to be clear about what can be done, using existing staff and resources, to procure them. This question also begins to force people to put their money where their mouths are. As the precise shape and content of strategy implementation emerges, it will become clear who is willing to go ahead and who is not. The final question asks strategists to be even more specific about what must be done and who must do it. The implications of strategy implementation will become quite real for organizational members at the conclusion of this step. Defining specific actions and assigning responsibilities to particular individuals are requisites of successful strategy implementation (Joyce, 1999; Randolph and Posner, 2002). In addition, such specificity will often determine *exactly* what people are willing and not willing to live with. Often such details prefigure the emerging future better than any grand vision. To paraphrase the novelist Gustave Flaubert, the divine is in the details.

The fourth and fifth questions involve the group in the work of step 9 (implementation), but that is desirable, because strategies should always be developed with implementation in mind. Actually, steps 6 and 9 may be merged in some circumstances: for example, when implementation must be understood clearly before key decision makers or policy boards, within an organization or across organizations, are willing to act, or when a small, single-purpose or single-function organization is involved.

A strategic planning team can use the snow card technique to answer each question. This technique allows for great creativity, and it facilitates development of organization-specific categories to hold the individual ideas. Using this five-part process together with the snow card technique has several other advantages. First, relatively large numbers of people can be involved (broken into subgroups of five to twelve people). Second, the process keeps people from jumping immediately to solutions, a typical failing of problem-solving groups (Janis, 1989; Nadler and Hobino, 1998; Nutt, 2002). Third, it keeps people from overevaluating their ideas; it keeps idea creation and evaluation in a reasonable balance. Fourth, it forces people to build a bridge from where they are to where they would like to be. Fifth, it forces people to deal with implementation difficulties directly.

Finally, a particular advantage of this five-part technique is that a great deal of unnecessary conflict is avoided simply because alternatives proposed in answer to one question will drop out if no one suggests a way to handle them in response to the next question. For example, instead of leaving the group members to struggle over the advantages and disadvantages of some major proposal for realizing an alternative, the process simply asks the group what has to happen in the next year or two, with existing staff working within existing job descriptions, to implement the proposal. If no one can think of a reasonable response, then an unnecessary struggle never happens, and strategy remains tied to what people can actually imagine themselves doing. Strategy formulation thus remains more realistic and grounded. Of course the group needs to make sure that answers in previous steps are linked to answers in subsequent steps to ensure that no proposal is unintentionally dropped from sight.

But there is a caveat: the five-part process is very useful for developing the broad outlines of a strategy and for engaging fairly large groups of people, but it does not promote much understanding of the relationships among ideas. Categories of ideas are created in response to the five questions, but the connections among ideas within categories or across responses to the five questions remain unclear. Care should be taken to ensure that important connections are made. It may be necessary to develop logic models to tie together key elements of desirable strategies (Millar, Simeone, and Carnevale, 2001; Poister, 2003).

Some groups may find that it is not necessary to answer all five questions; they may be able to collapse the last three questions into two questions or even a single question. The important point is that the specifics of implementation must be clarified as much as necessary to allow effective evaluation of options and to provide desired guidance for implementation. Recall that a strategy has been defined as a *pattern* of purposes, policies, decisions, actions, and resource allocations that effectively links the organization to its environment. The purpose of these questions, whether or not all five are used, is to get the organization to clarify exactly what that pattern has to be and who has to do what to make the pattern effective.

Some organizations (and communities), particularly larger ones, find it useful to have the strategic planning team answer the first two questions, using the snow card technique. The task of developing answers to the last three questions is then delegated to task forces, committees, or individuals. Those answers are brought back for review and perhaps decisions by the team. Alternatively, the entire task of answering all five questions may be turned over to a division, department, task force, committee, or individual that then reports back to the appropriate review or decision-making body. Yet another alternative is to use the two-cycle strategic planning process outlined in Chapter Two. In the first cycle, divisions, departments, or smaller units are asked to identify strategic issues (or goals or visions) and to prepare strategies, using the five-part process (or the oval mapping process, discussed later in this chapter), within a framework established at the top. The strategies are then reviewed by cross-divisional or cross-departmental strategic planning committees, perhaps including a cabinet. Once the committee agrees to specific strategies, detailed operating plans may be developed. These plans would involve a detailed elaboration of answers to the last two questions.

Once answers have been developed to deal with a specific strategic issue, the strategic planning team is in a position to make judgments about the strategies that should be pursued. In particular the team needs to ask:

- What is really reasonable?
- Where can we combine proposals, actions, and specific steps?
- Do any proposals, actions, or specific steps contradict each other, and if so what should we do about them?
- What (including the necessary resources) are we or the key implementers really willing to commit to over the next year?
- What are the specific next steps that would have to occur in the next six months for this strategy to work?

The five-part process also helps with ongoing strategy implementation efforts. Once specific strategies have been adopted and are being implemented, the organization should work its way back up the original set of five questions on a regular basis. Every six months the last question should be addressed again. Every year or two the fourth question should be asked again. Every two or three years the third question should be asked. And every three to five years, the first two questions should be addressed again as well.

Project for Pride in Living used aspects of the five-part process to develop the strategies it is pursuing to achieve the goals in its strategic plan (see Exhibit 7.2). The goals and strategies are introduced with statements about PPL's stakeholders' understanding of self-sufficiency, which is important because PPL's mission (Exhibit 4.3) is to assist low-income individuals and families to work toward self-sufficiency. The four goals correspond fairly directly to the four strategic issues PPL identified in step 5 of the strategic planning process (as discussed in Chapter Six).

The School District's task forces also used aspects of the five-part process to develop the strategies—*initiatives* in the district's terminology—included in the district's 1996 strategic plan (see Exhibit 7.3). (Recall that the oval mapping process was used to develop a new mission and overall goals for the district and to identify strategic issues; task forces were then formed to develop strategies to deal with the issues.) The ten initiatives integrated the results of the task forces' work. The last four initiatives were more student oriented, while the first six were more staff and community oriented. Initiative-specific goals were articulated, and actions were articulated for achieving the goals.

The Oval Mapping Process

The oval mapping process is a second helpful approach to formulating effective strategies. Oval mapping is based on the strategic options development and analysis (SODA) method developed by Eden and associates over the past twenty years (Eden and Ackermann, 2001; Bryson, Ackermann, Eden, and Finn, 2004). It involves creating options (phrased as actions) to address each issue. (The strategic planning team will already have done this if it used the oval mapping or indirect approaches to strategic issue identification.) The planning team should be as practical *and* creative as possible when brainstorming options. Specific options can be triggered by any number of considerations relevant to the issue at hand, including mission, mandates, and ideas for creating public value; stakeholder analyses; SWOCs; existing strategies; applicable reports and background studies; and knowledge of what other organizations are doing. Each option is written on a separate

EXHIBIT 7.2. STRATEGIES FOR PROJECT FOR PRIDE IN LIVING, 2003–2007.

PPL stakeholders confirmed that the essential elements of self-sufficiency are

- Economic independence
- Family stability
- The ability to manage crises

It is affirmed that self-sufficiency is a non-linear process of building skills and a support system. PPL can best assist participants by measuring their progress in aggregate, while also realizing that steps will differ with individuals.

Goal: Sustainability
Strategies:

- Focus on activities that are based on PPL's key strengths
- Develop viable business models for all programs and the organization as a whole
- Carefully assess opportunities for growth and fortify existing programs first

Goal: Measure effectiveness
Strategies:

- Define overall organization outcome measure(s) to show participants' progress toward self-sufficiency
- Develop measures for each program that reflect a unified definition of self-sufficiency
- Use measures to help PPL learn and be successful in the long term

Goal: Coordination
Strategies:

- Create improved internal and external communication strategies
- Integrate business operations

Goal: Increased leadership role
Strategies:

- Be proactive in bringing PPL's experience and perspective to public discussions on issues central to PPL's work
- Support the leadership of participants, community members, and other organizations in the communities we serve

Source: Project for Pride in Living, 2002.

EXHIBIT 7.3. INITIATIVES IN THE SCHOOL DISTRICT'S 1998 STRATEGIC PLAN.

Three initiatives are related to systems—how we operate and run our district:
- Using technology creatively
- Creating alternative sources of revenue
- Nurturing respect and creating a safe environment

Three initiatives are related to our community—how we work and communicate with the community:
- Enhancing relationships and trust within the community
- Standardizing and communicating processes and values
- Enhancing our prekindergarten through grade 12 School-to-Work commitment

Four of these initiatives relate to our mission of educating for success in a diverse and changing world. These initiatives include:
- Experiencing rich and challenging curricula
- Providing high-quality, future-oriented professional learning experiences for all employees
- Acquiring inter- and intrapersonal skills
- Ensuring that students feel they belong and learning is personalized

oval-shaped sheet of paper, 7½ inches wide and 4½ inches tall. (Experience indicates this is the best size for capturing one idea per card and allowing cards to be grouped and moved around easily; see Resource B for a pattern for ovals and for detailed instructions in the use of the oval mapping process; see Bryson, Ackermann, Eden, and Finn, 2004, and Ackermann, Eden, and Brown, 2004, for more examples and guidance.) If ovals are not available, snow cards or large Post-It notes can be used.

Once a set of options written on ovals is in hand, the options are stuck on a wall covered with flipchart sheets or on a whiteboard by means of adhesive putty or tape. The options are then arranged by a facilitator or the team members and linked with arrows indicating which options cause or influence the achievement of other options. An option may be part of more than one influence chain. The result is a *map* of action-to-outcome (cause-to-effect, means-to-end) relationships among the options intended to address the issue at hand. The team is then asked to develop options that outline consequences (desired or otherwise) of effectively addressing the issue. These options are used to extend the action-to-outcome relationships in order to develop goals for the organization in each issue area. Options toward the end of a chain of arrows (usually placed near the top of the map) are likely to be goals and are likely to be closely related to the organization's mission. Once a draft map has been prepared, it can be discussed further, reviewed, and revised until the full range of options for addressing each issue is articulated and the full range of possible goals for each issue area is understood. Particular action-to-outcome sets can then be selected as strategies for addressing each issue. Like the five-part process, this method shades over into the work of step 9.

Maps can get quite large, and computer support may be needed to understand, analyze, and manage the resulting complexity. Decision Explorer software is specially designed for this purpose (Banxia Software, 2004). (More information on the software is offered in Resource B.)

NSG relied on oval mapping and Decision Explorer software (among other techniques) to develop strategies designed to deal with the strategic issues it faced (discussed in Chapter Six). NSG strategies were grouped into *strategic thrusts* (Exhibit 7.4).

Strategic Plans

Strategic plans can vary a great deal in their form and content. The simplest form of strategic plan may be nothing more than an unwritten agreement among key decision makers about the organization's mission and what the organization should do given its circumstances. This is the most common form of strategic plan and clearly reflects a basic premise of this book—that shared strategic thinking, acting, and learning are what count, not strategic plans in and of themselves. As Mintzberg (1994, p. 252) notes, "Organizations function on the basis of commitment and mindset."

But coordinated action among a variety of organizational actors over time usually requires some kind of reasonably formal plan so that people can keep track of what they should do and why (Bolman and Deal, 2003; Daft, 2004). For one thing, people forget, and the plan can remind them of what has been decided. The plan also sets a baseline for judging strategic performance. And the plan serves a more overtly political purpose: it usually amounts to a "treaty" among key actors, factions, and coalitions. Finally, the plan (or a simplified version of it) can serve as a communications and public relations document for internal and external audiences.

The simplest written strategic plan consists of the organization's final versions of several of the worksheets in the workbook that is a companion to this book (Bryson and Alston, 2004):

EXHIBIT 7.4. STRATEGIC THRUSTS FOR THE NAVAL SECURITY GROUP, 1994.

Strategic Thrust 1: Influencing relations with the Navy
- Expand on NSG knowledge and experience in the emerging concept of Information Warfare
- Gain a formal charter for acquiring cryptologic systems
- Influence key internal stakeholders on Navy Pentagon staff
- Invest NSG cryptologic personnel at joint and other external commands for influence and expertise

Strategic Thrust 2: Dealing with the National Security Agency (NSA)
- Choose issues wisely in which to engage NSA (focus on those truly critical to success)
- Position our personnel at NSA for competency, not for control
- Recognize jointness as inevitable and be proactive in meeting it
- Focus on leveraging NSA technology and expertise in cryptology to support naval fleet operations

Strategic Thrust 3: Dealing with maintaining and assessing readiness for cryptologic operations
- Define critical operational processes and develop higher level metrics to gauge NSG "readiness" for these critical cryptologic operational processes (performance measurements)
- Focus on developing a responsive training requirement generation process that supports our critical operational processes

Strategic Thrust 4: Reorganizing internally to facilitate staff teamwork
- Organize horizontally by end-to-end process rather than vertically by function
- Explore visionary concepts (for example, outsourcing)
- Institutionalize strategic planning
- Continue redefining cryptologic occupational specialties in light of the information age and the end of the Cold War

Source: Frentzel, Bryson, and Crosby, 2000, pp. 418–419.

- Mission statement
- Mandates statement
- Vision of success, if one has been prepared
- SWOC analysis (perhaps as an appendix)
- Strategic issues (or a set of goals or a scenario outlining the preferred future)
- Strategies—grand; subunit; program, service, product, and business process; and functional—including especially information technology, human resource, and financial strategies (indeed, for many organizations pursuing e-commerce or e-government strategies, the IT strategy, even though functional, is becoming paramount and must be aligned with the organization's fundamental strategies)

Most organizations will prefer, however, to use their final versions of these worksheets as background material for preparation of a written strategic plan. When this approach is taken, the table of contents for the plan might include the following headings (Barry, 1997; Bryson and Alston, 2004):

- Executive summary (the mission and strategy statements and also the vision of success, if one has been prepared)
- Introduction (including purpose, process, and participation, as well as a brief organizational history)
- Mission statement (including meeting the mandates)
- Mandates statement (may be presented as an appendix)
- Vision of success (if one has been prepared)
- Values and guiding principles
- Situation analysis (including SWOCs; may be presented as an appendix)
- Goals, performance indicators, and grand strategy statement
- Issue-specific goals, performance indicators, and strategy statements
- Subunit goals, performance indicators, and strategy statements (if applicable)
- Program, service, product, or business process plans, including goals, performance indicators, and strategy statements
- Functional goals, performance indicators, and strategy statements
- Implementation plans (including action plans)
- Staffing plans (including needed full-time staff, part-time staff, and volunteers)
- Financial plans (including operating budgets for each year of the plan, plus any necessary capital budgets or fundraising plans)
- Monitoring and evaluation plans
- Plans for updating all parts of the strategic plan
- Appendices

The plan itself need not—and should not—be overly long. If it is, it will be put aside or forgotten by key staff.

Additional sections that might be included, perhaps as appendices, are the following:

- A review of needs, problems, or goals to be addressed
- A description of the organization's structure, either current or proposed, or both
- Governance procedures (current, proposed, or both)
- Key organizational policies (current, proposed, or both)
- Relationships with key stakeholders (current, proposed, or both)
- Assumptions on which the plan is based
- Marketing plans (Stern, 2001)
- Facilities plans
- Contingency plans to be pursued if circumstances change
- Any other sections deemed important

The task of preparing a first draft of the strategic plan should usually be assigned to a key staff person. Once the draft is prepared key decision makers, including the strategic planning team, the governing board, and possibly several external stakeholders, should review it. Several modifications are likely to be suggested by various stakeholders, and modifications that improve the plan should be accepted. After a final review by key decision makers the revised plan will be ready for formal adoption. Once the plan is adopted the planning team can move on to implementation, although many implementing actions may have occurred already, as they have become obvious and necessary over the course of the planning process.

Plan Adoption

The purpose of step 7 is to gain an official decision to adopt and proceed with the strategies and plan prepared and informally reviewed in step 6. For the proposed plan to be adopted, it must address issues that key decision makers think are important with solutions that appear likely to work. Also, the political climate and stakeholder opinion must be favorable, and the barriers to effective action must be down. There must be a *coupling*, in other words, of problems, solutions, and politics (Kingdon, 1995).

The planning team should keep step 6 *conceptually* distinct from step 7, because the dynamics surrounding the two steps may differ—even though in practice steps 6 and 7 may merge (as they may, for example, when planning is done in small, hierarchically organized, single-purpose or single-function organizations).

Step 6 may be quite collegial, as the team engages in dialogue in forums about what might be best for the organization. Step 7, however, can be quite conflictual, particularly when formal adoption must take place in legislative arenas such as city councils, multiorganizational confederations, or the various boards and organizations necessary for effective implementation of community plans. (Readers seeking more detailed advice on this step should see Bryson and Crosby, 1992, pp. 246–280.)

In order to gain the necessary support, key decision makers and important stakeholders must be open to the idea of change, and they must be offered specific inducements to gain their support. The arguments and inducements likely to produce support must be geared to the decision makers' and stakeholders' values, interests, and frames of reference, because they will choose on the basis of their own judgment whether or not to support the proposal (Bryson, 2004b). Considerable bargaining, negotiation, and invention of items to trade may be necessary in order to find the right combination of exchanges and inducements to gain the support needed without also bargaining away key features of the proposed strategies and plans (Susskind and Cruikshank, 1987; Susskind and Field, 1996; Thompson, 2001).

Formal adoption is likely to occur at a *window of opportunity*, an occasion when action favoring change is possible. There are three kinds of windows of opportunity: those opened by the emergence of pressing issues, those opened by important political shifts (newly elected or appointed policymakers, new executive directors, changed priorities at funding agencies), and those opened by decision points (times when official bodies are authorized and empowered to act). A major purpose of the initial agreement step is to define the network of stakeholders likely to form the basis of a supportive coalition and to map out likely decision points in advance so that the full-blown coalition will be able to act at the time the specific, viable plan is ready for adoption. Steps 2 through 6 also are designed to prepare the way for formal plan adoption in step 7, through producing the appropriate array of tangible and intangible process and content outcomes needed to convince enough people to move ahead (see Figure 3.1).

Sometimes formal adoption of a strategic plan occurs in stages over many months. For example, I worked with a school board that broadly supported most features of a draft plan. But board members had sharply differing opinions about the desirability of relocating an old high school. The high school was obsolete and did not meet state standards but was important symbolically as a focus for much of the community. After much discussion, bargaining, and negotiation over the entire facilities section of the plan, deciding and then redeciding, the board finally approved building a new high school on a site adjacent to the old one. The old high school was then to be remodeled to become the district's headquarters. The strategic plan was then formally adopted six months after it was presented. The dynamics of this adoption process were often rocky—in sharp contrast to previous steps—except for the final stages of step 6. When the first-draft strategic plan was formulated for review by the board, the conflicts became clear, as did the challenge of resolving them in a way that would assure a supportive coalition on the board and in the community. The difficulties of that challenge carried all the way through step 7.

Process Guidelines

The following guidelines should be kept in mind as the strategic planning team formulates effective strategies to link the organization with its environment.

1. *Remember that strategic thinking, acting, and learning are more important than any particular approach to strategy formulation or the development of a formal strategic plan.* The way in which strategies are formulated is less important than how good the strategies are and how well they are implemented. Similarly, whether or not a formal strategic plan is prepared is less important than the effective formulation and implementation of strategies.

2. *Consider a variety of creative, even radical options during the strategy formulation process.* The broader the range of alternative strategies the team considers, the more likely it is to find supportable, implementable, and effective strategies (Nutt, 2002). Constant awareness of the variety of options available will help ensure that a diverse set of possible strategies is considered before final choices are made. Recall the advice of the late Nobel Prize laureate Linus Pauling: "The best way to have a good idea is to have lots of ideas." Or consider the advice of the great German philosopher Johann Wolfgang von Goethe: "When ideas fail, words come in very handy." Keep talking and bouncing ideas off one another; keep your eye open for nascent, useful, but nonmainstream ideas in the organization; pay attention to what might be going on elsewhere that is good; and do not become a victim of "hardening of the categories" (Mintzberg, Ahlstrand, and Lampel, 1998). Another way of making this point is to argue that an organization should not engage in strategic planning unless it is willing to consider alternatives different from "business as usual." If the organization is interested only in minor variations on existing themes then it should not waste its time on a full-blown strategic planning exercise. Instead it should concentrate on programming existing strategies (the main focus of Chapter Nine) and making quality improvements in those strategies. Or the organization may wish to pursue a strategy of *logical incrementalism,* that is, a number of small changes organized around a general sense of direction

(Quinn, 1980; Bryson, 2003a). Or it might wish to give up on strategic planning altogether and pursue traditional incremental decision making, or *muddling through* (Lindblom, 1959), as a way of finding an acceptable fit with its environment.

David Osborne and Peter Plastrik (1997, 2000) offer a range of strategy options for public organizations. Exhibit 7.5 groups these strategies according to type and source of leverage. The *core* strategy focuses on clarifying purpose, direction, and roles. The *consequences* strategy makes use of incentives, forcing reliance on markets, competitive contracting, and benchmarking and using performance-oriented rewards. *Customer-focused* strategies create accountability to key stakeholders by inducing competition for customers, offering customers choice, and emphasizing service quality. The *control* strategy shifts power away from the top and center by empowering managers, frontline staff, and communities. Finally, the *culture* strategy emphasizes creation of an entrepreneurial and service-oriented culture. Osborne and Plastrik (2000) offer superb practical advice on when and how to pursue these strategies. Bryan Barry, one of the Amherst H. Wilder Foundation's premier consultants, presents an array of strategies typically pursued by nonprofit organizations (Exhibit 7.6). These strategies represent a compilation of the experience of the Wilder Foundation's nonprofit management consulting service, an industry leader. Unlike the strategies in Osborne and Plastrik's typology, these strategies are not grouped according to sources of leverage, but there are some clear similarities between the two lists. Barry also identifies the importance of attending to the environment; clarifying purpose, role, and market; doing the job well; being entrepreneurial and innovative when needed; and attending to key stakeholders.

3. *Remember that logical incrementalism can be very effective, but sometimes a big win is the way to go.* Incrementalism guided by a sense of mission and direction can result in a series of small decisions that accumulate over time into major changes. Karl Marx is perhaps the progenitor of this line of thought with his observation that changes in degree lead to changes in kind. Indeed, Mintzberg, Ahlstrand, and Lampel (1998) indicate that most strategic changes in large corporations are in fact small changes that are guided by and that result in a sense of strategic purpose. And Neustadt (1990), in his study of U.S. presidential power observes, "Details are of the essence in the exercise of power, day by day, and changes of detail foreshadow institutional development; they cumulate and thus suggest the system's future character" (p. 192). In general, realization of a new future is easier when that future can be shown to be a continuation of the past and present, even if the new future is ultimately qualitatively different (Neustadt and May, 1986; Weick, 1995).

In effect there are two sets of polar opposite strategies—big wins and small wins (Bryson, 1988), and knowledge exploration and knowledge exploitation (March, 1991; Benner and Tushman, 2003). I will consider the big win–small win

EXHIBIT 7.5. OSBORNE AND PLASTRIK'S TYPOLOGY OF PUBLIC SECTOR STRATEGIES.

Type of Strategy	Source of Leverage	Approaches
Core strategy	Clarifying purpose	Use strategic management to create clarity of direction
		Eliminate functions that no longer serve core purposes
		Clarify roles by separating policymaking and regulatory roles from service delivery and compliance roles; also separate service delivery from compliance
Consequences strategy	Making use of incentives	Use markets to create consequences
		Use competitive contracts and benchmarks
		Use performance-oriented rewards as incentives
Customer strategy	Making public organizations accountable to their key stakeholders	Induce competition Offer customers choice Emphasize service quality
Control strategy	Shifting power away from the top and center	Give managers the power to manage
		Give frontline employees the power to improve results
		Give communities the power to solve their own problems
Culture strategy	Developing an entrepreneurial and service-oriented culture	Change habits by introducing new experiences
		Create emotional bonds among employees
		Change employees' mental models

Source: Adapted from Osborne and Plastrik, 1997, p. 39, 2000, pp. vii–ix.

EXHIBIT 7.6. BARRY'S TYPOLOGY
OF NONPROFIT STRATEGIES.

Sharpen the organization	Gain greater clarity about mission and goals, program effectiveness, accountability, funding and resource management, and marketing
Rekindle the fire	Reinvigorate the organization around purpose and mission
Find a niche	Clarify the organization's role and market
Focus on one or two success factors	Be a leader around one or two factors critical for success
Plan the mix of programs and funding	Carefully plan the mix of programs and funding to keep programs fresh and enhance responsiveness to community needs
Gain advantages associated with size	Pursue growth, including alliances and mergers
Simplify or downsize	Eliminate activities not directly related to the core; wisely deploy the remaining resources
Replicate	Build on proven approaches and best practices; do not reinvent the wheel
Balance exploration with getting it done	Balance innovation in new and unproven areas with refining performance in time-tested strategy areas
Make relationships central	Concentrate on building strong relationships with staff, board, and other key stakeholders
Engage the community as an ally	Tap the resources of the community through better working relationships
Focus on root causes of social problems	Focus on prevention, research, advocacy, community organizing, or public policy work to get at root causes
Become entrepreneurial	Undertake new ventures or increase earned income

EXHIBIT 7.6. BARRY'S TYPOLOGY
OF NONPROFIT STRATEGIES, CONT'D.

Become *chaos pilots*	Emphasize responsiveness and adaptability through creating flexible organizational designs and cultures and hiring people who thrive on ambiguity
Pay attention to your organization's stage of development	Attend to issues of founding, growth, institutionalization, and leadership transition
Note sweeping trends	Focus on big changes and whether the organization is catching the wave, on the crests, or about to be in the outwash; decide what to do about it

Source: Adapted from Barry, 1997, pp. 65–69. Copyright 1997 Amherst H. Wilder Foundation. Used with permission.

dichotomy first. A *big win* is "a demonstrable, completed, large-scale victory accomplished in the face of substantial opposition" (Bryson and Crosby, 1992, p. 229), whereas a *small win* is "a concrete, completed, implemented outcome of moderate importance" (Weick, 1984, p. 43). The strategic planning process outlined in this book, because it highlights what is fundamental, may tempt organizations always to go for the big win. But the big-win strategy may be a mistake. Although big-win moves should be considered, the organization should also consider how a whole series of small wins might add up one or more big wins over time. A small-win strategy reduces risk, eases implementation, breaks projects into doable steps, quickly makes change real to people, releases resource flows and human energy, empowers people, encourages participation, boosts people's confidence and commitment, provides immediate rewards, and preserves gains (Weick, 1984; Kouzes and Posner, 2002). Nonetheless a big-win strategy may be best when a small-win strategy is unworkable or undesirable for some reason. For example, Britain and France did not first try out a tiny tunnel under the English Channel. Big wins might also be pursued when the time is right—for example, when the need is obvious to a large coalition, the proposed strategy will effectively address the issue, solution technology is clearly understood and readily available, resources are available, and there is a clear vision to guide the changes (Bryson and Crosby, 1992, p. 235). Big-win strategies probably must be controlled by senior decision makers in fairly hierarchical organizations, although they may also emerge through the loosely coordinated actions of many people moving in the same direction at the operating level (Mintzberg, Ahlstrand, and Lampel, 1998). Similarly, a big win in a collaborative setting may require the relatively tightly coordinated efforts of senior leaders (Milward and Provan, 2003; Huxham, 2003) but in a community setting may emerge from the relatively loosely coordinated efforts of many organizations (Wheeland, 2003). The School District and Project for Pride in Living pursued small-win strategies; each sought significant but not frame-changing improvements. Even so each still encountered some opposition internally or externally over specific strategy choices. For example, the School District faced some opposition over the size of its high school (the largest in the state in terms of population and square footage), but decisions made prior to the strategic planning process meant that the district could not afford another high school. Instead, strategies had to focus on how to make the high school *seem* smaller, making sure that students were connected with their teachers and one another and that no one fell through the cracks. As noted earlier, Project for Pride in Living faced some opposition over how to acknowledge and incorporate prior divisional strategic planning efforts and how to incorporate into the plan existing strategies that were working well. Ultimately, the Naval Security Group pursued a big-win strategy and became the Navy's executive agent for information warfare, in the process changing NSG's mission, basic strategies, key stakeholder alignments, and human resource policies.

The second set of opposing strategies is knowledge exploitation and knowledge exploration. *Knowledge exploitation* involves getting the most out of existing technologies (broadly conceived). Major repositioning of the core business, major stakeholders, basic strategies, or key practices is not required. Most of the decision premises can be inferred from much of current practice. Strategy improvement in these circumstances depends primarily on systematic pursuit of quality improvements via process management, which involves mapping processes, improving the processes, and adhering to systems of improved processes (Benner and Tushman, 2003). Issues of knowledge exploitation tend to be more operational than strategic. In contrast, issues requiring *knowledge exploration* tend to be more strategic and involve tensions that pull the organization in many directions (Nutt, 2001b). Changes implied by the knowledge exploration activities of the organization—or provoked by the results of knowledge exploration by other organizations—often require substantial repositioning of the core business, key stakeholders, basic strategies, and important practices (Benner and Tushman, 2003). However, organizations get into trouble when they invest excessively in knowledge exploitation activities to the detriment of knowledge exploration. For example, the U.S. Defense Department knows a great deal about fighting wars, as its military victories in Iraq in 1991 and 2003 demonstrate. What the Defense Department knows far less about is nation building and the creation of vibrant civil societies. There was no doubt which fighting force would win Gulf War II on the battlefield. There is considerable reason for caution in predicting what will happen in the aftermath of that war—particularly because senior civilian officials in the Bush administration apparently failed to appreciate the need for such planning for postwar Iraq and even ignored or undermined needed planning that was under way prior to the war. This was a serious mistake, and the military services and the rest of the U.S. government have had to scramble to catch up (Rieff, 2003; Fallows, 2004). A key point then is that an adaptive organization must preserve a balance between knowledge exploitation and knowledge exploration. Too much knowledge exploitation will blind the organization to impending frame-breaking changes in its environment and cripple it when the changes do occur. Too much knowledge exploration will not pay the bills fast enough, because almost by definition a lot of effort will be wasted before effective answers or operational formulas can be found. To paraphrase Benner and Tushman (2003, p. 242), an organization's dynamic capabilities depend on simultaneously exploiting current technologies and resources to gain efficiency benefits and creating new possibilities through exploratory innovation. The Naval Security Group faced precisely this challenge as it relied on legacy missions, technologies, and staffing while it built bridges to a new mission, technologies, capabilities, strategies, human resource management practices, and funding arrangements.

4. *Be aware that effective strategy formulation can be top-down or bottom-up.* The organizations that are best at strategic planning seem to deftly combine these two approaches into an effective strategic planning system (Mintzberg, Ahlstrand, and Lampel, 1998). Usually some sort of overall strategic guidance is given by top management, but detailed strategy formulation and implementation typically occur deeper in the organization. Detailed strategies and their implementation may then be reviewed at the top for consistency across strategies and with organizational purposes. (Chapter Ten contains more information on strategic planning systems.)

5. *Decide how to link strategy development with the strategic issues identified in step 6.* Planners need to determine whether strategies should be formulated in response to strategic issues, or to achieve goals, or to realize a vision. Most organizations probably will choose to develop strategies in response to strategic issues, at least at first. Smaller, single-function, or hierarchically organized organizations, organizations that have engaged in strategic planning for some time, or communities with significant value consensus may find it easier to develop strategies to achieve goals or a vision. Nonprofit organizations are more likely than governments or public agencies to be able to develop strategies in response to goals or a vision. But other organizations too may decide that they need more clarity about goals or visions before proceeding very far with strategy development.

It is important to repeat a point made in the previous chapter: the various ways of developing strategies are interrelated. For example, an organization may start by developing strategies in response to strategic issues identified directly or indirectly or through the vision of success approach, oval mapping, the tensions approach, or systems analysis and then develop goals based on its strategies. Goals then would represent the strategy-specific states desired as a result of effective strategy implementation. Mission, goals, and strategies then can be used as the basis for development of a full-blown vision of success. Alternatively, an organization may go through several cycles of strategic planning using various approaches to issue identification and strategy development before it decides to develop a vision of success (if indeed it ever chooses to do so) to guide subsequent rounds of issue identification and strategy development. Or an organization may start with the ideal scenario approach and expand the scenario into a full-blown vision of success after it completes the strategy development step. Or an organization may identify strategic issues using various means and then develop goals or idealized scenarios to guide strategy development in each issue area. No matter which approach is chosen, the five-part process outlined in this chapter provides an effective way to formulate strategies, particularly if the snow card technique is employed in each step. The questions will change only slightly depending on the approach. The strategic planning team may wish to assign different questions to different groups or individuals. If, for example, the team wishes to identify major alternatives and barriers to their achievement, it might ask task forces to develop major proposals and work programs to achieve the alternatives or to overcome the barriers. This is the approach the school board took. The oval mapping process is also an effective way to develop strategies to deal with issues, achieve goals, or realize visions. Again the questions asked will vary slightly depending on the approach taken. The team may wish to develop the broad outlines of a strategy map and then delegate detailed development of strategies and work programs to individuals or task forces. The School District took this approach when the board, with the help of the superintendent and cabinet, developed a map that clarified mission, goals, and strategic issues. The board then authorized the creation of five focused task forces to develop strategies to address the issues.

6. *Describe strategic alternatives in enough detail to permit reasonable judgments about their efficacy and to provide reasonable guidance for implementation.* For example, strategy descriptions might be required to include the following information:

- Principal components or features
- Intended results or outcomes, along with performance measures
- Timetable for implementation

- Organizations and persons responsible for implementation
- Resources required (staff, facilities, equipment, training)
- Costs (start-up, annual operating, capital)
- Estimated savings, if any, over present approaches
- Flexibility or adaptability
- Effects on other organizations, departments, persons, or communities
- Effects on other strategies
- Rule, policy, or statutory changes required
- Procedures for debugging the strategy during implementation (that is, formative evaluation plans) and for conducting subsequent evaluations to see whether or not the strategy has worked (*summative evaluation* plans; Scriven, 1967; Bryson and Cullen, 1984; Patton, 1997)
- Other important features

Financial costs and budgets deserve special attention. Readers are encouraged to look at the section on budgets in Chapter Nine.

7. *Evaluate alternative strategies against agreed-upon criteria prior to selection of specific strategies to be implemented.* As a set the criteria should reveal the extent to which possible strategies are

- Politically acceptable: for example, to key decision makers, stakeholders, and opinion leaders and to the general public
- Administratively and technically workable: in terms, for example, of technical feasibility; coordination or integration with other strategies, programs, and activities; cost and financing; staffing, training, information technology requirements, facilities, and other requirements; flexibility and adaptability; and timing
- Results oriented: in terms, for example, of consistency with mission, values, philosophy, and culture; relevance to the issue; client or user impact; long-term impact; availability or at least possibility of performance measures; and cost effectiveness
- Legally, ethically, and morally defensible: in terms, for example, of all applicable laws, rules, policies, and guidelines and of commonly held ethical and moral frameworks and standards

(For more about criteria see Joyce, 1999, pp. 50–60.) Those involved in strategy formulation should probably know in advance what criteria will be used to judge alternatives.

8. *Consider development of a formal strategic plan.* Such a plan may not be necessary, but as the size and complexity of the organization grows, a formal, written strategic plan is likely to become increasingly useful. The members of the strategic

planning team should agree on major categories and approximate length so that the actual preparer has some guidance. Indeed, a general agreement on the form of the strategic plan probably should be reached during the negotiation of the initial agreement (step 1), so that key decision makers have some sense of what the effort is likely to produce and surprises are minimized. It is conceivable of course that preparation and publication of a formal strategic plan would be unwise politically. Incompatible objectives or warring external stakeholders, for example, might make it difficult to prepare a rational and publicly defensible plan. Key decision makers will have to decide whether a formal strategic plan should be prepared, given the circumstances the organization faces.

9. *Even if a formal strategic plan is not prepared, consider preparing a set of interrelated strategy statements describing the grand strategy; subunit strategies; program, service, product, or business process strategies; and functional strategies.* To the extent they are agreed upon, these statements will provide extremely useful guides for action by organizational members, from top to bottom. Again, remember that it may be politically difficult or dangerous to prepare and publicize such statements.

10. *Use a normative process to review strategy statements and formal strategic plans.* Drafts typically should be reviewed by planning team members, other key decision makers, governing board members, and at least selected outside stakeholders. Review meetings need to be structured so that the strengths of the statements or the plan are recognized and modifications that would improve on those strengths are identified. Review sessions may be structured around the following agenda (Barry, 1997, p. 70; Crosby and Bryson, 2004):

1. Overview of plan.
2. General discussion of plan and reactions to it. Is it in the ballpark?
3. Brainstorming to produce a list of plan strengths. What plan elements do people like?
4. Brainstorming to produce a list of plan weaknesses. What are the problems, soft spots, or omissions?
5. Brainstorming to produce a list of modifications that improve on strengths and minimize or overcome weaknesses.
6. Agreement on next steps to complete the plan.

All modifications that actually improve the statements or plan should be accepted. When the review process is nearing completion, planning team members and key decision makers should ask themselves what risks are entailed in the plan. They should then ask whether the level of risk is acceptable, if something should be done to reduce the risk, or if the plan should not go forward.

11. *Discuss and evaluate strategies in relation to key stakeholders.* Strategies that are unacceptable to key stakeholders will probably have to be rethought. Strategies that do not take stakeholders into consideration are almost certain to fail. A variety of stakeholder analysis techniques can help, including stakeholder support versus opposition grids, stakeholder role plays, and ethical analysis grids. (More information on these techniques can be found in Resource A.)

12. *Have budgets and budgeting procedures in place to capitalize on strategic planning and strategic plans.* This may include making sure that monies tied to implementation of strategic plans are *flagged* so that they always receive special attention and treatment. It may also mean attempting to develop a special contingency fund to allow *bridge* funding, so that implementation of strategies or portions of strategies can begin out of sequence with the normal budgeting process. Most important, however, is the need to make sure strategic thinking precedes, rather than follows, budgeting. This is the key idea behind *performance budgeting* and *entrepreneurial budgeting* (Osborne and Plastrik, 1997, 2000). Unfortunately, the only strategic plans many organizations have are their budgets, and those budgets have typically been formulated without benefit of much strategic thought. Attention to creating public value and to mission, mandates, situational assessments, and strategic issues should precede development of budgets.

13. *Be aware that the strategy formulation step is likely to proceed in a more iterative fashion than previous steps because of the need to find the best fit among elements of strategies, among different strategies, and among levels of strategy.* Additional time and iterations are likely to be needed when an interorganizational network or community-based strategic planning effort is involved (Chrislip, 2002; Linden, 2002; Huxham, 2003). Strong process guidance and facilitation, along with pressure from key decision makers to proceed, will probably be necessary in order to reach a successful conclusion to this step. Process sponsors and champions, in other words, will be especially needed if this step is to result in effective strategies. The issue often is one of appropriately aligning new strategies with existing strategies, and some special planning sessions may be needed to work things out. For example, it is very important that information technology, human resource, and financial strategies support the organization's overall strategy and supporting strategies. Barry (1997, pp. 59–60) suggests a four-step process:

- Provide a written or graphic depiction (such as a logic model or oval map) of existing and proposed strategies in terms of their mission and desired impacts, program elements, and required support and resources.
- Identify what is working well with existing strategies and what needs adjusting, and identify what will need to work well with proposed strategies and what

adjustments might be needed. Focus as well on the integration of existing strategies with new strategies.

- Determine how the needed adjustments can be made.
- Incorporate these revisions into the strategy statements or strategic plan.

This same process is often very useful in implementation, step 9, when issues of alignment often became apparent.

14. *Allow for a period of catharsis as the organization moves from one way of being in the world to another.* Strong emotions or tensions are likely to build up as the organization moves to implement new or changed strategies, particularly if these strategies involve fairly drastic changes and challenge the current culture. Indeed, the buildup of emotions and tensions may prevent successful implementation. These emotions and tensions must be recognized, and people must be allowed to vent and deal with them (Spencer and Adams, 1990; Marris, 1996; Schein, 1997). Such emotions and tensions must be a legitimate topic of discussion in strategic planning team meetings. Sessions designed to review draft strategy statements or a strategic plan can be used to solicit modifications in the statements or plan that will deal effectively with these emotional concerns.

15. *Remember that completion of the strategy development step is likely to be an important decision point.* The decision will be whether to go ahead with the strategies or the strategic plan recommended by the strategic planning team. When a formal strategic plan has not been prepared, a number of decision points may ensue. The strategies proposed to deal with the various strategic issues are likely to be presented to the appropriate decision-making bodies at different times. Thus there will be an important decision point for each set of strategies developed to deal with each strategic issue.

16. *Ensure that key decision makers and planners think carefully about how the formal adoption process should be managed, particularly if it involves formal arenas.* Formal arenas typically have specific rules and procedures that must be followed. These rules must be attended to carefully so that the plan is not held hostage or overturned by clever opponents. Bargaining and negotiation over the modifications and inducements necessary to gain support and minimize opposition are almost certain to be needed. Obviously, any modifications that improve the proposal should be accepted, and agreements reached through bargaining and negotiation should not sacrifice crucial plan components.

17. *Provide some sense of closure to the strategic planning process at the end of step 7 or, when no formal plan is prepared, at the end of step 6.* Formal adoption of a strategic plan provides a natural occasion for developing such a sense of closure. But even when there is no strategic plan, some sort of ceremony and celebration may be required

to give participants in the process the sense that the strategic planning effort is finished for the present and that the time for sustained implementation is at hand.

18. *When the strategic planning process has been well designed and faithfully followed, but the strategies and plans are nevertheless not adopted, consider the following possibilities:*

- The time is not yet right.
- The draft strategies and plans are inadequate or inappropriate.
- The issues the strategies and plans purport to address are simply not real enough or pressing enough.
- The organization (or community) cannot handle the magnitude of the proposed changes, and they need to be scaled back.
- The strategies and plans should be taken to some other arena, or the present arena should be redesigned in some way.

Summary

This chapter has discussed strategy formulation and adoption. Strategy is defined as a *pattern* of purposes, policies, programs, actions, decisions, and resource allocations that defines what an organization is, what it does, and why it does it. Strategies can vary by level, function, and time frame; they are the way an organization (or community) relates to its environment.

Two approaches to developing strategies are suggested: a five-part process and the oval mapping process. This chapter also offers suggestions for the preparation of formal strategic plans, although once again I emphasize that strategic thinking, acting, and learning are the most important results, not any particular approach to strategy formulation or even the preparation of a formal strategic plan. Suggestions are also offered to guide the formal adoption of the plan when that step is necessary or desirable.

CHAPTER EIGHT

ESTABLISHING AN EFFECTIVE ORGANIZATIONAL VISION FOR THE FUTURE

You must give birth to your images. They are the future waiting to be born.

RAINER MARIA RILKE

The purpose of step 8 in the strategic planning process is to develop a clear and succinct description of what the organization (or community) should look like as it successfully implements its strategies, achieves its full potential, and creates significant public value. This description is the organization's *vision of success.* Typically, this vision of success is more important as a guide to implementing strategy than it is to formulating it. For that reason the step is listed as optional in Figure 2.1, and it comes after strategy and plan review and adoption. However, Figure 2.1 also indicates that under the right circumstances, visioning might occur at many places in the strategic planning process (see also Figure 2.4).

Although many—perhaps most—public and nonprofit organizations have developed clear and useful mission statements in recent years, fewer have a clear, succinct, and useful vision of success. Part of the reason for this is that a vision, even though it includes mission, goes well beyond mission. A mission outlines the organizational purpose, whereas a vision goes on to describe how the organization should look when it is working extremely well in relation to its environment and key stakeholders. Developing this description is more time consuming than formulating a mission statement (Senge, 1990; Angelica, 2001). It is also more difficult, particularly because most organizations are coalitional (Pfeffer, 1992; Bolman and Deal, 2003), and thus the vision must usually be a treaty negotiated among rival coalitions.

Other difficulties may hamper construction of a vision of success. People are often afraid of how others will respond to their vision. Professionals are highly vested in their jobs, and to have one's vision of excellent organizational performance criticized or rejected can be trying. People may also be afraid of that part of themselves that can envision and pursue excellence. First of all, they can be disappointed in their pursuit, which can be painful. Their own competence can be called into question. And second, being true to the vision can be a very demanding discipline, hard work that they may not be willing to shoulder all the time.

Key decision makers must be courageous in order to construct a compelling vision of success. They must envision and listen to their best selves in order to envision success for the organization as a whole. And they must be disciplined enough to affirm the vision in the present, to work hard to make the vision real in the here and now (Collins and Porras, 1997; Terry, 1993, 2001).

It may not be possible, therefore, to create an effective and compelling vision of success for the organization. The good news, however, is that although a vision of success may be very helpful, it may not be necessary in order to improve organizational performance. Agreement on strategy is more important than agreement on vision or goals (Bourgeois, 1980; Mintzberg, Ahlstrand, and Lampel, 1998). Simply finding a way to frame and deal with a few of the strategic issues the organization faces often markedly improves organizational effectiveness.

Desired Outcomes

Even though it may not be necessary to have a vision of success in order to improve organizational effectiveness, it is hard to imagine a truly high-performing organization that does not have at least an implicit and widely shared conception of what success looks like and how it might be achieved (see, for example, Knauft, Berger, and Gray, 1991; Collins and Porras, 1997; Rainey and Steinbauer, 1999). Indeed, it is hard to imagine an organization surviving in the long run without some sort of vision to inspire it—hence the merit of filmmaker Federico Fellini's comment, "The visionary is the only realist." Recall as well the famous admonition in Proverbs 29:18: "Where there is no vision, the people perish." Thus a vision of success might be advantageous.

Assuming key decision makers wish to promote superior organizational performance, the following outcomes might be sought in this step. First, if it is to provide suitable guidance and motivation, the vision should probably detail the following attributes of the organization:

- Mission
- Basic philosophy, core values, and cultural features
- Goals, if they have been established
- Basic strategies
- Performance criteria (such as critical success factors)
- Important decision-making rules
- Ethical standards expected of all employees

The vision statement should emphasize purposes, behavior, performance criteria, decision rules, and standards that serve the public rather than the organization and create public value. The guidance offered should be specific and reasonable. The vision should include a promise that the organization will support its members' pursuit of the vision. Further, the vision should clarify the organization's direction and purpose; be relatively action oriented and future oriented; reflect high ideals and challenging ambitions; and capture the organization's uniqueness and distinctive competence as well as desirable features of its history, culture, and values (Shamir, Arthur, and House, 1994; Weiss and Piderit, 1999; Kouzes and Posner, 2002). The vision should also be relatively short and inspiring.

Second, the vision statement should be widely circulated among organizational members and other key stakeholders after appropriate consultations, reviews, and sign-offs. A vision of success can have little effect if organizational members are kept in the dark about it.

Third, the vision should be used to inform major and minor organizational decisions and actions. Preparing the vision will have been a waste of time if it has no behavioral effect. If, however, copies of the vision are always handy at formal meetings of key decision makers and if performance measurement systems are explicitly attuned to the vision, then the vision can be expected to affect organizational performance.

Benefits

At least a dozen benefits flow from a clear, succinct, inspiring, and widely shared vision of success.

First, a fully developed vision of success provides a capsule theory of the organization: that is, its theory of what it should do and how it should do it to achieve success by altering the world in some important way (Bryson, Gibbons, and Shaye, 2001). The vision helps organizational members and key stakeholders understand why and how things should be done. Knowing this basic theory allows organizational members to act effectively without everything spelled out in detail and rules written to cover every possible situation. To paraphrase the great psychologist Kurt Lewin, "There is nothing quite so practical as a good theory" (Johnson and Johnson, 2000, pp. 42–44). Beyond that, the organization's theory of success articulates the way in which people can participate in creating a new and more desirable order. In a follow up to his remarkable study (Krieger, 1996) of some of the world's great entrepreneurs (Moses, Oedipus, Antigone, and Augustine, among others), Martin Krieger (2000) argues that, "redemptive order, what we might call theory, allows us to be involved in the world, to have a sense of what we are doing here" (p. 263). Such a theory and actions based on it are designed to "manufacture transcendence"—to excel, surpass, and go beyond the range of current experience (pp. 258–259).

Second, organizational members are given specific, reasonable, and supportive guidance about what is expected of them and why. They see how they fit into the organization's big picture. Too often the only guidance for members—other than hearsay—is a job description (which is typically focused on the parts and not on the whole). In addition, key decision makers are all too likely to issue conflicting messages to members or simply to tell them, "Do your best." A widely accepted vision of success records enough of a consensus on ends and means to channel members' efforts in desirable directions while it also provides a framework for improvisation and innovation in pursuit of organizational purposes (Collins and Porras, 1997; Osborne and Plastrik, 1997). In this way the vision serves primarily as an aid to strategy implementation, rather than formulation. Specifically, the two things that most strongly determine whether goals are achieved appear to be the extent to which the goals are specific and reasonable and the extent to which people are supported in pursuit of the goals (Locke, Shaw, Saari, and Latham, 1981; Behn, 1999a). It seems reasonable to extend the same argument to a vision of success and claim that the more specific and reasonable the vision, and the more supported organizational members are in pursuit of the vision, the more likely the vision is to be achieved or realized.

As noted earlier, conception precedes perception (Weick, 1995). People must have some conception of what success and desirable behavior look like before they can actually see them and thus strive toward achieving them. So a third benefit is that a vision of success makes it easier for people to discriminate between preferred and undesirable actions and outcomes and thus produce more of what is preferred.

Fourth, if there is an agreement on the vision and if clear guidance and decision rules can be derived from that vision, the organization will gain in power and efficiency. Less time will be expended on debating what to do, how to do it, and why, and more time devoted to simply getting on with it (Pfeffer, 1992; Weiss and Piderit, 1999).

Fifth, a vision of success provides a way to claim or affirm the future in the present and thereby to invent one's own preferred future. If the future is at least in part what we make it, then development of a vision outlines the future we want to have and forces us to live it—create it, *realize* it—in the present. It has been pointed out that "prediction is difficult—especially of the future." What is being said here is different: a vision of success helps not with *predicting* the future but with *making* it (Gabor, 1964).

Sixth, a clear yet reasonable vision of success creates a useful tension between *is* and *ought,* the world as it is and the world as we would like it to be. If goals are to motivate, they must be set high enough to provide a challenge but not so high as to induce paralysis, hopelessness, or too much stress. A well-tuned vision of success can articulate reasonable standards of excellence and motivate the organization's members to pursue them. The vision can provide what Ludema, Wilmot, and Srivastva (1997, p. 1025) call a "textured vocabulary of organizational hope."

Seventh, a well-articulated vision of success will help people implicitly recognize the barriers to realizing that vision. (That is, the vision can function in much the same way as the first step in the five-part strategy formulation process outlined in Chapter Seven.) Recognizing barriers is the first step in overcoming them.

Eighth, an inspiring vision of success can supply another source of motivation: clarification of a vocation tied to a calling. When a vision of success becomes a *calling,* jobs and careers can become *vocations* that release enormous amounts of individual energy, dedication, power, and positive risk-taking behavior in pursuit of the vision of a better future. A vocation creates meaning in workers' lives and fuels a justifiable pride. Noted theologian Frederick Buechner defines vocation as "the place where your deep gladness meets the world's deep need" (quoted in Palmer, 2000, p. 16). Consider, for example, that most remarkable of nonprofit organizations, the Society of Jesus (the Jesuits), founded in 1534 in Paris by Saint Ignatius of Loyola. The order's vision was first formulated in Ignatius's *Spiritual Exercises* (Guibert, 1964). The worldwide success of order members as missionaries, teachers, scholars, and spiritual directors is a tribute to how much they have been guided by their ideal, to be a disciplined force on behalf of the Roman Catholic Church. The fact that they have succeeded for so long against often incredible odds and trials is in part due to the power of their vision. They clearly have been called for a very long time to their vocation. These references to vocation and calling may seem odd to some, but it is becoming increasingly clear that attention to the broadly spiritual aspects of work matters enormously (Bolman and Deal, 2001). Paul Light (1998) finds that public and nonprofit organizations that are able to sustain innovations give witness to a deep and abiding faith (albeit a usually secular one). In other words it may well be that doubt is overvalued in management thought and guidance, and belief is seriously undervalued. Or as

Weick (1995) might say, believing is seeing, not the reverse. A well-crafted vision can become a shared statement of belief—a creed—that starts out as a desire and becomes a fact through action.

Ninth, a clear vision of success provides an effective substitute for leadership (Kerr and Jermier, 1978; Manz, 1986; Kouzes and Posner, 2002). People are able to lead and manage themselves when they are given clear guidance on the organization's direction and behavioral expectations. More effective decision making can then occur both at a distance from the center of the organization and from the top of the hierarchy.

Although constructing a vision of success may be difficult in politicized settings, the task may nonetheless be worth the effort, leading to a tenth benefit. An agreed-upon vision may contribute to a significant reduction in the level of organizational conflict. It can function as a set of overarching goals that can channel conflict in useful directions (Fisher and Ury, 1981; Thompson, 2001; Terry, 1993, 2001).

Eleventh, a well thought out vision can help the organization stay attuned to its environment and develop its capacities to deal with the almost inevitable crises characteristic of organizational life these days. The vision can promote the learning and the adaptation to a changing environment typically necessary to avoid catastrophic failure (Mitroff and Pearson, 1993; Pearson and Clair, 1998; Weick and Sutcliffe, 2001). In particular, a good vision should help the organization distinguish between strategic (or developmental) issues and operational (or nondevelopmental) issues (Nutt, 2001b; Benner and Tushman, 2003). A good vision, in other words, can help the organization thrive over the long term by being ambidextrous, by being good at both strategy implementation and strategy formulation, both knowledge exploitation and knowledge exploration, both making routine changes within the existing architecture and changing the architecture, both maintaining organizational identity and subtly changing it, both avoiding decision failures and learning from mistakes, and both being very serious and not taking itself too seriously. A good vision will provide the overarching framework and the detail necessary if the organization is to purposefully yet flexibly respond to changes in its environment—to hold tightly to its core while being willing to change the rest (Collins and Porras, 1997).

And twelfth, to the extent that the vision of success is widely shared, it lends the organization an air of virtue. It is not particularly fashionable to talk about virtue, but most people wish to act in morally justifiable ways in pursuit of morally justified ends (Frederickson, 1997). A vision of success provides important permission, justification, and legitimation to the actions and decisions that accord with the vision at the same time that it establishes boundaries of permitted behavior. This facilitates the normative self-regulation necessary for any moral community to survive and prosper (Kanter, 1972; Mandelbaum, 2000), and as a result the legitimacy of the organization in the broader community may be enhanced (Suchman, 1995).

An Example

The "2003–2008 Vision of Success" of The Royal Hospitals ("the Royal") of Belfast, Northern Ireland, provides an excellent example of what a vision might contain (The Royal Hospitals, 2003). The Royal comprises four internationally known hospitals: the Royal Victoria, the Royal Maternity Hospital, the Royal Belfast Hospital for Sick Children, and the Dental Hospital. In 2002, a staff of more than 6,700 treated 520,000 patients (332,000 as outpatients, 117,000 as accident and emergency cases, and the remainder as inpatients). The annual budget is approximately £250 million (US$437.5 million). The Royal is one of the best hospitals in the United Kingdom. If you suffer some sort of physical trauma, you stand a better chance of becoming healthy again at the Royal than you do at almost any other hospital in the UK.

The Royal's current vision is in effect its strategic plan for the period from 2003 to 2008, and the vision statement serves as the prime source document for the Royal's annual management (operational) planning cycle. The statement starts with an introduction to the vision and a description of the changing health care environment the Royal faces. Then come sections on mission, role, aims (goals), ethical standards and values, basic strategies, and accountabilities and decision rules. The statement ends with a listing of the Royal's noteworthy accomplishments since the previous vision was published. It is a glossy twelve-page document, with ten pages of text, lots of pictures, and a graphic representation of what should result from implementation of the ten-year physical development plan for the Royal's site. The vision serves primarily as a guide for implementation, but it is written in a way that prompts the Royal's staff to attend to their environment, to keep learning, and to stay open to change.

The Royal's vision statement begins by noting that this is the third such statement; its predecessors were issued in 1994 and 1998. The first vision statement was written primarily by the Royal's chief executive, William McKee, and was an effective but essentially one-way leadership and communication tool. The next vision statement was reviewed by a substantial number of people and organizations in its almost final draft form. The current vision statement was produced only after the Royal involved far larger numbers of people far earlier in the process—long before a draft of the vision was produced. Extensive consultations occurred internally and with numerous key external partners. The document was produced collaboratively because the health care environment increasingly demands health and social care delivery through collaborative networks of providers and caregivers in big institutions, clinics, the community, and families. The introduction notes how the document was produced, what it contains, and what its purpose is: "The aim is to offer guidance and inspiration to all staff in the Royal Hospitals and enable and empower all of us to work within a framework of innovation and ingenuity. We will also share this vision with our patients and all those who have an interest in the future of the Royal" (The Royal Hospitals, 2003, p. 3).

The next section, "Facing the Challenge," refers to changes and mandates in the broader environment. Government policy is mandating major improvements in health and a reduction in health inequalities both geographically and by demographic group. European Union directives are affecting working conditions for health care professionals, especially doctors. The nature of health care delivery is changing. Specifically, the focus is shifting away from individual hospitals and toward networks of clinical teams providing services across a number of locations, which requires more teamwork and partnership with others. In addition, the focus is increasingly on health rather than illness, which means the Royal needs to play its part in dealing with health risks from smoking, alcohol, and obesity. Further, the increased emphasis on service quality means the Royal will continue to emphasize quality improvement processes. The section concludes by praising the government for its financial support and other help (the Royal is part of the National Health Service) and requesting adequate levels of government funding: "We trust and hope that we are given enough resources to allow us to fulfill our role within this system" (The Royal Hospitals, 2003, p. 4).

The next section of the vision presents the Royal's mission, role, aims, and ethical standards and values. The mission states: "It is our fundamental purpose in the Royal Hospitals to improve public health and well-being by providing the highest quality healthcare as acute general hospitals and tertiary referral centers in an environment of learning, innovation and research." The mission emphasizes the Royal's role as a group of specialized hospitals and also the Royal's intended contribution to public health and well-being; this draws the attention of staff to broader concerns than medical care alone. And the mission statement is followed by several statements about the Royal's role in the broader area of health care and promotion. The foundation of what the Royal does is its role as a preeminent acute care hospital. As a tertiary treatment center the Royal has a crucial role in systems of hospital care across the province. The Royal also has a major teaching role. And finally, the Royal is called on to be a leader in changing the future pattern of health services. Reflecting the fact that in Northern Ireland (unlike in the rest of the UK) state-mandated and supported health services and social services are integrated, the document notes, "In fulfilling these complementary roles, we acknowledge the interdependence of the wider health and social care system, and our interlocking roles" (p. 5).

The Royal's *aims* are in part what we in the United States would call *goals* and in part what we would likely call a short vision statement. The goals are to

- Provide the highest quality healthcare in the best possible environment for our patients
- Deliver our services in collaboration with others, as parts of a system promoting optimum care for patients
- Ensure the care we provide is based on objectively assured standards delivered within a culture fostering continuous improvement
- Recognize the contributions of carers, families and communities and work in partnership with them in the care of patients
- Recruit and retain the highest caliber staff
- Promote an environment for staff that is safe, productive and characterized by fair treatment, teamwork, open communication, personal accountability and development opportunities
- Provide training, education and learning opportunities in collaboration with educational bodies and other agencies
- Promote research, an ethos of thoughtful enquiry and creative action
- Make best use of all our resources
- Fulfill our social and environmental responsibilities, promote equality of opportunity and target health and social needs as an employer, a deliverer of healthcare and as part of the community of Northern Ireland
- Further involve the users of our services in their organization and planning

This section concludes with a statement of things the Royal would like to have happen. The statement resembles the short vision statements often found in strategic plans. The Royal wants

- Our staff, our patients and the communities we serve to feel proud of the services we provide
- Excellence in all we do
- Acknowledgement of our success and the success of others
- Balanced working and personal lives
- Satisfaction from our work
- A healthier and more equitable society

The next major section lists the Royal's major strategies, grouped into the following categories: clinical services; learning, research, and development; social and environmental responsibilities; delivering excellence (meaning quality assurance and improvement); developing clinical service networks and systems of service; human resources; resources and property; and information and knowledge management. Three aspects of the strategies are particularly worthy of note. The section on learning, research, and development keeps the Royal open to the future and what cannot be known at present. The section on social and environmental responsibilities commits the Royal to more collaboration in the planning and delivery of services than it has practiced in the past, a consequence of the changing environment noted earlier. And the heightened emphasis on information and knowledge management is crucial to effective service delivery in a networked environment and in a context of continuous process improvement and learning.

The vision statement's penultimate section outlines accountabilities and decision rules. The roles of the board, chief executive, and clinical leadership are emphasized, along with the role of the executive team in clarifying and resolving tensions around maintaining corporate control and delegating freedom and responsibility. The final section, as mentioned earlier, highlights noteworthy accomplishments of the Royal since the 1998 publication of the previous vision.

Only one of the items that I suggest be included in a vision of success is missing: a set of performance criteria. A number of reasons might explain this omission. First, there may simply be too many criteria to list in a short document. Second, it is hard to develop performance criteria collaboratively (Huxham, 2003) although that is what the Royal is being called on to do. Third, publishing performance criteria—particularly when they must be met through collaborative work with outsiders—can leave an organization hostage to fortune. Further negotiations with involved and affected stakeholders may be necessary before the Royal is willing to commit to a number of key collaborative performance indicators. Once collaborative performance indicators are developed and agreed on, a logical next step would be to produce a set of complementary balanced scorecards to further clarify the operational aspects of the vision—that is, to clarify exactly what realizing the vision should mean in terms of performance. Nonetheless, it is important to emphasize that as the Royal Hospitals embark on realizing this new vision, they are starting with what is widely acknowledged to be one of the best developed performance management systems in the UK public sector (and one of its many strengths is that it is rooted in the Royal's visioning efforts).

The vision statement provides much specific and reasonable advice to employees and other stakeholders and indicates that the Royal will support and reward those who act in accord with the vision. Because much of the Royal's success depends on the actions and decisions of others whom it does not control, including those in governmental departments and ministries above the organization, the importance of wide circulation of and agreement on this document is hard to overestimate. It is also important to emphasize that this vision is no mere public relations ploy. Key decision makers and opinion leaders are committed to it. The vision codifies much that the Royal already does, but it also charts some new agreed-upon directions necessary to achieve excellence and serves as the basis for the organization's annual management planning cycle. In particular, the heightened emphasis on working in networks, collaborating, and promoting health is noteworthy.

Process Guidelines

The following guidelines are intended to help a strategic planning team formulate a vision of success.

1. *Remember that in most cases a vision of success is not necessary to improve organizational effectiveness.* Simply developing and implementing strategies to deal with a few important strategic issues can produce marked improvement in the performance of most organizations. An organization should therefore not worry too much if it seems unwise or too difficult to develop a vision of success. Nevertheless it seems unlikely that an organization can achieve truly superior performance without a widely shared, at least implicit vision of success—what theologian Teilhard de Chardin called "a great hope held in common" (quoted in Nanus, 1992, p. 15).

2. *In most cases, wait until the organization goes through one or more cycles of strategic planning before trying to develop a vision of success.* Most organizations need to develop the habit of thinking about, acting on, and learning from the truly important aspects of their relationships internally and with their environments before a collective vision of success can emerge. In addition, it is likely to require more than one cycle of strategic planning for a consensus on key decisions and an ability to resolve conflicts constructively to emerge, and both are necessary for developing an effective vision of success. For example, the School District did not develop a vision of success for itself until 2003, as it was moving toward an updated version of its 1998 strategic plan. By then considerable effort had gone into clarifying, developing, and embedding the district's core values, developing suitable performance indicators and measurement systems, and building teamwork and cohesion across the district. Of course this guideline may not apply if the organization has decided to proceed with strategic planning using the idealized scenario or goals approaches and if the organization has developed and is implementing effective strategies based on those approaches. If key decision makers have enough capacity for consensus to make either of these approaches possible, then the organization may also succeed in developing a viable, detailed vision of success.

3. *Include in the vision of success the desired outcomes listed earlier in this chapter.* The vision itself should not be long, preferably no more than ten double-spaced pages and ideally less. Organizations should think about making the published versions of their strategic plans serve as their visions of success, as the Royal does.

4. *Ensure that the vision of success grows out of past decisions and actions as much as possible.* Past decisions and actions provide a record of pragmatic consensus about what the organization is and should do. Basing a vision on a preexisting consensus avoids unnecessary conflict. Also, the vision should effectively link the organization to its past. Realization of a new future is facilitated to the extent that it can be shown to be a continuation of the past and present (Weick, 1995; Marris, 1996; Fiol, 2001, 2002). However, a vision of success should not be merely an extension of the present. It should be an affirmation in the present of an ideal and inspirational future. It should encourage organizational members to extrapolate backward from an image of that ideal future to the present; this will help them determine which actions today can best help the organization achieve success tomorrow. A vision of success should also encourage organizational members to keep their eyes open for new knowledge and changes in their environment.

5. *Remember that a vision of success should be inspirational.* It will not move people to excel unless it is. And what inspires people is a clear description of a desirable future, backed up by real conviction. An inspirational vision (Shamir, Arthur, and House, 1994; Kouzes and Posner, 2002)

- Focuses on a better future
- Encourages hopes, dreams, and noble ambitions
- Builds on (or reinterprets) the organization's history and culture to appeal to high ideals and common values
- Clarifies purpose and direction
- States positive outcomes
- Emphasizes the organization's uniqueness and distinctive competence
- Emphasizes the strength of a unified group
- Uses word pictures, images, and metaphors
- Communicates enthusiasm, kindles excitement, and fosters commitment and dedication

Just recall Martin Luther King Jr.'s "I Have a Dream" speech, and you have a clear example of an inspirational vision of success, focused in this instance on the better future of an integrated society.

6. *Remember that an effective vision of success will embody the appropriate degree of tension to prompt effective organizational change.* On the one hand too much tension will likely cause paralysis. On the other hand too little tension will not produce the challenge necessary for outstanding performance (Fiol, 2002; Light, 2002b). If

there is not enough tension, the vision should be recast to raise organizational sights.

7. *Consider starting the construction of a vision of success by having strategic planning team members draft visions of success (or at least relatively detailed outlines) individually* (perhaps using the relevant worksheets in this book's accompanying workbook, Bryson and Alston, 2004). The team may find it useful to review the discussion of the vision of success approach to strategic issue identification in Chapter Six before starting their individual drafts. Team members should then share and discuss their responses with each other. After the discussion the task of drafting a vision of success should be turned over to an individual, because an inspirational document is rarely written by a committee. Special sessions may be necessary to develop particular elements of the vision of success. For example, the organization's performance criteria or success indicators may not yet be fully specified. They might be developed out of the mandates, stakeholder analyses, SWOC analysis, or strategy statements or by using the snow card technique or oval mapping. Wherever there are gaps in the vision, special sessions may be necessary to fill them.

8. *Use a normative process to review the vision of success.* Drafts typically are reviewed by planning team members, other key decision makers, governing board members, and at least selected outside stakeholders (Nutt, 2001b). Review meetings need to be structured to ensure that the vision's strengths and any possible improvements are identified and listed. Review sessions can be structured according to the agenda suggested for the review of strategic plans (see Chapter Seven).

9. *Be aware that consensus on the vision statement among key decision makers is highly desirable but may not be absolutely necessary.* It is rarely possible to achieve complete consensus on anything in an organization, so all that can be realistically hoped for is a fairly widespread general agreement on the substance and style of the vision statement. Deep-seated commitment to a vision statement emerges slowly over time.

10. *Arrange for the vision of success to be widely disseminated and discussed.* This makes it more likely that the vision will be used to guide organizational decisions and actions. The vision statement probably should be published as a booklet and given to every organizational member and to key external stakeholders. Discussion of the vision should be made a part of orientation programs for new employees, and periodically the vision should be discussed in staff meetings.

A vision of success can become a living document only if it is referred to constantly as a basis for discerning and justifying appropriate organizational decisions and actions. When a vision statement does not regularly inform organizational decision making and actions, then preparation of the statement was probably a waste of time.

Summary

This chapter has discussed developing a vision of success for the organization. A vision of success is defined as a description of what the organization will look like after it successfully implements its strategies and achieves its full potential. A vision statement should include the organization's mission, its basic philosophy and core values, its basic strategies, its performance criteria, its important decision rules, and its ethical standards. The statement should emphasize the important social purposes that the organization serves and that justify its existence. In addition, the statement should be short and inspirational.

For a vision of success to have a strong effect on organizational decisions and actions it must be widely disseminated and discussed, and it must be referred to frequently as a means of determining appropriate responses to the various situations that confront the organization. Only when the vision statement is used as a basis for organizational decision making and action will it have been worth the effort of crafting it.

CHAPTER NINE

IMPLEMENTING STRATEGIES
AND PLANS SUCCESSFULLY

---

*You give an order around here, and if you can figure out what happens to it after that,
you're a better person than I am.*

HARRY S. TRUMAN

Well-executed implementation (step 9) completes the transition from strategic planning to strategic management by incorporating adopted strategies throughout the relevant system. Creating a strategic plan can produce significant value—especially in terms of building intellectual, human, social, political, and civic capital—but that is not enough. Developing effective programs, projects, action plans, budgets, and implementation processes will bring life to the strategies and create more tangible value for the organization (or community) and its stakeholders as mandates are then met and the mission fulfilled (see Figure 2.4). Programs, projects, action plans, and budgets are necessary in order to coordinate the activities of the numerous executives, managers, professionals, technicians, and frontline practitioners likely to be involved. The implementation process itself should allow for adaptive learning as new information becomes available and circumstances change. Such learning will lead to more effective implementation and to a cognitive, emotional, and practical basis for emergent strategies and new rounds of strategizing. Recall that *realized* strategies are a blend of what is intended with what emerges in practice (Mintzberg and Westley, 1992; Mintzberg, Ahlstrand, and Lampel, 1998).

Desired Outcomes

The most important outcome that leaders, managers, and planners should aim for in this step is *added public value* resulting from greater achievement of the organization's goals and heightened stakeholder satisfaction. To paraphrase Karl Weick (1995, p. 54), a presumed order of greater public value becomes a tangible order "when faith is followed by enactment." Or to paraphrase Mark Moore (2000, p. 179), with effective implementation the value proposition embodied in the strategic plan moves from being a hypothetical story to being a true story.

This outcome will be achieved via more instrumental outcomes. The first of these subordinate outcomes is the reasonably smooth and rapid introduction of the strategies throughout the relevant system. Typically, a broad repertoire of approaches is necessary in order to bring all relevant entities on board, or at least to get them to do what needs doing (for example, Light, 1998; Borins, 1998; Abramson and Lawrence, 2001; Peters and Pierre, 2003, pp. 205–256). The second subordinate outcome is the development of a clear understanding by implementers of what needs to be done and when, why, and by whom. Statements of goals and objectives, a vision of success, and educational materials and operational guides all can help. If they have not been created already, they may need to be developed in this step.

A third subordinate outcome is the use of a debugging process to identify and fix difficulties that almost inevitably arise as a new solution is put in place. As political scientist and anthropologist James Scott (1998) notes, "Designed or planned social order is necessarily schematic; it always ignores essential features of any real, functioning social order" (p. 6). Or to put it in less academic terms, implementers should recall that well-known administrative adage Murphy's Law: "Anything that can go wrong will go wrong." They should also recall the quip, "Murphy was an optimist"! The earlier steps in the strategic planning process are designed to ensure, insofar as possible, that the adopted strategies and plans do not contain any major flaws. But it is almost inconceivable that some important difficulties will not arise as strategies are put into practice. Key decision makers should pay regular attention to how implementation is proceeding in order to focus on any difficulties and plan how to address them. *Management by wandering around* (Peters and Waterman, 1982) can help decision makers gather information and solve difficulties on the spot. *Managing by groping along* can also help if it leads to useful adaptive learning (Behn, 1991; Borins, 1998). Also, as mentioned briefly in Chapter Seven, a conscious formative evaluation process is needed to help implementers identify obstacles and steer over, around, under, or through them to achieve—or if necessary, modify—policy goals during the early stages of implementation (Bryson and Cullen, 1984; Patton, 1997). A good formative evaluation will also provide useful information for new rounds of strategizing.

Fourth, successful implementation is also likely to include summative evaluations (Scriven, 1967; Patton, 1997), to find out whether strategic goals have actually been achieved once strategies are fully implemented. Summative evaluations often differentiate between outputs and outcomes. *Outputs* are the actual actions, behaviors, products, services, or other direct consequences produced by the policy changes. *Outcomes* are the benefits of the outputs for stakeholders and the larger meanings attached to those outputs. Outputs, in other words, are substantive changes, and outcomes are both substantive improvements and symbolic interpretations. Both outputs and outcomes are important in determining whether a change has been worth the expenditure of time and effort (Lynn, 1987; Frumkin, 2001; Poister, 2003). (Balanced scorecards can help implementers make the link between outcomes, which are customer oriented, and outputs, which are results produced by internal processes—particularly given that customer-oriented outcomes tend to be *lagging* indicators whereas internal process outputs are *leading* indicators.) Summative evaluations may be expensive and time consuming. Further, they are vulnerable to sabotage or attack on political, technical, legal, or ethical grounds. Nonetheless, without such evaluations it is very difficult to know whether things are "better" as a result of implemented changes and in precisely what ways they are better.

A fifth subordinate desired outcome is retention of important features of the adopted strategies and plans. As situations change and different actors become involved, implementation can become a kind of *moving target* (Wittrock and deLeon, 1986). It is possible that a mutation developed during the course of implementation can do a better job of addressing a strategic issue than can the originally adopted strategy or plan. In general, however, it is more likely that design distortions will subvert the avowed strategic aims and gut their intent, so it is important to make sure important design features are maintained.

A sixth subordinate outcome of successful implementation is the creation of redesigned organizational (or interorganizational or community) settings that will ensure long-lasting changes. These settings are marked by the institutionalization of implicit or explicit principles, norms, rules, decision-making procedures, and incentives; the stabilization of altered patterns of behaviors and attitudes; and the continuation or creation of a coalition of implementers, advocates, and supportive interest groups who favor the changes. For example, the School District embarked on a process of clarifying its core values as part of implementing one of its ten strategy initiatives (Exhibit 7.3), rather than doing this earlier as part of a mission clarification process. Hundreds of staff, students, and community members participated in suggesting values and refining the final list of five values: *honesty, integrity, caring, trust,* and *respect.* Now, visible signs of these values abound: they are emblazoned on posters, coffee cups, documents, wall murals, and the like. More important, serious discussions of the values and what they mean occur frequently across the district. Children write about the values. Employees approach the superintendent to commend or criticize the way the values have or have not been reflected in district decisions and practices. And the board, other decision makers, staff, students, and members of the community refer frequently to the values whenever important issues come up and decisions are made.

The Naval Security Group (NSG) made lasting changes in its own organization and in its relations with its major Navy and national stakeholders to implement its new mission of information warfare (currently called *information operations*). NSG revitalized its core competency of cryptology and applied it to the information warfare mission. NSG saw to it that information warfare (IW) modules were included in Navy entry-level officer and enlisted personnel training courses to foster knowledge about IW throughout the Navy. NSG also realigned its physical infrastructure to facilitate delivery of IW products and services, created special end product delivery relationships with Navy field commanders, and placed NSG officers in key positions on the staff of the Joint Chiefs of Staff, in major theater joint commands, in newly created fleet IW centers, and in the Office of the Secretary of Defense. As part of the implementation, NSG defined its critical IW operational processes and prepared a balanced scorecard of strategic measures and targets for the top leadership. And in perhaps the most lasting outcome of all, NSG redefined most of its enlisted personnel occupational specialties in light of the new IW mission. Recently, NSG has expanded this implementation by becoming a full partner in the Navy's new warfare strategy and by providing key officers and enlisted personnel to the Naval Network Warfare Command, whose mission is to act as the Navy's central operational authority for space, network management, and information operations in support of naval and joint forces afloat and ashore.

If the redesign of the settings is significant, the result may in fact be a new organizational regime. Regime construction is not easy and therefore will not happen unless relevant implementers believe the changes are clearly worth the effort. A variety of new or redesigned settings that allow the use of a range of tools, techniques, and positive and negative sanctions or incentives may be necessary in order to shape behaviors and attitudes in desired directions (Osborne and Plastrik, 2000), as was clearly the case for the implementation of NSG's strategies. A vision of success (discussed in Chapter Eight) may be highly desirable to outline what the new regime would look like if the purpose of the changes is realized and strategies are fully implemented.

The last subordinate desired outcome is the establishment or anticipation of review points, during which strategies may be maintained, significantly modified, or terminated. The Strategy Change Cycle is a series of loops, not a straight line. Politics, problems, and desired solutions often change (Kingdon, 1995). There are no once-and-for-all solutions, only temporary victories. Leaders, managers, and planners must be alert to the nature and sources of possible challenges to implemented strategies; they should work to maintain still desirable strategies, to replace existing strategies with better ones when possible or necessary, and to terminate completely outmoded strategies.

Benefits

A number of important benefits flow from effective implementation. Obviously, the first is the creation of real public value as changes are introduced smoothly and rapidly, worthwhile goals are achieved, and stakeholder satisfaction is enhanced. People's attention will be focused on making the changes that make a difference as adopted strategies are reconciled with existing and emergent strategies. As Mintzberg, Ahlstrand, and Lampel (1998) note, "We function best when we take some things for granted. And that is the major role of strategy in organizations: it resolves the big issues so that we can get on with the little details" (p. 17). Of course what they call "details" may not be so "little," but their point is still well taken.

The second benefit is in many ways the reverse of the first—namely, the avoidance of the typical causes of failure. These causes are legion but include the following:

- Resistance arising from attitudes and beliefs that are incompatible with desired changes. Sometimes these attitudes and beliefs stem simply from the resisters' not having participated in strategy or plan development.
- Personnel problems such as inadequate numbers of personnel, poorly designed incentives, inadequate orientation or training, or people's overcommitment to other activities or uncertainty that involvement with implementation can help their careers.
- Incentives that fail to induce desired behavior on the part of implementing organizations or units.
- Implementing organizations' or units' preexisting commitment of resources to other priorities and a consequent absence of uncommitted resources to facilitate new activities; in other words, there is little resource "slack" (Cyert and March, 1963).

- The absence of administrative support services.
- The absence of rules, resources, and settings for identifying and resolving implementation problems.
- The emergence of new political, economic, or administrative priorities.

A third significant benefit is increased support for the leaders and organizations that have successfully advocated and implemented the changes and who are now seen as having more legitimacy (Bryson and Kelley, 1981; Bartlett and Ghoshal, 1994; Burns, 2003). Real issues have been identified and effectively addressed; public value has been created. That is what public and nonprofit organizational or community leadership is all about. In addition, leaders who advocate and implement desired changes may reap career rewards. Their formal or informal contracts may be extended. They may receive pay raises or other perks, as well as attractive job offers from elsewhere. Further, because organizations are externally justified by what they do to address basic social or political problems or needs, advocating organizations should also experience enhanced legitimacy and support (Suchman, 1995).

Fourth, individuals involved in effective implementation of desirable changes are likely to experience heightened self-esteem and self-confidence (Dalton, 1970; Schein, 1997). If a person has done a good job of addressing real needs and of creating real public value, it is hard for him or her *not* to feel good about it. Effective implementation thus can produce extremely important *psychic income* for those involved. Finally, organizations (or communities) that effectively implement strategies and plans are likely to enhance their capacities for action in the future. They acquire an expanded repertoire of knowledge, experience, tools, and techniques and an expanded inventory of capital (intellectual, human, social, political, civic), and are therefore better positioned to undertake and adapt to future changes.

For these various benefits to accrue, a number of implementation vehicles are likely to be necessary. They include programs, projects, and budgets.

Programs and Projects

New or revised programs and projects are a component of many strategic change efforts (Koteen, 1989; Joyce, 1999; Randolph and Posner, 2002). The School District, Project for Pride in Living, and the Naval Security Group have implemented many aspects of their strategic plans as projects. Creation of programs and projects is a way of *chunking* (Peters and Waterman, 1982, pp. 126–134) changes, breaking them down into smaller pieces to address specific issues. Koteen (1989) refers to program and project management as a form of "bite-sized management" (pp. 133–134) because the creation of programs and projects can clarify the overall design of a change initiative, provide a vehicle for obtaining the necessary review and approval, and establish an objective basis for evaluation of progress (pp. 162–163). Programs and projects can also focus attention on strategic initiatives, facilitate detailed learning, build momentum behind changes, provide increased accountability, and allow easier termination of initiatives that turn out to be undesirable (Peters and Waterman, 1982; Randolph and Posner, 2002). When drawing attention to the changes is unwise for any reason, decision makers can still use a program or project management approach, but they will need an astute public relations strategy to defuse the ire of powerful opponents.

Program and project plans are a version of action plans. They should have the following components:

- Definition of purpose
- Articulation of the logic model guiding the initiative (Millar, Simeone, and Carnevale, 2001; Poister, 2003)
- Clarification of program or project organization and mechanisms for resolving conflicts
- Calculation of the inputs desired, including financial, human resource, information technology, and other resource inputs
- Definition of the outputs to be produced
- Identification of target clients
- Clarification of the process by which inputs are to be converted to outputs
- Timeline of activities and decision points
- Specification of objectively verifiable indicators of key aspects of the logic model
- Indicators or assumptions that are key to the success of the program

The Special Role of Budgets

Budget allocations have crucial if not overriding significance for the implementation of strategies and plans. Budgets often represent the most important and consequential policy statements that governments and nonprofit organizations make. Not all strategies and plans have budgetary significance, but enough of them do that public and nonprofit leaders and managers should consider involving themselves deeply in the process of budget making. Doing so is likely to be a particularly effective way to affect the design, adoption, and execution of strategies and plans (Lynn, 1987, pp. 191–193).

The difficulty of using budgets for planning purposes results partly from the political context in which budgeting takes place. The hustle, hassle, and uncertainty of politics means that budgeting typically tends to be short term, incremental, reactive, and oriented toward tracking expenditures and revenues rather than long term, comprehensive, innovative, proactive, and oriented toward accomplishment of broad purposes, goals, and priorities (Osborne and Hutchinson, 2004). The political side of budgeting is likely to be especially pronounced in the public sector, where adopted budgets record the outcomes of a broad-based political struggle among the many claimants on the public purse (Wildavsky, 1984; Rubin, 2000). But the same difficulties emerge (though perhaps in more muted form and for somewhat different reasons) in the private and nonprofit sectors as well (Mintzberg, 1994).

Another fundamental reason for the gap between budgeting and planning is that planning for control and planning for action are so fundamentally different, as Mintzberg (1994, pp. 67–81) argues, that a "great divide" exists between them. What can be done about this great divide, given that performance control on the one hand and strategies and programs on the other are equally important? Here are several suggestions:

1. Have strategic planning precede the budget cycle (Osborne and Plastrik, 2000, pp. 43–53). Budgeting is more likely to serve overall organizational purposes when environmental assessments, strategic issue identification, and strategy formulation precede rather than follow it. The City of Milwaukee, Wisconsin, provides an excellent example of how this can be done for a large public organization (Hendrick, 2003).

2. To make strategic planning precede the budget cycle, gain control of the master calendar that guides formal organizational planning and budgeting efforts. As Lynn argues (1987): "the master calendar is the public executive's most important device for gaining ascendancy over the process of budget making in the organization . . . [because it] puts public executives in a position to spell out the assumptions, constraints, priorities, and issues they want each subordinate unit to consider in developing its program, budget, and policy proposals. In the process, they can define the roles of the various staff offices . . . and indicate when and how they will make decisions and hear appeals" (pp. 203–205).

3. Build a performance budgeting system (using the master calendar and any other available tools and resources). As Osborne and Plastrik (2000) note: "performance budgets define the outputs and outcomes policymakers intend to buy with each sum they appropriate. . . . This allows both the executive and the legislature to make their performance expectations clear, then track whether they are getting what they paid for. It also helps them learn whether the strategies and outputs they

are funding are actually producing the outcomes they want. If not, they can ask for an evaluation to examine why—and what to do about it" (p. 43). A key point, however, is that the policymakers should stop at direction setting, budgeting, and evaluation—performance control—and leave the detailed specification of strategies and actions—action planning—to the managers responsible for producing the outputs and outcomes.

4. Be aware that prior strategic planning efforts can provide many of the premises needed to try to influence budgeting in strategic directions (Bryson and Crosby, 1992, pp. 81–117). In addition, the short-term, incremental nature of budgeting can be a source of opportunity rather than constraint for the strategically minded public and nonprofit leader and manager (Lynn, 1987, p. 203; Moore, 1995). This system is a natural setting for organizing a series of small wins informed by a strategic sense of direction—especially when some of that direction can come from prior planning efforts.

5. Pick your budget fights carefully. Given the number of players that budgeting attracts, particularly in the public sector, you cannot win every battle. Focus your attention on those budget allocation decisions that are crucial to moving desired strategies forward. Use the master calendar and preexisting decision premises to anticipate when and how potential budget fights are likely to arise. Lynn (1987, pp. 208–209) argues that there are three basic approaches to budgetary allocations and that each one handles issues differently:

- Each budget issue can be treated separately. This typically means that issues are framed and forwarded by subunits. Therefore cross-issue and cross-unit comparisons are avoided, and it may be possible to hide particular choices from broad scrutiny. If resolution of the individual issues leads to exceeding the total resources available, across-the-board cuts or selective comparisons on the margin are possible.
- Particular issues can be selected in advance for detailed consideration during budget preparations. The strategic planning process can be a likely source of candidate strategic issues for careful review. The incremental process of budgeting might be influenced by the general sense of direction that emerges from addressing these issues.
- Budgetary issues can be examined in light of a comprehensive analytical framework, benchmarks or performance measures, or strategy. Here the attempt is to influence budgetary allocations by means of a larger strategic vision. This approach is most likely to work when the strategic planning process can be driven by a vision of success, balanced scorecard, or other boundary spanning, integrative device and there is strong leadership in place to follow through with the more detailed vision of success or balanced scorecard that is likely to result (Osborne and Hutchinson, 2004).

6. Consider implementing *entrepreneurial budgeting* concepts to advance strategic purposes. A number of governments around the world are experimenting with reforms likely to facilitate implementation of intended strategies, help new strategies emerge via innovation, enhance managerial autonomy along with accountability for results, and promote an entrepreneurial culture (Osborne and Gaebler, 1992; Osborne and Plastrik, 1997; Osborne and Hutchinson, 2004). This approach can involve creating *flexible performance frameworks* that split policymaking from implementation and then use written agreements to spell out the implementing organization's or department's purposes, expected results, performance consequences, and management flexibilities (Osborne and Plastrik, 2000, pp. 124–148). Governments using this approach begin by establishing broad strategic goals and then setting overall expenditure limits along with broad allocations for specific functions such as health, public safety, or roads. Operating departments are given substantially increased discretion over their use of funds in order to achieve their portion of the strategic goals, "subject to the usual constraints of legality and political prudence" (Cothran, 1993, p. 446). This move significantly decentralizes decision making. In a further shift from traditional practice, departments are allowed to keep a significant fraction of any funds left at the end of the fiscal year, without having their budget base cut. Cost savings and wise management can be rewarded, and the phenomenon of foolish buying sprees at the end of the fiscal year, spurred by use-it-or-lose-it policies, is avoided. In a further move to enhance cost savings and wise management, some governments add to employees' paychecks a fraction of any savings they produce as individuals or through teamwork. The final feature of entrepreneurial budgeting is an emphasis on accountability for results. In return for increased discretion at lower levels, higher-level decision makers want greater evidence of program achievement and efficiency gains. An almost contractual agreement is negotiated between the policymakers or the central budget office and the operating departments. In this agreement each department lists and ranks its objectives, specifies indicators for measuring the achievement of those objectives, and quantifies the indictors as much as possible. If objectives are not achieved, serious questioning of managers by policymakers can ensue (Cothran, 1993; Osborne and Plastrik, 2000, pp. 126–128).

Entrepreneurial budgeting thus involves a blend of centralization *and* decentralization. Control over broad-scale goal setting and monitoring for results is retained by policymakers, and managerial discretion over how to achieve the goals is decentralized to operating managers. Authority is delegated without being relinquished, and both policymakers and managers are therefore better able—empowered—to do their jobs more effectively (Carver, 1997). In effect, as Cothran (1993) observes, "entrepreneurial budgeting, and decentralized management in general, can lead to an expansion of power, rather than a redistribution of power" (p. 453). The changes that entrepreneurial budgeting are intended to induce are so profound that a shift in organizational culture is likely to result. Indeed a major reason for moving to entrepreneurial budgeting is to create a culture of entrepreneurship, particularly in government (Osborne and Gaebler, 1992). This change in culture itself needs to be thought about in a strategic fashion (Hampden-Turner, 1990; Schein, 1997; Khademian, 2002).

7. Make sure you have good analysts and wily and seasoned veterans of budgetary politics on your side (Lynn, 1987, p. 207). Budgeting is a complicated game, and having a good team and good coaches can help. There is really no substitute for having a savvy insider who can both prepare and critique budgets effectively. But even though it is important to have good analysts and advisers, it is also important not to become their captive (Meltsner, 1990). The wise leader or manager will make sure that a sense of the organization's desired strategy informs the analysts' and advisers' work.

8. Develop criteria for evaluating the budgets for all programs—preexisting and new—and then to the extent possible make budgetary allocations on the margin away from lower-priority existing programs toward higher-priority new initiatives. This is one way of coping with the enormous difficulty in tight budgetary times of getting adequate budgets for new programs approved without first offering up for sacrifice worthy existing programs—and then running the risk of losing both (William Y. Frentzel II, personal communication, February 2004).

9. Finally, involve the same people in both strategy formulation and implementation if you can. This tactic can bridge the action-control gap. There are two approaches to it, centralized and decentralized (Mintzberg, 1994, pp. 286–287). In the centralized approach, which is most closely associated with strong entrepreneurial or visionary leaders of small organizations, the strategy formulator does the implementing. By staying in close contact with the intimate details of implementation, the implementer can continuously evaluate and readjust strategies during implementation. The decentralized approach is more suitable for highly complex situations in which many people are involved and "strategic thinking cannot be concentrated at one center" (pp. 286–287). In this case the implementers must become the formulators, as when "street-level bureaucrats" determine a public service agency's strategy in practice (Lipsky, 1980; Vinzant and Crothers, 1998). At the extreme this becomes what Mintzberg (1994, pp. 287–290) refers to as a "grass-roots model of strategy formation."

Process Guidelines

Successful implementation of strategies and plans will depend primarily on the design and use of various *implementation structures* that coordinate and manage implementation activities, along with the continuation or creation of a coalition of committed implementers, advocates, and supportive interest groups (Hjern and Porter, 1981; Peters and Pierre, 2003, pp. 205–255). These structures are likely to consist of a variety of formal and informal mechanisms to promote implementation-centered discussion, decision making, problem solving, and conflict management. New attitudes and patterns of behavior must be stabilized and adjusted to new circumstances, particularly through the institutionalization of shared expectations among key actors around a set of implicit or explicit principles, norms, rules, and decision-making procedures; positive and negative sanctions and incentives; and the continuation or creation of a supportive coalition.

The following leadership guidelines should be kept in mind as the adopted strategies or plans move to implementation. After the general guidelines, additional guidelines are offered for managing communication and education, personnel, and direct and staged implementation.

General Guidelines

1. *Consciously and deliberately plan and manage implementation in a strategic way.* Change implementers' attitudes and interests may be very different from those of the members of the advocacy coalition that adopted the changes. This is often the case when changes are imposed on implementers by legislative or other decision-making bodies. Implementers may thus have little interest in making implementation flow smoothly and effectively (Pressman and Wildavsky, 1973). Further, even when implementers are interested in incorporating adopted changes within their respective systems, any number of things can go wrong. Implementation is hardly ever automatic—Harry Truman's discovery quoted at the beginning of this chapter should be kept in mind. Also consider the aphorism that "history is one damn thing after another," and poet William Blake's eloquent "Help! Help!" Implementation therefore must be explicitly considered prior to the implementation step, as a way of minimizing later implementation difficulties, and it must be explicitly considered and planned for during the implementation step itself. Change implementers, particularly when they are different from the change formulators, may wish to view the changes as a mandate (step 2) and go through the process outlined in Chapter Two to figure out how best to respond to them. This process should include efforts to understand and accommodate the history and inclinations of key implementing individuals and organizations (Neustadt and May, 1986). Programs and projects must be organized carefully in order to effectively implement desired strategies. Budgets will also need to be given careful attention. (Additional detailed advice can be found in Elmore, 1982; Yin, 1982; Nutt and Backoff, 1992; Barry, 1997; Friend and Hickling, 1997; Bardach, 1998; Borins, 1998; Rosenhead and Mingers, 2001; Nutt, 2002; Bryant, 2003.) If implementation will occur in a collaborative setting, a great deal of time and effort will be

necessary to plan and manage implementation in a strategic way (Huxham, 2003; see also Resource C).

The board and cabinet of the School District thought quite strategically about implementation during the strategy and plan formulation and plan adoption steps. Of particular concern was how to deal with the size of the high school—the largest in the state in terms of student population and square feet. The district developed a variety of approaches to personalizing the educational experience and making sure the students were connected with each other and their teachers— approaches intended not just for this high school but for use throughout the district. Similarly, Project for Pride in Living had to make sure key implementers, often PPL staff, were engaged throughout the process. And the Naval Security Group's planning team pursued its plans in light of anticipated positive and negative stakeholder reactions. Each planning group was willing to deal with resistance in pursuit of desirable ends but also thought carefully about how to anticipate and accommodate stakeholder concerns constructively so as not to needlessly undermine the change effort.

2. *Develop implementation strategy documents and action plans to guide implementation and focus attention on necessary decisions, actions, and responsible parties.* Recall that strategies will vary by level. The four basic levels are the organization's or network's grand or umbrella strategy; the strategy statements for constituent units; the program, service, product, or business process strategies designed to coordinate relevant units and activities; and the functional strategies, such as finance, human resource, information technology, facilities, procurement strategies, also designed to coordinate the units and activities necessary to implement desired changes. It may not be possible to work out all these statements in advance, so the implementation step is the time to finish this task in as much detail as is necessary to focus and channel action without also stifling useful learning. Recall also that strategies may be long term or short term. Strategies may provide a framework for tactics—the short-term adaptive actions and reactions used to accomplish fairly limited objectives. Strategies may also provide the "continuing basis for ordering these adaptations toward more broadly conceived purposes" (Quinn, 1980, p. 9). (Recall of course that tactics can embody emergent strategies as well as implement intended strategies, making it difficult at times to know what the difference is between strategies and tactics; see Mintzberg, 1994, p. 243.) Action plans are statements about how to implement strategies in the short term (Frame, 1994; Randolph and Posner, 2002; Bryson, 2004a). Typically, action plans cover periods of one year or less. They outline

- Specific expected results, objectives, and milestones
- Roles and responsibilities of implementation bodies, teams, and individuals

- Specific action steps
- Schedules
- Resource requirements and sources
- A communication process
- A review and monitoring process
- Accountability processes and procedures

Without action planning, intended strategies are likely to remain dreams rather than becoming reality. The intentions will be overwhelmed by already implemented and emergent strategies.

3. *Try for changes that can be introduced easily and rapidly.* Implementers may have little room for maneuvering when it comes to the basic design of the proposed changes and the accompanying implementation process. Nonetheless, they should take advantage of whatever discretion they have to improve the ease and rapidity with which changes are put into practice, while still maintaining the basic character of the changes. Implementation will flow more smoothly and speedily when the changes (Gladwell, 2000; Rogers, 2003)

- Are conceptually clear
- Are based on a well-understood theory of cause and effect relations
- Fit with the values of all key implementers
- Can be demonstrated and made real to the bulk of the implementers prior to implementation (in other words, people have a chance to see what they are supposed to do before they have to do it)
- Are relatively simple to grasp in practice, because the changes are not only conceptually clear but also operationally clear
- Are administratively simple, entailing minimal bureaucracy and red tape, minimal reorganization of resource allocation patterns, and minimal retraining of staff
- Allow a start-up period in which people can learn about the adopted changes and engage in any necessary retraining, debugging, and development of new norms and operating routines
- Include adequate attention to the payoffs and rewards necessary to gain implementers' wholehearted acceptance (in other words, incentives are designed to favor implementation by relevant organizations and individuals)

Of course some changes will not be implemented smoothly and will take considerable time. For example, NSG was able to fairly quickly implement tangible programs and actions related to IW. The really crucial strategies, however, involved influencing key stakeholders, and these took years to implement before the full effects were realized.

4. *Use a program and project management approach wherever possible.* Chunking the changes, by breaking them down into clusters or programs consisting of specific projects, is typically an important means of implementing strategic changes. It also makes it easier to tie resources to specific programs or projects and therefore get budget approval for the efforts. Use standard program and project management techniques to ensure that the chunks actually add up to useful progress (Koteen, 1989; Randolph and Posner, 2002).

5. *Build in enough people, time, attention, money, administrative and support services, and other resources to ensure successful implementation.* If possible, build considerable redundancy in places important to implementation, so that if something goes wrong—which it no doubt will—there is adequate backup capacity. Almost any difficulty can be handled with enough resources—although these days budgets typically are exceedingly tight unless money can be freed from other uses. Think about why cars have seat belts, airbags, and spare tires; jetliners have copilots; and bridges are built to handle many times more weight than they are expected to carry: it is to ensure enough built-in capacity to handle almost any contingency. Tight resources are an additional reason to pay attention to the earlier steps in the Strategy Change Cycle. In order to garner sufficient resources, the strategic issue should be sufficiently important, the adopted strategies should be likely to produce desirable results at reasonable cost, and the supportive coalition should be strong and stable. When these elements are present, the chances of finding or developing the necessary resources for implementation are considerably enhanced. Nonetheless, those who must supply the resources may resist, and considerable effort may be needed to overcome that resistance. In almost every case, careful attention will need to be paid to budgeting cycles, processes, and strategies. Implementation plans should include resources for

- Key personnel
- *Fixers*—people who know how things work and how to fix things when they go wrong (Bardach, 1977)
- Additional necessary staff
- Conversion costs
- Orientation and training costs
- Technical assistance
- Inside and outside consultants
- Adequate incentives to facilitate adoption of the changes by relevant organizations and individuals
- Formative evaluations to facilitate implementation, and summative evaluations to determine whether the changes produced the desired results
- Unforeseen contingencies

6. *Link new strategic initiatives with ongoing operations.* Establishing new units, programs, projects, products, or services with their own organizational structures and funding streams is a typical strategy in the public sector. That way, overt conflicts with ongoing operations can often be minimized. But in an era of resource constraints new initiatives must often compete directly with, and be merged with, ongoing programs, products, services, and operations. Unfortunately, the implications of a strategic plan for an organization's ongoing operations may be unclear, particularly in the public sector where policymaking bodies may impose vague mandates on operating agencies. Somehow new (and often vague) initiatives must be blended with ongoing operations in such a way that internal support is generated from those persons charged with maintaining the organization's ongoing activities. However, the people working in existing operations are likely to feel overworked and undervalued already, and they will want to know how the changes will help or hurt them. Typically, they must be involved directly in the process of fitting desired strategic changes into the operational details of the organization, both to garner useful information and support and to avoid sabotage. One effective way to manage the process of blending new and old activities is to involve key decision makers, implementers, and perhaps representatives of external stakeholder groups in evaluating both sets of activities using a common set of criteria. At least some of these criteria are likely to have been developed earlier as part of the strategic planning process; they may include key performance indicators, client and organizational impacts, stakeholder expectations, and resource use. Once new and old activities have been evaluated, it may be possible to figure out how to fit the new with the old, what part of the new can be ignored, and what part of the old can be dropped. Again, recall that *realized* strategy will consist of some combination of the strategic plan, ongoing initiatives, and unexpected occurrences along the way. (Worksheets that may help with this process can be found in Bryson and Alston, 2004. Process guideline 13 in Chapter Seven provides additional guidance on how to align new strategies with existing ones.)

7. *Work quickly to avoid unnecessary or undesirable competition with new priorities.* The economy can always go bad, severely damaging financial support. Those who remember the recessions of the early 1980s, 1990s, and 2000s know this. In addition, tax revolts, tax indexing, tax cuts, and large state and federal deficits have greatly constricted public funds for new initiatives. For these and other reasons, it is wise to build in excess implementation resources to provide some slack. A poverty budget can turn out to be a death warrant. Cheapness should not be a selling point. Instead, program designers and supporters should sell cost effectiveness—that is, the idea that the program delivers great benefits in relation to its costs. A change in the policy board or administration is also likely to bring a change in priorities (Kingdon, 1995; Schein, 1997). New leaders have their own conception of which

issues should be addressed and how. For example, the new superintendent of the School District was hired by the board because of his interest in making major changes in many areas. The strategic planning effort was one consequence of the board's hiring him and giving him a mandate to pursue changes. Further, the anticipation of a new administration often paralyzes any change effort. People want to see what will happen before risking their careers by pushing changes that may not be desired by new leaders. So, once again, leaders and managers must move quickly to implement new strategies and plans before actual or impending change occurs in the economy or the authorizing environment (Moore, 1995).

8. *Focus on maintaining or developing a coalition of implementers, advocates, and interest groups intent on effective implementation of the strategies and willing to protect them over the long haul.* One of the clear lessons from the past three decades of implementation research is that successful implementation of programs in shared-power situations depends on developing and maintaining such a coalition (Baumgartner and Jones, 1993; Sabatier and Jenkins-Smith, 1993; Bardach, 1998; O'Toole, 2000, 2003). Coalitions are organized around ideas, interests, and payoffs, so leaders and managers must pay attention to aligning these elements in such a way that strong coalitions are created and maintained (Kotter and Lawrence, 1974). Strong coalitions will result when those involved see that their interests are served by the new arrangements (May, 2003).

9. *Be sure legislative, executive, and administrative policies and actions facilitate rather than impede implementation.* It is important to maintain a liaison with decision makers in arenas such as state legislatures, governors' offices, and key administrators' offices if their decisions can affect the implementation effort. Leaders and managers must also pay attention to the development and use by implementers of supplemental policies, regulations, rules, ordinances, articles, guidelines, and so on, that are required for implementation to proceed. Operational details must be worked out, and many of these ancillary materials will need to pass through specific processes before they have the force of law. For example, before implementing regulations can become official at the federal level, they must be developed following the procedures outlined in the Administrative Procedures Act (Cooper, 1996). States have their own administrative procedures, and localities and nonprofit organizations may have analogous routines. Change advocates should seek expert advice on how these processes work and attend to the ways in which supplemental policies are developed. Otherwise, the promise of the previous steps may be lost in practice.

10. *Think carefully about how residual disputes will be resolved and underlying norms enforced.* This may mean establishing special procedures for settling disputes that arise. It may also mean relying on the courts. It is preferable to rely on *alternative dispute resolution* methods if possible, to keep conflicts out of formal courts, and to

encourage all-gain solutions that increase the legitimacy and acceptance of the policy, strategy, or plan and of the outcomes of conflict management efforts (Fisher and Ury, 1981; Thompson, 2001). It is also important to remember that the court of public opinion is likely to be important in reinforcing the norms supporting the new changes.

11. *Remember that major changes, and even many minor ones, entail changes in the organization's culture.* Changes in strategy almost inevitably prompt changes in basic assumptions about how to respond to changes in the internal and external environments. Leaders, managers, and planners should facilitate necessary changes in cultural symbols and artifacts, espoused values, and underlying assumptions, recognizing that it is far easier to change the first two than it is to change the third. Indeed, heavy-handed attempts to change underlying assumptions are more likely to promote resistance and rejection than acceptance (Schein, 1997; Khademian, 2002).

12. *Emphasize learning.* The world does not stop for planning. Nor does it stop once the planning is done. Situations change, and therefore those interested in change must constantly learn and adapt. Formative evaluations can facilitate necessary learning, but learning should also become a habit—part of the culture—if organizations are to remain vital and of use to their key stakeholders (Schein, 1997; Crossan, Lane, and White, 1999). Said differently, strategies are hardly ever implemented as intended. Adaptive learning is necessary to tailor intended strategies to emergent situations so that appropriate modifications are made and desirable outcomes are produced (Mintzberg, Ahlstrand, and Lampel, 1998).

13. *Hang in there!* Successful implementation in complex, multiorganizational, shared-power settings typically requires large amounts of time, attention, resources, and effort (Kingdon, 1995; Nutt, 2001b, 2002). Implementers may also need considerable courage to fight resisters. The rewards, however, can be great—namely, effective actions addressing important strategic issues that deeply affect the organization and its stakeholders. The ultimate result can be the creation of substantial public value.

Communication and Education Guidelines

1. *Invest in communication activities.* This means giving attention to the design and use of communication networks and the messages and messengers within them (Goggin, Bowman, Lester, and O'Toole, 1990; Huxham, 2003). Particularly when large changes are involved, people must be given opportunities to develop shared meanings and appreciations that will further the implementation of change and the achievement of goals (Bryson and Anderson, 2000; Barzelay and Campbell, 2003). These meanings will both guide and flow out of implementation activities

(Lynn, 1987). People must *hear* about the proposed changes, preferably hearing the same messages through multiple channels many times to increase the chances that the messages will sink in. Further, people must be able to *talk* about the changes, in order to understand them, fit them into their own interpretive schemes, adapt them to their own circumstances, and explore implications for action and the consequences of those actions (Trist, 1983; Johnson and Johnson, 2000). Educational programs, information packets, and guidebooks can help the organization establish a desirable frame of reference and common language for addressing implementation issues. The School District, Project for Pride in Living, and the Naval Security Group have all held numerous workshops and other educational sessions with key implementers, organized information sessions for key stakeholders, and used a variety of other media to build understanding around concepts central to their strategic plans.

2. *Work to reduce resistance based on divergent attitudes and lack of participation.* Actions likely to reduce resistance on the part of implementers include providing those implementers with supportive orientation sessions, training materials and sessions, problem-solving teams, one-to-one interactions, and technical assistance. Ceremonies and symbolic rewards that reinforce desired behaviors are also helpful.

3. *Consider developing a guiding vision of success if one has not been developed already.* Developing a vision of success is an exercise in *rhetorical leadership* (Doig and Hargrove, 1987). Chapter Eight discusses visions of success and offers guidance on how to develop one.

4. *Build in regular attention to appropriate indicators.* This will ensure attention to progress—or lack thereof—against the issues that prompted the strategic planning effort. For example, the School District undertook a major effort to clarify the concepts and develop standards of measurement for each of its ten strategy initiatives (see Exhibit 7.3). The administration regularly reports on progress against the measures to the board, staff, and other key stakeholders. The Naval Security Group has developed a list of indicators tied to each of its strategic goals. Project for Pride in Living is in the process of identifying and developing measures linking its key inputs, activities, outputs, and outcomes—thus meeting one of the four goals in its strategic plan (see Exhibit 7.2). Many public and nonprofit organizations are creating balanced scorecards that help them pay attention to key performance indicators (Niven, 2003).

Personnel Guidelines

1. *As much as possible, fill leadership and staff positions with highly qualified people committed to the change effort.* As previously noted, changes do not implement themselves—people make them happen. This is particularly true for major changes. When

minor changes are required, systems and structures can often be substitutes for leadership. But when significant changes are involved, there are no substitutes for the many kinds of leadership needed. People—intelligent, creative, skilled, experienced, committed people—are necessary to create the new order, culture, systems, and structures that will focus and channel efforts toward effective implementation. In order to attract and retain such people, at least three things are necessary:

- People must be adequately compensated for their work. Fortunately, compensation does not always have to mean money. Psychic income—the reward that comes from doing good and being part of a new and important adventure— can count as well. Such income is traditionally extremely important in parts of the nonprofit world, and the fact that people are often willing to commit themselves to altruistic pursuits is one of that world's distinguishing features (Light, 2002b).
- People must see how involvement in implementation can advance their careers. The most intelligent and able people are likely to take a long view of their careers and will avoid what may be dead-end jobs. Instead, they are likely to choose jobs that can improve their skills, responsibilities, and long-term job prospects (Dalton and Thompson, 1993; Raelin, 2003).
- People want to have viable "escape routes" that they can use if things go bad or if they want to leave on their own. Many mechanisms can achieve this end—for example, an option of returning to prior jobs, the availability of outplacement services, or generous severance packages.

2. *Give the strategic planning team the task of planning and managing implementation or establish an implementation team that has a significant overlap in membership with the planning team.* As indicated, successful implementation typically requires careful planning and management. In complex change situations a team is likely to be necessary to help with this effort. Including some planning team members on implementation teams ensures that important learning from earlier steps is not lost during implementation. For example, when the School District moved to implement its plan, it created the Organizational Improvement Committee (OIC) by expanding its twenty-four-member strategic planning team to forty members. The OIC has been in place since and played a key role in developing the 2004 district "strategic framework" (discussed in Chapter Twelve).

3. *Ensure access to and liaison with top administrators during implementation.* This task is easy when the change advocates themselves are or become the top administrators. But even when this is not the case, the implementation team may find that administrators are interested in maintaining regular contact with the team.

4. *Give special attention to the problem of easing out, working around, or avoiding people who are not likely to help the change effort for whatever reason.* Standard practice in the public sector, of course, is to start a new agency rather than give implementation responsibilities to an existing agency whose mission, culture, personnel, and history are antagonistic to the intent of the changes. For example, President Lyndon Johnson insisted on establishing the Office of Economic Opportunity rather than turn over implementation responsibilities for many of his Great Society programs to established agencies such as the Departments of Labor or Health, Education, and Welfare. He remarked at one point, "The best way to kill a new idea is to put it in an old line agency" (Anderson, 1990, p. 180). Or, as management theorist Frederick Herzberg often says, "It is easier to give birth than to resurrect." But even when a new organization is started, leaders and managers may still be stuck with personnel who might be detrimental to achievement of the policy goals. For example, in the aftermath of September 11, 2001, President George W. Bush supported a Democratic proposal to create the Department of Homeland Security (DHS). DHS is made up of twenty-two previously separate domestic agencies. The merger of these agencies is one of the most significant transformations of U.S. government since 1947, when Harry Truman oversaw the merger of the various branches of the U.S. armed forces into the Department of Defense in order to better coordinate defense against military threats. DHS represents a similar consolidation, both in style and substance. Formation of DHS represents a dramatic change involving 180,000 employees and other stakeholders and a host of different structures, systems, and cultures (U.S. Department of Homeland Security, 2004). Not everyone involved was or is happy with the change, and creation of an effective new department is going very slowly (Crowley, 2004).

There are several options for dealing with such people. First, help them get jobs to which they are more suited. This may take considerable time initially—for establishing people's skills, ascertaining their goals, and writing favorable letters of recommendation—but the resulting increase in the remaining staff's morale and productivity is likely to be worth the effort. Second, have a policy of awarding merit pay only to people who actively implement policy goals. Third, place people who are resisting the change in jobs where they cannot damage the change effort. Fourth, buy these people off with early retirement or severance packages. And finally, if all else fails, work around them or ignore them.

Direct and Staged Implementation Guidelines

There are two basic approaches to implementation, direct and staged. Direct implementation incorporates changes into all relevant sites essentially simultaneously, and staged implementation incorporates changes sequentially, into groups of sites (Bryson and Delbecq, 1979; Joyce, 1999, pp. 81–82).

1. *Consider direct implementation when the situation is technically and politically simple, immediate action is necessary for system survival in a crisis, or the adopted solutions entail some "lumpiness" that precludes staged implementation.* When situations are simple, direct implementation can work if enough resources are built in to cover costs and provide sufficient incentives and if resistance to change is low. Therefore leaders and managers must try to reduce any resistance to change resulting from divergent attitudes and lack of earlier participation. A crisis can simplify a situation politically in that people become more willing to defer to top positional leaders and accept centralized decision making (Bryson, 1981; Alterman, 1995; Hunt, Boal, and Dodge, 1999). Thus a crisis often makes direct implementation feasible. However, the strategies adopted to address crises must still be technically workable, or at least practical enough that difficulties can be worked out without weakening people's support for change. Unfortunately, few organizations have an effective crisis management system in place (Mitroff and Pearson, 1993; Heath, 1997; Weick and Sutcliffe, 2001). Finally, "lumpy" solutions—that is, wholes that cannot easily be implemented a piece at a time—may demand direct implementation. For example, new buildings, information technology systems, and products or services often must be created all at once rather than piecemeal.

2. *In difficult situations, consider staged implementation.* Staged implementation presumes that implementation will occur in waves, that initial adopters will be followed by later adopters and that finally even most of the laggards will adopt the changes. The result is the familiar S-shaped curve associated with the adoption of most innovations over time. Early on there are few adopters, so the area under the curve is small. As time progresses more and more adoptions occur, the area under the curve increases geometrically, and it begins to assume an S shape. Later fewer and fewer adoptions occur, partly because there are fewer people, units, or organizations left to adopt the changes and partly because of deep-seated resistance on the part of the laggards. The curve levels off as the top of the S is completed (Gladwell, 2000; Rogers, 2003).

The exact nature of the staged process will depend on the difficulties faced. When facing technical difficulties, consider beginning with a pilot project designed to discover or prove cause and effect relations between particular solutions and particular effects. The more technically difficult the situation is, the more necessary it is to have a pilot project to figure out what techniques do and do not work. Once the technical difficulties are resolved, transfer of the implementation process to the remaining potential implementers can be pursued. For example, in the United States, pilot tests of new agricultural products and services occur regularly at experiment stations that involve universities, the U.S. Department of Agriculture, and often businesses in cooperative partnerships. Similarly, before settling on its preferred approaches, the Naval Security Group makes sure there have been pilot tests of the various computer hardware and software designs and deployments it is considering. When facing political difficulties, consider beginning staged implementation with demonstration projects to make it clear that solutions known to work in benign and controlled conditions can work in typical implementation settings. Once the applicability of the changes is demonstrated, transfer to the remaining implementers can be pursued. Demonstration projects are most likely to work when existing or potential opposition is not well organized; changes can then be put in place before effective opposition can materialize. When there is organized opposition to the proposed changes, demonstration projects may succeed in convincing at least some opponents of the merits of the changes, thereby dividing the opposition. But when there is a well-organized *and* implacable opposition, direct and massive implementation efforts may be warranted to expand the front and overwhelm opponents, rather than giving them a limited number of smaller targets to oppose (Bryson and Delbecq, 1979; Benveniste, 1989). However, even though that may be the best approach, the chances of success in such situations are still not great (Bryson and Bromiley, 1993). When facing both technical and political difficulties, consider beginning with a pilot project, following it with demonstration projects, and then moving on to the rest of the implementers. In general the more difficult the situation, the more important it is to promote education and learning, offer incentives for desired changes, and develop a shared sense of commitment to successful implementation and long-term protection of the changes among all interested parties.

3. *Design pilot projects to be effective.* Consider doing the following:

- Test the scientific validity of the proposed changes, probably using experimental or quasi-experimental designs. In other words, test whether the proposed changes actually produce the desired effects. The classic source of advice for such testing is Campbell and Stanley (1966), but any good contemporary evaluation text will provide the necessary information.
- Perform the test in a safe and controlled environment with access to a rich set of resources. The ideal test for causation matches a control group against an experimental group that differs from the control group *only* in that it will experience the policy change, or *treatment,* being tested. Only with such controlled trials can plausible rival hypotheses be ruled out.
- Test several possible changes, and search for their different strengths and weaknesses.
- Use skilled technical specialists to evaluate cause and effect relationships. If the specialists' credibility is a concern, consider using outside experts or an inside-outside team whose objectivity will not be questioned.
- Design tests that are concerned with the effectiveness of the changes, not their efficiency. In other words, tests should measure whether the changes produce

the desired effects or not, not whether they do so cheaply. Attention should be on both outputs and outcomes (as defined earlier in this chapter).

4. *Design demonstration projects to be effective.* Consider employing the following procedures:

- Test for the applicability of proposed changes to typical implementer settings, probably through the use of quasi-experimental designs. True experiments are rarely possible in the field, but it is still important to have some sort of control group, if possible, in order to determine what works under what circumstances and why. Quasi-experimental designs can make it possible for such learning to occur.
- Test in easy, average, and difficult implementation settings in order to gauge the robustness of the changes and the possibilities for handling a range of implementation difficulties.
- Test several possible changes in order to determine their comparative strengths and weaknesses.
- Use a two-cycle process: implementers learn how to work with the changes in the first cycle, and the effects of the changes are monitored in the second cycle.
- Use a qualitative evaluation (Patton, 2001) along with quantitative studies to reveal the different strengths and weaknesses of different solutions. Pay attention to outcomes as well as outputs.
- Remember that what is being tested in the demonstration stage is a process that is already known to work in a technical sense: that is, it can produce the desired effects.
- Assemble a special monitoring team, if necessary, to carry out the monitoring task.
- Provide opportunities for future implementers to witness the demonstrations.
- Develop a media strategy to communicate the desirability of the changes and the best way they might be implemented.

5. *Carefully transfer tested changes to other implementers.* Follow these steps:

- Commit substantial resources to communication tactics, including cycling in observers likely to influence subsequent implementer adoptions and to facilitate word-of-mouth information exchanges.
- Promote the visibility of the demonstration projects.
- Produce, emphasize, and disseminate educational materials and operational guides designed to make adoption and implementation easier.
- Develop credible and easily understood models that show clearly how the desired changes work and how they can be implemented.

- Provide additional resources for technical assistance and problem solving.
- Provide incentives for adopting the changes.
- Be flexible.

6. *Finally, when the implementation process is staged, give special attention to those who will implement the changes in the early stages.* In the early stages, when the practical nature of the changes still needs to be worked out, it is important to attract implementers with enough experience, skill, and desire to make the changes work. These people are likely to be ones who have firsthand experience with the strategic issue and understand the need for an adequate response to it, above-average ability, and experience with prior major change efforts. Furthermore, later adopters will be watching to see whether they wish to embrace the changes or resist them. Therefore early implementers should be valued and persuasive role models. They are more likely to be effective salespersons for change if they do not mindlessly charge after every new whim and fad that comes over the horizon. Instead they should be seen as courageous, wise, able, and committed to addressing the issue in a reasonable way. Further, they should be able to describe their experience to effectively educate the next wave of adopters.

Summary

Desired changes are not completed with the formal adoption of strategies and plans. Without effective implementation, important issues will not be adequately addressed, and lasting, tangible public value will not be created. Implementation therefore should be viewed as a continuation of the Strategy Change Cycle toward its ultimate goal of addressing the issues that prompted change in the first place in such a way that real public value is produced.

Implementation must be consciously, deliberately, and strategically planned, managed, and budgeted. Further, when major changes are required, successful implementation typically involves creation of a new regime to govern decisions and behavior. Elements of this new regime will include new or redesigned settings; new or revised implicit or explicit principles, norms, rules, and decision-making procedures; supportive budgets that also provide both substantive and symbolic incentives promoting the new arrangements; institutionalization of altered patterns of behavior and attitudes; and a supportive coalition of implementers, advocates, and interest groups. The new regime may also incorporate a widely shared vision of success.

Successful implementation introduces desired changes quickly and smoothly and overcomes the typical causes of implementation failure. Implementation may be either direct or staged. Direct implementation works best when the time is right, the need is clear to a strong coalition of supporters and implementers, critical issues and adopted strategies are clearly connected, solution technology is clearly understood, adequate resources are available, and a clear vision guides the changes. (These are also the conditions that favor big-win strategies.) Staged implementation is advisable when policymakers, leaders, and managers are faced with technical or political difficulties. It often involves pilot projects, to determine or to prove the cause and effect relations between particular solutions and desired effects, or demonstration projects, to show the applicability of adopted solutions to typical implementer settings and to diffuse knowledge to later waves of adopters, or both pilot and demonstration and projects. Staged implementation involves organizing a series of small wins.

Learning is a major theme underlying successful implementation efforts. It is not possible or desirable to plan everything in advance. People must be given the opportunity to learn new procedures and adapt them to actual situations. More effective implementation is likely to result, and the next round of strategizing is likely to be better informed.

CHAPTER TEN

REASSESSING AND REVISING STRATEGIES AND PLANS

What's past is prologue.

WILLIAM SHAKESPEARE, THE TEMPEST

The Strategy Change Cycle is not over once strategies and plans have been implemented. Ongoing strategic management of strategy implementation must ensue to take account of likely changes in circumstances, to ensure that strategies continue to create public value, and as a prelude to the next round of strategic planning. Times change, situations change, and coalitions change. Strategies that work must be maintained and protected through vigilance, adaptability, and updated plans. Doing so is particularly important when networks are needed for successful strategy implementation. For example, Milward and Provan (2000) found that "human service systems that are stable are more likely to perform well than systems in a state of flux" (p. 253). Thus, ironically, changes of some sort are probably in order if you want things to remain the same. But not all strategies continue to work as well as they should. These strategies must be bolstered with additional resources, significantly modified or succeeded by a new strategy, or else terminated. In each case, "What's past is prologue." In addition, ongoing strategic management these days also often means building and maintaining an organization-wide strategic management system (Poister and Streib, 1999).

Strategies cease to work for four main reasons. First, a basic strategy may be good but have insufficient resources devoted to its implementation, and therefore insufficient progress is made toward resolving the strategic issue it was meant to resolve. For example, the School District has often had to resort to special levy elections in order to fund its strategies. The success of each election has depended on developing a good plan for the use of the money, persuasive arguments on behalf of the levy, and a lively grassroots campaign involving board members, administrators, parents, the media, and other advocates.

Second, problems change, typically prompting a need for new strategies, on the one hand, and making what was once a solution itself a problem, on the other hand. For example, the Naval Security Group lost its enemy (the Soviet Union), witnessed dramatic changes in information technology and the theory of warfare, was required to cooperate more extensively with the other services, and faced serious budget difficulties. Existing strategies had to be changed if the group was to survive and the nation's security defended in the face of new threats and enemies.

Third, as substantive problem areas become crowded with various policies and strategies, their interactions can produce results that no one wants and many wish to change. Indeed, the need to sort out the various inconsistencies, misalignments, and unintended consequences of crowded policy and strategy areas is one of the compelling reasons for creating an organization-wide performance management system.

And fourth, the political environment may shift. As strategies become institutionalized, people's attention may shift elsewhere. Or supportive leaders and managers may be replaced by people who are uninterested or even hostile to the strategy, and they may change elements of it or appoint other people who undermine it. Or people may reinterpret history—"play tricks on the dead," to use historian Charles Beard's phrase—ignoring the facts to support their position. For example, the United States has probably the least cost-effective health care system in the developed world, and yet proposals to create a single-payer system or national health service are quickly labeled "socialized medicine"—like the British system, for example—by their opponents, and "we all know socialism doesn't work." Meanwhile the British allocate only 6.8 percent of their GDP for health care and cover everyone, whereas the United States allocates 14 percent of its GDP to health care and leaves out almost over a million people. Annual per capita health care spending is two and one-half times greater in the United States than in Britain ($4,100 versus $1,400), and administrative costs are more than twice as great in the United States (11.4 percent of total health care spending versus 5 percent). But in spite of all this spending and administration, the infant mortality rate is higher in the United States than in Britain (7.8 per 1,000 births versus 5.9 per 1,000 births) and life expectancy is lower (76.8 years versus 77.2 years). In addition, cancer and heart disease mortality rates, as well as many other population-level outcome statistics, are often either about the same in both countries or better in Britain (Frederickson, 2003). My own conclusion, based on having used the British system as a patient and on having been a management consultant to it for almost two decades, is that we should be cautious about letting ideologically loaded labels get in the way of the facts. And the facts are that the British system does as well or better than ours in most cases at a fraction of the cost. If we could simply replace our system with theirs, we would have virtually the same population-level health outcomes and 7.2 percent of our GDP left over *every year* (almost $800 billion out of an almost $11 trillion economy in 2004) to fix any remaining problems; to give back to businesses, employees, and taxpayers; or to do both. For any of these four reasons, therefore, policy and strategy can become their own cause—the proximate reason for the initiation of a new round of strategy change (Wildavsky, 1979).

Many organizations are now building and maintaining an organization-wide *strategic management system* (SMS) as a way of fostering greater rationality, coherence, and cost effectiveness in their strategies and operations. (Strategic management systems are often also called *performance management systems.*) An SMS may be thought of as an organizational design for strategically managing the implementation of agreed-upon strategies, assessing the performance of those strategies, reconciling inconsistencies and misalignments, and formulating new or revised strategies. An SMS in practice will describe the organization and its possibilities. The focus should be on increasing the technical rationality *and* political reasonableness of both the organization as a whole and its constituent parts—no easy task in the best of circumstances. And the SMS should ensure that maximum public value is and continues to be created. There are many different kinds of SMSs, and they are discussed later in this chapter.

Desired Outcomes

The purpose of this phase of the Strategy Change Cycle (step 10) is to review implemented policies, strategies, plans, programs, or projects and to decide on a course of action that will ensure public value continues to be created. Desired outcomes include the maintenance of good strategies, modification of less successful strategies through appropriate reforms or plan revisions, and elimination of undesirable strategies. In many cases another desired outcome is construction and maintenance of a strategic management system to ensure ongoing effective strategic management of the organization. A final desired outcome is the mobilization of energy and enthusiasm to address the next important strategic issue that comes along.

Benefits

Several benefits flow from successful action in this phase. First is the assurance that institutionalized capabilities remain responsive to important substantive and symbolic issues. Organizations often become stuck in permanent patterns of response to "old" issues. When the issues change, the institutions often do not and therefore become problems themselves (Schön, 1971; Wilson, 1989). A sort of goal displacement occurs, in which the institution ceases to be a means to an end and instead becomes an end in itself (Merton, 1940; Schön, 1971). Ensuring that organizations remain responsive to real issues and problems—and therefore produce better services and get better results—takes considerable effort. Periodic studies, reports, conferences, hearings, fact-finding missions and on-site observation, and discussions with stakeholders are necessary to stay in touch with the "real world" (Mintzberg, Ahlstrand, and Lampel, 1998; Weick and Sutcliffe, 2001; Zollo and Winter, 2002).

A second important benefit is the resolution of residual issues that occur during sustained implementation. Even if implemented strategies remain generally responsive to the issues that originally prompted them, inevitably there will be a host of specific difficulties that must be addressed if the strategies are to be highly effective. Attention and appropriate action over the long haul are necessary to ensure that strategies in practice remain as effective and efficient as they were in concept.

A third important benefit should be the continuous weeding, pruning, and shaping of crowded strategy areas (Wildavsky, 1979). Although there may be an appropriate *micro-logic* to individual strategy elements, element piled upon element often creates a kind of unintended and unwanted *macro-nonsense* (Peters and Waterman, 1982). Excessive bureaucracy and red tape often have their source in the foolishness that results from the interaction of individual rules that make sense individually but not collectively (Barzelay, 1992; Bozeman, 1999). Public and nonprofit leaders and managers must discover how to talk about the system as a whole in order to figure out what should stay, what should be added, and what should be dropped so that greater alignment results among desired public value, mission, mandates, strategies, and operations (Terry, 2001; Cleveland, 2002).

A fourth important benefit is improved organizational knowledge and collaboration across all levels of the organization. Information on progress and achievement should result in better identification of remaining or new issues, better networks of interaction among key actors, more effective decision making, and generally increased organizational learning, which should be useful in this step and in the next round of strategic planning. A fifth and related benefit is an increased ability to tell the organization's story to internal and external audiences, accurately describing what it does, how it does it, and what the results are.

Finally, this step should foster development of the energy, will, and ideas for significant reform of existing strategies. Minor difficulties can be addressed through existing administrative mechanisms, such as regular staff meetings, *management by exception* routines, administrative law courts, periodic strategy review and modification exercises, and routine access channels to key decision makers for advocates and advocacy groups. Major change, however, will not occur without the development of a substantial coalition in favor of it. And such a coalition will not develop unless there are real issues to be addressed, and the energy, will, and ideas for doing so can be harnessed. However, this is the step in which the beginnings of such a coalition are likely to emerge; in other words, this "end" to the Strategy Change Cycle is often the "beginning" of the next Strategy Change Cycle.

Examples

The Naval Security Group (NSG) provides the most dramatic example in this book of how things can change over time. As described previously, in early 1992 NSG headquarters had done no formal strategic planning, and the organizational culture was reactive and crisis driven. The Cold War strategy was still in place, and the group was successful in accomplishing its mission and enjoyed strong support from its two major stakeholders, the Navy and the National Security Agency (NSA). Thus NSG senior leadership had never been forced to consider major changes in direction, although it had introduced new cryptological systems periodically. In July 1992, NSG did draft a strategic plan in response to the Navy's first attempts at Total Quality Management (TQM). But the plan was prepared mainly to fulfill a step in the TQM process and not to serve as a carefully thought through guide to strategic action. In addition, the six functional departments (administration, training, communications, operations, logistics, and programs and budget) at NSG headquarters provided separate inputs to the plan, which meant the plan had no common goals and objectives and no integrated strategies.

But the environment was changing rapidly. The collapse of the Soviet Union in August 1991 probably marked the turning point, but NSG had not taken that change and its consequences fully into account when it prepared its 1992 strategic plan. The consequences included a dramatic downsizing of the Department of Defense, which meant a serious reduction in personnel was a possibility. Another consequence was a change in basic Navy doctrine from focusing on fighting open ocean conflicts to an expeditionary warfare strategy. NSG thus had to confront at least two strategic issues: how to protect its personnel and how to simultaneously reorient NSG strategy in response to changes in Navy strategy.

Another major issue concerned NSG's other major stakeholder, the National Security Agency. NSA needed to invest in new technology and was likely to cut funding for military cryptological personnel dedicated to the old technologies. And finally, in the Goldwater-Nichols Act of 1986, Congress had mandated joint operations involving collaboration across the armed services. Implementation had initially been sparse, but increasing budget cuts and base closings forced the issue, and intense interservice rivalry erupted over control of the remaining infrastructure.

NSG was thus forced into taking strategic planning seriously or running the risk of becoming irrelevant and at risk of elimination. The NSG comptroller initiated what eventually turned into a full-blown strategic planning process in October 1992, when he asked his subordinates to focus on the issues around reinvesting personnel resources. Eventually, the entire headquarters staff and senior cryptological officers on the major fleet staffs engaged in a full-blown, coordinated strategic planning process. Along the way, major refocusing, restructuring, and reinvesting occurred—and ultimately a new mission emerged.

In contrast to NSG, Project for Pride in Living (PPL) had a habit of developing a new strategic plan every five years. It was therefore not caught off guard the way NSG was—both because it practiced strategic planning and because its environment did not change as dramatically. When PPL began work on the plan discussed in this book, it did not have any specific strategic issues highlighted. It was just clear that a new plan was needed to better reflect the emerging environment and PPL capacities. For example, the board, president, and staff all knew that competition for funding was increasing, pressure for accountability was rising, maintaining dynamism and sustainability was a real challenge, the organization's core competencies needed attention, and something needed to be done to affect the broader policy environment in which PPL had to operate. Over the course of the planning process—from September 2001 to September 2002—the issues that the organization faced were clarified and often redefined. Extended discussions of the organization's mission, its core competencies, and the meaning of self-sufficiency occurred. A deeper understanding by key stakeholders resulted, and greater integration across organizational functions occurred. Not all discussions were finished, however, before the new plan was adopted at a board meeting in September 2002. The debate on many points continues, which is healthy and to be expected.

In 1996, the School District's existing strategic plan was seven years old, and a number of changes were prompting a new round of planning. First, the fact that 60 percent of the students were in grade 6 or below indicated that a significant population bulge, with major consequences for personnel and facilities, was working its way through the system. Second, changes in information hardware and software technology and physical facilities were changing ways of working and interacting and producing a range of new opportunities and challenges. Third, a new superintendent had been hired in late 1995. The school board was intent on making sure the new superintendent was committed to quality education as well as to partnerships; two-way, open communications; effective decision making; and a customer service orientation. The new superintendent was committed and saw strategic planning as an important way to pursue improvements in those areas; the process was initiated in the fall of 1996. The new strategic plan was finalized and adopted in the spring of 1998 and implemented in subsequent years. Now the time has arrived to produce a new plan, because even though the district continues to be extremely successful, the world continues to change.

All three organizations thus provide good examples of how environments can change and how strategies and plans need to change in response. There are no strategies or plans that will work forever, because environments do not remain stable forever. Strategic plans are ultimately ephemeral; what matter most are strategic thinking, acting, and learning and the ways in which strategic planning can promote them. Former president Dwight D. Eisenhower, who was also supreme allied commander in Europe in World War II, captured this best when he said, "Plans are nothing, planning is everything" (quoted in Linden, 2002, p. 199).

Building a Strategic Management System

Strategic management systems (or performance management systems) are ongoing organizational mechanisms or arrangements for strategically managing the implementation of agreed-upon strategies, assessing the performance of those strategies, and formulating new or revised strategies. These systems, in other words, are themselves a kind of organizational (or interorganizational) strategy. As Poister and Streib (1999, p. 311) assert, "Strategic management requires the following":

1. Continual monitoring of the "fit" between the organization and its environment and tracking external trends and forces that are likely to affect the organization
2. Shaping and communicating to both internal and external audiences a clear vision of the type of organization the unit is striving to become
3. Creating strategic agendas at various levels, and in all parts of the organization, and ensuring that they become the driving force in all other decision making, and

4. Guiding all other management processes in an integrated manner to support and enhance these strategic agendas.

Poister and Streib go on to assert that the strategic management process is organized around mission, vision, and values and includes strategic planning, results-oriented budgeting, performance management, and strategic measurement and evaluation (1999, pp. 316–319).

There appear to be six main types of systems, although any strategic management system in practice will probably be a hybrid of the six types. The types, or models, therefore refer to dominant tendencies. The types are

- Integrated units of management approach
- Strategic issues management approach
- Contract approach
- Collaboration approach
- Portfolio management approach
- Goal or benchmark approach

Before describing each approach I must express the ambivalence I have about attempts to institutionalize strategic planning and management. Although it is often important to create and maintain a strategic management system, it is also important to guard against the tendency such systems have of driving out wise strategic thought and action—precisely those features that strategic planning (at its best) promotes. In practice the systems often become excessively formal and bureaucratic, driven by the calendar and not events, numbers-oriented, captured by inappropriate forecasts, and conservative. The reader therefore is advised to recall the admonition in Chapter Two: whenever any strategic management system (or strategic planning process) threatens to drive out wise strategic thought, action, and learning, you should scrap the system (or process) and get back to promoting effective strategic thought, action, and learning.

It is also important to realize that each system embodies a set of arrangements that empowers particular actors, makes particular kinds of issues more likely to arise than others, and makes particular strategies more likely to be pushed rather than others.

Integrated Units of Management Approach

The purpose of this approach to strategic management is to link inside and outside environments in effective ways through development and implementation of an integrated set of strategies across levels and functions of the organization.

Figure 2.2 outlines a possible two-cycle, integrated strategic management system. It represents the classic, private sector, corporate-style, top down–bottom up strategic planning process. In the first cycle, there is a bottom-up development of strategic plans within a framework of goals, objectives, and other guidance established at the top, followed by reviews and reconciliations at each succeeding level. In the second cycle, operating plans are developed to implement the strategic plans. In each cycle, efforts are made to relate levels, functions, and inside and outside environments in effective ways. The process is repeated each year within the general framework established by the organization's grand or umbrella strategy. Periodically the overarching strategy and subordinate strategies are reviewed and modified based on experience, changing conditions, and the emergence of new strategies that may or may not have been planned in advance.

Public and nonprofit organizations have also used variants of this approach to advantage (Boschken, 1988; Hendrick, 2003; Bryson, 2003a, 2003b). Nevertheless it is precisely this sort of system that is most prone to drive out strategic thought and action when it is excessively formal and also underpinned by a belief that the future can be predicted accurately—a belief detached from the messiness of operational reality (Roberts and Wargo, 1994; Mintzberg, Ahlstrand, and Lampel, 1998). Such systems are very likely to be blindsided by unpredictable events. They therefore must be used with extreme caution, because they can take on a life of their own, promote incremental change when major change might be needed, and serve only the interests of the planners who staff them and the leaders and managers who wish to resist—not promote—major change.

With those caveats in mind, consider the useful example of the integrated strategic management system created by Hennepin County, Minnesota. Outside the military, this county government has gone about as far as any large local governmental unit has gone to date (but see also City of Charlotte, 2004). In 2004, the county had a population of over 1.1 million and the county government had a budget of approximately $1.65 billion and 11,000 employees. There are several elements to the Hennepin County strategic management framework, which is known as "Hennepin Results." Some of the elements are essentially guiding principles; others affect the sequence of activities (Hennepin County, 2002b). The principles appear to be the following:

- The system is guided by the county's vision. Overarching goals are derived from the vision. The system is focused on realizing the vision through achieving "key results" and improving customer outcomes linked to the results (see Figure 7.1).
- The system is meant to encompass the entire organization, which is seen holistically as consisting of interdependent parts.

- The system emphasizes a *lines of business* approach. Lines of business are similar services with common customers, which means that lines of business cross departmental lines and may involve independently elected county officials other than the county commissioners (for example, the county sheriff, county judges, and the county attorney and their staffs). There are six lines of business: public works, health, human services, justice, library, and general government.
- Balanced scorecards are used for the county government as a whole and for each department; the departmental scorecards are aligned with the county-wide scorecard. Each scorecard emphasizes results and the things that need to be done to achieve those results from four perspectives: customer, financial, internal processes, and learning and growth. The balanced scorecards promote measurement and communications designed to focus efforts and resources countywide on desired results for the population of Hennepin County and the region. The use of balanced scorecards is meant to align everyone in the organization in order to achieve desired results using coordinated strategies.
- The county focuses strategic and operational planning on identifying and achieving the results the county, its departments, and its partners believe they should focus on to change the condition, behaviors, and attitudes of the people in Hennepin County and the region in order to enhance their health, safety, and quality of life. Desired results are identified for the county as a whole, each line of business, and individual departments. The county calls this "planning for results."
- The meaning of *accountability* is intended to shift toward *accountability for results.* The idea is to hold programs accountable for the best possible performance while ensuring that their performance is aligned with and supports overall efforts of the county as a whole.

The following Hennepin County strategic management system elements focus on the sequence of activities (see Figure 10.1):

- Strategic planning precedes operational planning ("plan for results").
- Priorities among results are established ("plan for results").
- Strategic partnerships are identified and engaged ("plan for results").
- Strategic initiatives are undertaken, as appropriate, on a countywide and departmental basis or with one or more strategic partners ("plan for results").
- Results-based budgeting is emphasized ("budget for results"). This means allocating resources to make it more likely that the most important results will be achieved by the county as a whole, by departments, and by programs and services. Planning thus precedes budgeting.

FIGURE 10.1. INTEGRATED STRATEGIC MANAGEMENT APPROACH OF HENNEPIN COUNTY.

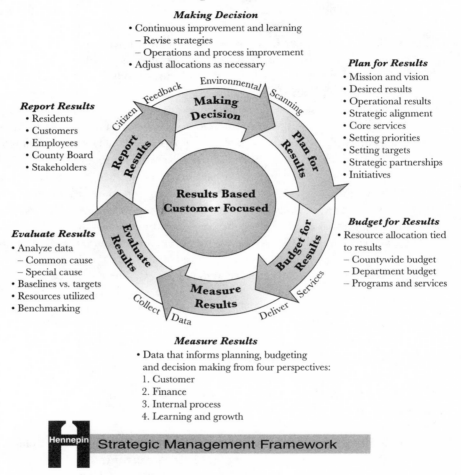

Hennepin Results

Making Decision
- Continuous improvement and learning
  - Revise strategies
  - Operations and process improvement
- Adjust allocations as necessary

Report Results
- Residents
- Customers
- Employees
- County Board
- Stakeholders

Evaluate Results
- Analyze data
  - Common cause
  - Special cause
- Baselines vs. targets
- Resources utilized
- Benchmarking

Plan for Results
- Mission and vision
- Desired results
- Operational results
- Strategic alignment
- Core services
- Setting priorities
- Setting targets
- Strategic partnerships
- Initiatives

Budget for Results
- Resource allocation tied to results
  - Countywide budget
  - Department budget
  - Programs and services

Results Based Customer Focused

Feedback · Citizen · Environmental Scanning · Report Results · Making Decision · Plan for Results · Evaluate Results · Budget for Results · Measure Results · Collect Data · Deliver Services

Measure Results
- Data that informs planning, budgeting and decision making from four perspectives:
  1. Customer
  2. Finance
  3. Internal process
  4. Learning and growth

Hennepin Strategic Management Framework

Source: Vargas, 2003.

- Measuring for results is emphasized ("measure results"). Baseline measurements are or will be established, and indicators and performance measures identified. Measures are tied to the balanced scorecards.
- Evaluation is standard practice ("evaluate results").
- Evaluation elements include examining baseline versus target performances, finding causes of results, and examining resource utilization.
- Results will be reported to board members, employees, residents, and other stakeholders ("report results").
- Decision making is meant to be as informed as possible and to include attention to continuous improvement and learning. Strategies, initiatives, and activities will be judged based on results and evaluation findings; necessary revisions and reallocations will be made ("decision making"). Decision making completes the circle that begins with planning.

Work on this system began in 2000—although it builds on the county's decades of experience with strategic planning, operational planning, budgeting, measurement, and evaluation (Hennepin County, 2003). In 2000, the lines of business were created and began developing their strategic plans. In 2001, a county strategic leadership team (SLT) was created, consisting of the county administrator; deputy county administrator; assistant county administrators for human services and public works; department heads representing the lines of business in justice and the library; directors of budget and finance, human resources, information technology, and planning and development; and union representatives. The SLT identified a set of overarching goals for the county and key results (Figure 7.1). Also in 2001, a working group was organized to identify guiding principles and key elements of a countywide performance measurement and management system. The group recommended a balanced scorecard approach. In 2002, work began on balanced scorecards for the county. The county board adopted new mission and vision statements for the county (Exhibit 4.5 and Figure 7.1). Drafts of countywide strategies (in the form of maps) for achieving the overarching goals were prepared by the SLT, district court, county attorney's office, and the sheriff's office, with input from relevant departmental staff. In 2003, the vast majority of departments had balanced scorecards in the works. The countywide strategy map was presented and work begun to identify performance measures for each of the strategic objectives on the strategy map. Guidelines were released for the 2004 results-based budget, the county's first; the guidelines link the budget to the countywide balanced scorecard. A county budget reduction plan was adopted. A balanced scorecard advisory group and user groups were established. The 2004 results-based budget was presented to the county board. All departments identified key results, selected strategic objectives, and key performance measures as part of the budget. In 2004, the system will be finalized—as much as any of these systems ever are—with the formal publication of *Hennepin Results: Strategic Management Framework* (Hennepin County, 2004). An expanded version of the county executive team will identify priorities and initiatives, link the budget with the scorecard, and collect information tied to countywide performance measures. (The expanded executive team includes the county administrator, associate county administrator, two assistant county administrators, director of human resources, director of budget and finance, public defender, director of community corrections, and director of the county medical center.) Attention will be paid to making sure departmental scorecards are aligned with the countywide scorecard. And instructions will be released for the 2005 plan and budget cycle.

The Hennepin County experience makes it clear that building a strategic management system is a long-term construction project. It takes time to change a large organization with multiple stakeholders, systems, structures, processes, and cultures (Abramson and Lawrence, 2001; Khademian, 2002). It is also important to incorporate as much as possible of what already exists into the new system; change becomes more manageable when much remains familiar (Mangham and Overington, 1987). Successful change is more likely to result from recombination than mutation (Kingdon, 1995). The big changes in the Hennepin County experience would appear to be the creation of the SLT as an initiating, adjudicating, and oversight body and its replacement in 2004 by an expanded executive team; the establishment of lines of business that crossed departmental lines; the introduction of balanced scorecards; and the insistence that planning be tied to results and the balanced scorecards and precede budgeting. Each of these changes was years in coming and often involved more than one false start. But the county in recent years has also emphasized the importance of becoming a *learning organization*. The county accepts that strategic management is a continuous process, that it takes time to create a good strategic management system, and that those involved can learn as much from a failure as they can from a success (Vargas, 2003).

Strategic Issues Management Approach

The strategic issues management system is the most common form of institutionalized strategic planning and management system in public and nonprofit organizations. This system does not attempt to integrate strategies across levels and functions to the extent layered or stacked units of management approaches do. The reason for this is that the various issues are likely to arise in different time frames, involve different constituencies and politics, and do not need to be considered in light of all the other issues. Figure 10.2 provides a schematic of a fairly

FIGURE 10.2. STRATEGIC ISSUES MANAGEMENT APPROACH.

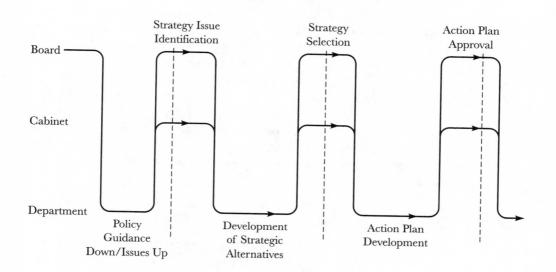

standard strategic issues management system (Eckhert, Haines, Delmont, and Pflaum, 1993). In this system, strategic guidance is issued at the top, and units further down are asked to identify issues they think are strategic. Leaders and managers at the top then select the issues they wish to have addressed, perhaps reframing the issues before passing them on to units or task forces. Task forces then present strategic alternatives to leaders and managers, who select which ones to pursue. Strategies are then implemented in the next phase. Each issue is managed relatively separately, although it is necessary to make sure choices in one issue area do not cause trouble in other issue areas.

As noted in Chapter Two, Baltimore and a number of other cities have institutionalized strategic issues management through use of the CitiStat system. A central analysis staff uses geographically coded data to spot trends, events, and issues that need to be addressed by line departments. The heads of the relevant units meet regularly (once or twice a month) with the mayor and his key advisers, including the heads of finance, human resources, and information technology, to examine the data and address the issues face to face. Actions and follow-up procedures (including the times when units heads are expected to report back on results) are agreed to on the spot. Several important successes have occurred in which better outcomes were produced, money was saved, or teamwork and competence were enhanced, and in some instances all three results occurred (Schachtel, 2001; Linden, 2002).

Although many public and nonprofit organizations have several task forces in operation at any one time, fewer take the next step of designing and using a strategic issues management system. They do not establish an overall framework of organizational goals or policy objectives, nor do they seek out issues to address or make sure their various issues management activities add up to increased organizational effectiveness. To make this approach work, organizational leaders and managers should consider taking this last step, keeping in mind that the resulting centralization of certain key decisions at the top is likely to draw the attention and resistance of those who do not want to see power concentrated in that way or who dislike the resulting decisions. Interestingly, Hennepin County relied on a strategic issues management system before it moved on to create an integrated units of management system.

Contract Approach

The contract approach (Figure 10.3) is another popular system of institutionalizing strategic planning and management, especially in simple to moderately complex shared-power environments. In the United States the contract approach is employed for much of the planning and delivery of many publicly financed so-

FIGURE 10.3. CONTRACT APPROACH.

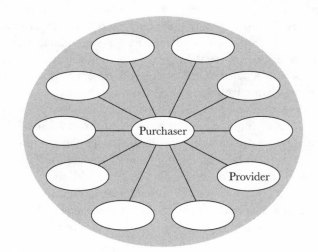

cial services via either public or nonprofit service providers (Milward and Provan, 2003). This system is also used to institutionalize strategic planning and management in school districts with site-based management.

In this system there is a *center* that establishes strategic objectives for the jurisdiction or organization as a whole, negotiates contracts with individual units of management, monitors performance, and ensures the integrity of the system. In the language of economics the center is the *principal,* and the individual units of management are the *agents.* In the language of reinventing government, the center *steers* while the units *row* (Osborne and Plastrik, 1997). The contract between the center and a unit outlines the unit's expected performance, defines its resources, lists other support the unit can expect from the center, and describes a review and renegotiation sequence. Within the framework and legal strictures of the contract, general managers of individual units and their staffs are free to do whatever they think is necessary or desirable to ensure adequate performance. At its best this approach allows both the center and the individual units to focus on what is important for them—both are empowered to do their jobs better. In such a system there is a strategic plan for the center and one for each of the units. Key system concerns include the content and approach embodied in the center's plan, the center's difficulties in acquiring adequate information, the proper alignment of incentives for the principal and the agents, the difficulties the center may have in exercising control in the face of a large number of contractors, and ways to ensure adequate investments by the units if they cannot be sure of a long-term contract with the center.

Collaboration Approach

Collaboration is a fourth type of strategic management system. Like contracting, collaboration is increasingly being used to govern and manage in shared-power environments. In fact the contract system represents a classic form of collaboration, but there are many different and often more complicated approaches to collaboration that are more suitable than competitive contracting for situations involving moderate to high levels of complexity and ambiguity (Alexander, 1995; Gray, 1996; Light, 1998; Milward and Provan, 2003). Human service systems often embody contracting and additional collaboration approaches—contracts for what can be specified and governed with reasonable ease, and supplemental collaboration for those situations involving higher levels of complexity and ambiguity and therefore requiring greater reliance on trust, shared norms, professionalism, and learning by doing for effective governance and management (Romzek, 1996; Huxham, 2003).

Collaboration involves varying degrees of sharing power and resources (such as information, money, clients, and authority) between units to achieve common ends that each unit could not achieve separately. The gain beyond what could be achieved separately is the *collaborative advantage* (Huxham, 1993, 2003), and the often elusive pursuit of this advantage is behind the persistent calls for more collaboration.

Collaboration is particularly useful when addressing problems for which no organization is fully in charge. Situations of this sort occur when, for example, a marked degree of separation exists between the source and user of funds; services are jointly produced (that is, service recipients are at least partly responsible for effective production, as occurs in mental health services); or the key governance and management task is arranging networks rather than managing hierarchies (Milward and Provan, 2003). Milward and Provan (2003), in their longitudinal study of mental health service delivery networks, found that network effectiveness is greatest when there is a strong central integrating unit, clear and consistent lines of authority and accountability embodied in contracts, aligned incentives that give everyone a stake in the success of the network, system stability, and munificent resources. These factors allowed constructive norms, social capital, and network learning capabilities to develop and needed incremental investments and changes to be made. Interestingly, the contracts in these situations are what economists call *relational contracts,* as opposed to *competitive contracts* (Milward and Provan, 2003, p. 10). Relational contracting involves infrequent rebidding and instead focuses on maintaining an effective relationship between buyer and seller—because there are only a few sellers to begin with; the production function is ambiguous; and effective performance by the seller depends on trust, collaboration, and long-term investment in the network's infrastructure. A key collaboration system concern is how to achieve the right balance between network stability and adaptability. Milward and Provan (2003) found that the highest-performing mental health networks were the most stable, in the sense that there were no significant changes in any structural feature or funding relationships. Stability allows the all-important trust, shared norms, expertise, productive relationships, learning by doing, and long-term investments to occur (Huxham, 2003). However, if a network is too stable, learning and responsiveness to environmental changes will diminish and the network will be unlikely to respond effectively to unexpected changes (Weick and Sutcliffe, 2001; Zollo and Winter, 2002). Because of the importance of stability to performance, Milward and Provan (2000) say they "believe that if a system must be changed, it must be done infrequently and, if possible, incrementally" (p. 258). Another key concern is the continual need to make sure incentives are aligned properly, so that participants have an incentive to maintain the network and high performance levels.

Portfolio Management Approach

In the portfolio management approach entities of various sorts (programs, projects, products, services, or providers) are arrayed against dimensions that have some strategic importance. The dimensions usually consist of the attractiveness or desirability of the entity (from high to low) and the capability of the organization or community to deliver what is needed (also from high to low).

Figure 10.4 shows one of the portfolios used to develop a three-year marketing strategy for The Royal Hospitals in Belfast, Northern Ireland (the organization whose vision of success was discussed in Chapter Eight). The Royal is a self-governing trust that is part of the National Health Service system and must compete for the business it receives. The portfolio outlines the Royal's services in terms of desired market share in the Belfast (Eastern Health and Social Services Board [EHSSB]) region for the three years beginning with 1993. The Royal has or seeks a monopoly or near-monopoly in the services that fall in the upper right-hand quadrant of Figure 10.4, such as neurosurgery and neurology. It faces much more competition for delivery of the services that fall in the lower left-hand corner. The Royal therefore has to have different strategies to manage services that fall in different quadrants.

As the example from the Royal shows, portfolio methods are flexible in that any dimensions of interest may be arrayed against one another and entities then mapped on to the resulting matrix. Portfolio methods can also be used at suborganizational and supraorganizational levels as well to assess options against strategically important factors (Nutt and Backoff, 1992; Bryson, 2001, 2003a). Unfortunately, few public and nonprofit organizations (or communities) make formal use of the portfolio system, even though many probably use it informally. The problem of course with using this method in a formal way is that it creates comparisons that may be troubling for politically powerful actors.

Goal or Benchmark Approach

In general, the goal or benchmark approach is much looser than the integrated units of management approach and is generally applied at the community, regional, or state level. It is designed to gain reasonable agreement on overarching goals or indicators (benchmarks) toward which relatively independent groups, units, or organizations might then direct their energies. This consensual agreement on goals and indicators can function somewhat like the corporate control exercised in integrated models, although it is of course weaker. This system's looseness means that calling it a strategic management system may be an overstatement. Nonetheless, when agreement can be reached and support for implementation

FIGURE 10.4. PORTFOLIO MANAGEMENT
APPROACH OF THE ROYAL HOSPITALS.

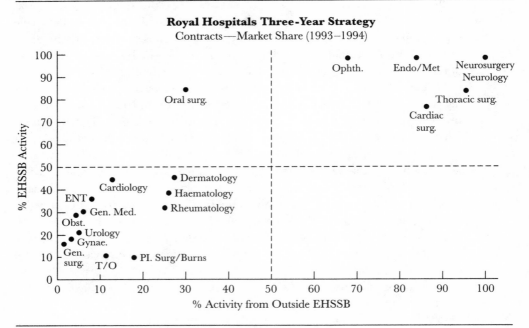

Royal Hospitals Three-Year Strategy
Contracts—Market Share (1993–1994)

Source: Reprinted with the permission of The Royal Hospitals Trust.

can be generated, this approach can work reasonably well. Besides, in the fragmented, shared-power environments in which most public problems occur, this approach may be the only viable approach. For example, most community strategic plans are implemented via goal or benchmark systems (Wheeland, 2003). Typically, large numbers of leaders and citizens are involved in the process of goal setting and strategy development. Then action plans outline what each participating organization might do to help implement the strategies and achieve the goals on a voluntary basis.

The Oregon Benchmarks program provides a state-level example (Oregon Progress Board, 2003). A statewide and inclusive effort was begun in Oregon in the early 1990s to develop a statewide strategic plan. The planning process was—and continues to be—managed by the Oregon Progress Board, an independent state planning and oversight agency established in 1989. The resulting plan was called Oregon Shines, and an updated version, Oregon Shines II, was published in 1997. The current plan includes three goals: quality jobs for all Oregonians; safe, caring, and engaged communities; and healthy, sustainable surroundings.

Goal achievement is measured using an extensive set of indicators called the Oregon Benchmarks. These indicators are also updated regularly. Every two years, the Progress Board issues the *Benchmark Performance Report,* which tracks statewide progress against the indicators. The logic of the system is outlined in Figure 10.5 (note that the figure is comparable to a very simple oval map). The statewide strategic plan includes a vision of "a prosperous Oregon that excels in all spheres of life." The three goals are meant to help agencies and organizations realize the vision. Each goal is broken down into a set of objectives. Progress toward accomplishing the objectives, goals, and vision is measured by a set of ninety benchmarks.

State agencies are expected by the governor and legislature to use benchmark-based planning, budgeting, and management systems geared to producing gains against the benchmarks. This feature is the tightest part of the system. Cities, counties, communities, and other entities throughout the state are also encouraged to do their part by developing their own benchmarks linked to the state benchmarks. The success of the system depends on broadly based, bipartisan political support. The desire to make progress against individual indicators or sets of indicators provides the basis for a large number of collaborative efforts throughout the state involving the public, private, and nonprofit sectors.

As I suggested earlier, although there are six general types of strategic management systems, any actual system is likely to be a hybrid of all six types. For example, in the School District some issues, such as overall staffing and finance, are handled in an integrated way. Others, such as issues involving curriculum reform, are handled on an issue-by-issue basis. Site-based management of individual schools fits the contract model—an agreement between the district office and individual schools outlines performance expectations; resource allocations; basic rules, regulations, and procedures; and a review schedule. Within the envelope provided by the agreement, individual schools have considerable freedom to manage their own affairs. The district is also engaged in a variety of collaborative efforts with other local governmental units, businesses, and nonprofit organizations. Community education staff use an informal portfolio approach to assess program offerings in terms of program desirability and the district's ability to deliver. And finally, the school board establishes an overall set of goals to which everyone is expected to contribute and around which the board hopes cross-sector collaborations will develop.

Process Guidelines

The following guidelines should be kept in mind by leaders and managers as they review implemented strategies and ponder what to do about them. General guidelines are presented first, and then specific suggestions are offered for strategy maintenance,

FIGURE 10.5. GOAL AND BENCHMARK APPROACH OF OREGON SHINES II.

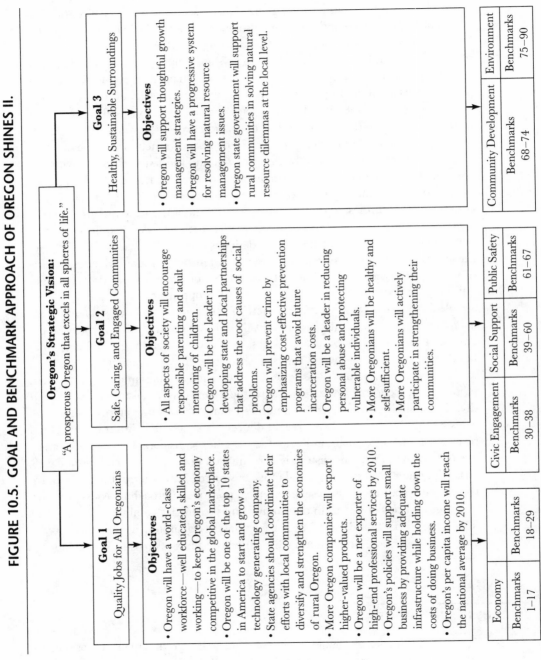

Oregon's Strategic Vision:
"A prosperous Oregon that excels in all spheres of life."

Goal 1
Quality Jobs for All Oregonians

Objectives

- Oregon will have a world-class workforce—well educated, skilled and working—to keep Oregon's economy competitive in the global marketplace.
- Oregon will be one of the top 10 states in America to start and grow a technology generating company.
- State agencies should coordinate their efforts with local communities to diversify and strengthen the economies of rural Oregon.
- More Oregon companies will export higher-valued products.
- Oregon will be a net exporter of high-end professional services by 2010.
- Oregon's policies will support small business by providing adequate infrastructure while holding down the costs of doing business.
- Oregon's per capita income will reach the national average by 2010.

Goal 2
Safe, Caring, and Engaged Communities

Objectives

- All aspects of society will encourage responsible parenting and adult mentoring of children.
- Oregon will be the leader in developing state and local partnerships that address the root causes of social problems.
- Oregon will prevent crime by emphasizing cost-effective prevention programs that avoid future incarceration costs.
- Oregon will be a leader in reducing personal abuse and protecting vulnerable individuals.
- More Oregonians will be healthy and self-sufficient.
- More Oregonians will actively participate in strengthening their communities.

Goal 3
Healthy, Sustainable Surroundings

Objectives

- Oregon will support thoughtful growth management strategies.
- Oregon will have a progressive system for resolving natural resource management issues.
- Oregon state government will support rural communities in solving natural resource dilemmas at the local level.

Economy		Civic Engagement	Social Support	Public Safety	Community Development	Environment
Benchmarks 1–17	Benchmarks 18–29	Benchmarks 30–38	Benchmarks 39–60	Benchmarks 61–67	Benchmarks 68–74	Benchmarks 75–90

Source: Oregon Progress Board, 2003, p. 7. Printed with permission.

succession, and termination (for additional details, see Hogwood and Peters, 1983; Baumgartner and Jones, 1993; Kingdon, 1995). A final section presents guidelines for building a strategic management system.

General Guidelines

1. *Stay focused on what is important.* Pay attention to the organization's mission and mandates and the social needs and political problems that justify its existence. Think about how to create public value. Pay attention to the fundamental challenges— strategic issues—that the organization faces as it tries to meet its mandates, pursue its mission, and create public value. Never let the organization and its strategies or plans become ends in themselves. Instead, leaders and managers should focus on key stakeholders and on their own ideals and how best to serve them.

2. *Focus on signs or indicators of success and failure.* Attention should be paid to changes in those signs or indicators that were used to argue for strategy change in the first place, to new indicators that are important to key stakeholders and that shed light on implementation effectiveness, and to results of any summative evaluations. To the extent that any or all of these indicators reveal valid signs of strategic progress or failure, they can support a decision to maintain, reform, or terminate a strategy or plan.

3. *Review the issue framings used to guide strategy formulation in the first place.* Are they still accurate and useful interpretations of reality? Have they led to constructive issue descriptions, strategies, and plans? Or has some reality—political, economic, social, technological, internal, or external—changed, making these issue framings into distortions that suggest unhelpful strategies and plans?

4. *Use existing review opportunities, or create new ones.* Periodic policy reauthorization sessions, strategic issue identification exercises, and annual budget review periods, for example, provide regular review opportunities (Feldman, 2000). Election campaigns and changes in top political or executive leadership present predictable occasions for strategy reviews in public organizations. Similarly, board member turnover and new executive appointments in nonprofit organizations can be occasions for review. For example, the new superintendent in the School District and the new president of Project for Pride in Living both pushed for a new round of strategic planning. However, leaders and managers can create strategy review opportunities almost anytime they wish. Conferences, hearings, study sessions or commissions, media events, investigative reporting, discussion groups, and so on can be arranged whenever leaders and managers wish to promote discussion and critique of strategies.

5. *Create a review group.* The composition of this review group may vary considerably depending on the nature of the review. Legislation and policies requiring

scheduled reviews may specify a particular group—for example, a legislative committee, city council, or nonprofit board of directors. Often, however, organizations have flexibility in choosing participants, and it is often wise to include outsiders with no vested interest in the status quo. They may be counted on to focus on important issues and can offer constructive suggestions for change.

6. *Challenge institutional and organizational rules that favor undesirable inertia.* Institutions have an uncanny ability to take on a life of their own, making constructive change extremely difficult (Wilson, 1989; Osborne and Plastrik, 1997; Kouzes and Posner, 2002). There are many political routines that challenge anything new but do not subject what is already in place to a searching critique. These routines and other rules—embedded in the design and use of existing forums, arenas, and courts—often make present arrangements the taken-for-granted "way things are." This can make a different future unlikely. If the future is to be what we want, these rules must be confronted and set aside when the need arises (Osborne and Plastrik, 1997). For example, the decision of School District's board and superintendent to engage in strategic planning was a signal to key stakeholders and the community that many of the existing rules and routines would be examined and innovative strategies explored.

7. *Remember that organizations usually have greater staying power than their strategies* (Hogwood and Peters, 1983). Typically, therefore, it is easier to change the strategies than the organizations. And typically, it is more productive to call into question or attack the strategies than the organizations. In other words it is likely to be more effective to praise the intentions and goodwill of an organization while attacking its strategies than to attack its motives and goodwill directly. Further, from a strategic standpoint it is often wise to figure out whether problems can be solved with existing organizational or network strategies, because strategies can be created or changed more easily than organizations and networks. Moreover, it is wise to figure out how existing organizations and their adherents might benefit from possible changes in strategy, so that allies can be created rather than opponents (Neustadt and May, 1986; Bryson, Cunningham, and Lokkesmoe, 2002). Sometimes this simply means organizing support for new units or programs within existing organizations. But given the distressing inertia of many organizations, change advocates may ultimately conclude that new organizations and networks are required to solve important issues. Community planning efforts, for example, often involve developing at least partially new networks to frame and address key issues (Kemp, 1993; Wheeland, 2003).

8. *Finally, stay fresh.* Build energy and enthusiasm for continuing with good strategies and addressing new strategic issues. Avoid letting efforts go stale. Issues will not be formulated and addressed effectively unless leaders and managers take responsibility for doing so. A statement attributed to Edmund Burke reminds us that the only thing necessary for the triumph of evil is for good people to do nothing.

Strategy Maintenance Guidelines

1. *To maintain existing strategies, seek little change in current organizational (interorganizational or community) arrangements.* Any significant change is likely to undermine the regime established in the previous phase. It is important, however, to find occasions in forums to recall or reinvigorate the organization's mission and the vision that originally inspired it and to validate the results of previous strategy formulation efforts.

2. *To maintain or marginally modify existing strategies, rely on implementers, invite focused input from consumers, and involve supportive advocates.* Project for Pride in Living made use of various stakeholder involvement mechanisms to evaluate its work and suggest possible changes. Its forty-six-member board was kept fully informed of the strategic planning process. These groups contained a number of community notables and representatives, but no one likely to propose radical and damaging changes, given the ongoing success PPL has had and its substantial support in the community. In contrast, broad involvement of elites and the public is likely to raise issues and conflicts that may require fundamental policy changes (Hogwood and Peters, 1983; Baumgartner and Jones, 1993).

3. *Invest in distinctive competencies necessary for the success of the strategies.* Continual investment is required to maintain the competency necessary for successful, ongoing strategy implementation. Depending on the strategy, this may mean, for example, staff education and professional development, investment in physical infrastructure, nurturance of networks of providers, or bolstering fundraising and marketing capabilities. If the organization must compete for resources, it is particularly important to invest in *distinctive* competencies—that is, those that differentiate the organization from its competitors (Eden and Ackermann, 2000; Johnson and Scholes, 2002).

Strategy Change or Succession Guidelines

1. *To facilitate a move to new strategies, significantly alter existing arrangements.* A new set of issues, decisions, conflicts, and policy preferences is then likely to emerge. For example, the arrivals of a new superintendent at the School District in 1995 and a new president at PPL in 2000 marked changes that along with board and key staff support led to new rounds of strategizing. In the early 1990s, the arrival at NSG headquarters of Captain William Frentzel and later of new senior leadership helped NSG grapple with the issues it faced as its environment changed and existing strategies could be expected to fail.

2. *Create occasions to challenge existing meanings and estrange people from them and to create new meanings and facilitate their enactment.* Leaders and managers may wish to estrange people from the missions, mandates, policies, and strategies that support

particular ways of being in the world for their organizations, networks, or communities (Mangham, 1986; Marris, 1996). New ways of interpreting reality may supply the seed from which a different configuration of policies, plans, programs, projects, products, services, and resource allocations grows. For example, a strategy reassessment may imply that a different set of external or internal categories, stakeholders, value judgments, signs or indicators, or comparisons is relevant. Change advocates may articulate a new or revised vision that inspires action. Leaders and managers must use available occasions and settings to estrange people from existing meanings, because "estrangement creates a circumstance in which *givenness* becomes *possibility*" (Mangham, 1986, p. 144). Often estrangement can occur as a result of altering the way issues are formulated, so that the formulations highlight certain features of the internal and external environments and not others. For example, the Naval Security Group used a set of scenarios to convince skeptics that cooperation with the other services was mandatory, and that realization helped the NSG figure out how best to arrange that cooperation, given that there was no going back to the way things once had been (Frentzel, Bryson, and Crosby, 2000, p. 412).

Even when change advocates are successful in challenging existing strategies on intellectual grounds, they should not expect new strategies to be adopted without a change in political circumstances, particularly in public organizations. As Kingdon (1995) notes, these changes may include public opinion swings, election results, administrative changes, ideological or partisan redistributions in legislative bodies, and interest group pressure campaigns. Before new strategy proposals can be adopted, key decision makers must be receptive, and political changes may be necessary before this is likely to occur. Major change may also depend on a successful search for important ideas and methods for operationalizing these ideas. For example, the School District has had to explore in detail the conceptual and practical meaning of a number of the concepts embodied in its ten strategic initiatives. The definitions and measurement approaches it decides on must address the issues the district faces and also be politically salable. NSG had to figure out what information warfare meant for it. Ongoing workshops and discussions are necessary for people to figure out what changes might mean in practice (Roberts, 2002). Project for Pride in Living, for example, has had an ongoing dialogue about the conceptual and practical meaning of the *self-sufficiency* it seeks for its program participants.

3. *Be aware that strategy succession may be more difficult than adoption of the existing strategy was because the existing strategy is now likely to have a coalition of supporters in place.* Hogwood and Peters (1983) add that the concessions and compromises embedded in the existing strategy are likely to prevent major reforms and reformers are likely to be disappointed with the gains achieved in relation to their efforts.

4. *Remember that both implementers and beneficiaries of existing strategies are likely to be more concerned with strategy implementation details than with policy innovation* (Hogwood and Peters, 1983; Roberts and King, 1996). Strategies themselves are often more symbolic than real. What counts is how they are implemented—what they mean in practice. That is where the real action is for implementers and beneficiaries. There is good news and bad news here. The good news for change advocates is that if the issues they are tackling stem mainly from existing strategies, strategy changes may be adopted before implementers and beneficiaries of the status quo know what is happening. The bad news is that implementers and beneficiaries may be able to kill any strategy they do not like during implementation. More good news for change advocates is that if the problem is not caused by existing strategy, only strategy implementers may need to be convinced of the virtues of the changes. The bad news is they may not be convinced. The School District's principals and teachers pay careful attention to any administrative and educational reforms. Their support had to be nurtured every step of the way, because they can successfully torpedo almost any major change.

5. *To make major strategy changes, rely on key decision makers, along with implementers and beneficiaries.* In all likelihood, to make substantial changes leaders and managers will need the support of a coalition different from the one that adopted and implemented existing strategies. A new constellation of ideas, stakeholder interests, and agreements will need to be worked out (Sabatier and Jenkins-Smith, 1993). For example, the School District relied on a relatively stable board, an incumbent superintendent and assistant superintendent, and the support of most staff and a substantial fraction of the community to formulate its reform agenda, embodied in its strategic plan, and to implement major portions of that plan. There was no effective opposition to the new strategic plan, in part because some important critics were engaged and became supporters. Any new opponents must be converted to become supporters or else kept at bay if the board, implementers, and beneficiaries are to succeed with implementing all of the plan.

6. *To achieve strategy succession, consider a move either to split aspects of the strategy or to consolidate strategies.* Splitting means carving off and eliminating, revising, or phasing in aspects of a strategy. Consolidation means joining together strategies not previously joined. Reframing the way issues and strategies are viewed can facilitate this splitting or consolidation. Moreover, key stakeholders will favor splitting or consolidation if it is in their interest. Splitting or consolidation can also resolve conflicts over areas of political influence through allowing either separate or combined budgetary allocations and, depending on the circumstances, allowing ambiguous or clear allocations of jurisdiction. For example, a move to budgeting based on site-based management will sharpen some conflicts between a school district's headquarters and individual schools, particularly those related to the fairness of

allocations across the district, but will redirect other conflicts, particularly those involving allocations within each school, to individual schools. Conflicts over ideas are less easily resolved, although good analysis may help. However, there may be strong coalitions in support of each position, and no amount of analysis may convince them to reassess their positions (Benveniste, 1989; Sabatier and Jenkins-Smith, 1993).

7. *Consider building a new system without dismantling the old system.* The result is parallel, redundant, or competing systems, but often there are overall net social gains through better market segmentation and the benefits of competition (Bendor, 1985). For example, the move to voucher systems and the creation of charter schools are ways to create new educational systems without directly taking apart the traditional public school system.

8. *Invest in distinctive competencies that continue to be relevant, and build the new competencies that are needed.* For example, the Naval Security Group continuously invests in the competency of its staff, particularly as technology changes. Its move to being the Navy's executive agent for information warfare has also required NSG to develop and maintain a new set of competencies. Put simply, you cannot get to where you are going without the ability to get there.

Strategy Termination Guidelines

1. *Think of strategy termination as an extreme version of strategy change.* Many of the strategy change or succession guidelines are applicable to strategy termination as well. And a new coalition organized around new ideas, stakeholder interests, and agreements is likely to be necessary. Given the probable resistance of current implementers and beneficiaries, leadership will be a crucial component of all strategy termination efforts. And a fundamental leadership task will be to estrange important stakeholders from strategies to be terminated (Mangham, 1986).

2. *Engage in cutback management when programs need to be eliminated or severely reduced.* A substantial literature has developed on how to manage cutbacks in general. Behn (1983) argues that there are typically two stages to cutback efforts in public organizations. In the first stage the organization typically borrows against the future to cover the gap between current revenues and needed expenditures. Yet if revenues are not increased in the future, this tactic merely makes the adjustments to retrenchment worse by postponing the second stage, or day of reckoning, when major cuts and redesigns are made. The following steps appear to be important cutback management tasks, but even though useful they obviously provide no panacea or quick fix (Behn, 1983; Nutt, 2001a; Holzer, Lee, and Newman, 2003):

- Take a long-term view.
- Develop the support of key leaders, decision makers, and constituencies, including legislators, if necessary, in the public sector.

- Emphasize the mission, vision, and values to be adhered to.
- Develop clear guidelines and goals for making reductions.
- Emphasize the importance of focusing on results, accountability, and integrity.
- Use strategic assessments and performance measures to determine what to cut and what to reward.
- Rely on transparent communications to build an understanding of the problems to be faced and to build cooperation among affected units, unions, employees, and other stakeholders.
- Maintain morale, in part by indicating what is off limits to cuts.
- Attract and keep quality people, which may be particularly difficult when people think the ship is sinking.
- Reinvest and redeploy staff based on a strategic vision, create opportunities for innovation, and emphasize continuous improvement in what remains.
- Create incentives for cooperation.
- Avoid mistakes.
- Be compassionate.

Guidelines for Building a Strategic Management System

Building an effective strategic management system is an evolutionary process and typically requires several successful cycles of strategic planning. The following guidelines are adapted from those followed by Hennepin County as it has gone about constructing its strategic management system (Hennepin County, 2001, pp. 8–9):

1. *Apply the strategic management system to the whole organization.* The system should provide a framework for linking strategic goals and performance indicators to operational results. It should provide a way to cascade high-level measures down to more specific operational measures and should allow the roll-up of operational results to higher levels where they can be analyzed and used to support strategic decision making.

2. *Build on performance measurement and management approaches already in use in the organization.* Do not reinvent any more wheels than you need for an effective vehicle.

3. *Focus on a small number of key results and indicators.* A few key indicators should be identified at each level of the organization. Using balanced scorecards is one way to do this, because they typically rely on a few key indicators. Development of the indicators should make use of stakeholder input, facilitate the identification of strategic issues, and allow for the measurement of success.

4. *Use a common set of categories for performance measures.* Again, use of a balanced scorecard can facilitate adoption of a common set of performance indicators because of the scorecard's emphasis on the learning and growth, internal process, financial, and customer and constituent categories of indicators. Using the same

set of categories across the organization will help the organization measure short- and long-term progress toward results and how best to allocate resources across strategies, functions, and levels.

5. *Connect performance measures to specific programs, services, and activities.* The performance measures should tell a story about the purpose of the activity, its implementation, and its effect on or benefit to the user.

6. *Support the linking of organizational performance and individual performance.* The use of a consistent and complementary set of performance indicators promotes alignment throughout the organization. As a result the linkage of individual goals and performance to the organization's strategic goals and performance is facilitated.

7. *Use the strategic management system to support planning, decision making, budgeting, evaluation, and learning.* A good system should provide a stream of strategic and operational data for planning, decision making, and budgeting purposes. The data should be available to inform regularly scheduled as well as ad hoc management processes and events. The system, in other words, should become a part of the way the organization does business and should underpin a culture of excellent performance. This will happen more quickly and effectively if the system is easy to use and makes ongoing evaluation and learning possible.

8. *Review and update the system on a regular basis.* The system should be adjusted as necessary in response to experience, changes in the organization, and changes in the environment.

Summary

In this last step in the Strategy Change Cycle, leaders, managers, and other stakeholders review strategies that have resulted from previous steps or emerged along the way to determine whether they should be maintained, significantly altered, or terminated. This chapter has discussed why strategies cease to work and outlined the benefits of moving successfully through this review step. The most important benefits are the assurance that the new strategy remains responsive to important issues, resolution of residual implementation difficulties, generation of needed energy for strategic renewal, and pruning of areas that are overcrowded with bits and pieces of assorted strategies. This step also addresses building an effective strategic management system.

In this step leaders and managers should focus on the issues that prompted the strategy under review and decide whether those issues are still relevant. They should rely on indicators of strategy success or failure to help them decide whether strategies should be maintained, reformed, or terminated. If the strategies have not been effective or if the situation has changed, it may be necessary to identify new strategic issues and modify or eliminate particular strategies. Whatever the cause of this changed approach, it may also be necessary to revise the understandings that underlie the adopted strategies. Leaders and managers must also recognize that working with existing organizational structures, rather than trying to change or replace them, may be very productive at this point. A review group and review opportunities must be established and institutional inertia must be overcome, however, in order to review and perhaps change or replace existing strategies.

The design and use of forums, arenas, and the like in this step will vary, depending on whether an existing strategy is to be maintained, reformed, or terminated. In order to maintain and incrementally improve the strategy, leaders and managers should seek little change in the existing settings. They may be able to involve mainly implementers and beneficiaries in the strategy review. If significant change is needed, the design and use of the pertinent forums, arenas, and such will have to be significantly altered. Leaders and managers will have to create or redesign forums to allow challenges to existing meanings and enactment of new meanings. Once again implementers and beneficiaries are the most likely participants in the review, although some key decision makers and probably a new supportive coalition will have to be enlisted as well. Possible approaches to strategy succession involve splitting or consolidating strategy elements or developing a parallel system. Strategy termination is an extreme version of strategy succession. Leaders and managers will need to employ cutback management strategies and techniques to minimize the resulting pain and dislocation and to make sure the organization continues to create public value. Finally, leaders and managers should renew their own energy for working on the important issues their organizations or communities face.

Strategic management systems (or performance management systems) are organizational arrangements meant to ensure ongoing strategic management of organizations and their strategies. There are various types of strategic management systems, but virtually every system in practice is a hybrid of two or more of the types. Construction, maintenance, and revision of a strategic management system is almost always an evolutionary process that unfolds as the organization gains experience with strategic planning, results-based budgeting, performance management, and strategic measurement and evaluation. It usually takes years of experience to build a really effective and vital system and to build the culture of outstanding performance that goes along with it.

PART THREE

MANAGING THE PROCESS AND GETTING STARTED WITH STRATEGIC PLANNING

Strategic planning is in no way a substitute for leadership. Nor does strategic planning implement itself. It is simply a set of concepts, procedures, and tools designed to help an organization's (or community's) leaders, managers, planners, and staff think, act, and learn strategically. People who want to use strategic planning must attend to a wide range of leadership concerns. This section addresses these needs.

Chapter Eleven addresses the leadership tasks that have to be accomplished to make strategic planning work. Leaders must understand the context; understand the people involved; sponsor and champion the process; foster collective leadership; design and use formal and informal settings for discussion, decision making, and conflict management; and put all the necessary understandings and efforts together over the course of the Strategy Change Cycle. Many different people will need to lead at times and follow at times to accomplish these tasks. When strategic planning does work, it is a collective achievement.

In Chapter Twelve, the final chapter, the three major examples of strategic planning used throughout this book—the School District, Project for Pride in Living, and the Naval Security Group—are summarized and discussed. Then a number of process guidelines are presented to help organizations (and communities) get started with their own strategic planning process.

CHAPTER ELEVEN

LEADERSHIP ROLES FOR MAKING STRATEGIC PLANNING WORK

John M. Bryson, Barbara C. Crosby

Leaders perform political, spiritual, and intellectual functions as well as managerial and group-maintenance tasks. These range from providing vision and strategies for change, to mobilizing a constituency, to facilitating group decisions or creating coalitions.

CHARLOTTE BUNCH, *PASSIONATE POLITICS*

As has been emphasized earlier, strategic planning is *not* a substitute for effective leadership. There is *no* substitute for effective leadership when it comes to planning. Strategic planning is simply a set of concepts, procedures, and tools designed to help executives, managers, and others think, act, and learn strategically on behalf of their organizations and their organizations' stakeholders. At its best, strategic planning helps leaders pursue virtuous ends in desirable ways so that public value is created and the common good is advanced. At its worst, strategic planning drives out strategic thought, action, and learning; makes it more difficult for leaders to do their job; and keeps organizations from meeting their mandates, fulfilling their missions, and creating public value. Whether strategic planning helps or hurts depends on how leaders at all organizational levels use it—or misuse it.

In each of the cases detailed in this book, executives, managers, and others had the ability to think, act, and learn strategically. They used strategic planning to tap this ability, canvass diverse views, build coalitions and commitment, and identify and address key organizational issues in order to enhance organizational performance in the eyes of key stakeholders. Without effective leadership focused on both content *and* process concerns, strategic planning simply would not have happened.

So what is leadership? We define it as "the inspiration and mobilization of others to undertake collective action in pursuit of the common good" (Crosby and Bryson, forthcoming). This definition suggests that *leadership* and *leaders* are not the same thing. Effective leadership in public and nonprofit organizations and communities is a collective enterprise involving many people playing different roles at different times, as the statement by Charlotte Bunch quoted at the head of this chapter emphasizes. Indeed, the same people will be leaders at times and followers at times over the course of a strategy change cycle.

Carrying out the following interconnected leadership tasks is important if strategic planning and implementation are to be effective:

- Understanding the context
- Understanding the people involved, including oneself
- Sponsoring the process
- Championing the process
- Facilitating the process
- Fostering collective leadership
- Using dialogue and discussion to create a meaningful process, clarify mandates, articulate mission, identify strategic issues, develop effective strategies, and (possibly) develop a vision of success
- Making and implementing policy decisions
- Enforcing norms, settling disputes, and managing residual conflicts
- Putting it all together

Understanding the Context

Leaders should help constituents view the organization and organizational change in the context of relevant social, political, economic, and technical systems and trends. They should take a long view backward over the organization's history and even its prehistory in order to help people in the organization think more wisely about the future. At the same time, they must avoid being captured by that history (Burns, 1978; Hunt, 1991). They must see history as the interplay of continuity (or stability) and change, and recognize how best to balance these forces in a given context. They will need insight about how today's major global developments—such as the global marketplace, the information revolution, the push for democratization and human rights, and the attention to multiculturalism—affect the organization (Handy, 1996; Lipman-Blumen, 1996; Rifkin, 2000; Cleveland, 2002). They must also have an intimate knowledge of the organization in order to make sense of that organization in relation to the broader context (Mintzberg, Ahlstrand, and Lampel, 1998).

An understanding of the external and internal context of the organization is important for recognizing emergent strategies, understanding how strategic planning might help the organization, tailoring the process to the organization's circumstances, negotiating the initial agreement, framing issues effectively, developing viable strategies for addressing the issues, and getting the strategies adopted and implemented. The leaders in each of the three cases described in this book were very attentive to their organization's internal and external contexts, the sweep of history within which the organization existed, and the possibilities for change presented by the context.

External and internal organizational assessments, stakeholder analyses, and special studies are all designed to attune strategic planning participants to important specifics of the context within which the organization exists. But those explorations typically occur *after* the process has started. Leaders also need some understanding of the context *before* the process begins—in order to know when the time is right to initiate strategic planning, how to organize it, and how to promote it. Leaders can stay attuned to the organization's external and internal environment through personal contacts and observation, broad reading, continuing education, use of the organization's monitoring systems, and reflection.

Leaders should be especially attentive to the possibilities for rather dramatic strategic change. Organizational strategies typically remain stable over long periods and then suddenly change all at once in response to cumulative changes in the environment (Gersick, 1991; Baumgartner and Jones, 1993; Kingdon, 1995; Mintzberg, Ahlstrand, and Lampel, 1998). Leaders need to be in touch with the possibilities for significant change in order to know whether strategic planning should be used to formulate major intended strategy changes—typically through raising the visibility and priority of particular strategies already present in nascent form— or whether strategic planning should be primarily a tool to program improvements in stable strategies. Without leaders' intuitive sense of whether big or small changes are in the cards, strategic planning might be used inappropriately. Hopes for big changes might be raised when they are not possible, or time might be wasted in programming strategies when drastic change is needed.

Understanding the People Involved, Including Oneself

Understanding oneself and others is particularly important for developing the strength of character and insight that invigorates leadership and increases the chances that strategic planning and implementation will help the organization. Leaders should seek to understand the strengths and weaknesses of the people who are or should be involved in strategic planning and implementation, including themselves. Perhaps the most important strength is a passion for fulfilling the organization's mission and contributing to the well-being of multiple stakeholders. Other strengths are professional or technical competencies, interpersonal skills and networks, and a feel for complexity—that is, the ability to view the organization from multiple perspectives and choose from a repertoire of appropriate behaviors (Luke, 1998; Cleveland, 2002; Bolman and Deal, 2003). In strategic planning the personal qualities of integrity, self-efficacy, and courage are especially important in helping participants develop the trust and determination to take risks, explore difficult issues and new strategies, and pursue what might be unpopular causes. Additional personal leadership assets include a sense of humor, awareness of one's habitual ways of learning and interacting with people, commitment to continual learning, possession of power and authority, supportive personal networks, ability to balance competing demands, and awareness of how leadership is affected by one's location in major social hierarchies. Leaders should remember that an understanding and marshaling of personal assets is perhaps the most powerful instrument of all (Lipman-Blumen, 1996).

Useful approaches to understanding oneself and others range from formal assessments to deep study and reflection to informal storytelling. Feedback from others is often highly useful. Effective strategic thinking, acting, and learning seem to depend a great deal on intuition, creativity, and pattern recognition, none of which can be programmed although they may be recognized, facilitated, and encouraged (Mintzberg, Ahlstrand, and Lampel, 1998). Knowing people well, relying on the nominations of trusted colleagues, and betting on the basis of past performance thus may be about the only ways of finding people who are effective strategists. The process of understanding oneself and others can be used to establish personal development plans, choose team members, and gear messages and processes to different styles of learning and interacting.

Sponsoring the Process

Process sponsors typically are top positional leaders. They have enough prestige, power, and authority to commit the organization to undertaking strategic planning and to hold people accountable for doing so. They are not necessarily involved in the day-to-day details of making strategic planning work—the champions do that—but they do set the stage for success and pay careful attention to the progress of the process. They have a vested interest in a successful outcome and do what they can to make sure of that outcome. They also typically are important sources of knowledge about key strategic issues and effective strategies for addressing them. The information they have about the organization and its environment is invaluable. They also are likely to be especially knowledgeable about how to fit the process to key decision points, so that strategic planning dialogue and discussion can inform decisions in the relevant arenas.

Leaders interested in sponsoring a strategic planning process should consider the following guidelines:

1. *Articulate the purpose and importance of the strategic planning effort.* Many participants will need some convincing on the reasons for undertaking a strategic planning effort. Leaders can start by outlining their views of the organization's past, present, and future. They should invoke powerful organizational symbols as they link the strategic planning effort to the organization's mission and values and to the best aspects of the organization's culture (Schein, 1997; Bolman and Deal, 2003). They can also highlight core organizational competencies, key changes in the environment, significant strategic issues that the organization faces or will face, the importance of creating public value, possible actions the organization will need to consider, and the likely consequences of failure to engage in strategic planning. Working from this sketch, leaders should outline in general how they want the organization to engage in strategic planning and what they hope the outcomes and benefits of doing so will be. In doing so they will demonstrate a concern both for the content, process, and outcomes of strategic planning. Emphasizing the importance of the strategic planning effort is vital at the outset and also at points along the way, when participants' enthusiasm is dwindling and their spirits need to be raised and their energies restored.

2. *Commit necessary resources—time, money, energy, money, legitimacy—to the effort.* A crucial way of making the process real is to allocate resources to it. Nothing will demonstrate leaders' seriousness (or lack of it) about strategic planning more than that.

3. *Emphasize at the beginning and at critical points that action and change will result.* This is another crucial way of making the process real for participants and getting them to take it seriously. If they see that strategic planning is real in its consequences, they will invest the necessary effort in the process.

4. *Encourage and reward creative thinking, constructive debate, and multiple sources of input and insight.* Sponsors should emphasize the importance of creativity and constructive debate and the value of strategically significant ideas no matter what their origin. They should reward those who supply creative ideas. Otherwise, the leaders will be viewed as hypocrites and important sources of new ideas and information will be cut off. The School District's final strategic plan included virtually all the recommendations of the task forces charged with addressing the district's strategic issues. The district's culture of participative decision making was thereby enhanced, the plan was strengthened, and the superintendent and board gained credibility as decision makers who meant it

when they said they believed in inclusion and empowerment. Encouraging constructive debate also means anticipating where conflicts might develop and thinking about how those conflicts might be addressed productively. In particular, leaders must think about which conflicts can be addressed within the existing rules of the game and which can be managed effectively only if the rules of the game are changed. The School District's board and superintendent, for example, decided that they had to change the rules of the game regarding teachers' workloads. At the beginning of the process each year teachers were expected to teach ten classes out of sixteen possible teaching slots (four class sessions per quarter times four quarters). That was increased to twelve classes out of sixteen slots for financial reasons. There simply was no other way for the district to meet its educational goals and still remain financially viable. In the case of the Naval Security Group, after the Goldwater-Nichols Act of 1986 mandated collaboration across the military services, NSG planners had to work with many senior decision makers to get them and other internal stakeholders to realize that the rules of the game had changed.

5. *Be aware of the possible need for outside consultants.* Outside consultants may be needed to help design the process, facilitate aspects of it, do various studies, or perform other tasks. It is a sign of strength to ask for help when you need it. Enough money must be budgeted to pay for any consultants you may need.

6. *Be willing to exercise power and authority to keep the process on track.* Strategic planning is inherently prone to break down (Bryson and Roering, 1988, 1989). For one thing, effective strategic planning is a nonroutine activity, and as March and Simon (1958, p. 185) have pointed out, there is a sort of "Gresham's Law of Planning" at work in organizations: "Daily routine drives out planning." Another danger with strategic planning is that people are likely to fight or flee whenever they are asked to deal with tough issues or failing strategies, serious conflicts, or significant changes. Sponsors have a key role to play in keeping the process going through the difficult patches; they can provide a *holding environment* (Heifetz, 1994) that provides a measure of safety for participants as they are encouraged to face unpleasant challenges or dilemmas. How these difficulties are handled will say a lot about the leaders' and participant's characters. As Csikszentmihalyi (1990) points out, "The ability to persevere despite obstacles and setbacks is the quality people most admire in others, and justly so; it is probably the most important trait not only for succeeding in life, but for enjoying it as well." The challenges are opportunities to demonstrate courage, forge strong characters, and end up with a more effective organization to boot (Selznick, 1957; Terry, 1993). Wise dispute resolution and conflict management strategies are called for, but they may need to be backed up by power and authority to make them work well.

Championing the Process

The champions are the people who have primary responsibility for managing the strategic planning process day to day. They are the ones who keep track of progress and also pay attention to all the details. They model the kind of behavior they hope to get from other participants: reasoned, diligent, committed, enthusiastic, and good-spirited pursuit of the common good. They are the cheerleaders who, along with the sponsors, keep the process on track and push, encourage, and cajole the strategic planning team and other key participants through any difficult spots. Champions, especially, need the interpersonal skills and feel for complexity noted earlier. Sometimes the sponsors and champions are the same people, but usually they are not.

Champions should keep the following guidelines in mind:

1. *Keep strategic planning high on people's agendas.* Daily routine can easily drive out attention to strategic planning. Blocking out time in people's calendars is one way to gather participants together and focus their attention. Another is calling on sponsors to periodically emphasize the importance of the process. Yet another is to publish updates on the process in special memoranda or regular newsletters. Yet another is to circulate think pieces, special reports, relevant CDs and audiotapes, and so on, that encourage strategic thought and action. By whatever means, people will need to be reminded and shown on a regular basis that something good will come from getting together to talk about what is important and then doing something about it.

2. *Attend to the process without promoting specific solutions.* Champions are far more likely to gain people's participation and constructive involvement if they are seen as advocates more for the process than for specific solutions. When the champions are seen as committed partisans of specific solutions, other participants may boycott or torpedo the process rather than seek to find mutually agreeable strategies to address key issues.

3. *Think about what has to come together (people, tasks, information, reports) at or before key decision points.* When it comes to strategy formulation and strategic planning, time is not linear; instead it presents important junctures. The best champions think like theater directors, orchestrators, choreographers, or playwrights. They think about stage settings, themes, acts and scenes, actors and audiences, and how to get the *right people* with the *right information* on stage at the *right time*—and then get them off.

4. *Organize the time, space, materials, and participation needed for the process to succeed.* Without attention to the details of the process, its benefits simply will not be

achieved. The "trivialities" of the process matter a great deal—they are not trivial at all (Huxham, 1990). Effective champions therefore arrange the retreats, book the rooms, make sure any necessary supplies and equipment are handy, send out the meeting notices, distribute the briefing papers and minutes, oversee the production details of the draft and final plans, and keep track of the work program.

5. *Pay attention to the language used to describe strategic planning and implementation.* One function of strategic planning is to establish a vocabulary and format that allow people to share views about what is fundamental for the organization (Mintzberg, 1994, p. 352). At various points in the process participants are likely to wonder about the meaning of particular planning concepts (mission, vision, goals, issues, strategies) and how they relate to substantive matters of concern. An introduction to strategic planning, often in a retreat setting, is typically a useful way to begin developing a common vocabulary of concepts with which to organize efforts to plan strategically. As the process proceeds further, discussion will almost invariably focus again at various points on the meaning of planning concepts and how they relate to the subjects of group discussion and specific products of group work. Champions should be prepared to discuss similarities and differences among various concepts and how these concepts do or do not relate to substantive concerns, products, and outcomes. The specific vocabulary a group uses to label things does not matter as much as development of a shared understanding of what things mean.

6. *Keep rallying participants and pushing the process along.* The duration of a successful strategic planning process can vary from a few weeks or months to two or more years (Bryson and Roering, 1988, 1989). Some processes must fail one or more times before they succeed. Some never succeed. Champions should keep the faith and push until the process does succeed or until it is clear that it will fail and there is no point in continuing. At the same time, it is important to remember that strategic planning is likely to feel like a failure in the middle, as Kanter (1983) has said of innovations. Champions keep pushing to help the strategic planning team and organization move through the failure stage toward success. Champions also need to know when it is time to quit pushing, at least for a while, and when it is time to quit altogether.

7. *Develop champions throughout the organization.* A champion-in-chief may oversee the entire strategic planning process, but he or she should seek out champions throughout the organization to oversee parts of the process. Otherwise, the central champion may be in danger of burning out or may have no one to take over if he or she has to drop out of the process. Having multiple champions is especially important when the planning occurs in multiorganizational or community settings (Bardach, 1998; Huxham and Vangen, 2000; Huxham, 2003).

Facilitating the Process

Process facilitators are often helpful in moving a strategic planning process along because of their group process skills, the attention they can give to structuring and managing group interactions, and the likelihood that they have no stake in the substantive outcomes of the process, particularly if they are outsiders (Schwarz, 2002; Chrislip, 2002). The presence of a facilitator means that champions can be free to participate in substantive discussions without having to worry too much about managing the group process. A skilled facilitator also can help a group build trust, interpersonal skills, and conflict management ability. Building trust is important because the members of a strategic planning team often come from various functions and have never worked together before, let alone on fundamental strategic questions facing the organization.

Skilled facilitation usually depends on the establishment of a successful partnership among facilitators, sponsors, and champions. To do their work well, facilitators must learn a great deal very quickly about the organization and its politics, issues, culture, and secrets. They must quickly gain the trust of the sponsors and champions, learn the lay of the land, and demonstrate their ability to further the strategic planning effort. Their efforts will be thwarted, however, unless the sponsors and champions commit themselves to working closely with the facilitators. The sponsors, champions, and facilitators usually form the core group that moves the process forward with the help of the strategic planning team that is usually a part of most planning efforts (Bryson, Ackermann, Eden and Finn, 1996; Friend and Hickling, 1997; Schwarz, 2002).

Facilitators should come to any process with a well-developed set of group process skills (Kaner and others, 1996; Johnson and Johnson, 2000; Iacofano, 2001; Schwarz, 2002) and with skills especially applicable to strategic planning for public and nonprofit organizations (Nutt and Backoff, 1992; Friend and Hickling, 1997; Justice and Jamieson, 1999). In addition to employing these skills they should consider following these guidelines:

1. *Know the strategic planning process, and explain to others how it works, at the beginning and at many points along the way.* Participants will often be experiencing a new process at the same time as they are working on issues of real importance to the organization. Thus they can easily get lost. Facilitators play a key role in explaining to participants where they are, where they can head, and how they might get there.

2. *Tailor the process to the organization and the groups involved.* Planning processes must be fitted to the unique circumstances in which organizations and groups find

themselves (Nadler and Hobino, 1998; Christensen, 1999; Alexander, 2000). Facilitators, along with sponsors and champions, are in the best position to design the process so that it fits the organization, its circumstances, and the participants. Facilitators must pay careful attention to both the *tasks* of strategic planning and the *socioemotional maintenance* of the groups and teams involved in the process. Both content and process dimensions are crucial to effective group functioning and indeed are the basic elements of effective team leadership (Johnson and Johnson, 2000).

3. *Convey a sense of humor and enthusiasm for the process and help groups get unstuck.* Sponsors and champions can express humor and enthusiasm for the process but not in the ongoing way that a facilitator can. Strategic planning can be alternately tension-ridden and tedious. Good facilitators can help manage the tensions and relieve the tedium. Facilitators can also help groups confront the difficulties that arise over the course of a strategic planning process. By helping groups reframe their situations imaginatively; invent new options; channel conflict constructively; and tap hidden sources of courage, hope, and optimism, facilitators can provide or find important resources to help groups move forward (Buzan and Buzan, 1993; Terry, 1993; Seligman, 1998; Nelson and McFadzean, 1998; Schwarz, 2002; Bolman and Deal, 2003).

4. *Press groups toward action and the assignment of responsibility for specific actions.* Part of keeping the process moving is making sure that participants engage in timely action. Facilitators should maintain participants' interest, enthusiasm, and commitment. If the whole process is devoted entirely to talking and never gets to acting, people will quickly quit participating. Facilitators should emphasize that not all of the thinking has to take place before any of the acting can occur. Whenever useful and wise actions become apparent—as a result of attention to mission and mandates, stakeholder analyses, SWOC analyses, strategic issue identification, and various strategizing efforts—they should be taken, as long as they do not jeopardize possible choices that decision makers might want to make in the future. There are limits to thinking things out in advance. Often people can know what they think only by acting first, and often important strategies can emerge only by taking small steps and using adaptive learning to figure things out as one goes along (Weick, 1995; Mintzberg, Ahlstrand, and Lampel, 1998). Pushing people toward action does raise the danger of inducing premature closure. People may act on what is immediately at hand without thinking creatively about other options or waiting until the time is right. A good facilitator will have a well-developed intuitive sense about when to push for action and when to hold back. He or she will also be good at probing people and groups about the merits of options and the advisability of taking specific actions.

5. *Congratulate people whenever possible.* In our experience, most people in most organizations suffer from chronic—and sometimes acute—positive reinforcement deprivation. Yet people respond very favorably to kind words and praise from people who are important to them. Indeed, many excellently managed organizations are known for the praise and emotional support they offer their employees (Collins and Porras, 1997; Kouzes and Posner, 2002; Hesselbein and Johnston, 2002). Facilitators are in an especially good position to congratulate people and say good things about them in a genuine and natural way.

Fostering Collective Leadership

When strategic planning is successful for public organizations, it is a collective achievement. Many people contribute to its success, sometimes by leading, other times by following. Collective leadership may be fostered through the following approaches:

1. *Rely on teams.* The team is the basic vehicle for furthering strategic planning. Champions in particular will find much of their time is focused on making sure strategic planning teams or task forces perform well and make effective contributions. There are two reasons why teams are so important. The first is that no one person can have all the relevant quantitative and qualitative information, so forming a team is one way to increase the information available for strategic planning. The second reason is political. To be viable, strategic planning and strategies will need support at many points throughout the organization and from external stakeholders. A strategic plan and intended strategies will need the support of a critical coalition when they are adopted and during implementation. A wisely constructed strategic planning team can provide the initial basis for such a coalition, and team members can do much of the work leading to formation of the necessary coalition.

Team leaders naturally must focus on the accomplishment of team goals or tasks, but they must also attend to individual team members' needs and consciously promote group cohesion (Johnson and Johnson, 2000). Team leadership balances direction, mentoring, and facilitation, what Schaef (1985) describes as enabling "others to make their contributions while simultaneously making one's own" (p. 128). Leaders should help team members

- Communicate effectively (through active listening, dialogue, and other conflict management methods)

- Balance unity around a shared purpose with diversity of views and skills
- Define a team mission, goals, norms, and roles
- Establish an atmosphere of trust
- Foster group creativity and sound decision making
- Obtain necessary resources
- Develop leadership competencies
- Celebrate achievement and overcome adversity

2. *Focus on network and coalition development.* Coalitions are organized around ideas and interests that allow people to see that they can achieve together what they cannot achieve separately. The ways that issues, goals, or visions—and strategies for achieving them—are framed will structure how stakeholders interpret their interests, how stakeholders assess the costs and benefits of joining a coalition, and the form and content of winning and losing arguments. Therefore leaders should use the insights gained from various stakeholder analysis exercises to articulate a view of the world that will lie behind the ways issues, goals, visions, and strategies are framed and make these framings likely to draw significant support from key stakeholders. The worldview public, nonprofit, and community leaders should seek is one that will call up widely shared notions of what constitutes the public interest and the common good (Bryson, Cunningham, and Lokkesmoe, 2002; Chrislip, 2002; Stone, 2002; Crosby and Bryson, forthcoming). The political acceptability of a strategic plan or an individual strategy increases as the benefits of adopting and implementing it increase and the costs diminish for key stakeholders. As Light (1991) notes in relation to presidential agenda setting, it is primarily the issues with the greatest potential benefit for key stakeholders that get on the agenda, and among these, it is the ones that are the least costly for key stakeholders that receive prime consideration. Moreover, any proposal likely to be adopted and implemented will be a carefully tailored response to specific circumstances rather than an off-the-shelf solution imported from somewhere else (Kingdon, 1995; Nadler and Hobino, 1998; Nutt, 2002). And typically, not every member of a winning coalition will agree on every aspect of an entire plan or set of strategies, and that is OK.

Leaders should recognize that coalition development depends on following many of the same guidelines that help them develop effective teams. In particular, successful coalitions are probably more likely to form if organizers employ strategies for valuing the diversity of coalition members and their various ideas and special gifts. Acquiring the necessary resources is also vital to coalition development, and the coalition itself can become a major source of resources for implementing a strategic planning process. Rewarding and celebrating collective achievements and sharing credit for them broadly are also likely to help (Bardach, 1998). In a broader sense, public leaders should work to build a sense of community—that is, a sense of relationship, mutual empowerment, and common purpose—within and beyond their organizations. This is desirable because so many of the problems public and nonprofit organizations are called on to address require multiorganizational, or community, responses (Chrislip, 2002; Linden, 2002). Community may be tied to a place or be what Heifetz and Sinder (1988) and others have called a community of interest, an interorganizational network that often transcends geographical and political boundaries and is designed to address transorganizational problems (Trist, 1983). Leaders contribute to community building by facilitating communal definition and resolution of issues, fostering democratic leader-follower relations (Boyte and Kari, 1996), providing resources, and using their knowledge of group process to help people work together. Most important, Palmer (2000) suggests, leaders build community by "making space for other people to act" (p. 138).

3. *Establish specific mechanisms for sharing power, responsibility, and accountability.* Authority is not usually shared by policymaking bodies or chief executives—and often cannot be by law—but that does not mean power, responsibility, and accountability cannot be shared. Doing so can foster participation, trigger information and resource flows, and build commitment to plans and strategies and their implementation (Linden, 2002). Strategic planning teams, strategic issue task forces, and implementation teams are typical vehicles for sharing power. Action plans should indicate any shared responsibilities. Credit is something else that should be broadly shared.

Using Dialogue and Discussion to Create a Meaningful Process

Creating and communicating meaning is the work of visionary leadership. Sometimes visionary leadership results in a vision of success for the organization, but in the present discussion *visioning* covers a broader range of outcomes; it is meant more as an action than an object. Leaders become visionary when they play a vital role in interpreting current reality, fostering a collective group mission, articulating desirable strategies, and shaping a collective sense of the future (Denhardt, 1993; Hunt, Boal, and Dodge, 1999). Furthermore, visionary leaders must understand important aspects of their own and others' internal worlds, and they must also grasp the meaning of related external worlds. As truth tellers and direction givers, they help people make sense of experience, and they offer guidance for coping with the present and the future by helping people answer these questions: What's going on here? Where are we heading? And how will things look when we get there? They frame and shape the perceived context for action (Smircich and Morgan, 1989), and they "manage" important stakeholders' perceptions of the organization, its strategies, and the effects of these strategies (Lynn, 1987; Neustadt, 1990). In order to foster change, particularly major change, they become skilled in applying the following guidelines for creating and communicating new meanings:

1. *Understand the design and use of forums. Forums* are the basic settings we humans use to create shared meaning through dialogue and discussion (Crosby and Bryson, forthcoming). Much of the work of strategic planning takes place in forums, where fairly free-flowing consideration of ideas and views can take place before proposals are developed for adoption and action in decision-making arenas. The tasks of sponsoring, championing, and facilitating strategic planning are performed primarily in forums. Strategic planning retreats, team meetings, task force meetings, focus groups, strategic planning newsletters, conference calls, e-mail exchanges, and strategic plans themselves—when used as educational devices—are all examples of forums. These forums can be used to develop a shared understanding about what the organization is, what it does or should do, and why.

2. *Seize opportunities to be interpreters and direction givers in areas of uncertainty and difficulty.* Leadership opportunities expand in times of difficulty, confusion, and crisis, when old approaches are clearly not working and people are searching for meaningful accounts of what has happened and what can be done about it (Heifetz, 1994; Schein, 1997; Hunt, Boal, and Dodge, 1999; Kouzes and Posner, 2002). Focusing on strategic issues or failing strategies therefore provides opportunities for exercising leadership, for inspiring and mobilizing others to figure out what might be done to improve the organization's performance in the eyes of key stakeholders. Turning dangers, threats, and crises into manageable challenges is an important task for visionary leaders (Dutton and Jackson, 1987; Jackson and Dutton, 1988; Dutton and Ashford, 1993; Chattopadhyay, Glick, and Huber, 2001). Doing so not only promotes optimism and hardiness but also is likely to free up the necessary thinking, resources, and energy to confront the challenges successfully. The School District's superintendent used an impending financial and demographic crisis to mobilize action not only to address those issues but also to pursue the more inspiring goals of educational reform. NSG faced a far more serious set of challenges all around it and had to find ways to make these challenges manageable on its journey to a new mission, set of technologies, funding arrangements, stakeholder relationships, and distinctive competencies and as it negotiated other changes.

3. *Reveal and name real needs and real conditions.* New meaning unfolds as leaders encourage people to see the real situation and its portents. To illuminate real con-

ditions, leaders may use intuition or integrative thinking (Mintzberg, Ahlstrand, and Lampel, 1998; Cleveland, 2002). They formally or informally scan the organization's environment and discern the patterns emerging from local conditions, or they accept patterns and issues identified by other people such as pollsters or planners. Simply articulating these patterns publicly and convincingly can be an act of revelation. However, leaders cannot just delineate emerging patterns and issues; they must also explain them (Neustadt, 1990). They must relate what they see to their knowledge of societal systems and to people's experience (Boal and Bryson, 1987). Going further, leaders alert followers to the need for action by their "uncovering and exploiting of contradictions in values and between values and practice" (Burns, 1978, p. 43).

4. *Help followers frame and reframe issues and strategies.* In revealing and explaining real conditions, leaders are laying the groundwork for framing and reframing issues facing the organization and strategies for addressing them (Stone, 2002; Bolman and Deal, 2003). The *framing* process consists of naming and explaining the issue, opening the door to alternative ways of addressing it, and suggesting outcomes. The *reframing* process involves breaking with old ways of viewing an issue or strategy and developing a new appreciation of it (Mangham, 1986). As noted earlier, framing and reframing should be connected to stakeholder views and interests.

5. *Offer compelling visions of the future.* Leaders convey their visions through stories rooted in shared history yet focused on the future. These stories link people's experience of the present (cognitions), what they might do about the situation (behaviors), and what they might expect to happen as a result (consequences); in other words the stories help people grasp desirable and potentially real futures (Brickman, 1978; Boal and Bryson, 1987). Effective stories are rich with metaphors that make sense of people's experience, are comprehensive yet open ended, and impel people toward union or common ground (Terry, 1993; Gabriel, 2000). Finally, leaders transmit their own belief in their visionary stories through vivid, energetic, optimistic language (Shamir, Arthur, and House, 1994; Kouzes and Posner, 2002).

6. *Champion new and improved ideas for dealing with strategic issues.* Championing ideas for addressing issues is different from championing the process of strategic planning but is nonetheless important. Astute leaders gather ideas from many sources (Burns, 1978; Neustadt, 1990; Mintzberg, Ahlstrand, and Lampel, 1998). Within organizations and political communities, they foster an atmosphere in which innovative approaches flourish (Heifetz, 1994; Crossan, Lane, and White, 1999; Kouzes and Posner, 2002). Acting in the mode of Schön's *reflective practitioner* (1983), these leaders champion "improved" ideas, ones that have emerged from practice and been refined by critical reflection, including ethical analysis. In analyzing ideas, leaders keep strategic planning participants focused on the outcomes they seek (Nutt, 2002).

7. *Detail actions and expected consequences.* Often actions and consequences are an integral part of leaders' visions or organizational missions and strategies, and they become more detailed as implementation proceeds (Mintzberg and Westley, 1992). Crises, however, can necessitate reversing this sequence. When old behaviors are not working and disaster is imminent, followers may wish leaders to prescribe new behaviors and may be willing to try those behaviors without a clear vision of the outcome for the organization as a whole or its specific strategies. To sustain a leader-follower relationship founded on crisis, however, leaders must soon link the recommended course of action to a higher purpose (Boal and Bryson, 1987; Hunt, Boal, and Dodge, 1999), such as a shared sense of mission. Providing evidence of causal links between the new behaviors and desired outcomes is also critical.

Making and Implementing Decisions

Public and nonprofit leaders are also required to be political leaders—partly because all organizations have political aspects (Bolman and Deal, 2003) and partly because public and nonprofit organizations are inherently involved in politicized decision making much of the time. The key to success, and the heart of political leadership, is understanding how intergroup power relationships shape decision-making and implementation outcomes. Particularly important is understanding how to affect outcomes by having some things never come up for a decision. Specifically, political leaders must undertake the following responsibilities:

1. *Understand the design and use of arenas.* Political leaders must be skilled in designing and using formal and informal *arenas,* the basic settings for decision making (Crosby and Bryson, forthcoming). For the public sector these arenas may be legislative, executive, or administrative. For nonprofit organizations they will include board and management meetings. For interorganizational networks and communities there will be many relevant arenas. It is in arenas that the products of forums—such as strategic plans and important aspects of strategies—are adopted as is, altered, or rejected. A major issue in any strategic planning process is how to sequence the move from planning forums, particularly planning team meetings that include key decision makers, to decision-making arenas. A large fraction of the necessary strategic thinking will occur as part of the dialogue and discussion in forums. Once viable proposals have been worked out, they then can be moved to arenas for any necessary revision, adoption, and implementation— or else rejection. At a minimum, managing the transition from forums to arenas depends on figuring out when key decision points will occur and then designing

the planning process to fit those points in such a way that decisions in arenas can be influenced constructively by the work done in forums. A further issue is how to handle any residual conflicts or disputes that may arise during implementation. The decisions made in arenas usually cannot—and should not try to—cover all the details and difficulties that may come up during implementation. Some advance thinking is therefore almost always in order about the ways these residual or subsidiary conflicts might be handled constructively, either in other arenas or in formal or informal courts.

2. *Mediate and shape conflict within and among stakeholders.* Conflicts, or at least recognizable differences, are necessary if people are to be offered real choices in arenas (Burns, 1978) and if decision makers are to understand these choices and their consequences (Janis, 1989). Further, political leaders must possess transactional skills for dealing with followers, other leaders, and various key stakeholders who have conflicting agendas. To forge winning coalitions, they must bargain and negotiate, inventing options for mutual gain so that they can trade things of value that they control for others' support (Susskind and Field, 1996).

3. *Understand the dynamics of political influence and how to target resources appropriately.* The first requirement for influencing political decision making may be knowing whom to influence. Who controls the agenda of the relevant decision-making body—a city council, a board of directors, or some other group? Who chairs the group and any relevant committees? The next requirement is knowing how to influence. What forms of providing information, lobbying, vote trading, arm-twisting, and so on, are acceptable? Should change advocates try to change the composition of the decision-making bodies? Given the available time, energy, and resources, how might they best be spent (Kaufman, 1986; Benveniste, 1989; Bryson, 2004b)? Basically, political leaders manipulate the costs and benefits of actions so that supporters are more motivated to act in desired directions and opponents are less motivated to resist (Kaufman, 1986). Outcomes in arenas can be affected dramatically by influencing the agenda of what comes up for decision and what does not, thereby becoming a *non-decision* (Bachrach and Baratz, 1963; Crosby and Bryson, forthcoming). Decision outcomes can also be affected by *strategic voting,* in which participants use their knowledge of voting rules and manipulation of their vote resources to steer outcomes in directions they favor. Reshaping the way issues are viewed can also have dramatic effects on how people vote (Riker, 1986).

4. *Build winning, sustainable coalitions.* For strategic planning to be effective, a coalition of support must be built for the process and its outcomes (Bolman and Deal, 2003). There must be a coalition in place that is strong enough to adopt intended strategies and to defend them during implementation. Building winning coalitions can be gritty work. As Riker (1986) notes: "Politics is winning and losing, which depend, mostly, on how large and strong one side is relative to the other.

The actions of politics consist in making agreements to join people in alliances and coalitions—hardly the stuff to release readers' adrenaline as do seductions, quarrels, or chases" (p. 52). Finding ideas (visions, goals, strategies) that people can support that further their interests is a large part of the process but so is making deals in which something is traded in exchange for that support.

5. *Avoid bureaucratic imprisonment.* Political leaders in government particularly may find their ability to make and implement needed decisions severely constrained by the bureaucracies in which they serve. Those bureaucracies usually have intricate, institutionalized rules and procedures and entrenched personnel that hamper any kind of change. Leaders committed to change must continually challenge the rules or else find their way around them. Whenever possible, they should try to win over members of the bureaucracy—for example, by appealing to shared goals (Behn, 1999a). When necessary, they should appeal over the heads of resistant bureaucrats to high-level decision makers or to key external stakeholders (Burns, 1978; Lynn, 1987; Kouzes and Posner, 2002).

Enforcing Norms, Settling Disputes, and Managing Residual Conflicts

Leaders are always called upon to be ethical, not least when they are handling conflict. Disputes and residual conflicts are likely to arise during the implementation of strategies. The decisions made in arenas are unlikely to cover all the details and difficulties that may come up during implementation. These residual or subsidiary conflicts must be handled constructively, either in other arenas or in formal or informal courts, both to address the difficulty at hand *and* to reinforce or change important norms governing the organization. The following tasks are vital to exercising ethical leadership:

1. *Understand the design and use of formal and informal courts. Courts* operate whenever two parties having a conflict rely on a third party (leader, manager, facilitator, mediator, arbitrator, judge) to help them address it. Managing conflict and settling disputes not only takes care of the issue at hand but also reinforces the important societal or organizational norms used to handle it. Leaders must be skilled in the design and use of formal and informal courts, the settings for enforcing ethical principles, constitutions, and laws and for managing residual conflicts and settling disputes (Crosby and Bryson, forthcoming). Formal courts theoretically provide the ultimate social sanctions for conduct mandated or promoted through formal policymaking arenas, but in practice the informal "court of public opinion" can be even more powerful.

2. *Foster organizational integrity and the educating of others about ethics, constitutions, laws, and norms.* In nurturing public organizations that contribute to the common good, leaders must adopt practices and systems that nurture organizational integrity (Frederickson, 1997). Such leaders make a public commitment to ethical principles and then act on them. They involve the organization's stakeholders in ethical analysis and decision making, inculcate a sense of personal responsibility in followers, and reward ethical behavior.

3. *Apply constitutions, laws, and norms to specific cases.* Constitutions are usually broad frameworks establishing basic organizational purposes, structures, and procedures. Laws, although much more narrowly drawn, still typically apply to broad classes of people or actions; moreover, they may emerge from the legislative process containing purposeful omissions and generalities necessary to obtain enough votes for passage (Posner, 1985). Therefore both constitutions and laws require authoritative interpretation as they are applied to specific cases. In the U.S. judicial system, judges, jurors, and attorneys, and even interest groups filing amicus curiae briefs, all contribute to that authoritative interpretation. Outside the formal courts, leaders typically must apply norms rather than laws.

4. *Adapt constitutions, laws, and norms to changing times.* Judicial principles endure even as the conditions that prompted them and the people who created them change dramatically. Sometimes public leaders are able to reshape the law to current needs in legislative, executive, or administrative arenas; often, however, as Neely (1981) suggests, leaders must ask formal courts to mandate a change because vested interests that tend to oppose change hold sway over the executive and legislative branches.

5. *Resolve conflicts among constitutions, laws, and norms.* Ethical leaders working through the courts must find legitimate bases for deciding among conflicting principles. This may mean relying on judicial enforcement or on reconciliation of constitutions, laws, and norms. Conflict management and dispute resolution methods typically emphasize the desirability of finding principles or norms that all can support as legitimate bases for settling disputes (Fisher and Ury, 1981; Susskind and Field, 1996; Thompson, 2001). Obviously, these principles and norms should be applied in such a way that the public interest is served and the common good advanced. One of the best tests for discerning the public interest or common good is asking whether respect for future generations is implied in an outcome, which as Lewis (1991) points out, typically requires an understanding of the context and "accommodating rather than spurning the important values, principles, and interests at stake" (p. 47). Another test is to look for empathy: are public and nonprofit leaders acting as stewards of the "vulnerable, dependent, and politically inarticulate, those mostly likely to be overlooked in formulations of the public interest"? (Lewis, 1991, p. 47; see also Block, 1993).

Summary: Putting It All Together

The tasks of leadership for strategic planning are complex and many. Unless the organization is very small, no single person or group can perform them all. Effective strategic planning is a collective phenomenon, typically involving sponsors, champions, facilitators, teams, task forces, and others in various ways at various times. Over the course of a strategy change cycle, leaders of many different kinds must put together the elements we have described in such a way that organizational effectiveness is enhanced—thereby making some important part of the world outside the organization noticeably better.

CHAPTER TWELVE

GETTING STARTED WITH STRATEGIC PLANNING

With hope it is, hope that can never die,
Effort, and expectation, and desire,
And something evermore about to be.

WILLIAM WORDSWORTH, "THE PRELUDE"

Previous chapters have presented an overview of strategic planning, an introduction to the Strategy Change Cycle, detailed guidance on working through
the process, and a discussion of the leadership roles in strategic planning. This
chapter presents a number of guidelines that can help public and nonprofit organizations and communities interested in strategic planning to proceed with the
process.

The Three Examples Revisited

How have our three examples—two public organizations and one nonprofit—
fared with strategic planning? Each has achieved notable successes, and each also
has encountered challenges to its ability to think, act, and learn strategically. A
number of lessons can be drawn from each organization's experience. The lessons
have been discussed before, particularly in Chapters Two through Ten, but they
become more concrete in relation to specific cases.

School District

The School District passed an ambitious strategic plan in 1998, about a year and
a half after the planning process began. The plan included intended changes in
technology, curriculum, financing, safety, connections with the community,

school-to-work commitments, standardization of processes and values, professional development, inter- and intrapersonal skill building, and methods of ensuring that students felt they belonged and learning was personalized—ten initiatives in all, with goals and actions for each goal. By mid-2003, the plan had been virtually fully implemented. The district could demonstrate that fact because it had worked hard to clarify the concepts behind each of its initiatives along with performance measures to demonstrate progress. The district's performance management system allowed it to make regular progress reports to key stakeholders.

One especially noteworthy accomplishment involved the initiative to make sure students felt they belonged and that learning was personalized. The need to make gains in this area was most acute at the high school—which is, as I described earlier, the largest in the state in terms of student population and square feet. *Connections classes* have been created to make sure each student is part of a small group headed by the same teacher for all four years of high school. Teachers act as advisers, meeting with their groups once a week for half an hour for a check-in and to pursue a small curriculum. A more expensive model has been instituted in the middle schools, where teams of teachers have continuing groups of students. This model is more expensive because the teachers now teach for only five out of the seven periods available. They meet with their student group for the sixth period, and have the seventh for preparation. Without these teams, teachers would be teaching six periods rather than five. There clearly is a cost—which is an issue for some stakeholders—for making sure each student is connected with at least one adult (if not the whole team), linked with other students, and has his or her individual concerns addressed. But even though cost may be an issue, it is also true that the previous issue of kids falling through the cracks—an issue that helped prompt strategic planning in the first place—just does not come up anymore.

The School District case is clearly a strategic planning success story. The board mapped out the district's mission, goals, and key issue areas, charged task forces of insiders and outsiders to develop strategies to address them, adopted a strategic plan that incorporated most of the recommendations, and then worked hard to ensure the plan was implemented. The superintendent, his cabinet, and hundreds of other people were the implementers. Now, the initiatives, goals, and objectives of the strategic plan are close to being fully achieved.

The board has experienced substantial turnover since the planning process was implemented, but the new group remains committed to strategic planning—in part because the process of plan preparation and implementation was so inclusive that it was clear it was the *community's* plan. The superintendent who pushed the planning stepped down as superintendent in 2002 but remained on staff for a year to do some special projects for the district. The assistant superintendent—who was the process champion—is the new superintendent. She and the board initiated a new round of strategic planning in 2003, which was completed in the spring of 2004. In 2004, the district had 10,349 students—up from the 9,744 it had in 1996, but demographic projections indicate the numbers will decline over the next several years. It also had 1,422 employees (including part-timers), up from the 1,293 employees it had in 1996. This time the process was less intense, and the district calls the result the "Journey to Excellence Strategic Framework," rather than the "strategic plan." The framework was developed with the help of the Organizational Improvement Committee (OIC), which had responsibility for overseeing implementation of the 1998 strategic plan. The OIC took on some additional members to help with framework development. The framework reaffirms the district's mission statement and core values. It adds a vision statement, based on the language of the ten initiatives in the 1998 plan. The vision states that those in the School District will achieve the mission by

- Creating a safe and respectful learning environment
- Challenging all to become motivated, confident, ethical learners and responsible citizens with a passion for learning
- Providing a comprehensive curriculum, personalized learning, effective instruction, and support
- Using resources effectively and efficiently while promoting creativity and innovation

The framework also outlines five strategic directions:

- Having all students demonstrate academic growth and success (which means closing gaps in achievement)
- Embracing differences to improve learning (which means allowing schools to be different from one another to reflect the diversity of their student bodies)
- Ensuring high-quality, professional staff
- Developing broader community knowledge and partnerships
- Ensuring wise, proactive use of resources

In addition, the framework names seven categories of success indicators: student achievement, human development, rigorous and challenging curriculum, learning environment, fiscal responsibility, community connections and communication, and governance.

As of this writing the School District has been on its journey to excellence for almost eight years. All the advocates along the way were inspired by a hope of "something evermore about to be." William Wordsworth would be proud of them.

The lessons from the School District's experience seem clear. First, unless the top decision makers are fully committed to strategic planning, such planning is unlikely to succeed in the organization as a whole. Again, there is simply no substitute for that kind of leadership.

Second, one of the biggest innovations that strategic planning promotes is getting key decision makers into the habit of focusing attention on what is truly important. The planning process helped the board and staff identify the key issues, figure out what to do about them, and follow through. There is simply no substitute for that kind of dialogue and deliberation.

Third, if strategic planning is to be really effective in an organization that has a governing board, the board itself must understand and "own" the process.

Fourth, the board must understand what it means to be an effective policymaking body and must act the part (Carver, 1997; Robinson, 2001). The School District's board initiated the process in part to help it be a better policymaking body. One reason for engaging in a new, scaled-down version of strategic planning was to educate a board made up of mostly new members in how to be an effective policymaking body.

Fifth, strategic planning is an iterative process that can lead to surprising understandings—and to new and more effective rounds of strategic thought and action. The School District's board and superintendent underestimated how much mistrust of the administration there was in the district as a result of the previous superintendent's style. Fortunately, the new superintendent's open and engaging style helped overcome the mistrust, and the transparent, participative strategic planning process also built needed trust, along with intellectual, social, political, and civic capital.

Sixth, staff must be assigned to work on what is truly important. A good plan would not have been prepared and adopted and the plan's contents would not have been implemented had not the superintendent and staff followed through. Here is a place where process champions are again critical. The most important champion in this case was the assistant superintendent. She diligently and faithfully followed through and made sure that what was necessary occurred—no matter how overworked, tired, or frustrated she became. (This follow-through was particularly important during the ongoing discussion of the district's values. That conversation was really about changing the district's culture, and culture change happens only over the long haul.) Strong overall citizen support also helped. The strategic planning consultants also provided support, encouragement, and needed insights at key points. And facilitators were often used to help various task forces and focus groups work through difficult issues.

Seventh, if strategic discussions precede budgeting and bond referenda, budgets may be prepared and reviewed in light of their consequences for the organization as a whole, and these referenda are more likely to be passed, even in an era when the citizenry is opposed to new taxes in general. A persuasive case must be made in order to get citizen support.

Eighth, advocates of strategic planning and plans must be prepared for disruptions, delays, and unexpected events because they are almost bound to happen. The slowdown experienced in the School District as a result of teacher workload negotiations is one example. The minor disruptions caused by board turnover constitute another example. The district was lucky in that its disruptions and delays were comparatively minor.

Ninth, strategic planning by itself is not enough. The key decision makers in the system (in this case the board members and superintendent) must be willing to take effective political action to promote strategic thought, action, and learning. Although this did not happen in the School District's case, I have certainly seen instances where some decision makers needed to be "sacrificed" in order to get needed changes introduced. Hope and courage are necessary—but not costless—civic virtues. Public leaders must be willing to pay the price when necessary.

Project for Pride in Living

Project for Pride in Living used strategic planning to continue its strong tradition of public service. By providing housing, jobs, and training, the organization continues to be a leader in assisting lower-income individuals and families to work toward self-sufficiency. But the organization has had to come to terms both with its success—it was big and complex and needed to be better integrated—and with the changing environment's demands for greater accountability and the increased competition for funds. In this new environment the organization has to focus on how it will achieve organizational sustainability for the long haul, how it will measure effectiveness, how it will achieve greater internal and external coordination, and how it will affect the broader policy environment within which it operates.

Many of the lessons drawn from the School District case can be drawn from the example of Project for Pride in Living (and of the Naval Security Group [NSG]) as well. Rather than repeat them all, I will focus on five particularly apparent ones. First, leadership counts (Behn, 1991). PPL's top administrators are and have been thoughtful, service-oriented professionals deeply committed to the organization's mission. They are dedicated to providing high-quality, cost-effective service that creates substantial public value. They understand how to be effective sponsors and champions and know when to involve stakeholders, consultants, and facilitators. And they have tried to be wise in determining which projects to pursue, how to build public support, and how to garner needed resources. As former elected officials, PPL executive directors Jim Scheibel and Steve Cramer, in particular, have made use of their well-developed political instincts and relationships.

Second, strategic planning and strategy change are almost always about culture change. PPL founder Joseph Selvaggio was a typical iconoclastic, rule-defying social entrepreneur who got PPL going and on the map. When Steve Cramer took over as executive director, he had to repair relationships with public officials and be more of a manager as PPL kept being innovative and grew rapidly. When Jim Scheibel took over from Cramer, the challenge was to better integrate all the pieces of the organization, instill more financial discipline, work on measurement systems to enhance accountability and fundraising ability, and change the broad policy environment that made PPL's work more important and harder to do. Now that Scheibel has stepped down and Cramer has returned, those challenges are still on the table, and some newer ones have emerged. Major demographic changes are under way in Minnesota (particularly as more immigrants from many countries move to the state); the state has more need for affordable housing, especially in the suburbs surrounding Minneapolis; and PPL needs to cluster its activities geographically so its assistance will not be spread too thin and so that it can work to build neighborhoods, as a complementary way of helping individuals and families. All these changes have involved a host of culture changes over the organization's thirty-plus-year-existence. Unless an organization pays attention to its culture—what is good about it and what needs changing—strategy change is unlikely to succeed. And productive culture changes happen only when leaders are committed to such changes over long periods of time.

Third, it takes times and effort for all involved with an organization to gain widespread appreciation of that organization as a whole, and when the organization is involved in a host of collaborative relationships, it takes even longer. (This lesson also applies with special force to NSG.) A great deal of discussion and dialogue was necessary before a fuller understanding of PPL, its divisions, and its partnerships emerged. There is no substitute for this kind of conversation; people must reach their own conclusions in their own time through conversation with others—and it all takes time.

Fourth, it is important to blend what is ongoing with what is new. PPL divisions had to be assured that existing strategies that were working well would be maintained and that ongoing divisional planning efforts would be taken into account. In other words the strategic planning efforts had to be about what was existing and working, not just about what was new and what should stop. (NSG also had to deal with this issue of making effective use of the old while also attending to the new.)

Finally, it really helps to have a governing board that is also an effective policy board. The School District's board was well on its way to being an effective policy board when its planning process began, and the board used that process to become yet more effective. NSG planners had to really work to create an effective policy board through the education and engagement of NSG's superiors around the critical issues facing NSG. Sometimes the planners were surprised by the superiors' receptiveness to new ways of thinking about issues; sometimes they were surprised by the views of new superiors transferring into leadership positions. But eventually they got the policy board NSG needed. PPL began with a forty-six-member board. The size of the board was an issue because, even though the board had links to all segments of the community, it is hard for a group that size to be an effective policymaker. PPL made use of the board's planning and development committee to shepherd the planning process along, which was one way of getting a smaller group with which to work. Now the board has been slimmed down to thirty-three members, and it has very functional subcommittees and a seven-person executive committee that meets monthly.

The Naval Security Group

The Naval Security Group experienced the most dramatic changes among the three cases. What makes that fact especially interesting is that the strategic planning effort did not begin at the top—as it did in the School District and PPL—but was initiated in the middle of the organization. The first lesson, therefore, is that strategic planning can proceed in an evolutionary way and still have revolutionary consequences. Over the course of the strategy change effort, the focus moved from a functional focus toward an integrated focus involving a transformational strategy for NSG as a whole. It began with department heads and ended with department heads and top leadership working on the same page. Along the way, participants gained a far greater understanding of organizational strategic planning (as opposed to war planning) and of many different tools for doing it.

Second, the admonition to start where you are is particularly apt in NSG's case. The efforts of the department heads proved crucial in preparing NSG for changes prompted by the requirement to work jointly with other services. A number of NSG jobs were saved, and NSG was well positioned before its rivals were to be a major actor in the information warfare (IW) realm. Ultimately, once top leadership was on board, the strategies and strategic thinking, acting, and learning capacity of NSG were strengthened in ways that could not have been anticipated. Strategic planning thus is often a leap of faith that may well be justified by the outcomes of the effort (Frentzel, Bryson, and Crosby, 2000, p. 420).

Third, as was true in the School District and PPL cases, surprises should be expected. For example, the department heads were surprised and pleased by the efforts of the comptroller, deputy commander, and ultimately the admiral to foster strategic planning. They were also surprised by the transformation strategy that was adopted and implemented when it had not been clear that one was needed at the start. In other words, when everyone already knows what should be done strategically, then there is no need for strategic planning. When people do not know the answer and are open to new learning and possibilities, strategic planning can be of use. Furthermore, strategic planning can help the organization create its own desirable surprises, rather than having to respond to surprises sprung on it by someone else (Frentzel, Bryson, and Crosby, 2000, pp. 420–421).

Said differently, NSG's process facilitated an important shift in the planners' and others' thinking, to the point that some things that were once only possibilities became givens (Mangham, 1986; Isabella, 1990). Here is an example—and fourth lesson—that fits de Gues's observation (1988) that "the real purpose of strategic planning is not to make plans but to change the mental models decision makers carry in their heads" (p. 71). Recall Mintzberg's (1994) observation, noted earlier, that "organizations function on the basis of commitment and mindset" (p. 252). Strategic planning can alter the premises and binding choices that govern behavior.

Fifth, NSG's experience also strongly emphasizes a lesson about the importance of forums in any strategic planning process that bridges organizational boundaries. As an organization in which cross-departmental processes matter a great deal, NSG necessarily relies on discussion and dialogue to figure out what it should be doing and how. The department head meetings helped build cross-departmental understanding. As more and more senior leaders became involved in discussions focused on the organization as a whole, forum participants began to challenge various worldviews, orthodoxies, and existing strategies; consider new possibilities; and pursue them. A lot of talk occurred, and sometimes it seemed to group members to be going nowhere. But eventually the dialogue resulted in a plan to which people could commit that transformed NSG and enabled it to produce far greater public value.

Finally, of all the cases, the NSG's experience illustrates most strongly a lesson about the need to fit strategic planning to other ongoing processes in an organization. The process had to be compatible with Navy rules, regulations, and traditions; Department of Defense procedures and guidelines; Clinton administration "reinventing government" efforts; and various other federal rules, regulations, and guidelines governing budgeting, personnel, and contracting procedures. The lesson here is that if attention had not been paid to meshing the strategic planning effort with these other activities, that effort would have been useless.

General Lessons

Four additional lessons are not tied to any of the cases in particular but should nevertheless be emphasized. First, operational detail can overwhelm strategic planning efforts. Even though each organization discussed here has been successful at strategic planning, it still took each organization a fairly long time to get through the process. Often attention to the day-to-day simply drove out attention to the long term. It takes a real commitment to find the time to attend regularly to what is fundamental. Yet this regular attention may well be the most important discipline strategic planning is designed to promote. Without it, strategic thinking, acting, and learning among a group of senior decision makers is not likely to occur. Strategic planning cannot be simply an add-on for already overworked leaders, managers, and staff.

Both the difficulty and the importance of paying attention to what really matters are captured in this snippet of dialogue from Sue Monk Kidd's *The Secret Life of Bees* (2002, p. 147):

"The whole problem with people is—"

"They don't know what matters and what doesn't," I said, filling in her sentence and feeling proud of myself for doing so.

"I was gonna say, The problem is they *know* what matters, but they don't *choose* it. . . . The hardest thing on earth is choosing what matters."

Second, quicker really can be better. If the challenges are serious and imminent—bankruptcy, for example—a lengthy and elaborate strategic planning process can doom the organization to an early death. Third, simpler can be better too. Focusing on the most critical issues in a direct and timely way and developing effective strategies to address these issues may be all that is needed. Such a process will not be data heavy, although some key quantitative and qualitative data are likely to be necessary. Instead it will be heavy on strategic thinking, acting, and learning.

Finally, if there is no real reason to plan strategically—no major challenges or important opportunities—then *perhaps* strategic planning is a waste of time. Muddling through may work acceptably until strategic planning does become necessary.

Getting Started

These three cases along with the others cited in this book indicate that strategic planning can help public and nonprofit organizations and communities fulfill their missions, meet their mandates, create public value, and satisfy their key stakeholders more effectively. These cases also indicate that a number of difficulties and challenges must be overcome if strategic planning is to fulfill its promise for organizations. Let me conclude with some advice about how to get started with strategic planning:

1. *Start where you and the other people who might be involved in or affected by the process currently are.* This is one of the most important principles for organizing collective action (Kahn, 1991; Bobo, Kendall, and Max, 2001). You can always undertake

strategic planning for the part of the organization you control. Whatever you are in charge of—a unit, department, division, or a whole organization—you can always start there. But wherever you start, you must also keep in mind where the participants currently are. Other involved or affected parties are likely to need some education concerning the purposes, processes, and products of strategic planning. If they are important for the formulation or implementation of strategies, you will need to bring them along so that they can be effective supporters and implementers.

2. *Have a compelling reason to undertake strategic planning.* Otherwise, the process is not likely to be worth the effort or to reach a satisfactory conclusion. The obverse of this guideline is that people can create an infinite number of reasons *not* to engage in strategic planning, even when it would be the best thing for the organization or community; such reasons may be nothing more than excuses. The reasons that might be compelling are numerous. The organization or community may be performing well, but key decision makers may be fully aware of important strategic issues that must be addressed if the organization is to continue to do well. That was the case with the School District, where, for example, a big bulge in younger children was working its way through the school system and huge changes were occurring in information technology. Project for Pride in Living leaders saw that competition for funding and pressures for accountability were increasing and that PPL needed to maintain organizational dynamism and sustainability, to attend to its core competencies, and to try to change the broader policy environment within which it had to operate. Or the organization may feel threatened by the emergence of strong rivals. The School District faced competition as a result of the state's open-enrollment policy and from private schools. PPL faced competitors for funding. But the Naval Security Group faced the most serious competition, both for funding and from the other services that might be able to do NSG's work. Or an organization may be confronting a real turning point in its history— a point that might lead to success or extermination. Recall that organizational strategies are usually fairly stable for long periods of time, and during these periods, strategic planning is usually more concerned with programming strategy implementation than with formulating whole new strategies. Project for Pride in Living's efforts, for example, have been focused mostly on making marginal improvements in existing strategies, although efforts at integration across the organization may ultimately prove revolutionary. But after long periods of stability come significant shifts—either as a result of changes in the environment or new leadership visions. At such times strategic planning is much more concerned with enhancing strategy formulation (Gersick, 1991; Mintzberg and Westley, 1992; Mintzberg, Ahlstrand, and Lampel, 1998). That was the case with NSG, which faced dramatic changes in stakeholders, funding, technology, needed competencies, and operations. Cumulatively, NSG's strategy change process resulted in a

"quantum" change in the organization (Miller and Friesen, 1984), even though that result was not anticipated at the beginning of the process. Yet another compelling reason is that the organization may feel the need for strategic planning but not engage in the process until ordered to do so by decision makers further up the hierarchy. That was not the case with any of the three organizations discussed here, but it can happen; indeed, federal legislation and many states now require certain organizations to engage in strategic planning. But whatever the compelling reason, organizational or community members—especially key decision makers—must see some important benefits to be derived from strategic planning, or they will not be active supporters and participants. And if they do not support and participate, the process is bound to fail.

3. *Remember that there is no substitute for leadership.* The concepts, procedures, and tools that strategic planning comprises cannot think, act, or learn by themselves. Nor can they inspire and mobilize others to act on behalf of what is best for an organization (or community). Only concerned and committed people—leaders and followers—can do that. Broad-based, collective leadership spread throughout an organization is necessary to ensure that it fulfills its mission, meets its mandates, creates real public value, and satisfies the expectations of its key stakeholders. And when the organization succeeds, it is a collective accomplishment. Two leadership roles are especially important to the success of any strategic planning effort: *sponsoring* and *championing.* Unless the process is sponsored (ultimately, if not initially) by important and powerful leaders and decision makers, it is likely to fail. Only key decision makers who are also effective leaders will be able to motivate and guide their organizations through a successful strategic thinking, acting, and learning process. Leadership from the key decision makers is absolutely necessary if the organization itself must be changed as a result of strategic planning. A strategic planning process will also not succeed unless it is championed by someone. This person should believe in the process and see his or her role as promoting effective thinking, deciding, acting, and learning on the part of key decision makers. A process champion does not have a preconceived set of answers to the important issues the organization faces, but he or she pushes a process that is likely to produce effective answers. It certainly helps if the process champion is near the top of the organization chart. That was the case for the School District, Project for Pride in Living, and ultimately the Naval Security Group. But it does not hurt to have other champions at other levels. Indeed, the process is likely to be more effective when more than one champion is involved. A third leadership role—*facilitating*—can also be very important, though I would not place it in the same category as the first two. Facilitation is a special skill and can be very important at particular points, especially during the design of the process and as groups of participants learn how to work effectively together (Kaner and others, 1996; Iacofano, 2001; Schwarz, 2002).

4. *Tailor the process to the organization or community and situation.* Strategic planning efforts clearly must fit the situation at hand, even if the ultimate aim of the process is to change the situation (Mintzberg, Ahlstrand, and Lampel, 1998). The roles the official planners play in that process will also depend on the situation. In most cases involving strategic planning across units or levels within an organization or a community, planners will need to facilitate strategic thought, action, and learning by key decision makers. In other situations, planners will also be called on to serve as technical experts. Another key situational factor concerns the presence or absence of the necessary formal and informal forums (for discussion), arenas (for decision making and implementation), and formal or informal courts (for managing residual conflicts and enforcing underlying norms). These are the settings in which strategic planning and implementation will occur, and the ways they are designed and used are important to the success of the process. For example, if it is clear that key strategic issues bridge organizational boundaries, then it is probably necessary to create forums to discuss the issues that also bridge the boundaries. Forums might include strategic planning teams, task forces, or discussion groups. Similarly, if implementation will require coordinated action across boundaries, some sort of arena-like mechanism to manage the process across those boundaries may be necessary. Appropriate mechanisms might include a policy board, cabinet, interagency coordinating council, project management group, or community leadership council. Court-like vehicles to manage residual conflicts also are likely to be needed. Referral procedures for moving decisions up the administrative hierarchy, alternative dispute resolution mechanisms, administrative tribunals, or access to the formal courts may be needed.

The strategic plans themselves must also be tailored to fit the situation. It may be important, for example, not to prepare a written strategic plan. Indeed, some of the best strategic plans I have seen were unwritten agreements among key decision makers about what was important and what actions they would take. In other cases, plans will consist of informal letters, memoranda of agreement, issue-specific strategy documents, or full-blown glossy publications intended for public consumption. It all depends on the purposes to be served by the plan. A final area of needed situational sensitivity concerns the criteria used to assess strategies and plans. Viable strategies and plans will need to be politically acceptable, technically and administratively workable, and legally and ethically justifiable—a severe test given the many stakeholders who are likely to be involved or affected. To find strategies that can satisfy the many stakeholders, leaders, managers, and planners will need to be willing to construct and consider arguments geared to many different evaluative criteria.

5. *Remember that the big innovation in strategic planning is having key decision makers talk with one another about what is truly important for the organization or community as a whole.* A strategic planning process is merely a way of helping key decision makers think,

act, and learn strategically. The process can in no way substitute for the presence, participation, support, and commitment of key decision makers to raise and resolve the critical issues facing the organization or community. The initiation and institutionalization of the process can provide the occasions, settings, and justification for gathering key decision makers together to think, act, and learn strategically on behalf of the organization or community. In all too many organizations and communities, such occasions, settings, and justifications do not exist. Organizational and community performance and stakeholder satisfaction suffer accordingly.

6. *Be aware that the resource most needed to undertake strategic planning is not money but the attention and commitment of key decision makers.* Strategic planning is not expensive in dollar terms, but it is expensive when it comes to the resources that typically are most scarce—the attention and commitment of key decision makers. For organizations, strategic planning may involve having key decision makers spend up to 10 percent of their ordinary work time working together to identify and address fundamental policy questions. That may not seem like much. Indeed, one might argue that decision makers unwilling to devote up to 10 percent of their work time to what is truly important for the organization are either incompetent or disloyal and ought to be fired! But realistically, for a variety or reasons, it is hard to persuade key decision makers to commit more than 10 percent of their time to strategic planning. The reasons include the fact that the urgent often drives out the important and what is routine drives out what is nonroutine. But beyond that, because major strategy changes are relatively rare, many decision makers realize that strategic planning usually focuses on strategy implementation rather than strategy formulation. Thus strategic planning may seem redundant to them, repeating what they are already doing, or it may appear less glamorous and important than its sponsors and champions think. In addition, decision makers may be justifiably concerned that strategic planning will drive out strategic thought, action, and learning or may unreasonably or unwisely limit their own discretion. Or they may simply be afraid of the consequences, conflictual or otherwise, that may result from focusing on particular strategic issues. For whatever reason, it is hard to get much attention for the process in most organizational situations. And it may be even more difficult to get substantial blocks of time from community leaders for community strategic planning. Strategic planning processes are also likely to be thrown off track by various disruptions and delays. Strategic planning processes in which I have been involved have been thrown off course by elections, promotions, crises, scandals, deaths and life-threatening illnesses, planned and unplanned pregnancies, horrible public gaffes, and chance events both favorable and unfavorable of numerous sorts. Such eventualities are normal, and sponsors and champions should expect them. Also, strong sponsors and champions are necessary to keep key decision makers focused on what is important, so that wise strategic thought, action, and learning are not lost in the disruptions and delays.

Given the difficulties of getting key decision makers' attention, an effective strategic planning process is likely to be one that is fairly simple (simpler is better), quick (quicker is better), and treated in a special and sensitive way so that key decision makers will give the process the time and attention needed when it is needed. In addition, it is important that sponsors and champions think of *junctures* as a key temporal metric. Time in strategic planning is generally not linear (*chronos*) or characterized by peaks or optimal experiences (*kyros*). Instead, it is *junctural:* key people must come together at the right time with the right information in order to discuss what is important and do something effective about it (Albert and Bell, 2002). The ability to think juncturally, to think about timing, is a special skill that must be cultivated (particularly by sponsors and champions) if the strategic planning process is to be successful (Bryson and Roering, 1988, 1989).

7. *Remember that the biggest payoffs from strategic planning may come in surprising ways or from surprising sources.* For example, organizations often find that organizational development, team building, and heightened morale throughout the organization are among the greatest benefits derived from a strategic planning process. The School District found it needed to focus concentrated effort on its core values. The Naval Security Group planners were surprised and pleased when NSG's senior leadership finally got on board with strategic planning; almost everyone was surprised by the transformational strategy that resulted; many participants were surprised by the extent to which NSG needed to engage in stakeholder influence strategies in order to secure its future; and all were surprised and pleased when NSG was designated the Navy's executive agent for information warfare. There is no telling what will happen as a result of the strategic planning process. But the organization or community that is open to surprises may create and take advantage of its own opportunities. As Louis Pasteur said, "Fortune favors the prepared mind."

8. *Outside consultation and facilitation can help.* Often organizations and communities need some consultation, facilitation, and education from outsiders to help with the design and management of the strategic planning process. The School District, Project for Pride in Living, and the Naval Security Group each relied on outside help of various kinds at various points throughout the strategic planning process. If help is needed, try to get it.

9. *If the going gets tough, keep in mind the potential benefits of the process.* Recall that strategic planning can help organizations and communities in a number of ways. For example, strategic planning can help organizations and communities to

- Think, act, and learn strategically and develop effective strategies
- Clarify future direction and establish priorities
- Improve decision making by

Making today's decisions in light of their future consequences

Developing a coherent and defensible basis for decision making

Making decisions across levels and functions

- Exercise maximum discretion in the areas under organizational control
- Solve major organizational and community problems
- Improve organizational, community, or broader system performance
- Deal effectively with rapidly changing circumstances
- Build teamwork and expertise

But it may not be easy to achieve these benefits. The faith of process sponsors and champions is often sorely tried, particularly when the organization or community is engaged in strategic planning for the first time. For example, the process seems particularly prone to disintegration in the middle—the strategic issue identification and strategy development steps. And the big payoffs may take a long time to achieve. For instance, it may take several years to know whether some important strategy has worked or not. In the meantime, therefore, try to label as much as possible that comes out of the process a success—count every small win and work hard to improve the process along the way.

In order to maintain enthusiasm for the process until successes tied directly to implemented strategies began to appear, the School District emphasized—even celebrated—the achievements and benefits of the process as they occurred. Interim achievements were highlighted at meetings of the strategic planning team, school board, and community groups and in newsletters, glossy brochures, newspaper articles, and regular talks by the superintendent and assistant superintendent throughout the year. Thus the process was managed so that it was "successful" long before any strategies were implemented. It is also useful for sponsors and champions to do what they can to maintain an optimistic stance toward the world—to see difficulties as specific rather than pervasive, temporary rather than permanent, and as something that can be changed (Seligman, 1991, 1998). They should do what they can to build their own and others' psychological hardiness through building commitment to the organization's mission, building a sense of control over the organization's future, and seeing difficulties as manageable challenges (Kouzes and Posner, 2002). Sponsors and champions also should be realistic—at least with themselves—about what strategic planning might achieve. They might keep in mind, for example, what Sigmund Freud told doubting patients: "Much will be gained if we succeed in transforming your hysterical misery into common unhappiness." Strategic planning will not lead to perfection, but it can result in useful, implementable strategies for addressing a few key issues—and that is something worth pursuing. By organizing hope, strategic planning can make the courageous organization's hopes reasonable. Recall also Maya

Angelou's observation, "Courage is the most important virtue, because without courage you can't practice any other virtue consistently." Creating lasting public value almost always takes committed, courageous, hopeful people—and strategic planning is a set of concepts, procedures, and tools that can help such people make the world a better place.

10. *Lastly, keep in mind that strategic planning is not right for every organization or community.* In the following situations, strategic planning should perhaps not be undertaken (Barry, 1986, 1997):

- The roof has fallen.
- The organization or community lacks the necessary skills, resources, or commitment of key decision makers to produce a good plan.
- Costs outweigh benefits.
- The organization or community prefers to rely on the vision, intuition, and skill of extremely gifted leaders.
- Incremental adjustments or muddling through in the absence of a guiding vision, set of strategies, or plan are the only processes that will work.
- Implementation of strategic plans is extremely unlikely.

Nonetheless, although there may be *reasons* not to undertake strategic planning, those reasons all too easily become *excuses* for not paying attention to what is really important for the organization or community. An organization or community that gives in to excuses has suffered a failure of hope and courage. Wordsworth reminds us that "Our destiny, our being's heart and home" are with hope, effort, expectation, and desire. And Maya Angelou reminds us that only courage will get us there.

Strategic planning can help public and nonprofit organizations fulfill their missions, meet their mandates, and create real public value; it can also help communities serve important purposes, including the creation of public value. Said differently, strategic planning can help organizations and communities create a better, more productive, more effective, more satisfying value proposition for their key stakeholders. But strategic planning will work only if people want it to work. This book was written to help all those who want their organizations and communities to survive, prosper, and serve noble purposes. I hope it will prompt more than a few of these organizational and community citizens to proceed with strategic planning, because then significant change can occur. As Woodrow Wilson said long ago, "There is no higher religion than human service. To work for the common good is the greatest creed."

RESOURCES

Three resources are included in this book. Resource A presents an array of stakeholder identification and analysis techniques. Resource B describes how to use the oval mapping process to identify strategic issues and formulate effective strategies. And Resource C discusses how to adapt the Strategy Change Cycle to collaborative settings.

RESOURCE A

STAKEHOLDER IDENTIFICATION
AND ANALYSIS TECHNIQUES

This resource focuses on how and why leaders, managers, and planners might go about using stakeholder identification and analysis techniques in order to help their organizations meet their mandates, fulfill their missions, and create public value. A range of stakeholder identification and analysis techniques is reviewed. The techniques cover the functions presented in Figure 2.4: organizing participation; creating ideas for strategic action; building a winning coalition around proposal development, review, and adoption; and implementing, monitoring, and evaluating strategies. Wise use of stakeholder analyses can help planners frame issues that are solvable in ways that are technically and administratively feasible and politically acceptable, that are legally and morally defensible, and that create public value and advance the common good.

Figure A.1 shows how the stakeholder identification and analysis techniques fit with the simplified public and nonprofit sector strategic management theory summarized in Figure 2.4.

An Array of Techniques

Two techniques have already been discussed in detail: choosing stakeholder analysis participants (in Chapter Three) and the basic stakeholder analysis technique (in Chapter Four). This resource presents an additional thirteen stakeholder identification and analysis techniques. They are grouped according to the functions

FIGURE A.1. STRATEGIC MANAGEMENT PURPOSES AND FUNCTIONS AND STAKEHOLDER ANALYSIS TECHNIQUES TO ASSIST WITH FULFILLING THEM.

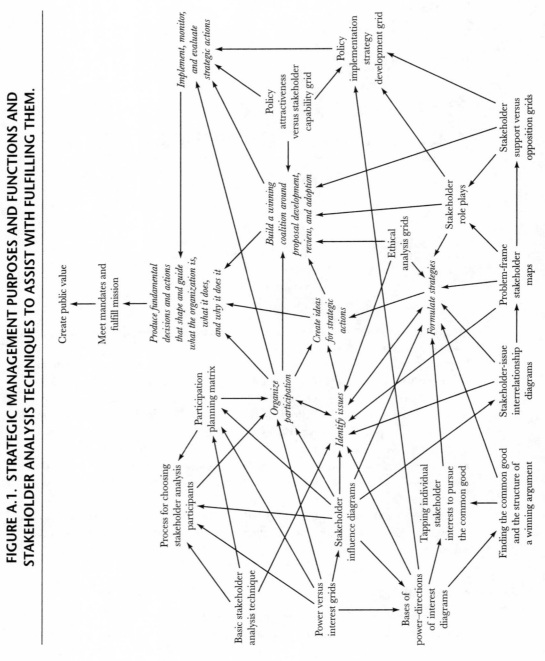

presented in Figure A.1. All the techniques are fairly simple in concept and rely on standard facilitation materials such as flipcharts, marking pens, tape, colored stick-on dots, and so on. All it takes to do them is some time and effort—an expenditure of resources that typically is miniscule when compared with the opportunity costs of the less than adequate performance, or even disaster, that typically follows in the wake of failing to attend to key stakeholders, their interests, and their information (Nutt, 2002).

Techniques for Organizing Participation. Stakeholder analyses are undertaken for a purpose and that purpose should be articulated as clearly as it can be before the analyses begin, with an understanding that purposes may change over time. The purpose should guide the choice of analysis participants and the ways in which they will be involved. Different analyses will be needed at different stages in the Strategy Change Cycle.

Deciding who should be involved in doing stakeholder analyses and how, when, and why is a key strategic choice. In general, people should be involved if they have information that cannot be gained otherwise or if their participation is necessary to ensure successful adoption and implementation of initiatives built on the analyses (Thomas, 1993, 1995). Can there be too much or too little participation in stakeholder analyses? The general answer to this question is yes, of course. But the specific answer depends on the situation, and there are no hard and fast rules, let alone good empirical evidence, on when, where, how, and why to draw the line. There may very well be important trade-offs between earlier and later participation and one or more of the following factors: representation, accountability, analysis quality, analysis credibility, analysis legitimacy, and the ability to act based on the analyses, and these and other factors will need to be thought through. Fortunately, this choice can be approached as a sequence of choices, so that an individual or small planning group begins the effort, and then others become participants later as the advisability of their doing so becomes apparent (Finn, 1996).

Five stakeholder identification and analysis techniques are particularly relevant to organizing participation: a process for choosing stakeholder analysis participants (discussed in Chapter Three), the basic stakeholder analysis technique (discussed in Chapter Four), the power versus interest grid, the stakeholder influence diagram, and the participation planning matrix.

Power Versus Interest Grid. The *power versus interest grid* (Figure A.2) is described in detail by Eden and Ackermann (1998, pp. 121–125, 344–346). This grid arrays stakeholders on a two-by-two matrix where the dimensions are the stakeholder's interest (in a political sense as opposed to simple inquisitiveness; see Campbell and Marshall,

FIGURE A.2. POWER VERSUS INTEREST GRID.

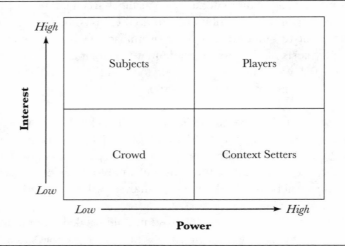

Source: Eden and Ackermann, 1998, p. 122. Reprinted with permission.

2002) in the organization or issue at hand and the stakeholder's power to affect the organization's or issue's future. Four categories of stakeholders result: *players,* who have both an interest and significant power; *subjects,* who have an interest but little power; *context setters,* who have power but little direct interest; and members of the *crowd,* who are stakeholders with little interest or power.

The power versus interest grid helps planners identify the players, the people whose interests and power bases *must* be taken into account in order to address the problem or issue at hand. It also highlights coalitions to be encouraged or discouraged, behavior that should be fostered, and people whose buy-in should be sought or who should be co-opted. Finally, it provides some information that can be used to convince stakeholders to change their views. Interestingly, the knowledge gained from this grid can be used to advance the interests of the relatively powerless (Bryson, Cunningham, and Lokkesmoe, 2002). Note that in some cases it may make sense to construct a *power versus identity grid,* as identity as well as interest can motivate stakeholder action (see Rowley and Moldoveanu, 2003).

A power versus interest grid is constructed as follows:

- The facilitator tapes four flipchart sheets to a wall to form a single surface two sheets high and two sheets wide.
- The facilitator draws the two axes on the surface, using a marking pen. The vertical axis is labeled *interest,* from *low* to *high,* and the horizontal axis is labeled *power,* from *low* to *high.*

- Planning team members brainstorm the names of the various stakeholders by writing these names as they come to mind on 1.5-by-2-inch (3.5-by-5-cm) self-adhesive labels, one stakeholder per label. Alternatively, if the basic analysis technique has been performed, the names can be taken from that list.
- The facilitator places each label in the appropriate spot on the grid, guided by the deliberations and judgments of the planning group members. Labels should be collected in round-robin fashion, one label per group member, until all labels (other than duplicates) are either placed on the grid or eliminated for some reason.
- Labels are moved around until all group members are satisfied with the *relative* location of each stakeholder on the grid.
- The group discusses the implications of the resulting stakeholder placements.
- The facilitator records the results of the discussion on flipchart sheets.

Stakeholder Influence Diagram. The *stakeholder influence diagram* indicates how the stakeholders on a power versus interest grid influence one another. The technique is taken from Eden and Ackermann (1998, pp. 349–350; see also Finn, 1996; Bryson, Cunningham, and Lokkesmoe, 2002) and begins with a power versus interest grid. The steps in developing a stakeholder influence diagram are as follows:

- The planning team starts with a power versus interest grid, and for each stakeholder on the grid, team members suggest lines of influence from one stakeholder to another.
- The facilitator draws in the lines with a soft-lead pencil. Two-way influences are possible, but the team should attempt to identify the primary direction in which influence flows in each case.
- Team members engage in a dialogue to determine which influence relationships exist, which are most important, and what the primary direction of influence is.
- Once final agreement is reached, the facilitator makes the lines of influence permanent with a marking pen.
- Team members discuss the results and implications of the resulting diagram, including identification of the most influential or central stakeholders.
- The facilitator records the results of the discussion on flipchart sheets.

Participation Planning Matrix. In a sense, all the techniques considered so far are relevant to planning for stakeholder participation. The *participation planning matrix*, however, is specifically designed for this purpose. The matrix incorporates ideas adapted from publications of the International Association for Public Participation (2004), specifically the association's notion of a spectrum of levels of public participation, and the strategic management functions identified in Figures 2.1

and A.1. The levels of participation range from a minimum level of simply informing stakeholders to the ultimate level of empowering them, giving stakeholders or some subset of them final decision-making authority. Each level has a different goal and makes a different kind of promise—implicitly if not explicitly (Exhibit A.1).

The matrix prompts planners to think about responding to or engaging different stakeholders in different ways over the course of a strategy change effort. As a result, planners may gain the benefits that arise from taking stakeholders seriously yet avoid the perils of responding to or engaging stakeholders inappropriately. The process for filling out the matrix is as follows:

- Begin using this matrix relatively early in the change effort, but not before some stakeholder analysis work has been done.
- Place stakeholders' names in the appropriate matrix boxes, and then develop action plans for following through with each stakeholder.
- Revise the matrix as the change effort unfolds.

Techniques for Creating Ideas for Strategic Actions. Creating ideas for strategic actions involves strategic issue identification and strategy development but also depends on understanding political feasibility. In other words, creating ideas that are worth implementing and also implementable depends on clearly understanding stakeholders and their interests, both separately and in relation to each other, so that issues can be formulated in such a way that they have a chance of being addressed effectively in practice (Wildavsky, 1979). Therefore techniques relevant to organizing participation also have something to contribute to the process of issue identification and strategy development. In turn, issue identification in conjunction with strategy development can have an impact on organizing participation. Six additional stakeholder identification and analysis techniques are particularly relevant to creating ideas for strategic actions. They are the bases of power–directions of interest diagram, the technique of finding the common good and the structure of a winning argument, the technique of tapping individual stakeholder interests to pursue the common good, the stakeholder-issue interrelationship diagram, the problem-frame stakeholder map, and the ethical analysis grid.

Bases of Power–Directions of Interest Diagram. This technique builds on the power versus interest grid and the stakeholder influence diagram and involves looking more closely at each of the stakeholder groups, including the most influential or central stakeholders. A *bases of power–directions of interest diagram* can be created for each stakeholder. The technique is an adaptation of Eden and Ackermann's *star diagrams* (1998, pp. 126–128, 346–349; see also Bryson, Cunningham, and Lokkesmoe, 2002). A diagram of this kind indicates the sources of power available to the

EXHIBIT A.1. PARTICIPATION PLANNING MATRIX.

	Which Stakeholders to Approach by Which Means				
	Inform	**Consult**	**Involve**	**Collaborate**	**Empower**
Strategic Management Function or Activity	Promise: We will keep you informed.	Promise: We will keep you informed, listen to you, and provide feedback on how your input influenced the decision.	Promise: We will work with you to ensure your concerns are considered and reflected in the alternatives considered and provide feedback on how your input influenced the decision.	Promise: We will incorporate your advice and recommendations to the maximum extent possible.	Promise: We will implement what you decide.
Organizing participation					
Creating ideas for strategic actions (including issue identification and strategy formulation)					
Building a winning coalition around proposal development, review, and adoption					
Implementing, monitoring, and evaluating strategic actions					

Source: Adapted from International Association for Public Participation, 2004; Bryson, 2004b. Copyright IAP2. All rights reserved.

stakeholder, as well as the goals or interests the stakeholder seeks to achieve or serve (Figure A.3). Power can come from access to or control over various support mechanisms, such as money or votes, or from access to or control over various sanctions, such as regulatory authority or votes of no confidence (Eden and Ackermann, 1998, pp. 126–127). Directions of interest indicate the aspirations or concerns of the stakeholder. Typically the diagrams focus on the stakeholder's bases of power and directions of interest in relation to a focal organization's purposes or goals: that is, they seek to identify the powers that might affect achievement of the focal organization's purposes.

There are two reasons for constructing this diagram for each stakeholder. The first is to help the planning team find the common ground—especially in terms of interest—across all the stakeholder groups. After exploring the power bases and interests of each stakeholder, the planning group will be in a position to identify commonalities across the stakeholders as a whole or across particular subgroups. This search will allow the group to find the common good and the structure of a winning argument (see next technique). Second, the diagrams are intended to provide background information on each stakeholder so the planning team knows how to tap into stakeholders' interests or make use of stakeholders' power to advance the common good. For example, this background information can be used in stakeholder role plays (discussed later in this resource) intended to help planners further understand stakeholder reactions to specific problem framings or proposals for change.

A bases of power–directions of interest diagram may be constructed as follows:

- The facilitator attaches a flipchart sheet to a wall, and writes a stakeholder's name in the middle of the sheet.
- The planning team brainstorms possible bases of power for the stakeholder (particularly as they affect the focal organization's purposes or interests), and the facilitator writes these bases on the bottom half of the sheet.
- Following team discussion, the facilitator draws arrows on the diagram from the power bases to the stakeholder and between power bases to indicate how one power base is linked to another.
- The planning team brainstorms the stakeholder's goals or interests (particularly those relevant to the focal organization's purposes or interests). The facilitator writes these on the top half of the sheet and draws arrows from the stakeholder to the goals or interests and, when appropriate, arrows linking goals or interests.
- The team engages in a thorough discussion of each stakeholder's diagram and its implications.
- The facilitator records the results of the discussion on flipchart sheets.

FIGURE A.3. BASES OF POWER–DIRECTIONS OF INTEREST DIAGRAM.

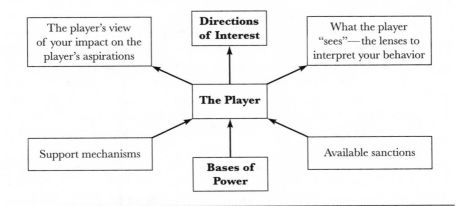

Source: Bryson, Cunningham, and Lokkesmoe, 2002, p. 576; adapted from Eden and Ackermann, 1998, p. 127.

Finding the Common Good and the Structure of a Winning Argument. Bryson, Cunningham, and Lokkesmoe (2002) created this technique and used it successfully in the development of a viable political strategy for producing better outcomes for young African American men in a large county in the United States. The technique builds on the bases of power–directions of interest technique. Bases of power–directions of interest diagrams can be explored in depth to determine which interests or themes appear to garner support from a significant number of stakeholders. Members of the planning team need to search for these common themes, which are called *supra-interests.* For each theme the team should construct a label that captures or integrates the specific interests that make up the theme. The identification of common themes is a subjective exercise calling for creativity, discernment, and judgment. After identifying these themes the team can construct a map that identifies all the supra-interests that tie together the individual stakeholders' interests and that indicates what the relationships among the supra-interests appear to be.

This map is called *finding the common good and the structure of a winning argument* because it indicates—at least in part—what the common good (the creation of real public value) *is* for this group of stakeholders and suggests how arguments will probably need to be structured to tap into the interests of enough stakeholders to create a winning coalition. In other words, if persuasive arguments can be created that show how support for specific policies and programs will further the interests of a significant number of important stakeholders, then it should be possible to forge the coalition needed to adopt and implement the policies and programs. Being relatively clear about goals or interests—although not always necessary (Bryson and Crosby, 1992; Bardach, 1998; Huxham, 2003; Crosby and Bryson, forthcoming)—does help when it comes to producing successful programs and projects (Nutt, 2002). Any difficulties that then arise are likely to concern the means to achieve specific ends rather than the nature of the ends themselves. Conflicts over means can be resolved through interest-based bargaining and through the creation of pilot projects or small experiments to identify the most effective approaches (Nutt, 1992). In addition, the structure of a winning argument outlines a *viable political rhetoric* around which a *community of interests* can mobilize, coalesce, and coalign to further the common good (Majone, 1989; Stone, 2002).

Tapping Individual Stakeholder Interests to Pursue the Common Good. Developing a viable political rhetoric is a key visionary leadership task (Bryson and Crosby, 1992, pp. 45–50; Crosby and Bryson, forthcoming) and should help public leaders, managers, staff, and their collaborators understand how they might "pursue significance" for themselves and their organizations (Denhardt, 1993). What still remains is the task of understanding how *specific stakeholders*—either separately, in coalitions, or in coaligned groups—might be inspired and mobilized to act in such a way that the common good is advanced. A further analysis is therefore needed in order to understand how *each stakeholder's interests* connect with the *supra-interests.*

Specifically, a set of diagrams is needed that shows how each individual stakeholder's bases of power–directions of interest diagram links to the supra-interests (Bryson, Cunningham, and Lokkesmoe, 2002). Once these diagrams are constructed, it is possible to see the ways in which policies, programs, and projects need to be found, tailored, or sold so that individual stakeholders perceive that their own interests are advanced. Developing these diagrams is a kind of research that helps the planning team create and market social programs successfully (Andreasen, 1995; Kotler, Roberto, and Lee, 2002). This research is designed to help the team understand the organization's audiences well enough to both satisfy their interests and advance the common good. Program design will be enhanced as a result of more clearly understanding stakeholder interests, and effective one- and two-way communication strategies can be created through developing and testing out these diagrams with key informants in the target audiences.

The techniques discussed so far have at least implicitly if not explicitly approached strategic issue identification and strategy formulation in terms of the common good or creating public value by searching for themes, concerns, or goals shared by key stakeholders. The analyses have tended to downplay the significance of opposition—including opposition to a specifically defined common good. The techniques that follow begin to address the ways in which opposition might need to be taken into account.

Stakeholder-Issue Interrelationship Diagram. The *stakeholder-issue interrelationship diagram* helps the planning team understand which stakeholders have an interest in which issues and how some stakeholders might be related to other stakeholders through their relationships with the issues (Figure A.4). (Bryant, 2003, pp. 190–197, calls this diagram the *preliminary problem structuring diagram.*) This diagram provides some important structuring of the issue areas, in which a number of actual or potential areas for cooperation—or conflict—may become apparent. An arrow indicates that a stakeholder has an interest in an issue, though the specific interest is likely to be different from stakeholder to stakeholder, and those specific interests may well be in conflict. The arrows should therefore be labeled to indicate exactly what the interest is in each case. In Figure A.4, stakeholders A, B, C, D, E, and F all have an interest, or stake, in issue 1, while subgroups of stakeholder A have a further issue between them, issue 2. Stakeholder A is also related to stakeholders E, G, H, and I through their joint relationship to issue 3. Again, in an actual case the arrows should be labeled so it is clear exactly what the interests are and whether they are in conflict.

A stakeholder-issue interrelationship diagram may be constructed as follows:

- The planning team starts with a power versus interest grid and stakeholder influence diagram and perhaps also with the basic stakeholder analysis technique.
- The facilitator tapes four flipchart sheets to a wall to form a single surface two sheets high and two sheets wide.
- Planning team members brainstorm the names of stakeholders by writing the names of different stakeholders as they come to mind on 1 1/2-by-2-inch self-adhesive labels, one stakeholder per label. Alternatively, the names may be taken from one of the previous analyses.
- Planning team members also brainstorm issues that appear to be present in the situation at hand. These are also are written on self-adhesive labels, preferably in a different color.
- The facilitator places the issues on the flipchart surface and, following team discussion, arrays the stakeholders around the issues. Each stakeholder may be involved in more than one issue.
- The facilitator draws arrows indicating which stakeholders have a stake in which issues; the content of each arrow—that is, the stake or interest involved—is also written in.
- The team thoroughly discusses each issue, stakeholder, and arrow, and any implications for the framing or reframing of issues and management of stakeholder relationships are noted.
- The facilitator records the results of the discussion on flipchart sheets.

Problem-Frame Stakeholder Map. The *problem-frame stakeholder mapping technique* was developed by Anderson, Bryson, and Crosby (1999) and is adapted from a technique

FIGURE A.4. STAKEHOLDER-ISSUE INTERRELATIONSHIP DIAGRAM.

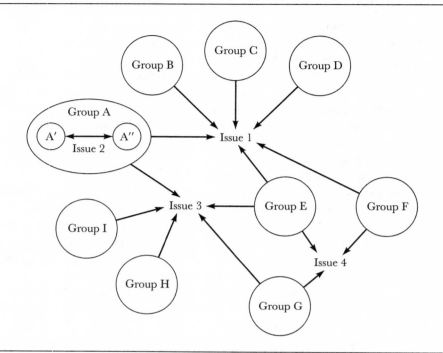

Source: Adapted from Bryant, 2003, pp. 196, 264. Copyright © 2003. This material is used by permission of John Wiley & Sons, Inc.

developed by Nutt and Backoff (1992). It is especially useful in developing problem (or issue) definitions likely to lead to a winning coalition. Careful analysis is usually necessary to find desirable problem definitions that can motivate action by a coalition of stakeholders large enough to secure adoption of preferred solutions and to protect them during implementation (Rochefort and Cobb, 1994; Schön and Rein, 1994; Jacobs and Shapiro, 2000). A crucial first step in this analysis is to link stakeholders to alternative problem definitions through a problem-definition stakeholder map (Figure A.5). Ideally, once a potentially winning frame has been identified, specific policy proposals can be developed within that frame.

These steps may be followed to construct a problem-frame stakeholder map:

- The facilitator tapes four flipchart sheets to a wall to form a single surface two sheets high and two sheets wide.
- The facilitator draws a two-by-two matrix on the surface, using a marking pen. The vertical axis on the left is labeled *problem frame*. The vertical axis above the

FIGURE A.5. PROBLEM-FRAME STAKEHOLDER MAP.

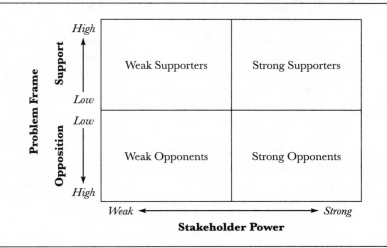

Source: Anderson, Bryson, and Crosby, 1999; adapted from Nutt and Backoff, 1992.

horizontal line that bisects the matrix is labeled *support,* from *low* at the horizontal line to *high* at the top of the axis. The vertical axis below that horizontal line is labeled *opposition,* from *low* at the horizontal line to *high* at the bottom of the axis. The horizontal axis at the bottom of the matrix is labeled *stakeholder power,* from *weak* on the left-hand side to *strong* on the right-hand side.

- On a second set of flipchart sheets, the planning group members brainstorm and write down the various problem frames, or definitions, that might apply to the case at hand. The whole range of frames or definitions should be recorded, including those favored by known critics or opponents. The snow card technique, nominal group technique, or other brainstorming method can be used.
- On a third set of flipchart sheets, the planning group brainstorms a list of the stakeholders likely to be implicated by the range of problem definitions.
- These stakeholder names are placed on 1.5-by-2-inch self-adhesive labels, one stakeholder per label. Alternatively, if the basic analysis technique has been performed, the names should be taken from that list.
- For each problem definition, the team considers the policy changes that are implied or likely to be needed, and then, guided by the deliberations and judgments of the planning group members, the facilitator arrays the stakeholders on the matrix that was created at the beginning of this process.
- Labels are moved around until all group members are satisfied with the *relative* location of each stakeholder on the grid.

- The group discusses the implications of the resulting stakeholder placements. Particular attention should be given to the stakeholders who show up in the right-hand quadrants for all definitions of the problem. In other words, attention should be devoted to the more powerful stakeholders. Emphasizing a problem frame that increases the number of strong supporters and reduces the number of strong opponents facilitates formation of a winning coalition.
- The facilitator records the results of the discussion on flipchart sheets.

Ethical Analysis Grid. Attending to stakeholders and to the common good certainly can be thought of as contributing to ethical behavior. But more is required in order to ensure the ethical appropriateness of whatever actions are ultimately taken. Lewis (1991) proposes use of a grid to clarify and prompt a dialogue about the ethics around *who* and *what.* Use of the grid helps the organization fulfill both deontological (duty-based) and teleological (results-oriented) obligations. Results of the analysis should indicate which proposals or options should be eliminated or altered on ethical grounds. A modified version of the grid Lewis proposes is illustrated in Exhibit A.2. The planning team members simply work together to fill it out and to discuss the results. It may be wise to involve others in this discussion as well. In general, Lewis's admonition would be to pursue the common good *and* avoid doing harm.

Techniques for Plan Development, Review, and Adoption

Once stakeholders and their interests have been identified and understood, it is typically still advisable to do additional analyses in order to develop proposals that can garner adequate support in the plan review and adoption process. Three techniques are considered here: the stakeholder support versus opposition grid, stakeholder role plays, and the policy attractiveness versus stakeholder capability grid.

Stakeholder Support Versus Opposition Grid. The *stakeholder support versus opposition grid* builds on the problem-frame stakeholder map, using the same grid and basic process. But this time specific proposals—rather than problem frames or definitions—are assessed in terms of stakeholder support, opposition, and importance. Nutt and Backoff (1992) developed the technique. The steps are simple. For each proposal:

- The facilitator constructs a separate grid.
- The planning team members brainstorm stakeholders' names and place them on self-adhesive labels, one name per label.
- The facilitator places the labels on the grid in the appropriate places.
- The team discusses the results in terms of the viability of specific proposals and the stakeholders requiring special attention.

EXHIBIT A.2. ETHICAL ANALYSIS GRID.

Stakeholder Name and Category		Description of Stake			
Internal stakeholder External stakeholder and direct External stakeholder and indirect					
Factors and Score		**High (3)**	**Medium (2)**	**Low (1)**	**None (0)**
Dependence of stakeholder on government (for example, alternative services are inaccessible)					
Vulnerability of stakeholder (for example, potential for injury)					
Gravity (versus triviality) of stakeholder's stake					
Likelihood remedy or relief will be unavailable to the stakeholder					
Risk to fundamental value					
Overall negative impact of policy on stakeholder					
Total scores: do they indicate obligatory action or relief?					

Note: Direct = directly affected by the proposed strategy change. Indirect = indirectly affected by the proposed strategy change.

Source: Adapted from Lewis, 1991, p. 122. Copyright © 1991. This material is used by permission of John Wiley & Sons, Inc.

- The facilitator records the results of the discussion on flipchart sheets.
- The team discusses and deploys specific tactics based on its analysis. Nutt and Backoff (1992; see also Bryson and Crosby, 1992, pp. 378–380) propose a set of tactics to deal with the different categories of stakeholders.

A serious question is how large a winning coalition should be. The political science literature on policy adoption tends to emphasize using a *minimum* winning coalition (that is, the smallest size feasible for victory), because creating a larger coalition is likely to entail so many concessions or trades that the proposal is watered down to the point where it cannot achieve its original purpose (Riker, 1962, 1986). Conversely, the literature on collaborative planning argues that a larger coalition probably should be pursued, because sustained implementation requires broad-scale support and the minimum winning coalition may not provide it (Margerum, 2002; Bryant, 2003). Obviously, in any specific case a thoughtful discussion should precede any answer to this question.

Stakeholder Role Plays. Eden and Ackermann (1998, pp. 133–134) show how *role plays*—in which different members of the planning team play the roles of different stakeholders—can be used to develop plans likely to address stakeholder interests, build a supportive coalition, and ensure effective implementation. Role plays have the special benefit of really enhancing the planning group's capacity to understand how other stakeholders think. Role plays build on the information revealed in bases of power–directions of interest diagrams and may also take advantage of the findings of problem-frame issue maps and stakeholder support versus opposition grids. In some cases it may be wise to use role plays to inform the issue identification and strategy development steps.

A stakeholder role play involves the following steps:

- Each member of the planning team reviews the problem-frame stakeholder maps and stakeholder support versus opposition grids, if they have been prepared.
- Each member of the planning team assumes the role of a different stakeholder.
- With the stakeholder's bases of power–directions of interest diagram as a guide, each team member should answer, from the stakeholder's point of view, two questions about each proposal:

     How would I react to this option?

     What would have to be done to increase my support or decrease my opposition?

- The facilitator uses flipchart sheets to record the responses.
- Team members do the exercise more than once as they repeatedly modify proposals to increase proposal robustness and political viability and then test each modification with role plays until they are satisfied with the result.

Policy Attractiveness Versus Stakeholder Capability Grid. The *policy attractiveness versus stakeholder capability grid* is discussed in Bryson, Freeman, and Roering (1986, pp. 73–76; see also Bryson, 1995, pp. 283–284) and involves assessing the attractiveness of policies, plans, proposals, or options in general against stakeholder capacities to implement these actions (Figure A.6). The grid reveals the proposals that are likely to be implemented successfully because they match stakeholder capacities and those that are likely to fail because of lack of capacity. The technique is therefore especially useful in shared-power, no-one-in-charge situations, where planners are necessarily led to focus on the proposals likely to be implemented successfully. Proposals that are high in attractiveness and capability certainly should be pursued. Proposals that are otherwise attractive but do not match up well with stakeholder capabilities will require a substantial buildup of those capabilities in order to be implemented. Where the organization might find the resources for the buildup should be explored and discussed during the proposal development review and adoption process. Low-attractiveness proposals are best discarded.

The process for constructing one of these grids is as follows:

- The facilitator constructs an attractiveness versus capability grid on flipchart sheets and has a list of proposals and a list of stakeholders ready.
- The planning team develops criteria to assess the *attractiveness of policies, plans, or proposals,* from *low* to *high* (in terms of mission, goals, results, outcomes, or stakeholder-related criteria) and criteria to assess *stakeholders' capability to implement policies, plans, or proposals,* from *low* to *high.*
- Team members write proposals on self-adhesive labels, one proposal per label, and the facilitator places each label on the grid in the appropriate position after the team has considered both the proposal's attractiveness and the various stakeholders' capacities to implement it.
- The team discusses the results and any implications for building necessary capability among stakeholders or for getting unattractive proposals off the agenda.
- The facilitator records the results of the discussion on flipchart sheets.

Techniques for Policy Implementation. In a sense, all the techniques considered so far are relevant to policy implementation because they are concerned with developing proposals likely to garner significant stakeholder support. But it is still important to focus directly on stakeholders during implementation (Goggin, Bowman, Lester, and O'Toole, 1990; Nutt, 2002). Developing a *policy implementation strategy development grid* can give planners and decision makers a clearer picture of what will be required for implementation and help them develop action plans that will tap stakeholder interests and resources. This technique is adapted from Meltsner (1972), Coplin and O'Leary (1976), Kaufman (1986), and Christensen (1993) and

FIGURE A.6. POLICY ATTRACTIVENESS VERSUS STAKEHOLDER CAPABILITY GRID.

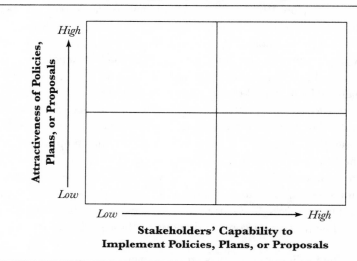

Source: Bryson, Freeman, and Roering, 1986, pp. 73–76; see also Bryson, 1995, pp. 283–284. Used with permission.

builds on information revealed by previously created bases of power–directions of interest diagrams, stakeholder support versus opposition grids, stakeholder role plays, and policy attractiveness versus stakeholder capability grids (Exhibit A.3).

The process for filling out one of these grids is fairly simple:

- The facilitator creates a grid on flipchart sheets and assembles previously done bases of power–directions of interest diagrams, stakeholder support versus opposition grids, stakeholder role plays, and policy attractiveness versus stakeholder capability grids.
- The planning team members fill out the policy implementation strategy grid.
- The team discusses next steps and prepares action plans.
- The facilitator records the results of the discussion on flipchart sheets.

Conclusions

As can be seen, a wide variety of techniques is available for performing the basic functions of strategic management. Each technique provides a different kind of information that can at times be of tremendous assistance.

Some might argue that stakeholder analyses involve a lot of rigmarole that produces not too surprising results. For example, Mintzberg, Ahlstrand, and Lampel

EXHIBIT A.3. POLICY IMPLEMENTATION STRATEGY DEVELOPMENT GRID.

Stakeholders	Stake or Interest	Resources	Action Channels Open to Stakeholder	Probability of Participation and Manner of Doing So	Influence (as a product of resources and participation)	Implications for Implementation Strategy	Action Plan Elements
Supportive stakeholders							
Opposing stakeholders							

Source: Adapted from Meltsner, 1972; Coplin and O'Leary, 1976; Kaufman, 1986; Christensen, 1993.

(1998, pp. 250–251) put little faith in such analyses, although their criticism seems to be based on a limited understanding of the full range of available stakeholder analysis techniques. However, Nutt's (2002) masterful study of 400 strategic decisions indicates that a failure to attend carefully to stakeholder interests and information can easily lead to disaster. Given Nutt's evidence and given how relatively simple and cheap the techniques are, doing stakeholder analyses certainly appears to be a clear candidate for what Bardach (1998) calls a *smart practice*. I would go further and assert that *not* doing stakeholder analyses often appears to be a *dumb practice*.

But whether the practice is as smart as it can be depends on which techniques are used for what purposes and when, where, how, by whom, and with what results. Each of the techniques has a different purpose and reveals some things while hiding, or at least not highlighting, others. Like any other technique designed to aid strategic thinking and acting, stakeholder analyses must be undertaken skillfully and thoughtfully, with a willingness to learn and revise along the way (Lynn, 1996; Bardach, 1998). For some smaller change efforts, a one-time use of one or two techniques may be all that is necessary; for larger change efforts, a whole range of techniques will be needed at various points throughout the process. Hybrid techniques or new techniques may need to be invented along the way. The key point is the importance of thinking strategically about why, when, where, how, and with whom the analyses are to be undertaken and about ways to change direction when needed.

It is also worth noting that stakeholder analyses can be used to advance causes that many people would believe do not serve the common good or create public value. Stakeholder analysis should never be seen as a substitute for virtuous and ethical practices, although it may be a part of promoting such practices. One way to avoid outcomes that do not create public value might be to begin with an inclusive definition of stakeholders, so that the net of considerations about who and what counts is cast widely to begin with. Another step might be to undertake enough stakeholder analyses to prompt the kind of strategic conversations needed to discover a morally and ethically sound version of the common good to pursue. In the end these analyses certainly do not guarantee that public value will be created, but they may well provide information that guides the organization toward creating such value.

THE OVAL MAPPING PROCESS: IDENTIFYING STRATEGIC ISSUES AND FORMULATING EFFECTIVE STRATEGIES

John M. Bryson, Fran Ackermann, Colin Eden, Charles B. Finn

A crucial strategic planning task is creating strategic ideas that are worth im - plementing and can be implemented (see Figure 2.4). In order to create these ideas, it is useful to think in terms of at least four subtasks:

1. *Brainstorming ideas.* Techniques such as straight brainstorming (Johnson and Johnson, 2000) or the nominal group technique (Delbecq, Van de Ven, and Gustafson, 1975) can be used to create lots of ideas.
2. *Clustering the resulting ideas into categories.* Brainstorming can produce numerous ideas, but usually it is the process of clustering and categorizing the ideas that starts to reveal their strategic significance. The snow card process (see Chapter Five) can help groups structure their brainstormed ideas as they group them into categories and then organize each category's contents into logical, priority, or temporal order. *Mind mapping* (Buzan and Buzan, 1993) does much the same thing.
3. *Clarifying specific action-to-outcome relationships among ideas.* Creating and catego- rizing ideas typically is not enough. It is also important to identify the causal relationships among ideas—in other words, what leads to what both within and across categories. A process is therefore needed to capture and map these relationships. The resulting causal map, or word-and-arrow diagram, consists of concepts (phrased as actions) recorded on oval-shaped pieces of paper and

linked by directional arrows indicating the cause and effect or influence relationships among them—such as A may cause or influence B, which in turn
may cause or influence C (Bryson, Ackermann, Eden, and Finn, 2004). These
maps may consist of hundreds of interconnected relationships, showing different areas of interest and their relationships to one another.

4. *Using the resulting map to inform strategic thinking, acting, and learning.* A causal map
   should help the group using it gain a more holistic understanding of what is
   going on in an area, what might be done about it, and why. As actions are taken
   they can be assessed in light of the predicted outcomes the map suggests,
   and then new actions can be taken or the map can be redone or both these
   steps can be undertaken.

The *oval mapping* process, which is a causal mapping technique, was developed
and refined over a number of years by Colin Eden and a large number of associates (Eden, Jones, and Sims, 1983; Eden and Huxham, 1996; Eden, Ackermann,
and Cropper, 1992; Ackermann, 1993; Bryson and Finn, 1995; Eden and Ackermann, 1998; Ackermann, Eden, and Brown, 2004). The process was developed
as part of an approach to strategic management called *strategic options development
and analysis* (SODA) (Eden, 1989; Eden and Ackermann, 2001) that has strongly
influenced my own approach to strategic planning (outlined in Chapter Two).
Bryson, Ackermann, Eden, and Finn (2004) summarize much of this work for
practitioners, and their work is a key source of material for this resource section.

The oval mapping process can be used with individuals or with groups. Nor-
mally, we suggest groups have no more than ten members, because in groups larger
than ten, participants can feel lost in the crowd rather than part of a group. But
groups larger than ten are possible, especially when there is a strong group facilitator or when smaller subgroups create their own maps and then these maps are
merged. Another advantage of dividing the team into subgroups, beyond increasing the sense of participation, is that these subgroups may produce different
interpretations of an issue area and the team may gain additional insights from
comparing and contrasting these interpretations. Subgroups may all be assigned
the same question or issue, or each can consider a different aspect of an issue.
Subgroups may be homogeneous, representing a single class of stakeholder or a
single organizational level, or heterogeneous, representing diverse interests. The
simplicity of the basic process means it can be adapted to a number of uses, including stakeholder analyses, scenario development, clarification of distinctive
competencies, strategic issue identification, strategy development, and clarification of symbolically or substantively important concepts. Several of these applications are discussed later in this resource.

Purpose, Desired Outcomes, and Benefits

The purpose of the oval mapping process is to make sense of an area of concern by capturing and structuring the ideas that compose it. The meaning of any particular idea consists of its context—that is, the ideas that influence it (*arrows in*) and the ideas that flow from it as consequences or outcomes (*arrows out*). Comparing and contrasting ideas and elaborating their connections establishes a rich context that makes understanding easier (Kelly, 1963; Weick, 1995; Schein, 1997). As ideas are explored, different interpretations are identified, leading to a more complete picture. The most important desired outcome of using the oval process thus is increased understanding of an important problem or issue area.

For example, a small nonprofit college was facing a serious financial crisis (see Bryson, Ackermann, Eden, and Finn, 2004, pp. 153–181, for more detail on this case). A team of fifteen persons was assembled to develop the basics of a strategic plan (mission, goals, and basic strategy areas) using the oval mapping process. The team included representatives of the board, faculty, administration, students, alumni, potential donors, and townspeople. The group (which was led by a strong facilitator and was not divided into subgroups) constructed a map of about 100 different ideas, all linked by arrows, in the space of a few hours. As the map was created, each idea was given its own number, in a sequence beginning with 1. These numbers had no meaning other than to indicate the sequence in which the ideas were created and to allow computer software (Decision Explorer) to keep track of each idea. In other words the numbers served as placeholders for the software, which is discussed further later.

One of the strategic issues the group identified was "generate more income, for example, tuition and fee income" (idea 2) (Figure B.1). This issue was affected directly by two other issues, "increase student enrollment" (28) and "increase tuition and fee income" (45), and indirectly by a third issue, "increase academic standards" (82). There is a negative link between "increase academic standards" and "increase student enrollment," because increasing academic standards might decrease, not increase, student enrollment unless the process is carefully managed. (Such management might include "convening meetings with teachers" [46] and "having meetings with parents" [14]—items not shown on the figure.) Generating more income would also require the school to "assess financial options" (38) and to look at two bundles of actions, "cut expenses" (56) and "engage in [a] fundraising campaign" (50). Cutting expenses might mean having to "close [the] college" (62), "mothball some buildings until finances/enrollment improve" (58), "vacate and lease building to local businesses" (60), "discontinue relationship with government agencies" (57), "reduce staffing" (78), "create cost-cutting teams" (79),

FIGURE B.1. SMALL COLLEGE STRATEGIC ISSUE: GENERATE MORE INCOME.

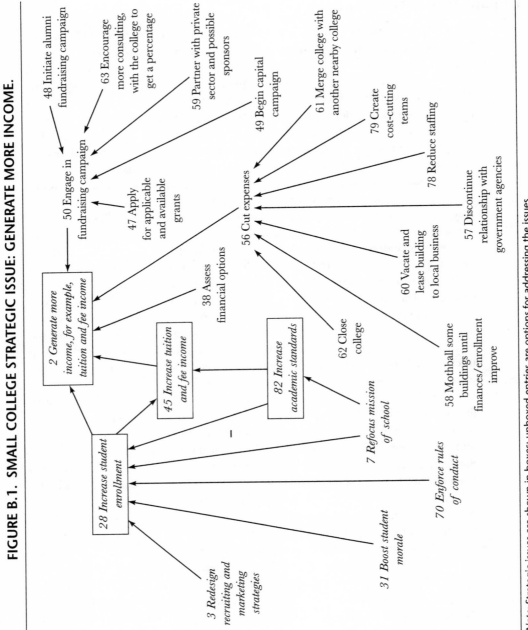

Note: Strategic issues are shown in boxes; unboxed entries are options for addressing the issues.

Source: Bryson, Ackermann, Eden, and Finn, 2004, p. 167.

or "merge [the] college with another nearby college" (61). Engaging in a fundraising campaign might require the college to "apply for applicable and available grants" (47), "begin [a] capital campaign" (49), "partner with [the] private sector and possible sponsors" (59), "encourage more consulting, with the college to get a percentage" (63), and "initiate [an] alumni fundraising campaign" (48).

The issue of generating more income fits into a wider network of issues and goals and mission in somewhat complex ways (Figure B.2). If the college could "generate more income, for example, tuition and fee income" (2), that would allow the college to see to it that "teachers are well paid" (55) and "classroom and physical facilities are excellent" (53). Paying teachers well would help ensure that "morale at the college is high" (51), which in turn would help the college achieve its mission, to "make lasting positive educational and civic contributions to our students, partners, and the community" (29). Having excellent classroom facilities would also be a direct means of raising morale, and helping "students achieve outstanding results" would also raise morale indirectly. Outstanding student results would also contribute directly to the mission. Other goals and other issues also contribute directly and indirectly to the mission.

There are a number of important benefits to using the oval mapping process, including its capacity to enhance reasoning ability, improve dialogue, manage complexity in issue areas, and build teamwork within the group. The process, in other words, offers an excellent technique for achieving many of the outcomes Figure 3.1 indicates are likely to be needed for a successful strategic planning process. Specific benefits are as follows:

First, the process is easy to understand, teach, and use, and thus complex maps can be developed relatively quickly. Mapping typically is a very efficient use of a group's time.

Second, structuring action-to-outcome relationships helps people figure out what they can do about an area of concern. This makes the process very useful to leaders and managers, who typically have an action orientation and often are uncomfortable with vague abstractions. It also promotes understanding as people work out what is necessary to make something happen.

Third, the process promotes a fuller understanding of an area of concern, which makes it more likely that any actions taken will be constructive rather than shortsighted, foolish, or downright damaging.

Much of the fuller understanding comes from the inclusion of many people's views. So a fourth benefit is that the process creates a *shared* view of the area of concern and what might be done about it. The process thus promotes intra- and interorganizational, as well as intra- and interdisciplinary, understanding and creativity. In most cases the shared view represents a reconstruing of reality (Kelly,

FIGURE B.2. SMALL COLLEGE ISSUES AND GOALS.

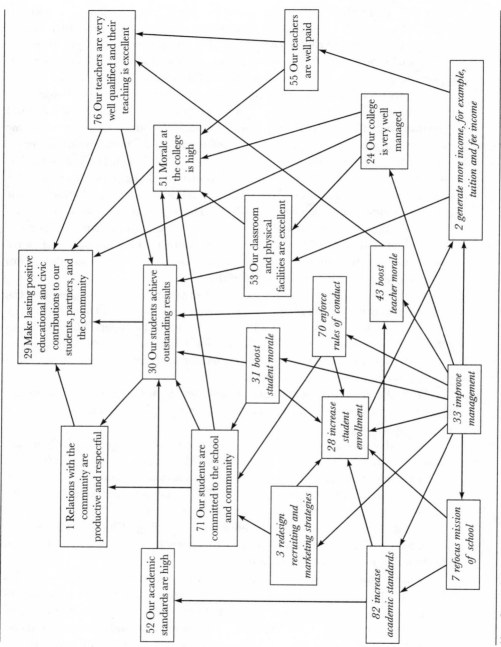

Note: Strategic issues are shown in italics; goals are shown in normal type.

Source: Bryson, Ackermann, Eden, and Finn, 2004, p. 176.

1963): that is, participants see the world differently from the way they saw it before they came together—not as a result of arguments—but through the way statements come to be linked together.

The process is highly participative and attends to the social aspects of group work. Thus a fifth benefit is that the process promotes participants' understanding of each other's ideas and roles. It also means the process can build cohesion and generate commitment to and ownership of subsequent actions. The process is thus an effective team-building tool.

Sixth, the process creates a forum for discussion and dialogue around important areas of concern, a fundamental feature of effective strategic planning and a crucial precursor of effective action (Bryson and Crosby, 1992; Crosby and Bryson, forthcoming).

Seventh, the process typically results in the creation of a tangible product—a map—that is a record of the participants' merged contributions. To the extent that the map represents a shared and agreed-upon view, it serves as a *transitional object* (de Gues, 1988), or bridge, to the next step in the strategic planning process. The map and the shared understanding of what it means can strongly influence mission formation, strategy development, and implementation.

Eighth, the process and the maps that result provide a useful way of managing complexity. The maps can incorporate broad and abstract general statements of desired states (goals) as well as clusters of more specific options (issues) and agreed-upon portfolios of actions (strategies and work programs). The general form and logic of a map intended for use as an action-oriented strategy map is presented in Figure B.3. Each small circle represents a different idea phrased as an action; in other words, each circle in an actual map would be a statement beginning with an imperative form of a verb. Goals are at the top, issues are below goals, options to achieve the issues are below issues, and statements of fact or assertions are at the very bottom. Typically, a workshop process is used to convert a draft map to an agreed-upon set of goals, strategies, actions, and assertions. Both the School District and the Naval Security Group made extensive use of mapping in their strategic planning processes.

Finally, the process enhances group productivity. Everyone can both "speak" (write on ovals) and "listen" (read ovals) in a full and broad context rather than having to hear one person's views at a time and in sequence. Further, participants can come and go without necessarily negatively affecting the process in significant ways.

Process Guidelines

Persons wishing to use the process may find the following guidelines useful.

FIGURE B.3. GENERAL SHAPE AND LOGIC OF AN OVAL MAP INTENDED FOR USE AS AN ACTION-ORIENTED STRATEGIC MAP.

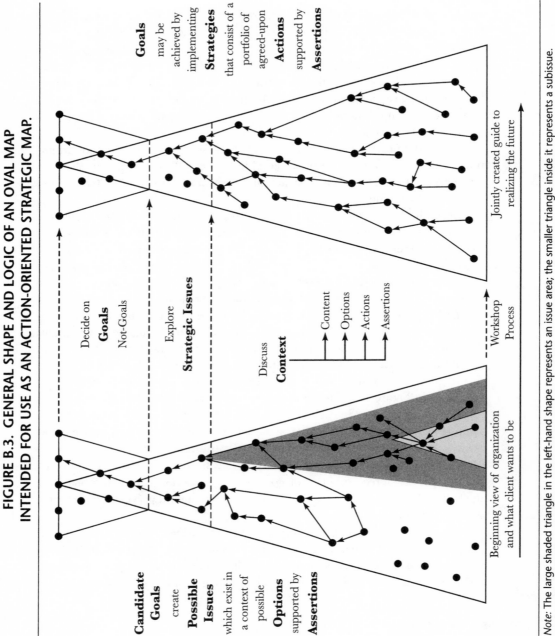

Note: The large shaded triangle in the left-hand shape represents an issue area; the smaller triangle inside it represents a subissue.

Source: Bryson, 1995. Copyright © 1989 by Fran Ackermann, 1995 by Real-izations, Inc. Reprinted with permission.

Equipment Needs. A large, smooth, unbroken wall space is needed for each map that will be constructed. The wall space should be approximately twenty feet wide and six to eight feet high. It is often difficult to find suitable wall space without some advance reconnaissance. This space will be papered over with flipchart sheets in two or three rows, one above the other. Each row should be six to nine flipchart sheets wide, depending on how many ideas are likely to be included on the map. The sheets should be hung with masking tape or self-adhesive putty so that they overlap each other by about an inch. When all the sheets are hung, the seams should be taped with masking tape so that when completed, the map can be taken off the wall in one piece and easily transported. It is also advisable to photograph the map before taking it down; each photograph should be of a single flipchart sheet. If the map does not need to be transported, it can be constructed on a large whiteboard (although it may be difficult to find one large enough), using whiteboard markers to indicate links among ideas.

It helps if the room is spacious and well lit, with easily accessible refreshments and restrooms. In addition, the following materials and equipment will prove useful:

- *A full flipchart pad.* Remember, each map will take twelve to eighteen sheets or more, so do not get caught short.
- *Masking tape or self-adhesive putty, such as Blu-Tack.* This is used to affix the flipchart sheets to the walls. Architect's drafting tape usually does not work as well because it is not as sticky.
- *A stack of ovals.* Cut out or have a commercial printer make oval-shaped pieces of paper, approximately 7 1/2 inches (20 cm) long and 4 1/2 inches (12 cm) wide. (A template is provided in Figure B.4.) Typically, the paper has the same weight as construction paper and is colored yellow or some other light color so that the ovals stand out against the flipchart sheets and at the same time the writing on them, in marking pen, can be read easily. Have twenty to thirty ovals per participant available. Precut, self-adhesive ovals may be purchased at www.banxia.com. (Alternatively, half-sheets of letter-sized paper, 3-by-5-inch cards, or large self-stick notes can be used. The difficulty with these alternatives, however, is that they usually result in ideas arranged in rows and columns rather than placed in visually meaningful relationships to other ideas.)
- *A bullet-tipped, water-based marking pen for each participant.* Bullet-tipped, water-based marking pens may be harder to find than chiselpoint pens, but they are easier to use and the writing is more legible. The pens should all be the same color—usually black—to promote anonymity and to contrast with the color of the ovals. Some additional marking pens in different colors should be available to highlight particular features of the map (links, titles, key observations) during

FIGURE B.4. TEMPLATE FOR AN OVAL.

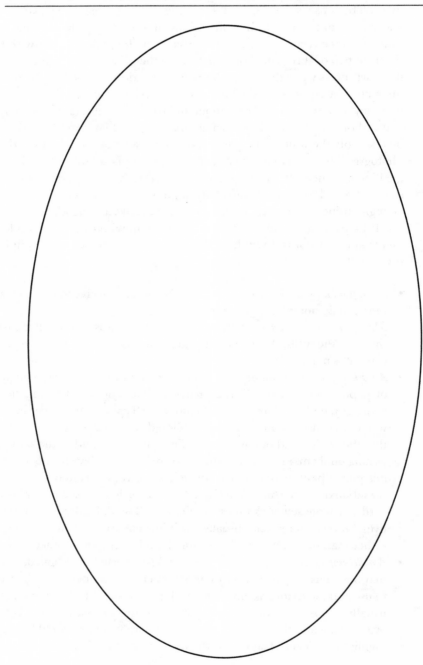

Note: Ovals are approximately 7.5 inches (20 cm) long and 4.5 inches (12 cm) wide.

group discussions. Do not use regular ballpoint pens, as the resulting writing will likely be impossible to read from a distance.

- *Self-adhesive putty (such as Blu-Tack) for attaching the ovals to the flipchart sheet.* You need only a small amount of putty to attach an oval. Larger amounts are a waste and make it harder to move the ovals around. Alternatively, have participants attach a tape roll to the back of each oval. A tape roll is a strip of tape with the ends stuck together to form a small cylinder, sticky side out. Drafting tape is better than masking tape for this purpose, because masking tape is too sticky and will likely tear the flipchart sheets if you try to move ovals around.
- *A sharpened, soft lead pencil with attached eraser for each participant.* These will be used for drawing arrows to tentatively link ovals and for making notes on the map.
- *Large erasers for use with the lead pencils.* These will be used for large erasing jobs.
- *Self-adhesive dots in various colors to identify the nature of particular ovals or clusters of ovals and for straw polls.* Have on hand packets of at least one hundred red, purple, blue, green, and orange dots, three-quarters of an inch in diameter. (Larger dots cover too much space, particularly when used for straw polling, and smaller dots are harder to see.)
- *Suitable refreshments.* Have a supply of coffee, tea, soft drinks, mineral water, fresh fruit, nuts, cookies, and pastry, if possible.
- *A fully automatic camera.* This is used to photograph the final map and the group as the process proceeds. The photographs can be used to remind participants of what happened during the process, and when discussing the nature of the process with others.

Preparing a Starter Question. Have a "starter" question (or set of questions) written out and clearly visible to participants as the process begins. *Starting with the "right" question is important* because it will have a dramatic impact on the answers. The question should be reasonably broad without being ambiguous. It should not be so narrow as to invite only yes or no answers. The planning team will probably need to devote considerable time to developing and pilot-testing the starter question(s) and may want to consult with key informants. Consider using a question like this: What should we do in the next three to five years?

Introducing the Process. Participants will want information about the purpose of the session and the process to be used. For example, if the purpose of the session is to develop a sense of the strategic issues that face the organization and the possible strategies that might address them, then the session might begin with this information:

1. Introduce the session by saying that the purpose of the session is to gather opinions about the issues the organization faces and what might be done about

them. All of the information created will be used to inform the strategic planning process. Be as specific as you can be about what will happen to the information and how it will be used; typically, the information is used to influence decisions rather than creating them directly.

2. All views must be written down on ovals, or they will get lost. This is an important opportunity for participants to have a significant influence on the identification of issues and development of strategies. Note that the process will result in an efficient use of participants' time, because they can all "speak" simultaneously when writing on ovals—thus increasing each person's airtime—and they can "listen" simultaneously when reading the ovals.

3. Ideas should be expressed in action terms, preferably starting with a verb, such as *do, buy, get, formulate, implement, achieve,* or some other imperative.

4. This process does not necessarily seek consensus or attempt to resolve conflict. Instead, the purpose is to clarify and understand how individuals and the group view the organization and its environment. If there are disagreements, it is important to clarify the rationales behind them and record these rationales on separate ovals. It is *not* acceptable to remove other participants' ovals, to edit them without the authors' consent, or to disparage the ovals or their authors. For example, in a recent exercise designed to address on a national basis the needs of students with disabilities, one group thought an oval labeled "have inclusive educational environment" meant having blind and hearing-impaired children in regular classrooms with sighted and hearing students. Another group thought it meant having separate schools for blind and hearing-impaired children so that they could experience being in the majority. Each view was placed on a separate oval, with an arrow going from the oval to the "have inclusive educational environment" oval.

5. Ideas should be put up on the wall as soon as they have been written down and not hoarded, so that others can see the ideas and build ("piggyback," "hitchhike") on them.

6. Either the facilitator or the participants themselves will sort the ovals into clusters that make sense. Clusters should be organized according to common themes or subjects. The advantage of using a facilitator is that all participants can observe and join in the discussion of where each idea belongs. A shared group understanding of what all the ideas are may therefore emerge more quickly than it would if participants work in subgroups of two or three. If a facilitator does do the sorting, however, all participants should be encouraged to offer advice on where ovals should go. If participants do not know where they should go, the ovals should be placed to one side, to be revisited by the group after all the clusters have been examined or else the facilitator should sort them into the appropriate clusters as those groupings become apparent. (Often, some combination of small-group and large-group work is desirable. For example, small groups may do the

initial clustering and then a facilitator may help the large group make sense of the initial clusters and do any regrouping that is necessary.)

7. Keep the statement of each idea to around eight to ten words. This will encourage participants to write only one idea per oval and make it easier for participants to read each other's ideas. The facilitator should encourage participants to lengthen short statements so that their meaning is clearer.

Facilitating the Process. 1. Some participants may grasp the process quickly, start writing and displaying their ideas, and actively participate in structuring clusters of ideas. Others may take longer before they feel comfortable with the process and actively engage in it. It usually takes no more than twenty minutes to half an hour for everyone to be on board.

2. Ideas are first sorted into clusters that make sense. The next step in structuring the clusters involves placing ideas that are more general, abstract, or goal oriented near the top of clusters. Ideas that are more concrete, specific, and detailed are placed toward the bottom. Also, assertions or statements of fact ("our budget will be cut 10 percent"; "client numbers are growing 20 percent per year"; "the executive director will retire in one year") are placed toward the bottom.

3. Encourage participants to elaborate on the ideas and emergent issue clusters by asking questions. Say, for example, "I do not really understand this, could you say more?" or, "How would you make this happen?" or, "What would you hope to get out of doing this?" Questions also prompt other participants to add alternative perspectives as they discover that their interpretation is different from the proponent's.

4. Make sure that ideas are worded in the imperative to suggest an action orientation.

5. Make sure each oval contains only one idea. If an oval contains multiple ideas, have participants make separate ovals for each idea. If an oval contains more than eight to ten words, it usually means two separate ideas are present.

6. Keep encouraging people to write their ideas down, especially those participants who are less verbally dominant. One way to do this is to write a person's ideas on ovals as he or she is speaking and then place the ovals on the wall, to give the person confidence that his or her ideas are worth including. When a group is discussing or debating ideas, group members can be encouraged to capture their views on ovals and attach them to the wall.

7. It can be helpful to number each oval as it is put up, to help participants locate ideas on the wall. Numbering also helps when computer support is used.

Further Structuring the Clusters. 1. Tentatively title the clusters. Once fairly stable clusters appear and the number of new ideas diminishes, review each cluster and give it a name that describes the theme or subject of the ovals inside it. Write the name, phrased in action terms ("get our finances sorted out," "improve board-staff relations") on a new oval and place it at the top of the cluster. The cluster label typically will be the name of a potential strategic issue—indicated by the content of the cluster—and all the ovals beneath it will state options for addressing the issue.

2. With the help of participants, pencil in links within clusters and across clusters. Arrows *to* an idea indicate causes, influences, or something that has to happen first (the rules for these arrows do not need to be absolutely precise). Arrows *from* an idea indicate effects, outcomes, or consequences. Using a pencil is a good idea, because the placement of arrows can change as a result of discussion. Use an eraser to get rid of unwanted arrows. The arrow placement shows participants which clusters or ideas are more important or "busy"—they are the ones with the largest numbers of cross-links to other clusters or ideas.

3. Decide whether the idea on an oval is an issue label, option, assertion, assumption, or statement of fact. Assertions, assumptions, or statements of fact are not directly actionable (except in that they may call for further research) and should be placed at the bottom of clusters. Typically, they provide premises for subsequent strings of possible actions. For example, if an oval says, "the executive director will retire in one year" (a statement of fact), then the job description may need to be reviewed, a search committee established, and a choice made whether to search for a replacement outside the organization as well as inside. Assertions or statements of fact also may lead to research (to find out whether they are true) or may be converted to options through new statements that turn their implied actions into possible actions.

Options are ideas that contribute to achieving the purpose of a cluster (as indicated by the cluster's title). They are actionable ("produce staff phone directory," "conduct focus groups," "use a telephone bank for fundraising") rather than being assertions or statements of fact.

Issues, the labels for clusters of options, are more complex. An issue is usually stated in the top oval in a cluster, although discussion may indicate that another existing oval or a new oval better captures the essence of the issue. Issues usually are broad based, long term, and highly consequential in terms of associated challenges or opportunities, effects on stakeholders, resource use, or irreversibility of the strategies used to address them. An asterisk or colored stick-on dot may be used to identify issues.

4. Once ovals are arranged hierarchically as issues, options, and assertions, assumptions, or statements of fact, decide on the relative importance of the issues. (This step may come after the following step if that change in order is thought desirable.) Colored stick-on dots may be used to graphically indicate the group's views of the issues' relative importance. For example, give each partici-

pant five dots and ask him or her to place a single dot on each of the five most important issues. Alternatively, participants might be allowed to put more than one dot on an issue label, to produce a measure of intensity of feeling. It may also be helpful to straw poll participants directly on the relative *unimportance* of the issues. Often it is important to know which issues participants think are most important in the short term and which are most important in the long term. Dots of one color can be used to identify important short-term issues, and another color can be used for long-term issues.

5. Identify goals by asking "so what" questions about the issue clusters. In other words, query participants about what they would hope to achieve (what arrows out they envision) by addressing the issues effectively. Usually this line of questioning (or laddering) leads participants to additional issues or options before the set of goals is fully specified. Ideas that are obviously good things in their own right and do not seem to need any further elaboration are candidates to be goals. Typically, goals are morally virtuous and upright and tap the deepest values and most worthy aspirations of the organization's (or community's) culture. For example, pursuing this line of questioning around the strategic issues facing it led the small college to the goals outlined in Figure B.2. Goals may be identified with stick-on dots in a new color or with a self-stick note to highlight their significance. Again, straw-polling procedures may be useful to identify the goals participants believe are the most important.

Formulating and understanding a goal system involves identifying linkages among goals, issue labels, and options that compose issues. When working in a large group divided into subgroups, it is often useful to have subgroups exchange maps with each other after strategic issues have been identified—that is, subgroups should try to figure out the goal system implied by some other subgroup's strategic issues. This procedure can open participants to one another's thinking, promote creativity, and lead to a convergence across groups on goals, issues, options, and assertions.

The superordinate goals in a strategy map usually outline the organization's mission. If there is little connection between these goals and the organization's existing mission statement, then the content of the organization's mission is probably a strategic issue.

6. Decide on actions for the immediate future to address the issues and achieve the goals. The group should review the options (and their resource implications) and identify the ones already being done and the new ones that should be pursued over the course of the next six to twelve months. Options that address more than one issue (*potent options*) are particularly desirable ones to choose. A straw-polling exercise—typically using green dots for "go"—may be used to pool participants' opinions about which items should be included in the action set. The

group may wish to place two dots on items it wishes to take responsibility for itself and single dots on items it wishes to delegate to others outside the group. Once actions to address an issue have been chosen, the broad outlines of a strategy should be reasonably clear from looking at the map. The action set also typically comprises the basic tasks to be included in a work program that names the responsible parties, reporting dates, resources needed, and expected products or outcomes (see Chapter Nine).

7. Provide closure to the session. Groups of five to approximately thirty participants (in several subgroups) can often get through the process of constructing a draft map (including identifying goals, strategic issues, options, assertions, and actions) in a retreat setting over the course of a long day—or as part of a two- or three-day retreat that includes other activities, such as stakeholder analyses and SWOC analyses. At the end of the mapping exercise some sort of closure is desirable, usually in the form of a review of what the group has done, what understandings or agreements have been reached, and a statement of what the next steps in the strategic planning process will be. For example, individuals or task forces may be assigned specific action items, or the task of developing the issues further and recommending strategies for dealing with them.

Recording the Work of the Map Construction Session. There are several ways to record the group's work:

1. The map can simply be taken off the wall and saved. Before doing so, however, it is advisable to run long strips of drafting tape across all the ovals so that they do not come loose. The saved map can be posted wherever it is convenient so that its contents can be recorded in outline form or used as the focus of follow-up sessions.

2. The contents of the map may be recorded with the aid of a computer as the group discusses them, either in map form, using software especially designed for the purpose (such as Decision Explorer, discussed at the end of this resource), or in outline form.

3. The map may also be photographed. A high-resolution digital camera with built-in flash (or a standard, fully automatic, 35 mm camera with built-in flash) can be used to photograph each flipchart sheet separately. As long as participants have written legibly on their ovals, the map's contents can be read from the photographs. Photographs are a useful backup in case the map itself gets lost. They can also be a reminder to participants of what the day was like and can help nonparticipants understand how the process progressed. The photographs can be imported into a text document and distributed electronically or can be mounted on sheets of letter paper (four to a page), inserted into transparent holders, and

put in a three-ring binder. A title page, the date of the process, and a list of those who attended should precede the photographs. Alternatively, a photocopying machine that can copy full flipchart sheets can be used, reducing each sheet to a smaller size if that is desirable.

Useful Variations on the Mapping Process

The mapping process is flexible and can be used in various ways over the course of a strategic planning process. For example, Chapters Two and Six discussed the indirect approach to identifying strategic issues. In that approach, options are identified that might make or keep stakeholders happy; build on strengths, take advantage of opportunities, and minimize or overcome weaknesses and challenges; capture action-oriented features of mission and mandates, existing strategies, and background studies or reports; and in general create public value. These options are then arranged into clusters in an effort to find issues that emerge indirectly, via the options. The mapping process can obviously be used to provide additional structure to the issues and options and to clarify the goal system that might be pursued by addressing these issues and options.

Stakeholder Analyses. Mapping may be used to develop a more integrated picture of an organization's stakeholders and how they relate to each other and to the organization. Many of the techniques presented in Resource A are forms of causal maps. For example, stakeholder influence diagrams are causal maps. Bases of power–directions of interest diagrams are also causal maps, in which the planning team tries to articulate each stakeholder's goal system and bases of power. The team can expand the map for each stakeholder by placing the team's own organization's goals on the map and indicating what the stakeholder does or can do to affect achievement of the organization's goals. Next, the team can identify what its own organization does or can do to meet the stakeholder's goals (or criteria or expectations regarding the team's organization). The pattern of influences and outcomes can then be explored and elaborated. The resulting map should help the team be clear about what the organization wants or needs from the stakeholder; what the stakeholder can do to give or withhold the wanted item (and why), and what the organization can do, if anything, about it.

These and other causal maps involving stakeholders should highlight potential strategic issues and the elements of useful strategies. They can also be used for strategic planning team role plays aimed at developing the strategic options most likely to address stakeholder interests effectively, build a supportive coalition, and ensure effective implementation. Resource A provides more information on how to conduct these role plays. The maps are also helpful for clarifying areas of potential collaboration with different stakeholders. In particular the maps can highlight potential collaborative advantages, that is, the likelihood that two or more stakeholders can achieve desirable outcomes jointly that they cannot achieve alone (Huxham, 1993, 2003).

Unpacking Loaded Concepts. Often strategic planning is temporarily stymied by the need to deal with issues that carry extraordinary emotional freight for various stakeholders. The need to address issues of gender, race, disability, or political ideology, for example, has given headaches (sometimes heartaches) to teams with which I have worked. Such issues are highly emotive because of the negative consequences people have already suffered or think they might suffer depending on how the issues are resolved (Ortony, Clore, and Collins, 1990; Goleman, 1995). Reasonable dialogue usually becomes difficult or impossible. For example, to return to a case mentioned briefly earlier, in the 1990s a group of seventy stakeholder representatives working under the auspices of the U.S. Department of Education was interested in developing a national agenda for better addressing the needs of students with disabilities. The group became stymied by what *inclusive* education meant for students with disabilities. The emotional temperature was high, and many people were willing to accuse others of pretty awful things. There was a certain humorous irony in the situation, in that what *divided* people was *inclusion,* but few present saw anything at all funny about it. Group members imagined the worst about each other, partly because in the absence of real dialogue no one really knew what others thought, and therefore many were prone to stereotype, project, and rationalize in inaccurate and unhelpful ways (Roberts, 2002). Eventually, the group was unwilling to proceed further until the facilitators helped them deal directly with this issue of inclusion. In response the facilitators invented a variant of the mapping process, employing the following guidelines:

1. Write the "loaded" concept on an oval, and place the oval in the middle of a wall covered with flipchart paper. In the case of the group formulating an agenda for children with disabilities, the loaded concept was "have inclusive educational environment."

2. Have participants seat themselves in a semicircle in front of the wall.

3. Ask each person to take out a sheet of scratch paper and draw a line down the middle, dividing it into two columns of equal size. Ask everyone to label the left-hand column "How?" and the right-hand column "Why?" Then have each person individually and silently brainstorm as many answers to the two questions as possible. In the case of the education group this meant brainstorming as many possible *means* to achieving inclusive education (how) and as many possible *ends* (outcomes, consequences, goals) of inclusive education (why) as each person could imagine.

4. Have each person select a specified number of his or her most important means and an equivalent number of most important ends and write each one on a separate oval. In the education case, participants were asked to select one item from each list, because with seventy people in the group, a greater number would have drawn the process out too much and probably generated redundant ideas.

5. Cluster the *means* ovals below the loaded concept, and cluster the *ends* ovals above it. Add structure if necessary to indicate how the various ideas within and across clusters are related.

6. Lead participants in a conversation about the resulting clusters. Add ovals, linkages, and clusters as necessary. As the precise nature of the disagreements become more clear, people are better able to discuss them and to discover additional options or goals along the way. Keep asking how and why questions to help people clarify their reasoning and to keep them from coming to blows over particular options. In other words, help people to be reason-*able*. Record key points right on the flipchart-papered wall or on a separate flipchart.

In most cases the major disagreements will be over means and not ends. The map will make this graphically clear. When people realize they actually *share* some important goals, they are far more likely to engage in constructive dialogue about how to achieve them (Fisher and Ury, 1981; Thompson, 2001). They are also less likely to stereotype, project, and rationalize in destructive ways (Fisher and Brown, 1988). In the educational group, many participants were surprised to find that the entire group really did share most of the goals even though people differed on the far more numerous means. Heightened respect emerged, along with a less fraught atmosphere and a commitment to problem solve. After a number of months the project ultimately resulted in a valuable report and sense of direction for the future (U.S. Department of Education, 1994).

Scenario Construction. The mapping process can also be used to develop the elements of scenario story lines. The main benefit of constructing scenarios is to promote learning by the planning team, sensitize team members to plausible though perhaps unlikely futures, and develop strategies better able to handle most eventualities (de Gues, 1988; Schwartz, 1991; Van der Heijden and others, 2002). The following guidelines may be used:

1. For each team member prepare a set of ovals with the organization's mission, mandates, and existing goal system stated in action terms. The writing on these ovals should be in a different color than that used by participants to create the ovals in guideline 3.

2. Have the planning team consider the three *external* assessment categories outlined in Chapter Five: forces and trends (political, economic, social, technological,

educational, physical); stakeholders who control key resources (clients, customers, payers, members of nonprofit organizations); and competitors, collaborators, and competitive and collaborative forces and advantages. Using three sheets of scratch paper, one for each category, each person brainstorms as many trends and events as he or she can imagine happening in each category. Then the team members should consider and write out on scratch paper the trends and events that might affect the *internal* assessment categories—resources, present strategy, and performance. By looking externally and internally, the team is likely to consider the organization and all its stakeholders.

3. Each participant places ten to twenty brainstormed entries onto ovals, one entry per oval. Each oval should indicate the source of the idea (forces and trends; resource controllers; competitors, collaborators, and competitive or collaborative force or advantages; resources; present strategy; performance).

4. The facilitator merges the participant-created ovals into a single set and shuffles them. Each participant (or small group) is given up to twenty ovals. The participants are then asked to arrange their ovals into a map, on a flipchart sheet–covered wall, in a way that indicates a plausible (though not necessarily likely) set of influence relationships and that connects these ovals positively or negatively to the ovals indicating the organization's mission, mandates, and goal system. Extra ovals may be added as necessary. In other words each participant should construct a *story* that links the ovals together and indicates the influence chains that would either help or hinder achievement of the organization's goals.

5. The team then reviews each story and answers the following questions:

- What opportunities or challenges are highlighted?
- Which stakeholders are affected by this story, and would they be happy or unhappy if it happened?
- What strengths might we draw on to deal with this scenario, and what weaknesses would hinder us in dealing with it?
- In the case of challenging stories (and especially those that are really threatening scenarios), what, if anything, can we do to keep this story from happening?
- If we cannot do anything to stop it, what can we do to defend against it? Or is there any way to turn it into an opportunity?
- What can we do, if anything, to make sure desirable stories happen?

6. The answers to these questions are recorded. If the team uses the indirect approach to strategic issue identification, many of the answers can be placed on ovals and used to construct issue clusters. Similarly, if the team develops a strategy map, many of the ovals can be included in that map.

Mapping Distinctive Competencies. As indicated in Chapters Two and Five, a consideration of the organization's strengths and weaknesses can also lead to an identification of its *distinctive competencies* (Selznick, 1957), or what have been termed more recently *core competencies* (Prahalad and Hamel, 1990; Johnson and Scholes, 2002). These are the organization's strongest capabilities or its most effective strategies and actions or the resources (broadly conceived) on which it can draw routinely to perform well. What makes these abilities *distinctive* is the inability of others to replicate them easily, if at all, because of the way they are interlinked with one another (Eden and Ackermann, 2000). Usually distinctive core competencies arise from the interrelationships of a set of competencies and core competencies. It is the interrelationships that are particularly hard for others to replicate because, for example, they are based on tacit knowledge and long-term relationships (Eden and Ackermann, 1998, pp. 102–110).

Eden and Ackermann (2000) and Ackermann, Eden, and Brown (2004) offer a very sophisticated approach to identifying distinctive competencies. Because of space limitations, this resource outlines a more rough-and-ready approach to identifying distinctive competencies that was provided by Johnson and Scholes (2002, pp. 156–159). They suggest taking the following steps:

1. Clarify the organization's *critical success factors.* These are the organizational performances or product or service features that matter the most to key stakeholders and at which the organization must excel, particularly against any competitors. They might include such features as range of product offerings, quality of products, reliable delivery, speed of delivery, price, and good service.

2. Use mapping to articulate the reasons why these features matter to stakeholders. These reasons would be arrows in to the relevant success factors. For example, good service might result from rapid response times, flexibility, and problem-solving ability.

3. Next, identify the competencies and resources the organization draws on (arrows in) to match the stakeholders' reasons. In other words, what does the organization do to meet the critical success factors that also matches up with the stakeholders' reasons for thinking those are critical success factors? These competencies and resources might include good personal relations with the stakeholders, fast turnaround on requests for service, the organization's distribution and logistics system, and willingness to redo jobs until stakeholders are satisfied.

4. Figure out which of these competencies are core competencies—that is, competencies "that critically underpin an organization's competitive advantage" (Johnson and Scholes, 2002, p. 156)—or, for most public and nonprofit organizations, that are absolutely central to the organization's ability to satisfy key stakeholders' expectations and create public value.

Eden and Ackermann (1998, 2000) (on whose work Johnson and Scholes' is based) advise looking for interrelationships among the competencies and resources to search for distinctive competencies: that is, those competencies that would be particularly hard for anyone else to replicate. They advise focusing next on core distinctive competencies. These are competencies that are both critical to success and hard for others to replicate—and therefore can provide suitable bedrock on which to build effective strategies.

Computer Support

Computer support becomes increasingly helpful as the number of ideas to be mapped, managed, and analyzed increases. Decision Explorer, developed by Colin Eden, Fran Ackermann, and associates, is extremely powerful and useful software designed to record, manage, and analyze causal maps. The software can handle maps containing thousands of concepts and their associated links. The concepts and links are stored in a central database and can be displayed in a format similar to that of an original hand-drafted map. The software operates in the Windows environment and can draw on Windows for program management, color graphics, printing, and data storage and transfer.

The software can be obtained from www.banxia.com. Training in the use of the software can be found through the same Web site or through www.visible-thinking.com.

RESOURCE C

STRATEGIC PLANNING IN COLLABORATIVE SETTINGS

John M. Bryson, Barbara C. Crosby, Fran Ackermann

To date, most of the theory and practice of strategic planning has been focused on enhancing the performance of single organizations. Increasingly, however, strategic planning is being used to help multiorganizational or community-based efforts be effective. An obvious issue is how to adapt strategic planning concepts, procedures, tools, and practices typically developed to address the needs of single organizations to multiorganizational settings. This resource section discusses how the development of collaborations is tied to the Strategy Change Cycle (SCC) and recent research on collaboration.

Achieving successful collaboration typically becomes harder as more organizations or other stakeholders become involved. There is probably a rough continuum of difficulty: intraorganizational collaboration (the focus of most of this book) is easiest to foster, then comes interorganizational or interagency collaboration, and finally there is community collaboration. In other words, collaboration becomes more difficult as it becomes more voluntary and as more stakeholders are also veto holders (Linden, 2002, p. 220; Crosby and Bryson, forthcoming). If an organization has a strong leader, it is likely that internal collaboration can be created—as it was, for example, in the case of Baltimore's Citi-Stat system (see Chapters Two and Ten). Interorganizational or interagency coordination efforts typically are focused on implementing policies adopted by others (Chrislip, 2002, p. 42), such as state social service policies. In these instances a superordinate authority often has substantial power to influence the course of collaboration efforts (see the discussion of collaboration in Chapter Ten). In the case of community collaborations, however, typically no one is "in charge," and therefore a great deal of effort will likely need to be expended to create visions, goals, and actions that are supported by enough autonomous actors to achieve collaboration success (Chrislip, 2002; Wheeland, 2003).

Research on collaboration has increased in recent years, and now much is known about the ways collaborations develop and the factors that contribute to their success (see, for example, Gray, 1989; Ring and Van de Ven, 1994; Mattessich, Murray-Close, and Monsey, 2001; Chrislip, 2002; Linden, 2002). Some of the best work has been done by Chris Huxham and her colleagues, who have developed what they call the *theory of collaborative advantage* (Huxham, 2003; Huxham and Beech, 2002; Vangen and Huxham, 2002, 2003a, 2003b). What Huxham and her colleagues' work and the SCC have in common is that each provides a set of guides for reflective practice (Huxham, 2003)—that is, each offers a framework designed to prompt discussion, dialogue, learning, decision, and action.

Two examples of collaborative strategic planning will ground this discussion. The first is the African American Men Project of Hennepin County, Minnesota, in which the county government engaged an array of stakeholders both internal and external to the county government in developing policies, programs, and activities that would produce better outcomes for African American men aged eighteen to thirty (Hennepin County, 2002a; Bryson, Cunningham, and Lokkesmoe, 2002; Crosby and Bryson, forthcoming). The second is the strategic planning effort of a major regional public health service in the United Kingdom. The first author of this resource was involved in the first effort, and all three authors have been involved in the second effort. Because of space and confidentiality considerations, the second case is used mainly as a contrast to the first one.

The Theory of Collaborative Advantage

The theory of collaborative advantage (TOCA) is aimed at understanding collaborative work in general. TOCA consists essentially of one overarching challenge, or tension, and a set of subsidiary challenges or tensions organized according to different themes. The overarching challenge pits *collaborative advantage* against *collaborative inertia*. Collaborative advantage, on the one hand, is the synergistic outcome gained through collaboration in which something is achieved that could not have been achieved by any organization acting alone (Huxham, 2003, p. 403). This idea captures the *spirit of collaboration* (p. 416)—that is, the hopes for, or even ideology of, embracing, empowering, involving, and mobilizing participants to achieve desired outcomes. Collaborative inertia, on the other hand, refers to "the oft-pertaining actual outcome, in which the collaboration makes only hard fought or negligible progress" and may well not have been worth the effort (p. 403). *Collaborative thuggery* (p. 410) is often needed to overcome the inertia, and consists of manipulating the collaborative agenda and playing politics (Vangen and Huxham, 2002). In practice, typically both the spirit of collaboration and collaborative thuggery are present and necessary in order for desired outcomes to be achieved. In other words the spirit is not enough if the body politic is unwilling; the body politic is often reluctant—and so a bit of thuggery is needed to overcome inertia and move the body along.

The subsidiary challenges, or themes, are leadership, managing aims, building trust, managing power, membership structures, appropriate working processes, accountability, communication, commitment and determination, resources, democracy, equality, and compromise (Huxham, 2003). This resource will deal with the first ten of these thirteen themes, the ones that seem most relevant to a discussion of strategic planning. *Leadership* is understood to mean "making things happen in a collaboration" (Huxham, 2003, p. 415; see also Vangen and Huxham, 2003a). And leadership is probably the theme area in which the conflict between the ideology (or spirit) of collaboration and pragmatism plays out most frequently. In the view of Huxham and her colleagues, leadership plays out in three media—structures, processes, and participants' actions—and is not just a person-centered phenomenon. Structures and processes are as important in shaping agendas as are participants' actions but are often not under the direct control of a collaboration's membership (Bryson and Crosby, 1992; Crosby and Bryson, forthcoming). Beyond that, participants' actions can and do affect collaborative outcomes but often not in the way that was intended because of important challenges or dilemmas that get in the way (Bryant, 2003).

Managing aims captures the tension between the commonsense notion that collaborative endeavors should have clear aims and the likelihood that multiple organizations' multiple agendas will hamper immediate agreement on aims. The result is that collaborations often need to act their way into shared goals. In other words, collaborators need to do something, see if it works, see if they all can agree, and then fashion a goal that justifies the action and makes it seem as though the members knew what they were doing collaboratively all along. *Building trust* pits the conventional wisdom that trust is a precondition of successful collaboration against the common reality that mistrust and suspicion are the usual starting points. Trust in practice must be built, which means there must be enough trust for collaborators to take a risk and do something together, and then if it turns out the trust was justified, more can be done together. Trust thus ends up being an outcome of collaboration as much as a precondition of it (Vangen and Huxham, 2003b).

The theme of *managing power* juxtaposes the conventional wisdom that whoever controls financial resources has the power, with the empirical observation that power is broadly dispersed and exercised and that the locus of power is constantly shifting. Huxham and Beech (2002) refer to these manifold exercises of power as *points of power* that make up a collaboration's *power infrastructure*. Recognizing the ubiquity of power and its exercise also leads to recognizing the need for manipulative behavior—collaborative thuggery—which some would argue is against the spirit of collaboration. The *membership structures* theme highlights the idea that collaborative structures are ambiguous, complex, and dynamic. Often it is unclear exactly who is a member. Overlapping collaboratives and hierarchies of collaboratives add complexity. And membership structures are dynamic: members of the collaborative come and go and relationships change, the agendas and staff of member organizations change, collaborative agendas change, and so on.

Appropriate working processes contrasts the conventional wisdom that collaborators need appropriate, well-understood, clear, and reasonable working processes with the common experience of difficulty in fashioning these processes. The difficulties highlighted by the previously discussed themes all make it hard to create appropriate working processes. Similarly, *accountability* is very difficult to ensure, given the divergent accountability expectations and structures of the member organizations. A fairly constant dialogue about what the collaborative is accountable for and how, why, and to whom it is accountable appears to be one of the few ways to achieve a workable convergence (Roberts, 1997; Behn, 2001). This last point is one of the reasons there is a need for effective *communication*. Everyone would agree that good communication is essential; most collaborators probably don't realize how *much* communication there must be and how much of it should be focused on building and maintaining good relationships, managing conflict, fostering useful feedback, discerning aims, exercising power responsibly, and so on. As a theme, communication thus pervades every other theme.

Commitment and determination are also widely perceived to be vital for successful collaboration. And yet there is a tension around commitment and determination similar to that around trust. Commitment and determination are more likely to develop as outcomes of collaboration than to occur as preconditions, and yet a certain amount of both is absolutely necessary to get anything done at all. One way to handle this tension is to have a monomaniac with a vision push the collaborative work ahead, so that trust, commitment, and determination can be built (Huxham and Vangen, 2000). Finally, the theme of *resources* presents a tension similar to that found in many of the other themes. Resources are crucial but are unlikely to be forthcoming all at once at the beginning of a collaboration. Instead, resource flows typically will grow based on demonstrated accomplishment and the achievement of members' separate and joint aims.

The Strategy Change Cycle

Several points can be made about the SCC in the context of collaboration. First, it is important to view the ten steps in the process (Chapters Three through Ten) as a set of occasions for discussion, dialogue, learning, decision, and action, because much effort will be needed to engage the various stakeholders and all will come with their own views. Second, the steps should most emphatically not be thought of as a rigid sequence, because participants typically rethink what they are doing several times. In other words the process is cyclic and iterative. Specifically, a sequence of agreements will likely be needed as collaboration emerges incrementally. For example, Chrislip (2002, p. 54) argues that in voluntary, consensus-based community or regional multistakeholder collaborations, a series of agreements will be needed that establish the existence of a shared concern, who will work on this concern, how they will work together, how to understand the relevant information, how to define the problem or vision for the future, what strategies should be pursued, and what the action steps and responsibilities for pursuing them will be.

Third, collaborative strategic planning is very likely to begin in the middle of the planning process (with issues or failing strategies) or at the end of the process (with reassessing where strategies, goals, and outcomes have been and where they may need to go), because those are the situations in which the parties are most likely to find compelling reasons to collaborate. Fourth, goals and vision can be developed in many different places in the process. Many community-based collaborative efforts begin with a visioning process, but in highly politicized, public settings *effective* visions are more likely to be developed toward the end of the process—*after* the necessary parties have signed on and at least nascent strategies have been developed to deal with the issues—than they are to be developed *before* strategies are formulated. And finally, there is absolutely no substitute for leadership when it comes to successfully pursuing strategic planning in collaborative settings. Without leadership, constant communication, and obsessive attention to detail, the process is likely to fall apart.

To summarize, the TOCA points to the broad context within which collaboration takes place, whereas the SCC identifies a set of activities that should be undertaken as part of a strategic planning exercise. We now use the two cases to illustrate how strategic planning might be undertaken in collaborative settings.

The Cases

Two cases of collaborative strategic planning show how the Strategy Change Cycle can be adapted for use in collaborative settings. Most attention is given to the African American Men Project of Hennepin County (Minneapolis), Minnesota, in which the county government engaged an array of internal and external stakeholders in developing policies, programs, and activities that would produce better outcomes for African American men aged eighteen to thirty (Hennepin County, 2002a). This case is compared with the strategic planning efforts of a major regional health service in the United Kingdom, part of the British National Health Service (NHS). In both cases a powerful *lead organization* initiated the planning effort for a network of public, nonprofit, and for-profit organizations in which it was central.

The African American Men Project. The county commissioners of Hennepin County mandated the African American Men Project (AAMP) in 1999, because county statistics showed that even though many African American men were prospering, many others were in trouble. Statistics across a range of areas showed the same disheartening outcomes for the county's African American population, and especially African American men, as are found nationally. In terms of economic status, concentration of poverty, education, health, housing, and criminal justice outcomes, African American men were significantly worse off than their white counterparts. Moreover, this discrepancy persisted despite the substantial efforts of the county, other governmental agencies, and nonprofit organizations to fund and manage numerous programs designed to help disadvantaged people.

The purpose of the AAMP therefore was to help the commissioners figure out how to frame the challenges, choose goals or desired outcomes, and identify politically and technically viable solutions likely to produce better outcomes for the African American men aged eighteen to thirty who live in the county. The AAMP thus was an exercise in data gathering and analysis, issue framing, and strategy development and implementation—that is, strategic planning by another name. The key task was to figure out how to frame the issues in such a way that broad support would be forthcoming for a broad-scale advance.

When the county commissioners authorized the AAMP by resolution in 1999, they also allocated $500,000 to support the project. The AAMP was guided by a thirty-seven-member steering committee representing major sections of the African American community, local business, government, and the University of Minnesota. The project was directed by Gary Cunningham, the county's director of planning and development. Internal county work teams were organized to examine particular issues. A variety of outside research partners and community partners also participated, including various academic institutions, businesses, news organizations, and nonprofit groups.

The steering committee presented its final report to the county commissioners in January 2002. The commissioners subsequently unanimously approved the report and directed the county administrator to implement those recommendations for which the county was responsible. In response to the report, the African American Men Commission, with more than 130 members, was created in 2002. A variety of county-initiated implementing actions are under way, mostly in partnership with a variety of organizations. The project has to be termed at least a provisional success.

On the face of it the AAMP did follow the SCC steps, although in truth what prompted the process was a set of failing strategies. As noted, outcomes were not very good for the public funds expended. Meanwhile, the county had just spent a huge amount of money on a new jail, and that expense plus rising criminal justice costs in general placed the rest of the county's budget and commitments in jeopardy. Failing strategies and a big issue got the county commissioners' attention. The resolution they adopted, along with the money to fund its implementation, in effect mandated a strategic planning process. A number of studies were commissioned that explored existing missions and mandates, external and internal environments, specific issues needing to be addressed, and possible strategies for doing so. The AAMP final report essentially painted a vision of success and offered a series of recommendations that the commissioners adopted. That vision is now guiding implementation.

In terms of the TOCA, the themes and tensions identified by Huxham and her colleagues clearly were present and needed to be managed. *Leadership* mattered but was broadly dispersed. The project would not have succeeded without the mandate from, support of, and funding by the county commissioners. The structure of the county government and the formal processes for working within it shaped the final project and its report but so did the politics of the African American community and of the county more generally. The leadership of specific county commissioners, Gary Cunningham, the broadly representative steering committee, and study team leaders (mostly outside county government) also made a difference.

Managing aims was a challenge. The project began with the rather nonspecific aim (concern) of figuring out what to do to improve outcomes for African American men. Only after the study teams had completed their work were more specific goals articulated. And only after considerable debate were final recommendations adopted. So the project began with only a general sense of direction and worked its way toward more specific goals. Throughout the project *managing power* was an issue. Debates within the steering committee and study teams over what to recommend and how to do so were often intense. And the debaters had to keep in mind the ideal of having the county commissioners adopt the final report unanimously; otherwise, implementation would be problematic. Thus there were numerous points of power throughout a broadly dispersed power infrastructure.

Given the uncertainty about aims and the issues around power, it is not surprising that *building trust* was a challenge. A pervasive issue was whether the African American participants in the project should trust the white participants. Many in the African American group were very suspicious of any project that might show the African American community in a bad light or jeopardize existing programs, even if those programs were not working well. The fact that Gary Cunningham was himself a well-respected member of the African American community was probably essential to trust-building efforts.

Membership structures probably also played a crucial role in building trust. The fact that over 90 percent of the members of the AAMP steering committee were African Americans helped assure them of having substantial control over the direction of the project. The structure also ensured that the final report would have substantial legitimacy and would assure county commissioners that the African American community was probably supportive of the report's recommendations. Meanwhile Gary Cunningham made sure that the leaders of the various project study efforts and their teams were credible and that they had enough resources to do the work.

Having *appropriate working processes* meant that the steering committee and its subcommittees and the study teams had to ensure that all the work was compatible with the county government's procedures and timetables for action. Gary Cunningham, in particular, paid careful attention to these procedural matters, because he knew he had to if the project were to succeed.

Accountability was complicated (Romzek, 1996; Behn, 2001). First was the project's need to be accountable to the county commissioners. Second was its need to be accountable to the county administration by following the rules and procedures for studies such as this. Third was the need for the AAMP to be seen as accountable to the African American community. Fourth was its need to be seen as credible to the various professional groups involved in or affected by the study. And finally, the project needed to be seen as accountable to the citizenry in general. Constant attention to these issues, or *mindfulness* about them (Weick and Sutcliffe, 2001), on the part of many individuals was necessary. Otherwise the legitimacy of the whole effort would have been put in jeopardy (Suchman, 1995).

As indicated by Huxham (2003), obsessive attention to *communication* was necessary throughout the project. The huge numbers of individuals and groups involved meant that without adequate communication the project would simply not have produced enough "glue" to hold itself together or to advance through the phases of the Strategy Change Cycle. Gary Cunningham's office was the central node in the communication network. The wisdom of Huxham's admonition to "nurture, nurture, nurture" was clearly evident throughout the process, and Cunningham was the chief nurturer.

Commitment and determination and the presence of *resources* were somewhat tentative at the beginning of the project. On the one hand, only over time did a fuller commitment and determination grow on the part of steering committee members and study teams. And only when the final report was presented to them did the county commissioners adopt its recommendations unanimously and provide additional resources for implementation. On the other hand, Gary Cunningham and some of his staff members were committed to the project from the start. Cunningham fits the classification of a monomaniac with a vision, one who pushes the collaborative work ahead so that the necessary trust, commitment and determination can be built (Huxham and Vangen, 2000). In sum, all of the themes identified by Huxham and her colleagues were present and played themselves out in much the way they suggest. Also as they would predict, no precise prescriptions were followed, and the tension between conventional wisdom and common practice was present throughout.

Regional Health Service Planning Effort. The collaborative project for the regional NHS in the United Kingdom was mandated by a government health department and featured two related strategic planning efforts. As of this writing, these efforts are incomplete and stalled, so the analysis that follows is of efforts still in progress. The first effort is being managed by a senior civil servant and was begun at the behest of a government minister who sought to have a set of initiatives pulled together as a *regional strategy*. The second effort is being called a *visioning exercise* and was authorized in 2002 at the behest of a discussion group of civil servants and chief executives. A second senior civil servant was appointed overall project manager. He contracted with the authors to perform various tasks, including facilitating several sessions of the discussion group. The second effort is the project focused on here.

The health service followed the Strategy Change Cycle only in the most general way. The process did begin with an initial agreement among key actors, an agreement prompted by a sense that current strategies were failing and a number of issues were looming. In this sense the process was like that of the AAMP. Unlike the AAMP's process, the public health service process next focused specifically on strategic issues and from them induced the desired goals for the system. The oval mapping process was used to identify issues and potential goals. Once the goal system is agreed to at some future point, then more work will be done on elaborating strategies to address the issues. The final write-up will be called a *vision* but in effect will probably be a strategic plan that includes mission, mandates, goals, strategies, and recommended implementing actions. Because the participants are also the most important implementation managers, this has no doubt been the best way of proceeding.

Leadership matters in this case as well. The project would not have gotten under way without the support of senior civil servants and the minister above them. In this case, too, the structure of government and its formal processes have shaped the project and its reports, and broader politics have affected the project as well. The leadership of specific civil servants and chief executives also has made a difference. The project manager, in particular, has been vital to the effort. But unlike the AAMP case, there has been less consistency in top leadership support over the course of the effort.

Managing aims has been a challenge. The project began with the general aim of figuring out a vision for the whole system within the framework of existing governmental policy and has worked its way toward more specific goals. *Managing power* has also been more of an issue throughout the project than it was for the AAMP. The participants have considerable but different power bases in the system and are protective of their prerogatives and their constituents. They have engaged in spirited debates over what to recommend and how to do so, with issues of power always explicitly or implicitly involved. Given the uncertainly about aims and the issues around power, it is not surprising that *building trust* has been a challenge. The existence of the discussion group has helped to build trust, and many participants knew and trusted the consultants, but skepticism is still prevalent.

Membership structures, and specifically the discussion group, have played a crucial role in building trust. The structures also ensure that the final report on a vision for the system will have substantial legitimacy and assures senior civil servants and ministers that a crucial set of stakeholders are behind the report's recommendations. Meanwhile the project managers of both strategic planning efforts (the regional strategy and the visioning project) have attended carefully to *appropriate working processes. Accountability* is at least as complicated as in the AAMP case. Attention to *communication* has been necessary throughout the project because of the substantial numbers of individuals and organizations involved. The visioning project manager's office is the central node in the communication network and, unfortunately, he has had a full agenda of other work to do. This has made it hard to do what the theory of collaborative advantage advises, namely, "nurture, nurture, nurture."

Commitment and determination and the presence of *resources* were tentative at the beginning of the project. The effort was authorized, and the money to proceed has apparently been available. But there was no commitment on the part of the department at the beginning to adopt the discussion group's recommendations regarding the plan. Quite understandably, the department's leadership first wants to see what is produced. Meanwhile many of the chief executives have also taken a wait-and-see attitude because they are not sure what the final report will contain or how the department will respond.

In sum, all the themes identified by Huxham and her colleagues are present and have played themselves out in much the way they suggest. Unlike the leadership for the AAMP, however, leadership support from the top has been inconsistent. As a result the project manager has found it difficult to devote constant attention to the effort, including maintaining desirable levels of communication and nurturance. Managing aims, managing power, and building trust remain issues with which to contend. The ultimate outcome of the effort is still very much in doubt.

Process Guidelines

Leaders, managers, and planners wishing to pursue collaboration should consider the following guidelines, in addition to those offered in Chapters Three through Twelve:

1. *Successful collaboration takes an immense amount of effort, communication, and nurturance, so be sure there is a good reason to collaborate* (Huxham, 2003). In practice, this means it may take a crisis to prompt the necessary action (Linden, 2002, pp. 110–113). It also means there should be a clear indication that real collaborative advantage can be gained, that public value can be created beyond what individual organizations can achieve acting alone (Huxham, 1993). In assessing the value of collaboration, be sure to look beyond the immediate situation and recognize the long-term benefits of community building. As Chrislip (2002) notes: "[Community] collaboration is not just another strategy or tactic for addressing public concerns. It is a means of building social capital, sustaining a democratic society, and transforming the civic culture of a community or region" (p. 5).

2. *Consider reframing existing reality in order to show how public value might be created through seeking collaborative advantage.* Part of the reason for pursuing a strategy of collaboration in the AAMP was the need to reinterpret reality so that progress could be made, because continuing the same attitudes and policies could only go on producing disaster for many African American men. A strategy of collaboration would refashion existing networks and open up the possibility of "new constituencies for change" (Chrislip, 2002, pp. 52–53). The stakeholder analysis team directed by the first author of this resource (Bryson, Cunningham, and Lokkesmoe, 2002) used a sequence of analyses and steps that reframed the problems of many African American men as *everyone's* problems and not just problems for the men themselves. This reframing helped lead to the unanimous adoption by the county commissioners of the AAMP final report in January 2002, which was a major political triumph. As Kingdon (1995) notes, "Getting people to see new problems, or to see old problems in one way rather than another, is a major conceptual

and political accomplishment" (p. 115). The reframing paid homage to the honest efforts of those in the past but also estranged people from those efforts as a step toward embracing new attitudes, policies, and actions (Bryson, Ackermann, Eden, and Finn, 1996).

3. *Do not underestimate the importance of leadership.* Successful collaborations depend on having strong sponsors, champions, and facilitators committed to collaborative ways of working. Collaborative, catalytic leadership is absolutely essential (Luke, 1998; Chrislip, 2002; Linden, 2002; Huxham, 2003). Successful collaboration may even require having at least one "monomaniac with a vision" who is single-mindedly focused on creating an effective collaborative effort. Obsessive commitment to working with diverse, often powerful, and fractious stakeholders to achieve a vision may seem foolhardy—and yet anyone with experience with collaboration knows precisely how important leaders committed to a collaborative effort are. These leaders provide the consistency of purpose needed for collaborative work and long-term collaborative success. Leadership committed to the long haul makes it easier to enforce collaborative norms, manage external stakeholder expectations, and deal with shifts and changes in key actors (Bryson, Ackermann, Eden, and Finn, 1996). The two cases discussed earlier illustrate the importance of committed, collaborative leadership. Both strategic planning efforts involved somewhat centralized systems, but the NHS clearly is more centralized than the system within which the AAMP took place. However, the AAMP to date has had more success, and the leadership theme points to a likely cause. The AAMP has had more leadership stability, consistency of purpose, and support at the very top. Leadership has also been more broadly shared in the AAMP. Other TOCA themes may well have been easier to manage—and broadly shared leadership more likely to be effective—because of this stability, consistency, and support at the top.

4. *Be prepared to devote huge amounts of attention to the initial agreement phase.* TOCA points to the relatively slow, incremental emergence of agreements on how to proceed, with whom, and why. Multiple agreements are likely to be made along the way from initiation through commitment to action. Given their extensive case study research, Chrislip (2002, pp. 46–47, 57) and Linden (2002, pp. 171–186) would agree. Extensive stakeholder analyses are useful in determining who should be involved in fashioning these agreements, deciding on the content of the agreements, and identifying implementation strategies (see Resource A). A major reason so much attention needs to be devoted to creating these agreements is to be sure all of the outcomes detailed in the strategic planning process outcomes matrix presented in Figure 3.1 are achieved. It simply takes time to build trust among the partners and to gain emotional and reasoned commitment to specific actions (Bryson, Ackermann, Eden, and Finn, 1996).

5. *Work to build a strong constituency for collaboration.* Linden (2002) defines a *constituency for collaboration* as "a group (or several groups) of people who strongly believe that the collaboration effort is in their interest, who want to support it, and who have influence over the parties involved" (p. 131). This constituency will include at least a convening group, steering group, and a broader group of stakeholders. The size of the needed constituency may be larger than the minimum winning coalition needed to adopt policy changes because simply adopting changes is not enough. Broad support and commitment will be needed to actually implement the policies; this often means added consultation and consensus-based decision making are needed, especially for community collaborations (Thomas, 1995; Chrislip, 2002).

6. *Develop a road map of the process.* Participants will want some sense of where they are going, what process they will follow, and what the desired outcomes are along the way. The Strategy Change Cycle can provide a rough sketch of how the road map might look. Chrislip (2002, pp. 49–59) and Linden (2002, pp. 169–186) provide complementary approaches. Whichever approach is taken the TOCA themes may be thought of as forming a *process agenda* that needs to be managed effectively if the chances of overall success are to be increased. As a consequence, successful collaborations are unlikely to follow a rigid sequence of steps unless those steps are legislated, and even then, circular flows of activity involving many of the themes are probably more likely than set sequences of activity that occur in lockstep fashion across the themes (Bryson, Ackermann, Eden, and Finn, 1996; Van de Ven, Polley, Garud, and Venkataraman, 1999).

7. *Create a governance structure.* If a collaborative effort is to be successful in the long run, it will need a governance structure appropriate to the context, purpose, and membership of the collaborative (Linden, 2002, p. 172; Milward and Provan, 2003). Like other aspects of a successful collaboration, agreements about the appropriate governance structure are likely to emerge and change incrementally over time. In the case of intra- or interorganizational collaboration the steering group may be the most important decision-making body. But in the case of community collaboration, Chrislip (2002, p. 89) argues that the steering group should have no authority for making decisions about the content of the issue at hand and should instead concentrate on organizing the work of the broader group of stakeholders. In community collaborations, "stakeholders do the real work of collaboration in defining problems and visions, solutions, and strategies. When collaboration works, stakeholders become a constituency for change who are able to hold decisions makers and implementing organizations accountable for action. The makeup of this group makes or breaks the collaboration" (p. 74). It is thus important to clarify the specific roles and responsibilities of the various groups involved.

8. *Remember that successful collaboration depends on effective meeting management.* Chrislip (2002) argues: "The work done ahead of time to create an environment for working together is as important as what is done in the engagement itself. . . . Experience demonstrates that planning a meeting or a series of meetings requires at least as much time as the meetings themselves. Collaborative processes cannot work unless the meetings themselves work" (pp. 46–47). In practice this means devoting considerable attention to tailoring tools and techniques, agendas, and stage management to specific situations. It also means setting expectations for social behavior and carefully attending to relationships within and outside the meetings (Bryson, Ackermann, Eden, and Finn, 1996). In addition, it makes sense to use large-group interaction methods at various points in the process, because effective collaboration often requires participants to engage in the same activities at the same time. These methods are structured ways of engaging very large groups of people in designing and managing change processes. The methods go by various names, including *future search, search conferences, preferred futuring, open space technology,* and a host of others. The basic elements are often fairly similar, but they are combined in different ways for different purposes. More information on the range of large-group interaction methods can be found in Bunker and Alban (1997), Holman and Devane (1999), and Bryson and Anderson (2000).

9. *To succeed in leaving a legacy coordinate staffing, budgeting, information systems, and performance measures and management.* Collaboration will break down if the basic systems needed to run it are not adequately integrated. This means involving and rewarding people committed to collaboration, making sure the money flows are adequate, and seeing that people have the information they need to function. It also means setting aside a pot of money that can be used to fix problems as they arise. Performance measures and management are important vehicles for achieving adequate integration because they provide a focus and discipline for creating it. Linden (2002, pp. 196–198) argues that

- A limited number of outcome-oriented performance measures should be used, and they should be ones that matter to important external constituencies
- People who actually do the work should be involved in determining the appropriate measures
- Measurements should be taken and publicized frequently
- Someone should be responsible for each area being measured
- Information should be used to learn how to perform better
- Financial consequences should not necessarily be tied to performance on the measures; consequences should depend on the measure, the purpose of the collaborative effort, and the causes of good or bad performance.

10. *Nurture, nurture, nurture* (Huxham, 2003). Attention to relationships and the collaborative effort as a whole is absolutely crucial to successful collaboration. Gaining the understanding, trust, and commitment of key collaborators and other stakeholders; building and maintaining a constituency for collaboration; and responding to the inevitable ebbs and flows of participation, changes in key personnel, and unexpected events all require strong relationships. Almost anything can be accomplished with the right people, good relationships, and adequate resources, but these necessities do not show up automatically. If they are to be available at all, constant nurturance is required.

REFERENCES

Abramson, M. A., and Harris, R. S., III (eds.). *The Procurement Revolution*. Lanham, Md.: Rowman & Littlefield, 2003.

Abramson, M. A., and Kamensky, J.M.E. *Managing for Results 2002*. Lanham, Md.: Rowman & Littlefield, 2001.

Abramson, M. A., and Lawrence, P. R. (eds.). *Transforming Organizations*. Lanham, Md.: Rowman & Littlefield, 2001.

Abramson, M. A., and Means, G. E. (eds.). *E-Government 2001*. Lanham, Md.: Rowman & Littlefield, 2001.

Abramson, M. A., and Morin, T. L. *E-Government, 2003*. Lanham, Md.: Rowman & Littlefield, 2002.

Ackerman, L. D. *Identity Is Destiny*. San Francisco: Berrett-Koehler, 2000.

Ackermann, F. "Strategic Direction Through Burning Issues: Using SODA as a Strategic Decision Support System." *OR Insight*, 1992, *5*(3), 24–28.

Ackermann, F. "Using Dominos—for Problem Structuring." Working Paper. Department of Management Science, University of Strathclyde, Glasgow, Scotland, 1993.

Ackermann, F., Eden, C., and Brown, I. *The Practice of Making Strategy*. London: Sage, 2004.

Albert, S., and Bell, G. G. "Timing and Music." *Academy of Management Review*, 2002, *27*(4), 574–593.

Alexander, E. R. *How Organizations Act Together: Interorganizational Coordination in Theory and Practice*. Sydney, Australia: Gordon and Breach, 1995.

Alexander, E. R. "Rationality Revisited: Planning Paradigms in a Post-Postmodernist Perspective." *Journal of Planning Education and Research*, 2000, *19*, 242–256.

Allison, M., and Kaye, J. *Strategic Planning for Nonprofit Organizations*. New York: Wiley, 1997.

Alterman, R. "Can Planning Help in Time of Crisis? Planners' Response to Israel's Recent Wave of Mass Immigration." *Journal of the American Planning Association*, 1995, *61*(2), 156–177.

Alvesson, M., and Wilmott, H. "Identity Regulation as Organizational Control: Producing the Appropriate Individual." *Journal of Management Studies*, 2002, *39*(5), 619–644.

Amherst H. Wilder Foundation. *2000–05 Strategic Plan*. St. Paul, Minn.: Amherst H. Wilder Foundation, 2000.

Amherst H. Wilder Foundation. "Our History." [www.wilder.org/strategicplan.html]. 2004.

Andersen, D. F., and Richardson, G. P. "Scripts for Group Model Building." *Systems Dynamics Review*, 1997, *13*(2), 107–129.

Anderson, J. E. *Public Policymaking*. Boston: Houghton Mifflin, 1990.

Anderson, S. R., Bryson, J. M., and Crosby, B. C. *Leadership for the Common Good Fieldbook*. St. Paul, Minn.: University of Minnesota Extension Service, 1999.

Andreasen, A. R. *Marketing Social Change: Changing Behavior to Promote Health, Social Development, and the Environment*. San Francisco: Jossey-Bass, 1995.

Angelica, E. *Crafting Effective Mission and Vision Statements*. St. Paul, Minn.: Amherst H. Wilder Foundation, 2001.

Ashforth, B. E., and Mael, F. "Social Identity Theory and the Organization." *Academy of Management Review*, 1989, *14*(1), 20–39.

Bachrach, P., and Baratz, M. S. "Decisions and Non-Decisions: An Analytical Framework." *American Political Science Review*, 1963, *57*, 632–642.

Bandura, A. *Self-Efficacy: The Exercise of Control*. New York: Freeman, 1997.

Banxia Software. "Decision Explorer." [www.banxia.com]. 2004.

Barber, B. *Strong Democracy: Participatory Politics for a New Age*. Berkeley: University of California Press, 1984.

Bardach, E. *The Implementation Game: What Happens After a Bill Becomes Law*. Cambridge, Mass.: MIT Press, 1977.

Bardach, E. *Getting Agencies to Work Together: The Practice and Theory of Managerial Craftsmanship*. Washington, D.C.: Brookings Institution Press, 1998.

Barkema, H. G., Baum, J.A.C., and Mannix, E. A. "Management Challenges in a New Time." *Academy of Management Journal*, 2002, *45*(5), 916–931.

Barry, B. W. *Strategic Planning Workbook for Nonprofit Organizations*. St. Paul, Minn.: Amherst H. Wilder Foundation, 1986.

Barry, B. W. *Strategic Planning Workbook for Nonprofit Organizations, Revised and Updated*. St. Paul, Minn.: Amherst H. Wilder Foundation, 1997.

Bartlett, C. A., and Ghoshal, S. "Changing the Role of Top Management: Beyond Strategy to Purpose." *Harvard Business Review*, Nov./Dec. 1994, 79–88.

Barzelay, M. *Breaking Through Bureaucracy: A New Vision for Managing in Government*. Berkeley: University of California Press, 1992.

Barzelay, M. *The New Public Management: Improving Research and Policy Dialogue*. Berkeley: University of California Press, 2001.

Barzelay, M., and Campbell, C. *Preparing for the Future: Strategic Planning in the U.S. Air Force*. Washington, D.C.: Brookings Institution Press, 2003.

Baum, H. S. "Social Science, Social Work, and Surgery: Teaching What Students Need to Practice Planning." *Journal of the American Planning Association*, 1997, *63*(2), 179–188.

Baum, H. S. "Forgetting to Plan." *Journal of Planning Education and Research*, 1999, *19*, 2–14.

Baum, H. S. "How Should We Evaluate Community Initiatives?" *Journal of the American Planning Association*, 2001, *67*(2), 147–158.

Baumgartner, F. R., and Jones, B. D. *Agendas and Instability in American Politics.* Chicago: University of Chicago Press, 1993.

Becker, E. *The Denial of Death.* New York: Free Press, 1997.

Beech, N., and Huxham, C. *Cycles of Identity Formation in Collaboration.* Glasgow, Scotland: Graduate School of Business, University of Strathclyde, 2003.

Behn, R. D. "The Fundamentals of Cutback Management." In R. J. Zeckhauser and D. Leebaert (eds.), *What Role for Government?* Durham, N.C.: Duke University Press, 1983.

Behn, R. D. "Management by Groping Along." *Journal of Policy Analysis and Management,* 1988, *7*(4), 643–663.

Behn, R. D. *Leadership Counts: Lessons for Public Managers from the Massachusetts Welfare, Training, and Employment Program.* Cambridge, Mass.: Harvard University Press, 1991.

Behn, R. D. "Do Goals Help Create Innovative Organizations?" In H. G. Frederickson and J. Johnston (eds.), *Public Management Reform and Innovation: Research, Theory, and Application.* Tuscaloosa, Ala.: University of Alabama Press, 1999a.

Behn, R. D. "The New Public-Management Paradigm and the Search for Democratic Accountability." *International Public Management Journal,* 1999b, *1*(2), 131–165.

Behn, R. D. *Rethinking Democratic Accountability.* Washington, D.C.: Brookings Institution, 2001.

Behn, R. D. "The Psychological Barriers to Performance Management, or Why Isn't Everyone Jumping on the Performance-Management Bandwagon?" *Public Performance and Management Review,* 2002, *26*(1), 5–25.

Behn, R. D. "Rethinking Accountability in Education." *International Public Management Journal,* 2003, *6*(1), 43–74.

Bendor, J. B. *Parallel Systems: Redundancy in Government.* Berkeley: University of California Press, 1985.

Benner, M. J., and Tushman, M. L. "Exploitation, Exploration, and Process Management: The Productivity Dilemma Revisited." *Academy of Management Review,* 2003, *28*(2), 238–256.

Benveniste, G. *Mastering the Politics of Planning: Crafting Credible Plans and Policies That Make a Difference.* San Francisco: Jossey-Bass, 1989.

Berger, P. L., and Luckmann, T. *The Social Construction of Reality.* New York: Doubleday, Anchor Books, 1967.

Berger, R. A., and Vasile, L. *Strategic Planning: A Review of Grantee Practices.* Los Altos, Calif.: The David and Lucile Packard Foundation, 2002.

Berman, E. M., and West, J. P. "Productivity Enhancement Efforts in Public and Nonprofit Organizations." *Public Productivity and Management Review,* 1998, *22*(2), 207–219.

Berry, F. S., and Wechsler, B. "State Agencies' Experience with Strategic Planning: Findings from a National Survey." *Public Administration Review,* 1995, *55*(2), 159–168.

Block, P. *The Empowered Manager: Positive Political Skills at Work.* San Francisco: Jossey-Bass, 1987.

Block, P. *Stewardship.* San Francisco: Berrett-Koehler, 1993.

Boal, K. B., and Bryson, J. M. "Charismatic Leadership: A Phenomenological and Structured Approach." In J. G. Hunt, B. R. Balinga, H. P. Dachler, and C. A. Schriescheim (eds.), *Emerging Leadership Vistas.* Elmsford, N.Y.: Pergamon Press, 1987.

Bobo, K., Kendall, J., and Max, S. *Organizing for Social Change.* Minneapolis, Minn.: Seven Locks Press, 2001.

Bolan, R. S. "Generalist with a Specialty—Still Valid? Educating the Planner: An Expert on Experts." In *Planning 1971: Selected Papers from the ASPO National Planning Conference, New Orleans, March 27–April 1, 1971.* Chicago: American Society of Planning Officials, 1971.

Bolman, L. G., and Deal, T. E. *Leading with Soul: An Uncommon Journey of Spirit.* (Rev. ed.) San Francisco: Jossey-Bass, 2001.

Bolman, L. G., and Deal, T. E. *Reframing Organizations: Artistry, Choice, and Leadership.* San Francisco: Jossey-Bass, 2003.

Borins, S. *Innovating with Integrity: How Local Heroes Are Transforming American Government.* Washington, D.C.: Georgetown University Press, 1998.

Borins, S. "Loose Cannons and Rule Breakers, or Enterprising Leaders? Some Evidence About Innovative Public Managers." *Public Administration Review,* 2000, *60*(6), 498–507.

Boschken, H. L. *Strategic Design and Organizational Change.* London: University of Alabama Press, 1988.

Boschken, H. L. "Organizational Performance and Multiple Constituencies." *Public Administration Review,* 1994, *54*(3), 308–312.

Boschken, H. L. *Social Class, Politics, and Urban Markets: The Makings of Bias in Policy Outcomes.* Palo Alto, Calif.: Stanford University Press, 2002.

Bourgeois, L.J.I. "Performance and Consensus." *Strategic Management Journal,* 1980, *1,* 227–248.

Boyne, G. A., and Gould-Williams, J. S. "Planning and Performance in Public Organizations: An Empirical Analysis." *Public Management Review,* 2003, *5*(1), 115–132.

Boyte, H. S., and Kari, N. N. *Building America: The Democratic Promise of Public Work.* Philadelphia: Temple University Press, 1996.

Bozeman, B. *Bureaucracy and Red Tape.* Upper Saddle River, N.J.: Prentice Hall, 1999.

Bozeman, B. "Public-Value Failure: When Efficient Markets May Not Do." *Public Administration Review,* 2002, *62*(2), 145–161.

Bracker, J. "The Historical Development of the Strategic Management Concept." *Academy of Management Review,* 1980, *5,* 219–224.

Brandl, J. *Money and Good Intentions Are Not Enough.* Washington, D.C.: Brookings Institution, 1998.

Braybrooke, D., and Lindblom, C. E. *A Strategy of Decision: Policy Evaluation as a Social Process.* New York: Free Press, 1963.

Brickman, P. "Is it Real?" In J. H. Harvey, W. Ickes, and R. F. Kidd (eds.), *New Directions in Attributional Research.* Vol. 2. Hillsdale, N.J.: Erlbaum, 1978.

Bromiley, P., and Marcus, A. "Deadlines, Routines, and Change." *Policy Sciences,* 1987, *20,* 85–103.

Broom, C. A. "Performance-Based Government Models: Building a Track Record." *Public Budgeting and Finance,* 1995, *15*(4), 3–17.

Brower, R. S. "'All the World's a Stage': A Theatrical Bridge Between Theory and Ethical Practice." *Public Integrity,* Summer 1999, pp. 221–238.

Brown, A. D., and Starkey, K. "Organizational Identity and Learning: A Psychodynamic Perspective." *Academy of Management Review,* 2000, *25*(1), 102–120.

Bryant, J. *The Six Dilemmas of Collaboration: Inter-Organizational Relationships as Drama.* New York: Wiley, 2003.

Bryce, H. J. *Financial and Strategic Management for Nonprofit Organizations.* (3rd ed.) San Francisco: Jossey-Bass, 2000.

Bryson, J. M. "A Perspective on Planning and Crises in the Public Sector." *Strategic Management Journal,* 1981, *2,* 181–196.

Bryson, J. M. "Strategic Planning: Big Wins and Small Wins." *Public Money and Management,* 1988, *8*(3), 11–15.

Bryson, J. M. *Strategic Planning for Public and Nonprofit Organizations.* (Rev. ed.) San Francisco: Jossey-Bass, 1995.

Bryson, J. M. (ed.). *Strategic Management in Public and Voluntary Services.* Oxford, England: Elsevier, 1999.

Bryson, J. M. "Strategic Planning." In N. J. Smelser and P. B. Baltes (eds.), *International Encyclopedia of the Social and Behavioral Sciences.* New York: Elsevier, 2001.

Bryson, J. M. "Strategic Planning and Management." In B. G. Peters and J. Pierre (eds.), *Handbook of Public Administration.* London: Sage, 2003a.

Bryson, J. M. "The Amherst H. Wilder Foundation Case, January 1, 1985/December 31, 1997 (A); January 1, 1998/December 31, 2002 (B); and Teaching Note." *Journal of Public Affairs Education,* 2003b, *3,* 193–220.

Bryson, J. M. "Strategic Planning and Action Planning for Nonprofit Organizations." In R. Herman and Associates, *The Jossey-Bass Handbook of Nonprofit Leadership and Management.* (2nd ed.) San Francisco: Jossey-Bass, 2004a.

Bryson, J. M. "What to Do When Stakeholders Matter: A Guide to Stakeholder Identification and Analysis Techniques." *Public Management Review,* 2004b, *6*(1), 21–53.

Bryson, J. M., Ackermann, F., Eden, C., and Finn, C. B. "Critical Incidents and Emergent Issues in Managing Large-Scale Change." In D. F. Kettl and B. Milward (eds.), *The State of Public Management.* Baltimore, Md.: Johns Hopkins University Press, 1996.

Bryson, J. M., Ackermann, F., Eden, C., and Finn, C. B. *Visible Thinking: Unlocking Causal Mapping for Practical Business Results.* New York: Wiley, 2004.

Bryson, J. M., and Alston, F. *Creating and Implementing Your Strategic Plan.* (2nd ed.) San Francisco: Jossey-Bass, 2005.

Bryson, J. M., and Anderson, S. R. "Applying Large-Group Interaction Methods in the Planning and Implementation of Major Change Effects." *Public Administration Review,* Mar./Apr. 2000, *60*(20), 143–162.

Bryson, J. M., and Bromiley, P. "Critical Factors Affecting the Planning and Implementation of Major Projects." *Strategic Management Journal,* 1993, *14,* 319–337.

Bryson, J. M., Bromiley, P., and Jung, Y. S. "Influences on the Context and Process on Project Planning Success." *Journal of Planning Education and Research,* 1990, *9*(3), 183–185.

Bryson, J. M., and Crosby, B. C. *Leadership for the Common Good: Tackling Public Problems in a Shared Power World.* San Francisco: Jossey-Bass, 1992.

Bryson, J. M., and Crosby, B. C. "Planning and the Design and Use of Forums, Arenas, and Courts." In R. Burchell, S. Mandelbaum, and L. Mazza (eds.), *Planning Theory for the 1990s.* New Brunswick, N.J.: Rutgers University/CIPR Press, 1996.

Bryson, J. M., Crosby, B. C., and Ackermann, F. "Strategic Planning in Collaborative Settings." In P. Hibbert (ed.) *Co-Creating Emergent Insight: Multi-Organisational Networks, Partnerships and Alliances.* Glasgow: University of Strathclyde, Graduate School of Business, 2003.

Bryson, J. M., and Cullen, J. W. "A Contingent Approach to Strategy and Tactics in Formative and Summative Evaluations." *Evaluation and Program Planning,* 1984, *7,* 276–294.

Bryson, J. M., Cunningham, G. L., and Lokkesmoe, K. J. "What to Do When Stakeholders Matter: The Case of Problem Formulation for the African American Men Project of Hennepin County, Minnesota." *Public Administration Review,* 2002, *62*(5), 568–584.

Bryson, J. M., and Delbecq, A. L. "A Continent Approach to Strategy and Tactics in Project Planning." *Journal of the American Planning Association,* 1979, *45*(2), 167–179.

Bryson, J. M., and Einsweiler, R. C. "Editors' Introduction to the Strategic Planning Symposium." *Journal of the American Planning Association,* 1987, *53,* 6–8.

Bryson, J. M., and Einsweiler, R. C. (eds.). *Strategic Planning—Threats and Opportunities for Planners.* Chicago: Planners Press, 1988.

Bryson, J. M., and Finn, C. B. "Development and Use of Strategy Maps to Enhance Organizational

Performance." In A. Halachmi and G. Bouckaert (eds.), *The Challenge of Management in a Changing World.* San Francisco: Jossey-Bass, 1995.

Bryson, J. M., Freeman, R. E., and Roering, W. D. "Strategic Planning in the Public Sector: Approaches and Directions." In B. Checkoway (ed.), *Strategic Perspectives on Planning Practice.* Lexington, Mass.: Lexington Books, 1986.

Bryson, J. M., Gibbons, M. J., and Shaye, G. "Enterprise Schemes for Nonprofit Survival, Growth, and Effectiveness." *Nonprofit Management and Leadership,* 2001, *11*(3), 271–288.

Bryson, J. M., and Kelley, G. "Leadership, Politics, and the Functioning of Complex Organizations and Interorganizational Networks." In A. Negandhi, G. England, and B. B. Wilpert (eds.), *The Functioning of Complex Organizations.* Cambridge, Mass.: Oelgeschlager, Gunn, and Hain, 1981.

Bryson, J. M., and Roering, W. D. "Applying Private Sector Strategic Planning to the Public Sector." *Journal of the American Planning Association,* 1987, *53*, 9–22.

Bryson, J. M., and Roering, W. D. "Initiation of Strategic Planning by Governments." *Public Administration Review,* Nov.–Dec. 1988, *48*, 995–1004.

Bryson, J. M., and Roering, W. D. "Mobilizing Innovation Efforts: The Case of Governments in Strategic Planning." In A. H. Van de Ven, H. Angles, and M. S. Poole (eds.), *Research on the Management of Information.* New York: HarperCollins, 1989.

Bunch, C. *Passionate Politics.* New York: St. Martin's Press, 1987.

Bunker, B. B., and Alban, B. T. *Large Group Interventions: Engaging the Whole System for Rapid Change.* San Francisco: Jossey-Bass, 1997.

Burby, R. J. "Making Plans That Matter: Citizen Involvement and Government Action." *Journal of the American Planning Association,* 2003, *69*(1), 33–49.

Burns, J. M. *Leadership.* New York: HarperCollins, 1978.

Burns, J. M. *Transforming Leadership: The Pursuit of Happiness.* New York: Atlantic Monthly Press, 2003.

Burns, L. E. *Busy Bodies.* New York: Norton, 1993.

Buzan, T., with Buzan, B. *The Mind Map Book: Radiant Thinking: The Major Evolution in Human Thought.* London: BBC Books, 1993.

Campbell, D. T., and Stanley, J. C. *Experimental and Quasi-Experimental Designs for Research.* Skokie, Ill.: Rand McNally, 1966.

Campbell, H., and Marshall, R. "Utilitarianism's Bad Breath? A Re-Evaluation of the Public Interest Justification for Planning." *Planning Theory,* 2002, *1*(2), 163–187.

Carver, J. *Boards That Make a Difference: A New Design for Leadership in Nonprofit and Public Organizations.* (2nd ed.) San Francisco: Jossey-Bass, 1997.

Cassidy, A. *A Practical Guide to Planning for E-Business Success: How to E-Enable Your Enterprise.* Boca Raton, Fla.: St. Lucie Press, 2002.

Chattopadhyay, P., Glick, W. H., and Huber, G. P. "Organizational Actions in Response to Threats and Opportunities." *Academy of Management Journal,* 2001, *44*(5), 937–955.

Chrislip, D. D. "The New Civic Leadership." In B. Kellerman and L. R. Matusak (eds.), *Cutting Edge: Leadership 2000.* College Park, Md.: James MacGregor Burns Academy of Leadership, 2000.

Chrislip, D. D. *The Collaborative Leadership Fieldbook.* San Francisco: Jossey-Bass, 2002.

Christensen, K. "Teaching Savvy." *Journal of Planning Education and Research,* 1993, *12*, 202–212.

Christensen, K. S. *Cities and Complexity: Making Intergovernmental Decisions.* Thousand Oaks, Calif.: Sage, 1999.

City of Charlotte, North Carolina. "City's Balanced Scorecard" and "Charlotte's Strategic Plan." [www.charmeck.nc.us/governing/home]. 2004.

Cleveland, H. *The Knowledge Executive.* New York: Dutton, Truman Talley Books, 1985.

Cleveland, H. *Nobody in Charge: Essays on the Future of Leadership.* New York: Wiley, 2002.

Coggburn, J. D., and Schneider, S. K. "The Quality of Management and Government Performance: An Empirical Analysis of the American States." *Public Administration Review,* 2003, *63*(2), 206–212.

Cohen, M. D., March, J. G., and Olsen, J. P. "A Garbage Can Model of Organization and Choice." *Administrative Science Quarterly,* 1972, *17,* 1–25.

Cohen, S., and Brand, R. *Total Quality Management in Government: A Practical Guide for the Real World.* San Francisco: Jossey-Bass, 1993.

Cohen, S., and Eimicke, W. *Tools for Innovators: Creative Strategies for Strengthening Public Sector Organizations.* San Francisco: Jossey-Bass, 1998.

Cohen, S., Eimicke, W., Kamlet, M., and Pearson, R. "The Information Resource Management Program: A Case Study in Distance Education." *Journal of Public Affairs Education,* 1998, *4*(3), 179–192.

Collins, J. C., and Porras, J. I. *Built to Last: Successful Habits of Visionary Companies.* New York: HarperBusiness, 1997.

Commander Naval Security Group (CNSG). "Command Mission." [www.hqcnsg.navy.mil/mission.htm]. 2004.

Cooper, P. J. "Understanding What the Law Says About Administrative Responsibility." In J. Perry (ed.), *Handbook of Public Administration.* San Francisco: Jossey-Bass, 1996.

Coplin, W., and O'Leary, M. *Everyman's Prince: A Guide to Understanding Your Political Problem.* Boston: Duxbury Press, 1976.

Cothran, D. A. "Entrepreneurial Budgeting: An Emerging Reform?" *Public Administration Review,* 1993, *53*(5), 445–454.

Crittenden, W. F. "Spinning Straw into Gold: The Tenuous Strategy, Funding, and Financial Performance Linkage." *Nonprofit and Voluntary Sector Quarterly,* 2000, *29*(1), 164–182.

Crosby, B. C., and Bryson, J. M. *Leadership for the Common Good.* (2nd ed.) San Francisco: Jossey-Bass, forthcoming.

Crossan, M. M., Lane, H. W., and White, R. E. "An Organizational Learning Framework: From Intuition to Institution." *Academy of Management Review,* 1999, *24*(3), 522–537.

Crowley, M. "Playing Defense: Bush's Disastrous Homeland Security Department." *New Republic,* Mar. 25, 2004, pp. 17–21.

Csikszentmihalyi, M. *Flow: The Psychology of Optimal Experience.* New York: HarperCollins, 1990.

Cyert, R., and March, J. *The Behavioral Theory of the Firm.* Upper Saddle River, N.J.: Prentice Hall, 1963.

Daft, R. L. *Organization Theory and Design.* (8th ed.) Marion, Ohio: Thomson/South-Western, 2004.

Dair, I. "Building a New Organization for Nature Conservation." In J. M. Bryson (ed.), *Strategic Management in Public and Voluntary Services: A Reader.* Amsterdam: Pergamon, 1999a.

Dair, I. "Cutting Back Bureaucracy in a Public Service." In J. M. Bryson (ed.), *Strategic Management in Public and Voluntary Services: A Reader.* Amsterdam: Pergamon, 1999b.

Dalton, G. W. "Influence and Organization Change." In G. Dalton, P. Lawrence, and L. Greiner (eds.), *Organization Change and Development.* Homewood, Ill.: Irwin-Dorsey, 1970.

Dalton, G. W., and Thompson, P. H. *Novations: Strategies for Career Management.* Salt Lake City, Utah: Novations Group, 1993.

de Gues, A. P. "Planning as Learning." *Harvard Business Review,* Mar./Apr. 1988, pp. 70–74.

Delbanco, A. *The Real American Dream: A Meditation on Hope.* Cambridge, Mass.: Harvard University Press, 1999.

Delbecq, A. L., Van de Ven, A. H., and Gustafson, D. *Group Techniques for Program Planning.* Glenview, Ill.: Scott, Foresman, 1975.

deLeon, L., and Denhardt, R. B. "The Political Theory of Reinvention." *Public Administration Review,* 2000, *60*(2), 89–97.

Denhardt, R., and Denhardt, J. "The New Public Service: Serving Rather Than Steering." *Public Administration Review,* 2000, *60,* 549–559.

Denhardt, R. B. *The Pursuit of Significance: Strategies for Managerial Success in Organizations.* Belmont, Calif.: Wadsworth, 1993.

Denis, J.-L., Lamothe, L., and Langley, A. "The Dynamics of Collective Leadership and Strategic Change in Pluralistic Organizations." *Academy of Management Journal,* 2001, *44*(4), 809–837.

Dewey, J. *The Public and Its Problems.* Athens, Ohio: Swallow Press, 1954.

Deyle, R. E., and Smith, R. A. "Local Government Compliance with State Planning Mandates: The Effects of State Implementation in Florida." *Journal of the American Planning Association,* 1998, *64,* 457–469.

Doig, J. W., and Hargrove, E. C. (eds.). *Leadership and Innovation: A Biographical Perspective on Entrepreneurs in Government.* Baltimore, Md.: Johns Hopkins University Press, 1987.

Dutton, J. E., and Ashford, S. J. "Selling Issues to Top Management." *Academy of Management Review,* 1987, *12*(1), 76–90.

Dutton, J. E., and Ashford, S. J. "Selling Issues to Top Management." *Academy of Management Review,* 1993, *18*(3), 397–428.

Dutton, J. E., and Dukerich, J. "Keeping One Eye on the Mirror: The Role of Image and Identity in Organizational Adaptation." *Academy of Management Journal,* 1991, *34,* 517–554.

Dutton, J. E., Frost, P., Worline, M., Kanov, J., and Lilius, J. "Leading in Times of Trauma." *Harvard Business Review,* 2002, *80*(1), 54–61.

Dutton, J. E., and Jackson, S. E. "Categorizing Strategic Issues: Links to Organizational Action." *Academy of Management Review,* 1987, *12*(1), 76–90.

Eckhert, P., Haines, K., Delmont, T., and Pflaum, A. "Strategic Planning in Hennepin County, Minnesota: An Issues Management Approach." In R. L. Kemp (ed.), *Strategic Planning for Local Government.* Jefferson, N.C.: McFarland, 1993.

Edelman, M. *Political Language.* New York: Academic Press, 1977.

Edelman, M. *Constructing the Political Spectacle.* Chicago: University of Chicago Press, 1988.

Edelman, M. *The Politics of Misinformation.* Cambridge, England: Cambridge University Press, 2001.

Eden, C. "Using Cognitive Mapping for Strategic Options Development and Analysis (SODA)." In J. Rosenhead (ed.), *Rational Analysis for a Problematic World.* New York: Wiley, 1989.

Eden, C., and Ackermann, F. *Making Strategy: The Journey of Strategic Management.* Thousand Oaks, Calif.: Sage, 1998.

Eden, C., and Ackermann, F. "Mapping Distinctive Competencies: A Systemic Approach." *Journal of the Operational Research Society,* 2000, *51*(1), 12–20.

Eden, C., and Ackermann, F. "SODA—The Principles." In J. Rosenhead and J. Mingers (eds.), *Rational Analysis in a Problematic World Revisited.* London: Wiley, 2001.

Eden, C., Ackermann, F., and Cropper, S. "The Analysis of Cause Maps." *Journal of Management Studies,* 1992, *29*(3), 309–324.

Eden, C., and Huxham, C. "Action Research for Management Research." *British Journal of Management,* 1996, *7,* 75–86.

Eden, C., Jones, S., and Sims, D. *Messing About in Problems.* Oxford, England: Pergamon Press, 1983.

Eden, C., and Sims, D. "On the Nature of Problems." *Omega,* 1978, *7*(2), 119–127.

Eitel, D. F. "Strategic Planning in Illinois: A State at the Crossroads." *International Journal of Organization Theory and Behavior,* 2003, *6*(4), 577–610.

Elmore, R. F. "Backward Mapping: Implementation Research and Policy Decisions." In W. Williams (ed.), *Studying Implementation.* Chatham, N.J.: Chatham House, 1982.

Emmert, M. A., Crow, M., and Shangraw, R. F., Jr. "Public Management in the Future: Post-Orthodoxy and Organizational Design." In B. Bozeman (ed.), *Public Management: The State of the Art.* San Francisco: Jossey-Bass, 1993.

Epstein, P. D., Wray, L. D., Marshall, M. W., and Griffel, S. S. *Works in Progress: Citizens Engaged in Performance Management in Their Communities.* Minneapolis, Minn.: Citizens League, 1998.

Fallows, J. "Blind into Baghdad." *The Atlantic,* Jan.–Feb. 2004, *293*(1), 52–74.

Faragher, J. M. *Daniel Boone: The Life and Legacy of an American Pioneer.* New York: Henry Holt, 1992.

Feldman, M. S. "Organizational Routines as a Source of Continuous Change." *Organization Science,* 2000, *11*(6), 611–629.

Feldman, M. S., and Khademian, A. M. "Managing for Inclusion: Balancing Control and Participation." *International Public Management Journal,* 2000, *3,* 149–167.

Feldman, M. S., and Khademian, A. M. "To Manage Is to Govern." *Public Administration Review,* 2002, *62*(5), 541–554.

Finn, C. "Stakeholder Influence Mapping." In C. Huxham (ed.), *Creating Collaborative Advantage.* Thousand Oaks, Calif.: Sage, 1996.

Fiol, C. M. "Revisiting an Identity-Based View of Sustainable Competitive Advantage." *Journal of Management,* 2001, *27,* 691–699.

Fiol, C. M. "Capitalizing on Paradox: The Role of Language in Transforming Organizational Identities." *Organization Science,* 2002, *13*(6), 653–666.

Fisher, R., and Brown, S. *Getting Together: Building a Relationship That Gets to Yes.* Boston: Houghton Mifflin, 1988.

Fisher, R., and Ury, W. *Getting to Yes: Negotiating Agreement Without Giving In.* New York: Penguin Books, 1981.

Flyvbjerg, B. *Rationality and Power: Democracy in Practice.* Chicago: University of Chicago Press, 1998.

Ford, J. D., and Ford, L. W. "The Role of Conversations in Producing Intentional Change in Organizations." *Academy of Management Review,* 1995, *20*(3), 541–570.

Forester, J. *The Deliberative Practitioner.* Cambridge, Mass.: MIT Press, 1999.

Fountain, J. E. *Building the Virtual State: Information Technology and Institutional Change.* Washington, D.C.: Brookings Institution Press, 2001.

Frame, J. D. *The New Project Management.* San Francisco: Jossey-Bass, 1994.

Frederickson, D. G. "The Potential of the Government Performance and Results Act as a Tool to Manage Third-Party Government." In M. A. Abramson and J. M. Kamensky (eds.), *Managing for Results 2002.* Lanham, Md.: Rowman & Littlefield, 2001.

Frederickson, H. G. *The Spirit of Public Administration.* San Francisco: Jossey-Bass, 1997.

Frederickson, H. G. "Lessons in Comparative Health Care Reform." *Public Administration Times,* Feb. 2003, pp. 11–12.

Frentzel, W. Y., Bryson, J. M., and Crosby, B. C. "Strategic Planning in the Military: The U.S. Naval Security Group Changes Its Strategy, 1992–1998. *Long Range Planning,* 2000, *33,* 402–429.

Friedman, T. L. *The Lexus and the Olive Tree: Understanding Globalization.* New York: Anchor Books, 2000.

Friedmann, J. *Good Society.* Cambridge, Mass.: MIT Press, 1982.

Friend, J. K., and Hickling, A. *Planning Under Pressure: The Strategic Choice Approach.* (2nd ed.) Oxford, England: Heinemann, 1997.

Frumkin, P. "Managing for Outcomes: Milestone Contracting in Oklahoma." In M. A. Abramson and J. H. Kamensky (eds.), *Managing for Results 2002.* Lanham, Md.: Rowman & Littlefield, 2001.

Gabor, D. *Inventing the Future.* New York: Knopf, 1964.

Gabriel, Y. *Storytelling in Organizations: Facts, Fictions, and Fantasies.* New York: Oxford University Press, 2000.

Gary, J. K. "PPL Strategic Planning: A Review of Key Decisions and Strategy Development." Unpublished and independent study paper, Hubert H. Humphrey Institute of Public Affairs, University of Minnesota, 2003.

Gersick, C.J.G. "Revolutionary Change Theories: A Multilevel Exploration of the Punctuated Equilibrium Paradigm." *Academy of Management Review,* 1991, *16,* 10–36.

Giddens, A. *Runaway World: How Globalisation Is Reshaping Our Lives.* (2nd ed.) London: Profile, 2002.

Gill, J., and Meier, K. J. "Ralph's Pretty-Good Grocery Versus Ralph's Super Market: Separating Excellent Agencies from the Good Ones." *Public Administration Review,* Jan./Feb. 2001, *61*(1), 9–17.

Gladwell, M. *The Tipping Point: How Little Things Can Make a Big Difference.* Boston: Little, Brown, 2000.

Glassner, B. *The Culture of Fear: Why Americans Are Afraid of the Wrong Things.* New York: Basic Books, 1999.

Gleick, J. *Chaos: Making a New Science.* New York: Penguin, 1988.

Gleick, J. *The Acceleration of Just About Everything.* New York: Pantheon Books, 1999.

Goffman, E. *Frame Analysis: An Essay on the Organization of Experience.* Boston: Northeastern University Press, 1986.

Goggin, M., Bowman, A., Lester, J., and O'Toole, L. *Implementation Theory and Practice: Toward a Third Generation.* Glenview, Ill.: Scott-Foresman, 1990.

Goleman, D. *Emotional Intelligence.* New York: Bantam, 1995.

Goleman, D., Boyatzis, R., and McKee, A. *Primal Leadership: Realizing the Power of Emotional Intelligence.* Boston: Harvard Business School Press, 2002.

Gould, S. *The Panda's Thumb: Reflections in Natural History.* New York: Norton, 1980.

Gray, B. *Collaborating: Finding Common Ground for Multiparty Problems.* San Francisco: Jossey-Bass, 1989.

Gray, B. "Cross-Sectoral Partners: Collaborative Alliances Among Business, Government and Communities." In C. Huxham (ed.), *Creating Collaborative Advantage.* Thousand Oaks, Calif.: Sage, 1996.

Grayling, A. C. *What Is Good? The Search for the Best Way to Live.* London: Weidenfeld & Nicholson, 2003.

Greenblat, C., and Duke, R. *Principles and Practices of Gaming Simulation.* Newbury Park, Calif.: Sage, 1981.

Grossback, L. J. "The Problem of State-Imposed Mandates: Lessons from Minnesota's Local Governments." *State and Local Government Review,* 2002, *34*(3), 183–197.

Guibert, J. D. *The Jesuits: Their Spiritual Doctrine and Practice: A Historical Study.* (W. J. Young, trans., G. E. Gauss, ed.) Chicago: Institute of Jesuit Sources, 1964.

Gurwitt, R. "Are City Councils a Relic of the Past?" *Governing,* Apr. 2003, pp. 20–24.

Hall, P. *Great Planning Disasters.* Berkeley: University of California Press, 1980.

Hamel, G., and Prahalad, C. K. *Competing for the Future*. Boston: Harvard Business School Press, 1994.

Hammer, M., and Champy, J. *Reengineering the Corporation*. New York: HarperBusiness, 1993.

Hampden-Turner, C. *Corporate Culture*. Hutchinson, England: Economist Books, 1990.

Handy, C. *Beyond Certainty*. Boston: Harvard Business School Press, 1996.

Healey, P. *Collaborative Planning*. Basingstoke, England: Macmillan, 1997.

Heath, R. L. *Strategic Issues Management: Organizations and Public Policy Challenges*. Thousand Oaks, Calif.: Sage, 1997.

Heifetz, R. A. *Leadership Without Easy Answers*. Cambridge, Mass.: Harvard University Press, Belknap Press, 1994.

Heifetz, R. A., and Sinder, R. M. "Political Leadership: Managing the Public's Problem Solving." In R. B. Reich (ed.), *The Power of Public Ideas*. New York: HarperBusiness, 1988.

Helling, A. "Collaborative Visioning: Proceed with Caution! Results from Evaluating Atlanta's Vision 2020 Project." *Journal of the American Planning Association*, 1998, *64*(3), 335–350.

Hendrick, R. "Strategic Planning Environment, Process, and Performance in Public Agencies: A Comparative Study of Departments in Milwaukee." *Journal of Public Administration Research and Theory*, 2003, *13*, 491–519.

Hennepin County, Minnesota. *Strategic Planning Manual*. Minneapolis, Minn.: Hennepin County Office of Planning and Development, 1983.

Hennepin County, Minnesota. "Focusing on Results: From Measurement to Management in Hennepin County Government." Unpublished manuscript, Hennepin County Office of Planning and Development, Minneapolis, Minn., 2001.

Hennepin County, Minnesota. *Crossroads: Choosing a New Direction. African American Men Project Final Report*. Minneapolis, Minn.: Hennepin County Office of Planning and Development, 2002a.

Hennepin County, Minnesota. "Hennepin Results: Strategic Management Framework." Unpublished manuscript, Hennepin County Office of Planning and Development, Minneapolis, Minn., 2002b.

Hennepin County, Minnesota. "Mission Statement of the Hennepin County Board of Commissioners." [www.co.hennepin.mn.us/vgn/portal/internet/hcdetailmaster/0,2300,1273_1728_103200504,00.html]. May 2002c.

Hennepin County, Minnesota. "Hennepin County Strategic Management Framework and the Balanced Scorecard." Unpublished manuscript, Hennepin County Office of Planning and Development, Minneapolis, Minn., 2003.

Hennepin County, Minnesota. *Hennepin Results: Strategic Management Framework*. Minneapolis, Minn.: Hennepin County Office of Planning and Development, 2004.

Herson, L.J.R. *The Politics of Ideas*. Prospect Heights, Ill.: Waveland Press, 1984.

Hesselbein, F., and Johnston, R. *On High-Performance Organizations*. San Francisco: Jossey-Bass, 2002.

Hjern, B., and Porter, D. O. "Implementation Structures: A New Unit of Administrative Analysis." *Organization Studies*, 1981, *2*(3), 211–227.

Hogwood, B. W., and Peters, B. G. *Policy Dynamics*. New York: St. Martin's Press, 1983.

Holman, P., and Devane, T. E. *The Change Handbook: Group Methods for Shaping the Future*. San Francisco: Berrett-Koehler, 1999.

Holzer, M., Lee, S.-H., and Newman, M. A. "Best Practices in Managing Reductions in Force." *Review of Public Personnel Administration*, 2003, *23*(1), 38–60.

Houle, C. O. *Governing Boards: Their Nature and Nurture*. San Francisco: Jossey-Bass, 1989.

Howe, E. "Role Choices of Urban Planners." *Journal of the American Planning Association*, 1980, *46*, 398–409.

Humphrey, H. H. "A Sense of Purpose." Remarks at a meeting of Democratic Party chairmen and chairwomen, Washington, D.C., Sept. 17, 1959.

Humphrey, H. H. Speech at the Young Democrats Convention, Las Vegas, Nev., Dec. 13, 1968.

Hunt, H. G. *Leadership: A New Synthesis.* Thousand Oaks, Calif.: Sage, 1991.

Hunt, J.G.J., Boal, K. B., and Dodge, G. E. "The Effects of Visionary and Crisis-Responsive Charisma on Followers: An Experimental Examination of Two Kinds of Charismatic Leadership." *Leadership Quarterly*, 1999, *10*(3), 423–448.

Huntingdon, S. *The Clash of Civilizations and the Remaking of World Order.* New York: Touchstone Books, 1998.

Huxham, C. "Our Trivialities in Process." In C. Eden and J. Radford (eds.), *Tackling Strategic Problems: The Role of Group Decision Support.* Thousand Oaks, Calif.: Sage, 1990.

Huxham, C. "Pursuing Collaborative Advantage." *Journal of Operational Research Society*, 1993, *44*(6), 599–611.

Huxham, C. "Theorizing Collaboration Practice." *Public Management Review*, 2003, *5*(3), 401–423.

Huxham, C., and Beech, N. *Points of Power in Interorganizational Forms: Learning from a Learning Network.* Glasgow, Scotland: Graduate School of Business, University of Strathclyde, 2002.

Huxham, C., and Vangen, S. "Leadership in the Shaping and Implementation of Collaboration Agendas: How Things Happen in a (Not Quite) Joined-Up World." *Academy of Management Journal*, 2000, *43*(6), 1159–1175.

Iacofano, D. *Meeting of the Minds: A Guide to Successful Meeting Facilitation.* Berkeley, Calif.: MIG Communications, 2001.

Ingraham, P. W., and Donahue, A. K. "Dissecting the Black Box Revisited: Characterizing Government Management Capacity." In C. J. Heinrich and L. E. Lynn, Jr. (eds.), *Governance and Performance: New Perspectives.* Washington, D.C.: Georgetown University Press, 2000.

Innes, J. E. "Planning Through Consensus Building: A New View of the Comprehensive Planning Ideal." *Journal of the American Planning Association*, Autumn 1996, *62*, 460–472.

Innes, J. E. "Information in Communicative Planning." *Journal of the American Planning Association*, 1998, *64*, 52–63.

Innes, J. E., and Booher, D. E. "Consensus Building and Complex Adaptive Systems: A Framework for Evaluating Collaborative Planning." *Journal of the American Planning Association*, 1999, *65*(1), 9–26.

Institute of Education. *Changing Britain, Changing Lives.* London: Institute of Education, 2003.

International Association for Public Participation. "IAP2 Public Participation Spectrum." [www.iap2.org/practitionertools/spectrum.html]. 2004.

Isabella, L. A. "Evolving Interpretations as a Change Unfolds: How Managers Construe Key Organizational Events." *Academy of Management Journal*, 1990, *33*(1), 7–41.

Isenberg, D. J. "How Senior Managers Think." *Harvard Business Review*, Nov./Dec. 1984, pp. 81–90.

Jackson, S. E., and Dutton, J. E. "Discerning Threats and Opportunities." *Administrative Science Quarterly*, 1988, *33*, 370–387.

Jacobs, L., and Shapiro, R. *Politicians Don't Pander: Political Manipulation and the Loss of Democratic Responsiveness.* Chicago: University of Chicago Press, 2000.

Janis, I. L. *Crucial Decisions: Leadership in Policymaking and Crisis Management.* New York: Free Press, 1989.

Jenster, P. "Using Critical Success Factors in Planning." *Long Range Planning,* 1987, *20*(4), 102–110.

Johnson, B. *Polarity Management: Identifying and Managing Unsolvable Problems.* Amherst, Mass.: HRD Press, 1996.

Johnson, D. J., and Johnson, F. P. *Joining Together: Group Theory and Group Skills.* (7th ed.) Boston: Allyn and Bacon, 2000.

Johnson, G. "Mapping and Re-Mapping Organisational Culture." In V. Ambrosini (ed.), *Exploring Techniques of Analysis and Evaluation in Strategic Management.* London: Prentice Hall, 1998.

Johnson, G., Melin, L., and Whittington, R. "Micro Strategy and Strategizing: Toward an Activity-Based View." *Journal of Management Studies,* 2003, *40*(1), 1–17.

Johnson, G., and Scholes, K. *Exploring Corporate Strategy.* (6th ed.) Harlow, England: Pearson Education, 2002.

Joyce, P. *Strategic Management for the Public Services.* Maidenhead, Berkshire, England: Open University Press, 1999.

Jurkiewicz, C., and Bowman, J. S. "Charlotte: A Model for Market-Driven Public-Sector Management." *State and Local Government Review,* 2002, *34*(3), 205–213.

Justice, T., and Jamieson, D. W. *The Facilitator's Fieldbook.* New York: American Management Association, 1999.

Kahn, S. *Organizing, A Guide for Grassroots Leaders.* Washington, D.C.: National Association of Social Workers, 1991.

Kaner, S., with Lind, L., Toldi, C., Fisk, S., and Berger, D. *Facilitator's Guide to Participatory Decision-Making.* Gabriola Island, B.C., Canada: New Society Publishers, 1996.

Kanter, R. M. *Commitment and Community: Communes and Utopias in Sociological Perspective.* Cambridge, Mass.: Harvard University Press, 1972.

Kanter, R. M. *The Change Masters.* New York: Simon & Schuster, 1983.

Kanter, R. M. *When Elephants Learn to Dance.* New York: Simon & Schuster, 1989.

Kaplan, R. S. "Strategic Performance Measurement and Management in Nonprofit Organizations." *Nonprofit Management and Leadership,* 2001, *11*(3), 353–370.

Kaplan, R. S., and Norton, D. P. *The Balanced Scorecard: Translating Strategy into Action.* Boston: Harvard Business School Press, 1996.

Kaplan, R. S., and Norton, D. P. *Strategy Maps: Converting Intangible Assets into Tangible Outcomes.* Boston: Harvard Business School Press, 2004.

Kaufman, G. *Shame: The Power of Caring.* Rochester, Vt.: Schenkman, 1992.

Kaufman, H. *Are Government Organizations Immortal?* Washington, D.C.: Brookings Institution, 1976.

Kaufman, J. L. "Making Planners More Effective Strategists." In B. Checkoway (ed.), *Strategic Perspectives on Planning Practice.* San Francisco: New Lexington Press, 1986.

Kearns, K. P. *Managing for Accountability: Preserving the Public Trust in Public and Nonprofit Organizations.* San Francisco: Jossey-Bass, 1996.

Kelly, G. A. *A Theory of Personality: The Psychology of Personal Constructs.* New York: Norton, 1963.

Kelly, K. *Out of Control.* Cambridge, Mass.: Perseus Books, 1994.

Kemp, R. L. (ed.). *Strategic Planning for Local Government: A Handbook for Officials and Citizens.* Jefferson, N.C.: McFarland & Company, 1993.

Kerr, S., and Jermier, J. "Substitutes for Leadership: Their Meaning and Measurement." *Organizational Behavior and Human Performance,* 1978, *22*, 375–403.

Kettl, D. F. *The Global Public Management Revolution: A Report on the Transformation of Governance.* Washington, D.C.: Brookings Institution Press, 2000.

Kettl, D. F. *Transformation of Governance: Public Administration for Twenty-First Century America.* Baltimore, Md.: Johns Hopkins University Press, 2002.

Khademian, A. M. *Working with Culture: How the Job Gets Done in Public Programs.* Washington, D.C.: CQ Press, 2002.

Kidd, S. M. *The Secret Life of Bees.* New York: Penguin, 2002.

Kim, S. "Participative Management and Job Satisfaction: Lessons for Management Leadership." *Public Administration Review,* 2002, *62*(2), 231–242.

King, C. S., Feltey, K. M., and Susel, B. O. "The Question of Participation: Toward Authentic Public Participation in Public Administration." *Public Administration Review,* 1998, *58*(4), 317–326.

Kingdon, J. W. *Agendas, Alternatives, and Public Policies.* (Rev. ed.) Boston: Little, Brown, 1995.

Knauft, E. B., Berger, R. A., and Gray, S. T. *Profiles of Excellence: Achieving Success in the Nonprofit Sector.* San Francisco: Jossey-Bass, 1991.

Koteen, J. *Strategic Management in Public and Nonprofit Organizations.* New York: Praeger, 1989.

Kotler, P., Roberto, N., and Lee, N. *Social Marketing: Improving the Quality of Life.* (2nd ed.) Thousand Oaks, Calif.: Sage, 2002.

Kotter, J. P. *Leading Change.* Boston: Harvard Business School Press, 1996.

Kotter, J. P., and Lawrence, P. *Mayors in Action.* New York: Wiley, 1974.

Kouzes, J. M., and Posner, B. Z. *The Leadership Challenge: How to Get Extraordinary Things Done in Organizations.* San Francisco: Jossey-Bass, 1987.

Kouzes, J. M., and Posner, B. Z. *The Leadership Challenge: How to Get Extraordinary Things Done in Organizations.* (3rd ed.) San Francisco: Jossey-Bass, 2002.

Krasner, S. D. "Structural Causes and Regime Consequences: Regimes as Intervening Variables." In S. D. Krasner (ed.), *International Regimes.* Ithaca, N.Y.: Cornell University Press, 1983.

Krause, H., and Milgrom, M. "Thirty Days Without: Public Participation Issues in the Minnesota Department of Transportation Ramp Meter Study." Unpublished study, Hubert H. Humphrey Institute of Public Affairs, University of Minnesota, Minneapolis, 2002.

Kretzmann, J. P., and McKnight, J. L. *Building Communities from the Inside Out: A Path Toward Finding and Mobilizing a Community's Assets.* Chicago: ACTA, 1993.

Krieger, M. H. *Entrepreneurial Vocations: Learning from the Callings of Augustine, Moses, Mothers, Antigone, Oedipus, and Prospero.* Atlanta: Scholars Press, 1996.

Krieger, M. H. "Planning and Design as the Manufacture of Transcendence." *Journal of Planning Education and Research,* 2000, *19*, 257–264.

Krogh, G., and Roos, J. "A Tale of the Unfinished." *Strategic Management Journal,* 1996, *17*, 729–737.

Kübler-Ross, E. *On Death and Dying.* New York: Macmillan, 1969.

Lake, K. E., Reis, T. K., and Spann, J. "From Grantmaking to Changemaking: How the W. K. Kellogg Foundation's Impact Services Model Evolved to Enhance the Management and Social Effects of Large Initiatives." *Nonprofit and Voluntary Sector Quarterly,* 2000, *29*(Supp.).

Land, G., and Jarman, B. *Breakpoint and Beyond: Mastering the Future—Today.* New York: HarperBusiness, 1992.

Lane, R. E. *The Loss of Happiness in Market Democracies.* New Haven, Conn.: Yale University Press, 2000.

Lauria, M. *Reconstructing Urban Regime Theory.* Thousand Oaks, Calif.: Sage, 1996.

Leidecker, J. K., and Bruno, A. V. "Identifying and Using Critical Success Factors." *Long Range Planning*, 1984, *17*(1), 23–32.

Lewin, K. *Field Theory in Social Science.* New York: HarperCollins, 1951.

Lewis, C. W. *The Ethics Challenge in Public Service: A Problem-Solving Guide.* San Francisco: Jossey-Bass, 1991.

Light, P. C. *The President's Agenda.* Baltimore, Md.: Johns Hopkins University Press, 1991.

Light, P. C. *The Tides of Reform: Making Government Work, 1945–1995.* New Haven, Conn.: Yale University Press, 1997.

Light, P. C. *Sustaining Innovation: Creating Nonprofit and Government Organizations That Innovate Naturally.* San Francisco: Jossey-Bass, 1998.

Light, P. C. *Making Nonprofits Work: A Report on the Tides of Nonprofit Management Reform.* Washington, D.C.: Brookings Institution Press, 2000.

Light, P. C. *Government's Greatest Achievements.* Washington, D.C.: Brookings Institution Press, 2002a.

Light, P. C. *Pathways to Nonprofit Excellence.* Washington, D.C.: Brookings Institution Press, 2002b.

Lindblom, C. E. "The Science of Muddling Through." *Public Administration Review*, 1959, *19*, 79–88.

Lindblom, C. E. *The Intelligence of Democracy.* New York: Free Press, 1965.

Lindblom, C. E. *The Policy-Making Process.* Upper Saddle River, N.J.: Prentice Hall, 1980.

Linden, R. M. *Working Across Boundaries: Making Collaboration Work in Government and Nonprofit Organizations.* San Francisco: Jossey-Bass, 2002.

Lipman-Blumen, J. *Connective Leadership: Managing in a Changing World.* New York: Oxford University Press, 1996.

Lipsky, M. *Street-Level Bureaucracy: Dilemmas of the Individual in Public Services.* New York: Russell Sage Foundation, 1980.

Locke, E. A., Shaw, K. N., Saari, L. M., and Latham, G. P. "Goal Setting and Task Performance: 1969–1980." *Psychological Bulletin*, 1981, *90*, 125–152.

Ludema, J. D., Wilmot, T. B., and Srivastva, S. "Organizational Hope: Reaffirming the Constructive Task of Social and Organizational Inquiry." *Human Relations*, 1997, *59*(8), 1015–1052.

Luke, J. S. *Catalytic Leadership: Strategies for an Interconnected World.* San Francisco: Jossey-Bass, 1998.

Lynn, L. E., Jr. *Managing Public Policy.* Boston: Little, Brown, 1987.

Lynn, L. E., Jr. *Public Management as Art, Science, and Profession.* Chatham, N.J.: Chatham House, 1996.

Majone, G. *Evidence, Arguments, and Persuasion in the Policy Process.* New Haven, Conn.: Yale University Press, 1989.

Mandelbaum, S. *Open Moral Communities.* Cambridge, Mass.: MIT Press, 2000.

Mangham, I. L. *Power in Performance in Organizations.* Oxford, England: Blackwell, 1986.

Mangham, I. L., and Overington, M. A. *Organizations as Theatre: A Social Psychology of Dramatic Appearances.* New York: Wiley, 1987.

Manz, C. C. "Self-Leadership: Toward an Expanded Theory of Self-Influence Processes in Organizations." *Academy of Management Review*, 1986, *11*, 585–600.

March, J. G. "Exploration and Exploitation in Organizational Learning." *Organization Science*, 1991, *2*, 71–87.

March, J. G., and Olsen, J. P. *Rediscovering Institutions: The Organizational Basis of Politics.* New York: Free Press, 1989.

March, J. G., and Olsen, J. P. *Democratic Governance.* New York: Free Press, 1995.

March, J. G., and Simon, H. A. *Organizations.* New York: Wiley, 1958.

Marcus, A. A., and Nichols, M. L. "On the Edge: Heeding the Warnings of Unusual Events." *Organization Science,* 1999, *10*(4), 482–499.

Margerum, R. "Collaborative Planning: Building Consensus and a Distinct Model of Practice." *Journal of Planning Education and Research,* 2002, *21,* 237–253.

Marris, P. *The Politics of Uncertainty: Attachment in Private and Public Life.* New York: Routledge, 1996.

Marshall, M., Wray, L., Epstein, P., and Grifel, S. "21st Century Community Focus: Better Results by Linking Citizens, Government, and Performance Measurement." *Public Management,* 1999, *81*(10), 12–18.

Mattessich, P., Murray-Close, M., and Monsey, B. *Collaboration: What Makes It Work.* (2nd ed.) St. Paul, Minn.: Amherst H. Wilder Foundation, 2001.

May, P. J. "Policy Design and Implementation." In B. G. Peters and J. Pierre, *Handbook of Public Administration.* Thousand Oaks, Calif.: Sage, 2003.

May, R. *Love and Will.* New York: Norton, 1969.

McCaskey, M. B. "A Contingency Approach to Planning: Planning with Goals and Planning Without Goals." *Academy of Management Journal,* 1974, *17*(2), 281–291.

McLaughlin, J. A., and Jordan, G. B. "Logic Models: A Tool for Telling Your Program's Performance Story." *Evaluation and Program Planning,* 1999, *22,* 65–72.

Medley, G. J. "Strategic Planning for the World Wildlife Fund." In J. M. Bryson (ed.), *Strategic Management in Public and Voluntary Services: A Reader.* Amsterdam: Pergamon, 1999a.

Medley, G. J. "WWF UK Creates a New Mission." In J. M. Bryson (ed.), *Strategic Management in Public and Voluntary Services: A Reader.* Amsterdam: Pergamon, 1999b.

Meltsner, A. J. "Political Feasibility and Policy Analysis." *Public Administration Review,* Nov./Dec. 1972, *32,* 859–867.

Meltsner, A. J. *Rules for Rulers: The Politics of Advice.* Philadelphia: Temple University Press, 1990.

Merton, R. K. "Bureaucratic Structures and Personality." *Journal of Social Forces,* 1940, *17,* 560–568.

Millar, A., Simeone, R. S., and Carnevale, J. T. "Logic Models: A Systems Tool for Performance Management." *Evaluation and Program Planning,* 2001, *24,* 73–81.

Miller, D., and Friesen, P. H. *Organizations: A Quantum View.* Upper Saddle River, N.J.: Prentice Hall, 1984.

Milward, H. B., and Provan, K. G. "How Networks Are Governed." In C. J. Heinrich and L. E. Lynn (eds.), *Governance and Performance: New Perspectives.* Washington, D.C.: Georgetown University Press, 2000, pp. 238–262.

Milward, H. B., and Provan, K. G. "Managing the Hollow State." *Public Management Review,* 2003, *5*(1), 1–18.

Milward, H. B., Provan, K. G., and Else, B. A. "What Does the 'Hollow State' Look Like?" In B. Bozeman (ed.), *Public Management: The State of the Art.* San Francisco: Jossey-Bass, 1993.

Mintzberg, H. *The Nature of Managerial Work.* New York: HarperCollins, 1973.

Mintzberg, H. "Crafting Strategy." *Harvard Business Review,* July/Aug. 1987, 66–75.

Mintzberg, H. *The Rise and Fall of Strategic Planning.* New York: Free Press, 1994.

Mintzberg, H., Ahlstrand, B., and Lampel, J. *Strategy Safari: A Guided Tour Through the Wilds of Strategic Management.* New York: Free Press, 1998.

Mintzberg, H., and Westley, F. "Cycles of Organizational Change." *Strategic Management Journal,* 1992, *13,* 39–59.

Mitchell, R. K., Agle, B. R., and Wood, D. J. "Toward a Theory of Stakeholder Identification and Salience: Defining the Principle of Who and What Really Counts." *Academy of Management Review,* 1997, *22*(4), 853–886.

Mitroff, I. I., and Anagnos, W. G. *Managing Crises Before They Happen: What Every Executive and Manager Needs to Know About Crisis Management.* New York: AMACOM, 2000.

Mitroff, I. I., and Pearson, C. M. *Crisis Management: A Diagnostic Guide for Improving Your Organization's Crisis-Preparedness.* San Francisco: Jossey-Bass, 1993.

Monbiot, G. "America Is a Religion." *The Guardian* (London), July 29, 2003, p. 19.

Montanari, J. R., and Bracker, J. S. "The Strategic Management Process at the Public Planning Unit Level." *Strategic Management Journal,* 1986, *7*(3), 251–265.

Moore, M. H. *Creating Public Value.* Cambridge, Mass.: Harvard University Press, 1995.

Moore, M. H. "Managing for Value: Organizational Strategy in For-Profit, Nonprofit, and Governmental Organizations." *Nonprofit and Voluntary Sector Quarterly,* 2000, *29*(1), 183–204.

Moore, T. *Care of the Soul.* New York: HarperCollins, 1992.

Morgan, G. *Images of Organization: The Executive Edition.* San Francisco: Berrett-Koehler, 1998.

Myers, D., and Kitsuse, A. "Constructing the Future in Planning: A Survey of Tools and Theories." *Journal of Planning Education and Research,* 2000, *19,* 221–231.

Nadler, G., and Hobino, S. *Breakthrough Thinking.* (Rev. 2nd ed.) Roseville, Calif.: Prima Publishing, 1998.

Nahapiet, J., and Ghoshal, S. "Social Capital, Intellectual Capital, and the Organizational Advantage." *Academy of Management Review,* 1998, *23*(2), 242–266.

Nanus, B. *Visionary Leadership: Creating a Compelling Sense of Direction for Your Organization.* San Francisco: Jossey-Bass, 1992.

National Center for Vital Statistics. *National Vital Statistics Reports,* Sept. 18, 2003, *52*(3), 8.

National Health Service. *Your Guide to the NHS.* [www.nhs.uk/nhsguide]. 2001.

Neely, R. *How the Courts Govern America.* New Haven, Conn.: Yale University Press, 1981.

Nelson, A. C., and French, S. P. "Plan Quality and Mitigating Damage from Natural Disasters." *Journal of the American Planning Association,* 2002, *68*(2), 194–208.

Nelson, B. J., Kaboolian, L., and Carver, K. A. *The Concord Handbook: How to Build Social Capital Across Communities.* Los Angeles: UCLA School of Planning and Social Policy Research, 2003.

Nelson, T., and McFadzean, E. "Facilitating Problem-Solving Groups." *Leadership and Organization Development Journal,* 1998, *19*(2), 72–82.

Neuman, M. "Does Planning Need the Plan?" *Journal of the American Planning Association,* 1998, *64,* 208–220.

Neustadt, R. E. *Presidential Power and the Modern President.* New York: Free Press, 1990.

Neustadt, R. E., and May, E. R. *Thinking in Time: The Uses of History for Decision-Makers.* New York: Free Press, 1986.

Niven, P. R. *Balanced Scorecard Step-by-Step for Government and Nonprofit Agencies.* New York: Wiley, 2003.

Nonaka, I., and Takeuchi, H. *The Knowledge-Creating Company.* Oxford, England: Oxford University Press, 1995.

Normann, R. *Service Management: Strategy and Leadership in Service Business.* (2nd ed.) New York: Wiley, 1991.

North Point Health and Wellness Center. "Stragety Map." Minneapolis, Minn.: Hennepin County, Minnesota, North Point Health and Wellness Center, 2004.

Nutt, P. C. "Types of Organizational Decision Processes." *Administrative Science Quarterly,* 1984, *29,* 414–450.

Nutt, P. C. *Managing Planned Change.* New York: Macmillan, 1992.

Nutt, P. C. "De-Development as a Way to Change Contemporary Organizations." In R. W. Woodman and W. A. Pasmore (eds.), *Research in Organizational Change and Development.* Vol. 13. New York: Elsevier, 2001a.

Nutt, P. C. "Strategic Decision Making." In M. A. Hitt, R. E. Freeman, and J. S. Harrison (eds.), *The Blackwell Handbook of Strategic Management.* Oxford, England: Blackwell, 2001b, 35–69.

Nutt, P. C. *Why Decisions Fail.* San Francisco: Berrett-Koehler, 2002.

Nutt, P. C., and Backoff, R. W. *Strategic Management of Public and Third Sector Organizations: A Handbook for Leaders.* San Francisco: Jossey-Bass, 1992.

Nutt, P. C., and Backoff, R. W. "Strategic Issues as Tensions." *Journal of Management Inquiry,* 1993, *2*(1), 28–42.

Nutt, P. C., and Backoff, R. W. "Walking the Vision and Walking the Talk: Transforming Public Organizations with Strategic Leadership." *Public Productivity and Management Review,* 1996, *19*(4), 455–486.

Nutt, P. C., Backoff, R. W., and Hogan, M. F. "Managing the Paradoxes of Strategic Change." *Journal of Applied Management Studies,* 2000, *9*(1), 5–31.

Olsen, J. B., and Eadie, D. C. *The Game Plan: Governance with Foresight.* Washington, D.C.: Council of State Planning Agencies, 1982.

Oregon Progress Board. *Oregon Benchmarks, Standards for Measuring Statewide Progress and Institutional Performance.* Salem: Oregon Progress Board, 1994.

Oregon Progress Board. "Oregon Benchmarks." [www.econ.state.or.us/opb]. 2003.

Ortony, A., Clore, G. L., and Collins, A. *The Cognitive Structure of Emotions.* New York: Cambridge University Press, 1990.

Osborne, D., and Gaebler, T. *Reinventing Government.* Reading, Mass.: Addison-Wesley, 1992.

Osborne, D., and Hutchinson, P. *The Price of Government: Getting the Results We Need in an Age of Permanent Fiscal Crisis.* New York: Basic Books, 2004.

Osborne, D., and Plastrik, P. *Banishing Bureaucracy: The Five Strategies for Reinventing Government.* Reading, Mass.: Addison-Wesley, 1997.

Osborne, D., and Plastrik, P. *The Reinventor's Fieldbook: Tools for Transforming Your Government.* San Francisco: Jossey-Bass, 2000.

Oshry, B. *Seeing Systems: Unlocking the Mysteries of Organizational Life.* San Francisco: Berrett-Koehler, 1996.

O'Toole, L. J., Jr. "Research on Policy Implementation: Assessment and Prospect." *Journal of Public Administration Research and Theory,* 2000, *10*(2), 263–288.

O'Toole, L. J., Jr. "Interorganizational Relations in Implementation." In B. G. Peters and J. Pierre (eds.), *Handbook of Public Administration.* Thousand Oaks, Calif.: Sage, 2003.

O'Toole, L. J., Jr., and Meier, K. J. "Plus ça change: Public Management, Personnel Stability, and Organizational Performance." *Journal of Public Administration Research and Theory,* 2003, *13*(1), 43–64.

Palmer, P. J. *Let Your Life Speak: Listening for the Voice of Vocation.* San Francisco: Jossey-Bass, 2000.

Parkinson, C. N. *Parkinson's Law and Other Studies in Administration.* Boston: Houghton Mifflin, 1957.

Patterson, K., Grenny, J., Macmillan, R., and Switzer, A. *Crucial Conversations.* New York: McGraw-Hill, 2002.

Patton, M. Q. *Utilization-Focused Evaluation: The New Century Text.* (3rd ed.) Thousand Oaks, Calif.: Sage, 1997.

Patton, M. Q. *Qualitative Research and Evaluation Methods.* (3rd ed.) Thousand Oaks, Calif.: Sage, 2001.

Pearson, C. M., and Clair, J. A. "Reframing Crisis Management." *Academy of Management Review,* 1998, *23*(1), 59–76.

Perrow, C. *Complex Organizations.* New York: Random House, 1986.

Peters, B., and Pierre, J. (eds.). *Handbook of Public Administration.* Thousand Oaks, Calif.: Sage, 2003.

Peters, B. G. *The Future of Governing: Four Emerging Models.* Lawrence: University Press of Kansas, 1996.

Peters, T. J., and Waterman, R. H., Jr. *In Search of Excellence: Lessons from America's Best-Run Companies.* New York: HarperCollins, 1982.

Pfeffer, J. *Managing with Power: Politics and Influence in Organizations.* Boston: Harvard Business School Press, 1992.

Pfeffer, J., and Salancik, R. *The External Control of Organizations: A Resource Dependence Perspective.* New York: HarperCollins, 1978.

Pflaum, A., and Delmont, T. "External Scanning: A Tool for Planners." *Journal of the American Planning Association,* 1987, *53*(1), 56–67.

Pinsonneault, A., and Kraemer, K. L. "Exploring the Role of Information Technology in Organizational Downsizing: A Tale of Two American Cities." *Organization Science,* 2002, *13*(2), 191–208.

Piotrowski, S. J., and Rosenbloom, D. H. "Nonmission-Based Values in Results-Oriented Public Management: The Case of Freedom of Information." *Public Administration Review,* 2002, *62*(6), 643–657.

Poister, T. H. *Measuring Performance in Public and Nonprofit Organizations.* San Francisco: Jossey-Bass, 2003.

Poister, T. H., and Streib, G. "Municipal Management Tools from 1976 to 1993: An Overview and Update." *Public Productivity and Management Review,* 1994, *18*(2), 115–125.

Poister, T. H., and Streib, G. D. "Strategic Management in the Public Sector: Concepts, Models, and Processes." *Public Productivity and Management Review,* 1999, *22*(3), 308–325.

Pollitt, C., and Bouckaert, G. *Public Management Report: A Comparative Analysis.* Oxford, England: Oxford University Press, 2000.

Porter, M. E. *Competitive Advantage: Creating and Sustaining Superior Performance.* New York: Free Press, 1985.

Posner, R. A. *The Federal Courts: Crisis and Reform.* Cambridge, Mass.: Harvard University Press, 1985.

Prahalad, C. K., and Hamel, G. "The Core Competence of the Corporation." *Harvard Business Review,* May/June 1990, 79–91.

Pressman, J., and Wildavsky, A. *Implementation.* Berkeley: University of California Press, 1973.

Project for Pride in Living. *Building on Our Strengths.* 2003–2007 Strategic Plan. Minneapolis, Minn.: Project for Pride in Living, 2002.

Provan, K. G., and Milward, H. B. "Do Networks Really Work?: A Framework for Evaluating Public Sector Organizational Networks." *Public Administration Review,* 2001, *61*(4), 414–423.

Putnam, R. D. *Bowling Alone: The Collapse and Revival of American Community.* New York: Simon & Schuster, 2000.

Quinn, J. B. *Strategies for Change: Logical Incrementalism.* Homewood, Ill.: Irwin, 1980.

Radin, B. "The Government Performance and Results Act (GPRA) and the Tradition of Federal Management Reform: Square Peg in Round Holes?" *Journal of Public Administration Research and Theory*, 2000, *10*, 111–135.

Raelin, J. A. *Creating Leaderful Organizations: How to Bring Out Leadership in Everyone.* San Francisco: Berrett-Koehler, 2003.

Rainey, H. G. *Understanding and Managing Public Organizations.* (2nd ed.) San Francisco: Jossey-Bass, 1997.

Rainey, H. G. *Understanding and Managing Public Organizations.* (3rd ed.) San Francisco: Jossey-Bass, 2003.

Rainey, H. G., and Steinbauer, P. "Galloping Elephants: Developing Elements of a Theory of Effective Government Organizations." *Journal of Public Administration Research and Theory*, 1999, *9*(1), 1–32.

Randolph, W. A., and Posner, B. Z. *Checkered Flag Projects: 10 Rules for Creating and Managing Projects That Win!* Upper Saddle River, N.J.: Financial Times Prentice Hall, 2002.

Ray, K. *The Nimble Collaboration: Fine Tuning Your Collaboration for Lasting Success.* St. Paul, Minn.: Amherst H. Wilder Foundation, 2002.

Rees, M. *Our Final Century: Will the Human Race Survive the Twenty-First Century?* London: Heinemann, 2003.

Rieff, D. "Blueprint for a Mess." *New York Times Sunday Magazine*, Nov. 2, 2003, pp. 28–78 passim.

Rifkin, J. *The Age of Access: The New Culture of Hypercapitalism Where All of Life Is a Paid-For Experience.* New York: Tarcher/Putnam, 2000.

Riker, W. H. *The Theory of Political Coalitions.* New Haven, Conn.: Yale University Press, 1962.

Riker, W. H. *The Art of Political Manipulation.* New Haven, Conn.: Yale University Press, 1986.

Ring, P. S., and Van de Ven, A. H. "Developmental Processes of Cooperative Interorganizational Relationships." *Academy of Management Review*, 1994, *19*(1), 90–118.

Roberts, N. C. "Public Deliberation: An Alternative Approach to Crafting Policy and Setting Direction." *Public Administration Review*, 1997, *57*(2), 124–132.

Roberts, N. C. "Innovation by Legislative, Judicial, and Management Design: Three Arenas of Public Entrepreneurship." In H. G. Frederickson and J. M. Johnston (eds.), *Public Management Reform and Innovation.* Tuscaloosa: University of Alabama Press, 1999.

Roberts, N. C. "The Synoptic Model of Strategic Planning and the GPRA: Lacking a Good Fit with the Political Context." *Public Productivity and Management Review*, 2000, *23*(3), 297–311.

Roberts, N. C. (ed.) *The Transformative Power of Dialogue.* Amsterdam: JAI, 2002.

Roberts, N. C., and King, P. J. *Transforming Public Policy: Dynamics of Policy Entrepreneurship and Innovation.* San Francisco: Jossey-Bass, 1996.

Roberts, N. C., and Wargo, L. "The Dilemma of Planning in Large-Scale Public Organizations: The Case of the United States Navy." *Journal of Public Administration Research and Theory*, 1994, *4*(4), 469–491.

Robinson, M. K. *Nonprofit Boards That Work: The End of One-Size-Fits-All Governance.* New York: Wiley, 2001.

Rochefort, D., and Cobb, R. (eds.). *The Politics of Problem Definition: Shaping the Policy Agenda.* Lawrence: University Press of Kansas, 1994.

Rogers, E. M. *Diffusion of Innovations.* (5th ed.) New York: Free Press, 2003.

Romzek, B. S. "Enhancing Accountability." In J. L. Perry (ed.), *Handbook of Public Administration.* (2nd ed.) San Francisco: Jossey-Bass, 1996.

Rosenhead, J., and Mingers, J. (eds.). *Rational Analysis in a Problematic World Revisited.* London: Wiley, 2001.

Rowley, T. J., and Moldoveanu, M. "When Will Stakeholder Groups Act? An Interest- and Identity-Based Model of Stakeholder Group Mobilization." *Academy of Management Review*, 2003, *29*(3), 488–502.

The Royal Hospitals. *A Vision of Success, 2003–2008*. Belfast, Northern Ireland: The Royal Hospitals, 2003.

Rubin, I. *The Politics of Public Budgeting: Getting and Spending, Borrowing and Balancing.* (4th ed.) Chatham, N.J.: Chatham House, 2000.

Rushdie, S. *Midnight's Children.* London: Jonathan Cape, 1981.

Sabatier, P. A., and Jenkins-Smith, H. D. *Policy Change and Learning: An Advocacy Coalition Approach.* Boulder, Colo.: Westview Press, 1993.

Salamon, L. M. *Partners in Public Service: Government-Nonprofit Relations in the Modern Welfare State.* Baltimore, Md.: Johns Hopkins University Press, 1995.

Sardar, Z., and Davies, M. W. *Why Do People Hate America?* Cambridge, England: Icon Books, 2002.

Sawhill, J. C., and Williamson, D. "Mission Impossible? Measuring Success in Nonprofit Organizations." *Nonprofit Management and Leadership*, 2001, *11*(3), 371–386.

Schachtel, M.R.B. "CitiStat and the Baltimore Neighborhood Indicators Alliance: Using Information to Improve Communication and Community." *National Civic Review*, 2001, *90*(3), 253–265.

Schaef, A. W. *Women's Reality.* San Francisco: HarperCollins, 1985.

Schein, E. H. *Process Consultation: Lessons for Managers and Consultants.* Reading, Mass.: Addison-Wesley, 1987.

Schein, E. H. *Organizational Culture and Leadership.* (2nd ed.) San Francisco: Jossey-Bass, 1997.

Schön, D. A. *Beyond the Stable State.* London: Temple Smith, 1971.

Schön, D. A. *The Reflective Practitioner.* New York: Basic Books, 1983.

Schön, D. A., and Rein, M. *Frame Reflection: Toward the Resolution of Intractable Policy Controversies.* New York: Basic Books, 1994.

Schwartz, P. *The Art of the Long View: Planning for the Future in an Uncertain World.* New York: Doubleday Currency, 1991.

Schwartz, P. *Inevitable Surprises: Thinking Ahead in a Time of Turbulence.* New York: Gotham Books, 2003.

Schwartz, P., Leyden, P., and Hyatt, J. *The Long Boom: A Vision for the Coming Age of Prosperity.* Cambridge, Mass.: Perseus Books, 1999.

Schwarz, R. *The Skilled Facilitator.* (Rev. ed.) San Francisco: Jossey-Bass, 2002.

Scott, J. C. *Seeing Like a State.* New Haven, Conn.: Yale University Press, 1998.

Scott, W. R. "The Adolescence of Institutional Theory." *Administrative Science Quarterly*, 1987, *32*, 493–511.

Scriven, M. S. "The Methodology of Evaluation." In R. E. Sake (ed.), *Curriculum Evaluation.* AERA Monograph Series on Curriculum Evaluation. Skokie, Ill.: Rand McNally, 1967.

Seligman, M.E.P. *Learned Optimism.* New York: Knopf, 1991.

Seligman, M.E.P. *Learned Optimism: How to Change Your Mind and Your Life.* Pocket Books, 1998.

Selznick, P. *Leadership in Administration: A Sociological Interpretation.* Berkeley: University of California Press, 1957.

Senge, P. M. "The Leader's New Work: Building Learning Organizations." *Sloan Management Review*, Fall 1990, pp. 7–23.

Shamir, B., Arthur, M., and House, R. "The Rhetoric of Charismatic Leadership: A Theoretical Extension, a Case Study, and Implications for Research." *Leadership Quarterly*, 1994, *5*(1), 25–42.

Smircich, L., and Morgan, G. "Leadership: The Management of Meaning." *Journal of Applied Behavioral Science,* 1989, *18,* 257–273.

Spencer, L. *Winning Through Participation.* Dubuque, Iowa: Kendall/Hunt, 1989.

Spencer, S. A., and Adams, J. D. *Life Changes: Going Through Personal Transitions.* San Luis Obispo, Calif.: Impact, 1990.

Stalk, G., Evans, P., and Shulman, L. E. "Competing on Capabilities: The New Rules of Corporate Strategy." *Harvard Business Review,* Mar./Apr. 1992, pp. 57–69.

Staw, B., Sandelands, L., and Dutton, J. "Threat Rigidity Effects in Organizational Behavior: A Multilevel Analysis." *Administrative Science Quarterly,* 1981, *26,* 501–524.

Steiner, G. A. *Strategic Planning: What Every Manager Must Know.* New York: Free Press, 1979.

Sterman, J. D. *Business Dynamics: Systems Thinking and Modeling for a Complex World.* New York: McGraw-Hill, 2000.

Stern, G. *The Drucker Foundation Self-Assessment Tool: Process Guide.* San Francisco: Jossey-Bass, 1998.

Stern, G. *Marketing Workbook for Nonprofit Organizations: Develop the Plan.* St. Paul, Minn.: Amherst H. Wilder Foundation, 2001.

Stiglitz, J. E. *Globalization and Its Discontents.* New York: Norton, 2002.

Stivers, C. "The Listening Bureaucrat: Responsiveness in Public Administration." *Public Administration Review,* 1994, *54*(4), 364–369.

Stone, D. A. *Policy Paradox and Political Reason.* (Rev. ed.) New York: Norton, 2002.

Stone, M. M. "Exploring the Effects of Collaborations on Member Organizations: Washington County's Welfare-to-Work Partnership." *Nonprofit and Voluntary Sector Quarterly,* 2000, *29*(1), 98–119.

Suchman, M. C. "Managing Legitimacy: Strategic and Institutional Approaches." *Academy of Management Review,* 1995, *20*(3), 571–610.

Sun Tzu. *The Art of War.* Boston: Shambhala, 1991.

Susskind, L., and Cruikshank, J. *Breaking the Impasse.* New York: Basic Books, 1987.

Susskind, L., and Field, P. T. *Dealing with an Angry Public: The Mutual Gains Approach to Resolving Disputes.* New York: Free Press, 1996.

Szulanski, G., and Amin, K. "Learning to Make Strategy: Balancing Discipline and Imagination." *Long Range Planning,* 2001, *34,* 537–556.

Tan, A. *The Bonesetter's Daughter.* New York: Penguin, 2001.

Terry, R. *Seven Zones for Leadership: Acting Authentically in Stability and Chaos.* Palo Alto, Calif.: Davies-Black, 2001.

Terry, R. W. *Authentic Leadership: Courage in Action.* San Francisco: Jossey-Bass, 1993.

Thomas, J. C. "Public Involvement and Governmental Effectiveness: A Decision-Making Model for Public Managers." *Administration and Society,* 1993, *24*(4), 444–469.

Thomas, J. C. *Public Participation in Public Decisions.* San Francisco: Jossey-Bass, 1995.

Thompson, J. D. *Organizations in Action.* New York: McGraw-Hill, 1967.

Thompson, L. *The Mind and Heart of the Negotiator.* (2nd ed.) Upper Saddle River, N.J.: Prentice Hall, 2001.

Toffler, A. *Future Shock.* New York: Bantam, 1971.

Tolkien, J.R.R. *The Fellowship of the Ring.* (2nd ed.) Boston: Houghton Mifflin, 1965.

Tolkien, J.R.R. *The Hobbit.* Boston: Houghton Mifflin, 1999.

Trist, E. "Referent Organizations and the Development of Interorganizational Domains." *Human Relations,* 1983, *36*(3), 269–284.

Tuchman, B. *The March of Folly: From Troy to Vietnam.* New York: Knopf, 1984.

Underhill, P. *Why We Buy: The Science of Shopping.* New York: Simon & Schuster, 1999.

U.S. Department of Education. *The National Agenda for Achieving Better Results for Children and Youth with Disabilities.* Washington, D.C.: Office of Special Education and Rehabilitative Services, U.S. Department of Education, 1994.

U.S. Department of Homeland Security. "DHS Organization." [http://www.dhs.gov/dhspublic/theme_home1.jsp]. 2004.

Ury, W. L., Brett, J. M., and Goldberg, S. B. *Getting Disputes Resolved: Designing Systems to Cut the Costs of Conflict.* San Francisco: Jossey-Bass, 1988.

Van de Ven, A. H., Polley, D. E., Garud, R., and Venkataraman, S. *The Innovation Journey.* New York: Oxford University Press, 1999.

Van der Heijden, K. *Scenarios: The Art of Strategic Conversation.* New York: Wiley, 1996.

Van der Heijden, K., Bradfield, R., Burt, G., Cairns, G, and Wright, G. *The Sixth Sense: Accelerating Organizational Learning with Scenarios.* New York: Wiley, 2002.

Van Horn, C. E., Baumer, D. C., and Gormley, W. T. *Politics and Public Policy.* (3rd ed.) Washington, D.C.: Congressional Quarterly Press, 2001.

Vangen, S., and Huxham, C. *Enacting Leadership for Collaborative Advantage.* Glasgow, Scotland: Graduate School of Business, University of Strathclyde, 2002.

Vangen, S., and Huxham, C. "Enacting Leadership for Collaboration Advantage." *British Journal of Management,* 2003a.

Vangen, S., and Huxham, C. "Managing Trust in Inter-Organisational Collaboration: Conceptualizations and Tools." In P. Hibbert (ed.), *Co-Creating Emergent Insight.* Glasgow, Scotland: Graduate School of Business, University of Strathclyde, 2003b.

Vargas, S. "Linking Performance to Outcomes." Unpublished manuscript, Hennepin County Office of the County Administrator, Minneapolis, Minn, 2003.

Vickers, G. *The Art of Judgment: A Study of Policy Making.* Thousand Oaks, Calif.: Sage, 1995.

Vinzant, J. C., and Crothers, L. *Street-Level Leadership.* Washington, D.C.: Georgetown University Press, 1998.

Warech, M. A., and others. "Self-Monitoring and 360-Degree Ratings." *Leadership Quarterly,* 1998, *9*(4), 449–473.

Watzlawick, P., Weakland, J., and Fisch, R. *Change, Principles of Problem Formation and Problem Resolution.* New York: Norton, 1974.

"The Way We Were and Are." *Governing,* Oct. 2002, pp. 37–39.

Wechsler, B., and Backoff, R. "The Dynamics of Strategy in Public Organizations." *Journal of the American Planning Association,* 1987, *53*(1), 34–43.

Weick, K. E. "Small Wins: Redefining the Scale of Social Problems." *American Psychologist,* 1984, *39*(1), 40–43.

Weick, K. E. *Sensemaking in Organizations.* Thousand Oaks, Calif.: Sage, 1995.

Weick, K. E., and Sutcliffe, K. M. *Managing the Unexpected: Assuring High Performance in an Age of Complexity.* San Francisco: Jossey-Bass, 2001.

Weimer, D. L., and Vining, A. R. *Policy Analysis: Concepts and Practice.* (3rd ed.) Englewood Cliffs, N.J.: Prentice Hall, 1998.

Weisman, C. *Secrets of Successful Retreats: The Best from the Non-Profit Pros.* St. Louis, Mo.: Robbins, 2003.

Weiss, J. A., and Piderit, S. K. "The Value of Mission Statements in Public Agencies." *Journal of Public Administration Research and Theory,* 1999, *9*(2), 193–223.

Wheeland, C. "Implementing a Community-Wide Strategic Plan: Rock Hill's Empowering the Vision 10 Years Later." *American Review of Public Administration,* 2003, *33*(1), 46–69.

Wildavsky, A. *Speaking Truth to Power: The Art and Craft of Policy Analysis.* Boston: Little, Brown, 1979.

Wildavsky, A. *The Politics of the Budgetary Process.* (4th ed.) Boston: Little, Brown, 1984.

Wilshire, B. "The Dramaturgical Model of Behavior: Its Strengths and Weaknesses." *Symbolic Interaction,* 1982, *5*(2), 287–297.

Wilson, J. Q. *Bureaucracy: What Government Agencies Do and Why They Do It.* New York: Basic Books, 1989.

Wittrock, B., and de Leon, P. "Policy as a Moving Target: A Call for Conceptual Realism." *Policy Studies Review,* 1986, *6*(1), 44–60.

Worldwatch Institute. *State of the World 2004: Richer, Fatter, and Not Much Happier.* Washington, D.C.: WorldWatch Institute, 2004.

Wright, B. E., and Davis, B. S. "Job Satisfaction in the Public Sector: The Role of the Work Environment." *American Review of Public Administration,* 2003, *33*(1), 70–90.

Yin, R. K. "Life Histories of Innovations: How New Practices Become Routinized." *Public Administration Review,* Jan./Feb. 1982, pp. 21–28.

Zollo, M., and Winter, S. G. "Deliberate Learning and the Evolution of Dynamic Capabilities." *Organization Science,* 2002, *13*(3), 339–351.

NAME INDEX

SUBJECT INDEX

A

Accountability: establishing mechanisms for sharing, 309; results using, 273

Action plans: characteristics of, 50, 250–251; developing effective, 50–51; shared responsibilities as part of, 309. *See also* Strategic plans; Strategy implementation

Activity-based view of strategizing, 32

Administrative Procedures Act, 254

American dream, 133–134

American tradition, 135

Amherst H. Wilder Foundation: mission statement of, 118, 119; strategic plan (2000–2005) for the, 188–191; strategies formulated and adopted by, 187; vision statement of, 53

Arenas, 312–313

The Art of War (Sun Tzu), 123

B

Banxia Software, 206

Basic analysis technique, described, 36–37

Benchmark or goal approach, 281–283, 284

Benchmark Performance Report (Oregon Progress Board), 283

Big win–small win dichotomy, 212, 215–216

The Bonesetter's Daughter (Tan), 70

Boundary spanners, 72

BSC (balanced scorecard), 55

Budgets: entrepreneurial budgeting as part of, 241, 247–248; performance, 245–246; special role in strategy implementation, 244–248; strategic planning/plans keeping in mind, 221

Bureaucratic imprisonment, 314

C

Camera exercise, 142

Care of the Soul (Moore), 3

Champions of process, 23, 82, 303–304, 327, 330

Change: chunking, 243–244; continuation of technological, 132;

entailing changes in organization culture, 255; entrepreneurial budgeting leading to, 221, 247–248; expectations during Strategy Change Cycle, 91; initial agreements with flexibility for, 91; in strategies, 186; window of opportunity for, 210

Chunking changes, 243–244

CitiStat system, 55, 58

Civic republicanism, 133

Collaboration approach, 279–280

Collaboration model, 58

Collaborative advantage, 37

Collective leadership, 307–309

Communication: among key decision makers, 328–329; dialogue/discussion as part of, 309–312; strategy implementation and, 255–256. *See also* Information

Community/communities: addressing stakeholder needs, 37–38; benefits of strategic planning to, 330–331, 332; defining, 9; School District strategic plan and, 318–319; tailoring strategic planning process to, 328

DATE DUE

APR 2 9 2010